RECORD COPY
DO NOT REMOVE
FROM OFFICE

RITUALS
of
THE PAST

RITUALS
of
THE PAST

PREHISPANIC AND COLONIAL CASE STUDIES
IN ANDEAN ARCHAEOLOGY

EDITED BY
SILVANA A. ROSENFELD AND STEFANIE L. BAUTISTA

UNIVERSITY PRESS OF COLORADO
Boulder

© 2017 by University Press of Colorado

Published by University Press of Colorado
5589 Arapahoe Avenue, Suite 206C
Boulder, Colorado 80303

All rights reserved
Printed in the United States of America

 The University Press of Colorado is a proud member of
Association of American University Presses.

The University Press of Colorado is a cooperative publishing enterprise supported, in part, by Adams State University, Colorado State University, Fort Lewis College, Metropolitan State University of Denver, Regis University, University of Colorado, University of Northern Colorado, Utah State University, and Western State Colorado University.

∞ This paper meets the requirements of the ANSI/NISO Z39.48-1992 (Permanence of Paper).

ISBN: 978-1-60732-595-6 (cloth)
ISBN: 978-1-60732-596-3 (ebook)

Library of Congress Cataloging-in-Publication Data

Names: Rosenfeld, Silvana A., editor. | Bautista, Stefanie L., editor.
Title: Rituals of the past : prehispanic and colonial case studies in Andean archaeology / edited by Silvana A. Rosenfeld and Stefanie L. Bautista.
Description: Boulder : University Press of Colorado, 2017. | Includes bibliographical references and index.
Identifiers: LCCN 2016049329| ISBN 9781607325956 (cloth) | ISBN 9781607325963 (ebook)
Subjects: LCSH: Indians of South America—Andes Region—Rites and ceremonies. | Indians of South America—Peru—Rites and ceremonies. | Excavations (Archaeology)—Andes Region. | Excavations (Archaeology)—Peru. | Andes Region—Antiquities. | Peru—Antiquities.
Classification: LCC F2229 .R56 2017 | DDC 985/.01—dc23
LC record available at https://lccn.loc.gov/2016049329

An electronic version of this book is freely available, thanks to the support of libraries working with Knowledge Unlatched. KU is a collaborative initiative designed to make high-quality books open access for the public good. The open access ISBN for the PDF version of this book is 978-1-60732-702-8; for the ePUB version the open access ISBN is 978-1-60732-724-0. More information about the initiative and links to the open-access version can be found at www.knowledgeunlatched.org.

Front cover illustrations, top to bottom: Motul Dictionary (courtesy of the John Carter Brown Library); Mount Maloney type bowl from Actuncan (photo by Lisa LeCount); Caste War defense work in Iturbide (photo by Ute Schüren); Creation Tablet from Palenque (rubbing by Merle Greene Robertson); Caste War fortifications in Bacalar (photo by Ute Schüren); Talking Cross in Felipe Carrillo Puerto (photo by Wolfgang Gabbert)

Contents

List of Figures	vii
List of Tables	xiii

1. An Archaeology of Rituals
   *Silvana A. Rosenfeld and
   Stefanie L. Bautista*   3

2. The Nature of Ritual Space at Chavín de Huántar
   John W. Rick   21

3. Not Just a Pyramid Scheme? Diversity in
   Ritual Architecture at Chavín de Huántar
   Daniel A. Contreras   51

4. From Ritual to Ideology: Ritual Activity and
   Artistic Representations in the Northern
   Highlands of Peru in the Formative Period
   Yoshio Onuki   79

5. Architecture and Ritual Practices at Huaca A
   of Pampa de las Llamas–Moxeke
   Rafael Vega-Centeno Sara-Lafosse   103

6. Territoriality, Monumentality, and Religion in
   Formative Period Nepeña, Coastal Ancash
   *David Chicoine, Hugo Ikehara,
   Koichiro Shibata, and
   Matthew Helmer*   123

7. Ritual Practice at the End of Empire: Evidence of an Abandonment Ceremony from Pataraya, a Wari Outpost on the South Coast of Peru
    Matthew J. Edwards   151

8. From the Domestic to the Formal: A View of Daily and Ceremonial Practices from Cerro de Oro during the Early Middle Horizon
    Francesca Fernandini and Mario Ruales   169

9. The Demise of the Ruling Elites: Terminal Rituals in the Pyramid Complexes of Panquilma, Peruvian Central Coast
    Camila Capriata Estrada and Enrique López-Hurtado   193

10. Reconstructing Early Colonial Andean Ritual Practice at Pukara, Peru: An Architectural Approach
    Sarah Abraham   217

11. Ritual as Interaction with Non-Humans: Prehispanic Mountain Pass Shrines in the Southern Andes
    Axel E. Nielsen, Carlos I. Angiorama, and Florencia Ávila   241

12. Mining, Ritual, and Social Memory: An Exploration of Toponymy in the Ica Valley, Peru
    Hendrik Van Gijseghem and Verity H. Whalen   267

13. Rituals of the Past: Final Comments
    Jerry D. Moore   295

List of Contributors   313
Index   315

Figures

1.1.	Procession of Virgen del Carmen, Chavín de Huántar, Peru, 2015	4
2.1.	Current interpretation of the architectural layout of Chavín de Huántar at about 600 BC cal.	22
2.2.	Map of relevant parts of the monumental core of Chavín de Huántar	27
2.3.	Sample of smashed, hammered, and scratched obsidian angular debris illustrating intentional destruction of this material in a number of Building C contexts	29
2.4.	Rare intact example of sacrifice ware found in a Building C subterranean canal below a vertical chimney	31
2.5.	Exploration of deep pit below the floor of the Plaza Mayor, capped by a huge spalled and burned boulder	33
2.6.	Location of galleries mentioned in text, and general gallery distribution in Buildings A-C	34
2.7.	Segment of Rocas Canal just west of the Circular Plaza	38
2.8.	Known canals in the north esplanade of Building C as of 2013	40
2.9.	Isometric drawing of Canal CE2 of the north esplanade of Building C	41
3.1.	Site sectors and major architectural features	53
3.2.	Visible architecture in the West Field	54

3.3.	West Field Mito structure	56
3.4.	Stratigraphic context of the West Field Mito structure	57
3.5.	Hypothesized processional paths through the monument, a selection of ritually significant locations, and a selection of canal access ways with evidence for ritual activity	70
4.1.	Chronological chart for some excavated sites in the northern highlands	81
4.2.	Temple of the Crossed Hands at Kotosh	82
4.3.	Several temples of the Kotosh Mito phase, showing the trace of renovation	83
4.4.	Location of some Formative sites in the Jequetepeque and Cajamarca Valleys	87
4.5.	Plan of the temple of the Kuntur Wasi phase	88
4.6.	Gold nose ornament of the monster face with two different eyes	90
4.7.	Stone sculpture with two different eyes	91
4.8.	Gold nose ornament of the monster and twins	93
4.9.	"Idol" figure of earth for the wall relief of the Idolo phase	95
5.1.	Air photo of Pampa de las Llamas–Moxeke	110
5.2.	Plan of Huaca A	112
5.3.	Plan of Huaca A indicating corridors, open spaces, and rooms	114
5.4.	Plan of Huaca A indicating possible movements	115
5.5.	Atrium U-shape forms at Huaca A	116
5.6.	Diagram of Gamma Analysis	117
5.7.	Plan of Huaca A and possible organization of groups within rooms	118

6.1.	Map of the Nepeña Valley showing the location of the Formative period sites mentioned in the text and other Formative sites with significant monumental architecture	128
6.2.	Photographs of Cerro Blanco de Nepeña and Huaca Partida, Cerro Blanco phase	129
6.3.	Photographs of Caylán's urban complex	130
6.4.	Photographs of Kushipampa	133
6.5.	Results of visual impact and isovistas with schematic representation of structures for Huaca Partida, Cerro Blanco, Caylán, Samanco, and Huambacho's Main Platform Complex	137
6.6.	Results of visual impact and isovistas with schematic representation of structures for Kushipampa, Virahuanca Bajo, Paredones, and Huancarpón	138
6.7.	Maps showing combined visibility from/of the monuments at Samanco, Huambacho, Caylán's Mound-A, Cerro Blanco, and Huaca Partida	142
6.8.	Maps showing combined visibility from/ of the monuments at Virahuanca Bajo, Paredones, Kushipampa, and Huancarpón	143
7.1.	Location map	152
7.2.	Access and circulation within the Pataraya enclosure	153
8.1.	Map showing the location of Cerro de Oro and neighboring valleys	171
8.2.	Map of Cerro de Oro showing SW Area and SE Area	172
8.3.	A and 8.3B. Fragments from bowl showing the different blends of Middle Horizon 1 styles	173

8.4.	Prehispanic settlements in the Lower Cañete Valley	174
8.5.	Remains inside Room A	185
8.6.	Composition of funerary associations found inside Room A at Cerro de Oro	187
9.1.	Map indicating location of Panquilma	200
9.2.	(A) Pyramid 1; (B) Pyramid 3, Panquilma	201
9.3.	Ceramic figurine	202
9.4.	*Spondylus* valves	203
9.5.	Upper platform of Pyramid 1 at Panquilma showing evidence of intense burning over the floor	204
9.6.	Drawing of unit placed on Pyramid 3 showing burned room remains over the bench and the floor of the upper platform	205
10.1.	Aerial photo of Pukara and its surroundings, showing the location of sites discussed in the text	225
10.2.	Site of Pukara with El Peñon in the background	226
10.3.	Late Formative sunken court	228
10.4.	La Quinta Chapel	229
10.5.	Plan of La Quinta chapel and surrounding architectural features	230
10.6.	Santa Isabel church, Pucará	234
11.1.	Invoking the assistance of mountains, San Rafael, and Pachamama during departure ceremony of a llama caravan in Cerrillos, Sud Lípez, Bolivia	244
11.2.	Apacheta in Abra de Sepulturas (Quebrada de Humahuaca) "dressed" during an enflorada ceremony	247
11.3.	Location of sites mentioned in the text	251

11.4.	Artificial hollow at Abra del Toro Muerto 1	252
11.5.	Common offerings at artificial hollows	253
11.6.	Artificial hollow with greenstone offerings on the top of Cerro Pan de Azúcar	258
11.7.	Offering of plastic beads at the apacheta of Abra del Cóndor	261
12.1.	Upper Ica Valley	277
12.2.	Mina Azurita, a mining complex with prehispanic and post-colonial occupations and architecture	278
12.3.	Panoramic ground-level view of the west side of the Ica Valley	285

Tables

3.1.	Mito-style structures in the Central Andes and associated dates	60
3.2.	Estimated areas and capacities of selected ritual spaces at Chavín	69
5.1.	Gamma Analysis results	117
6.1.	Chronological table for the Formative Period in Nepeña	126
6.2.	Total area from which the monuments are visible under the two proposed thresholds for analysis (7.07 km and 10 km)	141
6.3.	Results of GIS analysis of multiple visibilities of monuments in different cases	144
7.1.	Major use areas during occupation	155
7.2.	Abandonment features and activities	155
8.1.	Stratigraphy of the burned contexts at Cerro de Oro	177
8.2.	Stratigraphic sequence for Unit 22W at Cerro de Oro	179
8.3.	Schematic description of occupations at Cerro de Oro	181
8.4.	Description of the funerary contexts at Cerro de Oro	182
11.1.	Archaeological remains recorded on mountain passes of the triple frontier area	249
11.2.	Archaeological remains recorded on mountain tops of the Southern Pozuelos Basin	257
12.1.	Toponyms of the Ica Valley	280

RITUALS
of
THE PAST

1

An Archaeology of Rituals

Silvana A. Rosenfeld and
Stefanie L. Bautista

Every July 16, the people from the small town of Chavín de Huántar in Ancash, Peru, celebrate the Virgen del Carmen festival. A clear fusion between Catholic and Andean beliefs, the Virgen del Carmen celebration is a well-organized event that involves the entire community. Typically, two sponsors (*mayordomos*) are in charge of organizing the festivities, which include the procession of the Virgen (figure 1.1), a mass at the local church, a live music band, a potluck meal, and bullfighting. To prepare for this event, the community is divided to partake in particular activities, such as preparing *chicha* (a traditional alcoholic corn beverage), baking special breads, and sacrificing pigs and chickens for consumption. Some of the classic Andean principles of reciprocity, community, and duality can be seen during this celebration (Murra 1975; Rostworowski de Diez Canseco 2001). Locals and visitors clearly enjoy these days of praying, dancing, eating, drinking, and fireworks.

The Virgen del Carmen festival coincides with the beginning of the harvest season, the most important time in the agricultural cycle for farming communities. The celebrations, however, also renew ties with Catholic figures by attending mass, praying, and participating in the colorful procession while also strengthening relationships among local townspeople who must work together in preparing the food (e.g., meat, bread, and alcohol) for public consumption. Ethnographic and ethnohistoric studies have shown that the interplay of customary and collective actions among humans and

DOI: 10.5876/9781607325963.c001

FIGURE 1.1. *Procession of Virgen del Carmen, Chavín de Huántar, Peru, 2015*

between humans and non-humans or supernatural agents, through the ritual mixture of Catholicism and indigenous practices, has been central to many communities in both South America and Mesoamerica (e.g., Nutini 1988; Rostworowski de Diez Canseco 1992). This volume seeks to highlight, from different archaeological perspectives and contexts across the Andes, how ritual affected or was affected by the diverse groups of peoples in this region.

The practice of ritual across time has long fascinated anthropologists, as it can highlight some of the most integral, emotive, and elaborative practices of human life. The study of ritual can demonstrate the interconnections among the various aspects of society, such as religion, politics, and economy. Though ritual has long been important to anthropologists (e.g., Bastien 1978; Bolton 1979; Flores Ochoa 1977; Geertz 1973; Rappaport 1999; Turner 1967), archaeologists have only more recently recognized the importance of studying ritual and its role in past societies (e.g., Bauer and Stanish 2001; Benson and Cook 2001; Insoll 2004; Kyriakidis 2007). Ritual is now considered a major component in the development of some ancient sociopolitical systems, as it aided in their creation, maintenance, and change (DeMarrais, Castillo, and Earle 1996; Marcus and Flannery 2004; Moore 1996; Pauketat et al. 2002).

While there have been discussions of how different archaeological frameworks have approached the ideological dimensions of ritual (e.g., Hodder and Hutson 2003; Insoll 2004), a pertinent debate has also taken place over whether the practice of ritual is distinguishable from other everyday activities in the material record (e.g., Berggren and Stutz 2010). Whereas ritual can be very much interrelated with other everyday practices, it is clear that rituals can be studied from an archaeological perspective. The formal repetition of rituals can create patterns that materialize in the archaeological record, which archaeologists can trace using a variety of methods.

In the Andean region of South America, evidence of ritual activity can be seen in early Peruvian prehispanic sites such as Kotosh in the northern highlands of Huánuco. Beginning circa 2500 BC, the people of Kotosh built enclosed rooms with a central sunken space and a formal hearth to burn offerings. The walls of these rooms were usually plastered with fine clay and contained niches and reliefs (Izumi and Terada 1972). Kotosh residents then buried these rooms and constructed new temples over the interred structures. This practice of architectural renovation was key in the development of early Andean societies, as it served to integrate small communities during the relative absence of a centralized authority (Onuki, this volume). The numerous studies about ritual in the ancient Andes published since 2000 (e.g., Albarracin-Jordan, Capriles, and Miller 2014; Arkush 2005; Cutright, López-Hurtado, and Martin 2010; Dillehay 2004; Gamboa Velasquez 2015; Inomata and Coben 2006; Isbell and Groleau 2010; Jennings and Bowser 2009; Kantner and Vaughn 2012; Knobloch 2000; Moore 2005; Rick 2008; Rosenfeld 2012; Tantaleán et al. 2016; Swenson and Warner 2012; Tung 2007; Vaughn 2004) attest to the significance of ritual in the development of many past societies. All of these studies show the fruitfulness of studying ritual in various Andean archaeological contexts.

In the past few years, influential books have been published about Andean ritual that focus on a particular archaeological locality and time period, such as Inka (Meddens et al. 2014) and colonial ritual in Lake Titicaca (Bauer and Stanish 2001), or on certain rituals, such as sacrifice (Benson and Cook 2001), feasting (Klarich 2010), and the worship of Andean sacred entities, or *wak'as* (Bray 2015). The chapters in this volume address different dimensions and implications of ritual in the prehispanic, colonial, and post-colonial Andean world. Many contributors to this volume were inspired theoretically by studies in cultural anthropology (Alberti et al. 2011; Geertz 1973; Henare, Holbraad, and Wastell 2007; Rappaport 1999; Turner 1969), particularly those within the Andean realm (e.g., Allen 1988; Bastien 1978; Moore 1996; Weismantel 1988). The goal of this volume is to synthesize archaeological studies of ritual specifically for the Andes by (1) exploring the various methods (e.g., architecture, ceramic styles, Geographic Information Systems) with which archaeologists identify ritual in the material record and (2) discussing the influence ritual had on the formation of, reproduction of, and changes in community life in past Andean societies. This volume presents current research from various archaeological contexts and time periods in the Andean region of South America, including Peru, Bolivia, Chile, and Argentina.

RITUALS AND THE ARCHAEOLOGICAL RECORD

The use of the plural term *rituals* in the title of this volume points to the variety of theoretical and methodological approaches to the study of ritual in anthropology and archaeology. One approach to the study of ritual has been to follow a theoretical view based primarily on practice theory, which posits that the structure of daily life serves as a small-scale reflection of the broader organizational tenets of society (Bourdieu 1977). This perspective aligns with the argument made in religious studies by Bell (1992) and later reinforced in anthropology by Moore (2005) that ritual action and ritual belief cannot be separated. Ritual is viewed as more than just action, but one wholly embedded within the larger social structure of the particular society. In this sense, this practice approach opened the platform for studying ritual from an everyday life perspective and away from an emphasis on monumental archaeological sites. Some of the case studies in this volume, while not necessarily following this theoretical perspective, do discuss ritual in a variety of non-monumental contexts, including mountain-pass shrines (Nielsen, Angiorama, and Ávila), quarry mines (Van Gijseghem and Whalen), and small architectural structures (Contreras).

The approach to ritual followed by many contributors to this volume is the one exemplified by Rick, who defines ritual as customary actions that are effective in obtaining outcomes over which the participants have little controlling power. In this sense, many of the scholars in this volume understand ritual as a specific set of practices conducted to legitimize certain power relations. For some of these scholars, ritual is interpreted as an important medium of integration (Onuki, Vega-Centeno Sara-Lafosse), resistance (Capriata Estrada and López-Hurtado), assimilation (Abraham), decentralization (Contreras), and competition (Chicoine et al.). Rituals are also approached in this volume as social action that addresses non-human agents (Nielsen, Angiorama, and Ávila). In this regard, ritual can be seen as an enactment of relationships tying humans to spirits, gods, ancestors, animals, and objects. Because these relationships are acted out based on personal experience, every ritual can be acted out in unusual ways (Houseman 2004:76). As argued by Swenson (2011), the study of ritual can be particularly valuable when it is engaged with the historical specificities of political organizations as structured by unique cosmologies. In this sense, some of the case studies in this volume discuss particular Andean meanings to show how ritual worked actively in the construction of distinctive landscapes and worldviews (see Nielsen, Angiorama, and Ávila; Onuki; Rick; Van Gijseghem and Whalen, this volume).

Scholars have debated whether ritual should be understood as religious (e.g., Bell 2007; Bradley 2003; Fogelin 2007; Renfrew 2007). Bell, for instance, argues that we can identify ritualization if we can distinguish how a society made such distinctions as those between sacred and profane or domestic and ritual (Bell 2007:284–85). If not, Bell argues that it would be a challenge for archaeologists to argue for the presence of ritual (ibid.:285). Dualist models would separate religious from secular ritual (e.g., Renfrew 2007). Religious rituals imply the invocation of the supernatural, as when in a Catholic baptism God is invoked to bless the baptized. Secular rituals would not involve the supernatural; and they can be political (e.g., presidential inaugurations or monarch coronations), educational (e.g., raising the flag at school every morning), or social (e.g., civil marriage). As many scholars argue, however, the relationship between religious/sacred and secular/domestic is more complex, and each element cannot be disentangled from the other (Angelo 2014; Hastorf 2007:78; Hodder 2010:14; Iteanu 2004:99).

Bradley (2003), for example, argues that the opposition between ritual and everyday practice is not helpful in understanding later prehistoric European contexts. He understands ritual as an extension of daily life, a practice that affected the ways artifacts, food, and settlements were formally placed (ibid.:21). The excavations and research at Neolithic Çatalhöyük have also revealed evidence of ritual in domestic houses, such as repetitive and formal installations of wild animal skulls, claws, and teeth on the walls of houses (Hodder and Cessford 2004). Hodder has recently argued that all of the buildings in Çatalhöyük show ample evidence of both ritual and quotidian activity (Hodder 2010:16). Similarly, ethnographic and archaeological research in the Andes shows that many communities experience ritual as part of their daily life, in part because their material world is perceived as powerful, animated, and subjective to human agency; therefore, many quotidian activities are embedded with acts of ritual (e.g., Allen 1988; Hastorf 2007; Sillar 2004). Bolin (1998) demonstrates this when she discusses the sacrificial offerings of llamas made to the earth (*Pachamama*), the mountains (*apus*), and the Thunder God (*Qhaya*) to increase the size of the camelid herd.

While the distinction between religious and secular may not have been clear in prehistory, most rituals seem to involve the invocation of a greater power. As many studies have shown (e.g., Allen 1988; Bolin 1998; Fernandini and Ruales, this volume; Rick, this volume; Van Gijseghem and Whalen, this volume), the entanglement between ritual and domestic does not preclude scholars from understanding ritual in a variety of ways in different Andean societies across time.

More recently, Aldenderfer (2011:24) has criticized archaeologists for focusing too much on ritual at the expense of religion, creating what he calls a "disembodied ritual." According to Aldenderfer, what archaeologists seek to understand is "religion in action" (ibid.) and what it did for specific societies. Aldenderfer is not concerned with a definition of religion but rather with what religion does. Similar to Bell's (2007) argument about explaining religion in archaeology, Aldenderfer (2011:28) talks about recognizing "contrasts" in the archaeological record. One way to do this is through careful documentation of changes in the archaeological data across time (see, for example, Abraham, Chicoine et al., this volume).

The identification of ritual depends on the society and the culture. Hodder (2010:14) has argued for a contextual and interpretative approach in archaeology. Particular spaces, particular configurations of artifacts or other archaeological material can point to the presence of ritual activity in a contextually situated society. As mentioned, while ritual can be intertwined with everyday practice, Hodder observed that "some events stand out" (ibid.:16) in their context. From a different perspective, Handelman (2004:4) has claimed that it is possible and necessary to first separate ritual as a phenomenon from its sociocultural surrounding and then reinsert the ritual back into its environment to assess an interpretation. He has suggested thinking about ritual in its own terms. This perspective is not followed by most of the authors in this volume. For the most part it is argued here that ritual has been a motor of transformation in the past and present Andes in a variety of ways. This is also an interpretation seen in many ethnohistoric sources on the Andes. For example, provinces who rebelled against the Inka were punished, as the Inka would publicly insult the provincial gods until the rebellious group surrendered. At this time the non-Inka gods were restored to their places and properly honored (Cobo 1997 [1653]:3–4). Further, the Inka famously reordered and rebuilt ceremonial places during their conquests based on existing practices to facilitate the establishment of the new ideology and thus enact sociopolitical change through ritual practices (MacCormack 1991:88). This is not to say that ritual was always used to produce intentional outcomes; but in the Andean cases studies shown here, ritual is interpreted as more than ritual for its own sake.

At a methodological level, if ritual is understood as the performance of sequences of informal and formal acts (Marcus 2007:45; Rappaport 1999:24) to unfold action, its repetitive character should leave traces in the archaeological record and allow the identification of its performative location and related paraphernalia. Rituals can have a repetitive character because they tend to include formal aspects in terms of both action and time. Ritual participants may know the sequence of specific rituals and what to expect before they attend. The periodicity of ritual varies according to the specific practice, but participants usually know when to expect it. A ritual can be practiced daily (e.g., nightly prayer before bedtime), be seasonal (e.g., solstice festival), or be prompted by specific circumstances such as an individual's life cycle (e.g., birth, maturity, marriage, sickness, death) or extreme environmental factors (e.g., drought or flooding; see Fernandini and Ruales, Rick, this volume). Of course, not all repetitive activities should be interpreted as ritual, but repetition is one of the characteristics that helps archaeologists identify ritual in the archaeological record.

Since ritual is about social actions and performances, its recurrent patterns, while not static, can help archaeologists engage theory with evidence. There are at least three observations for the identification of ritual in the material record: (1) archaeologists can identify types of places where rituals tend to occur (e.g., burials under house floors or platforms in some Andean sites; see Onuki, this volume), and (2) archaeologists can identify the last ritual performed in an area in which the same type of ritual occurred multiple times. These areas may be key locations for ritual, but they may also be cleaned every time, leaving few traces until the last ritual is performed and the space is abandoned (e.g., open patios for sponsored state feasts, closure rituals; see Capriata Estrada and López-Hurtado, Edwards Fernandini and Ruales, this volume). Finally, (3) archaeologists can find an area of repetitive ritual performance that is used over and over again without being cleaned each time, and the archaeological material therefore accumulated over time (e.g., shrines; see Nielsen, Angiorama, and Ávila, this volume). Finally, we need to remember that archaeologists may only find a portion of the artifacts used in a ritual. Certain artifacts were probably used repeatedly but conservatively and were not left as dedication in the ritual area.

RITUAL IN THE ANDES

Andean life is imbued with ritual significance. Myths, meanings, and daily practices are linked to mountain peaks, rocks, caves, streams, and lakes, but also to field boundaries, canals, and houses, making the landscape as well as the environment a place of potency beyond resource potentials. (Hastorf 2007:78)

The Andes, a succession of parallel and transverse mountain ranges, or cordilleras, extend over the modern-day South American countries of Ecuador, Peru, Bolivia, Venezuela, Chile, and Argentina. The archaeological record demonstrates that the Andes were the backdrop of some of the world's best-known prehispanic cultures (e.g., Nasca, Moche, Inka). Moreover, we know from ethnohistorical, ethnographic, and anthropological sources that ritual was a key component in the formation and maintenance of many of these prehispanic societies, as well as of present-day Andean indigenous communities (Abercrombie 1998; Bolin 1998; Isbell 1978). Many scholars have observed that some of the ritual practices and traditions are continuations from prehispanic times. For example, the present-day worship of the Andean mountains (*apus*) has been documented throughout many Andean areas (Allen 1988; Anders 1986; Bolin 1998; Reinhard 1985), and ethnohistorical documents indicate that the Inka also practiced this type of ritual (Gose 1986; Kuznar 2001). Andean archaeologists have used this evidence to make archaeological inferences about pre-Inka apu worshipping practices for societies such as the Wari (AD 550–950) (e.g., Glowacki and Malpass 2003; Moseley 2001; Williams and Nash 2006). While the rituals may have continued through time, their meanings were constantly reconstructed. Following this tradition, some case studies in this volume deal with certain rituals (e.g., termination rituals, *apacheta/* cairn worship, and mountain worship) that appear to have been recurrent in many parts of the Andes as fluid and dynamic practices (Edwards; Nielsen, Angiorama, and Ávila, Van Gijseghem and Whalen, this volume).

Through the study of archaeological, ethnographic, linguistic, and historical evidence from northern Peru to northern Chile, Bolivia, and northwest Argentina, the authors in this volume show the significance of ritual from pre-contact to the present day in the Andes. The volume, however, does not follow one specific theoretical or methodological approach; instead, broad topics are of concern to many of the contributors. The analysis of Andean ceremonial architecture to infer power relationships is present in many of the case studies (e.g., Abraham, Chicoine et al., Edwards, Fernandini and Ruales, this volume). This is not surprising, given that the social effort implied in public construction can be understood as a reflection of power (Moore 1996:3) and also because people's values and beliefs shaped Andean architecture (ibid.:123). However, current research (Bray 2015; Meddens et al. 2014) has demonstrated that rituals can be performed beyond architectural walls and in a variety of entities. Some of the authors in this volume demonstrate this phenomenon; Nielsen and colleagues discuss rituals at mountain passes and apachetas, and Van Gijseghem and Whalen focus on rituals inside mines. Other scholars, while focusing mostly on architecture, connect rituals in human-nature engagements such as with canals and water (Rick, this volume) and floors and fire (Onuki, this volume). Another important topic is the relationship between Andean cosmologies and social memory (e.g., Onuki; Nielsen, Angiorama, and Ávila; Van Gijseghem and Whalen, this volume). The chapters in this book demonstrate how the archaeological study of ritual activity can help us better understand past ideology, site function, elite strategies of power, local adaptations to colonialism, and perceptions of space and landscape.

The chapters in this volume are organized based on common themes and loosely chronological associations. Of course, other divisions could have been possible, since some similar topics (e.g., the study of structured depositions) crosscut different theoretical approaches and time periods. However, a chronological order was needed since the essays deal with data from one large region: the Andes. The volume begins with a discussion of ritual to understand cosmologies and ideologies during Chavín times in present-day Peru. After discussing the taphonomy of ritual evidence at Chavín de Huántar, John Rick details a variety of ritual locations, which include pits, construction fills, and, most notably, underground galleries and canals. While the canals functioned to drain and supply water, Rick interprets the complex design and content of part of the canals as places where water-related rituals took place. The concentration of complete but smashed vessels at the conjunction of canals is understood as an indication of possible locations of ritual sacrifice. Situating his interpretation within specific Andean cosmology, Rick suggests that these particular contexts could have represented the Andean belief *tinku*: the ritual encounter of water and people. These water-related rituals were perhaps performed to control the risks and outcomes involving water's energy, which would have been part of the complex belief system at the temple of Chavín.

Both Onuki and Contreras analyze the relationship between Andean ideology and cosmology by studying the early ceremonial architectural style known as Mito. Daniel Contreras discusses the presence of Mito-style architecture at the margins of the site of Chavín de Huántar and its relationship to the contemporaneous use of monumental structures in the core of the Chavín landscape. Contreras argues that the diversity in ritual architecture demonstrates that a variety of social and religious sources existed contemporaneously at Chavín, which allowed authorities to reinforce different ritual practices at this early ceremonial complex. His work reminds us of the importance and complexity of understanding ritual architectural relationships and their social implications within one site.

Yoshio Onuki discusses ritual innovation and ideology during the early Formative in the northern highlands of Peru. He interprets the processes of temple burial and renovation of Mito ceremonial architecture at the site of Kotosh as part of an ideology that may have originated from Amazonian myths and the slash-and-burn agriculture practiced in the tropical lowlands. He also claims that the stone sculptures and gold objects found at the site of Kuntur Wasi show animal and plant themes in common with those of the tropical lowlands. Onuki concludes that these data could provide evidence of a pre-Chavín tropical forest/highland interaction.

Other contributors consider the relationship between architectural design and differential access to and control of ritual participation and performance. Rafael Vega-Centeno Sara-Lafosse analyzes spatial organization and the movement of people at the site of Pampa de las Llamas–Moxeke in the Casma Valley of Peru during the early Formative period (1800–1200 BC). Previously, archaeologists had hypothesized that the architectural complex Huaca A had mainly been used as an administrative center. Through the analysis of corridor and door arrangements, Vega-Centeno argues that it was used exclusively by small, elite groups of people to perform rituals. Furthermore, he suggests that Huaca A summit architecture had a system designed to congregate and integrate multiple social groups.

From a regional and diachronic perspective, David Chicoine, Hugo Ikehara, Koichiro Shibata, and Matthew Helmer use Geographic Information Systems (GIS) to reconstruct landscapes of ritual practices in the Nepeña Valley of coastal Ancash, Peru, and to monitor their changes during the second part of the Formative period (circa 1100–150 BC). They argue for the use of ceremonial monuments as tools for social control, political integration, and intercommunal competition. Their analysis of isovistas shows that the buildings of the middle Formative period were designed to impress large audiences and viewers beyond the immediate architectural precinct. Leaders were interested in reaching and integrating most of the plains communities. During the final Formative period, however, their isovista analysis reveals more restrictive viewsheds of the religious buildings, which suggests a marked concern toward increased control over and exclusivity of ritual spaces and performances. The causes of these changes are still under research.

In the next three chapters, termination rituals and structured depositions are discussed in connection to political relationships. Matthew Edwards focuses on ritual closure at the site of Pataraya in the Southern Nasca Region of the Peruvian South Coast around AD 950. He argues that the abandonment of Pataraya was planned during the time when the Wari Empire began to disintegrate. Edwards interprets a detailed sequence of closing ritual practices that includes burned offerings, smashed pottery, and obstructed passageways. The architectural analysis revealed a pattern that limited travel within the enclosure. This suggests the obstructed passageways were part of a sequence of ritual events that perhaps included a procession across the site. This chapter highlights particularly well the ways archaeology can reveal past ritual systems, as the Wari enacted a type of funeral service for the closure of Pataraya that gave architecture the same respect and farewell as would a human burial.

Francesca Fernandini and Mario Ruales analyze the archaeological evidence at Cerro de Oro, a Middle Horizon site in the Cañete Valley on the Central Coast of Peru. They discuss the permeable boundaries between the mundane and the eventful and focus their analysis on a series of practices that include offering pits, closure rites, and intrusive burials to understand the ritual spectrum occurring in this settlement. They compare these rituals in size and place across the site and conclude that they were regular and repetitive practices involving the community at many different scales.

Camila Capriata Estrada and Enrique López-Hurtado contribute to the topic of termination rituals by exploring the intentional burning of selected spaces at Panquilma, a Late Intermediate Period–Late Horizon settlement located in the Lurín Valley on the Peruvian Central Coast. They found no evidence of foreign vandalism or extensive destruction at the site; instead, evidence of burned roofs over the clean floors of ceremonial areas suggests that this destruction was carefully planned and executed by local people. Capriata Estrada and López-Hurtado suggest that this burning was part of a terminal ritual performed by local ruling elites before abandoning Panquilma at the time the Inka polity arrived in the area.

The chapters by Abraham, Nielsen and colleagues, and Van Gijseghem and Whalen discuss ritual in late prehispanic and colonial times in very particular places: chapels, shrines, and mines. Sarah Abraham examines religious architecture and different forms of religious practices during the colonial era. She discusses novel forms of worship in the early colonial Andes of southern Peru as the introduction of Christianity became entangled with local ritual practices. Abraham examines the religious architecture of the La Quinta chapel, which was built between two prehispanic sunken courts at the site of Pukara in the Titicaca Basin of the Peruvian Puno region. She argues that this chapel has hybridized architectural forms and designs, which suggests that a new type of ritual space and architectural style was created by the inclusion of Andean and European elements. This mixed architectural form may have represented Christianity in a more traditional Andean environment, and it suggests that religious practices may have been intentionally hybridized during early colonial times. Abraham contrasts these early colonial religious architectural designs and practices with those that occurred following the rigid Toledan reforms. To this end, she compares La Quinta with the church of Santa Isabel in the same town. Abraham's religious architectural analysis is an excellent example of the dynamic nature of traditional and European ritual practices in the Andes.

Axel Nielsen, Carlos Angiorama, and Florencia Ávila discuss the relationship between non-human agency and ritual practice. Using ethnographic, ethnohistorical, and archaeological data, they focus on the late pre-Hispanic shrines travelers left at mountain passes across the borders of Argentina, Bolivia, and Chile. Based on the location and material content of offering pits and *apachetas* (cairns), they offer several interpretations of their ritual symbolism: the union of resources from different productive and cultural areas, places where travelers left gifts for non-human beings to secure safe travels, or places where travelers "fed" the mountains and earth to secure health and fertility. The authors conclude with an account of the genealogy of ritual practices from hunter-gatherer to current times and discuss the unique ways in which travelers ritually engaged with non-human agents at these high mountain passes.

Hendrik Van Gijseghem and Verity Whalen use ritual and linguistic data from the Ica Valley of southern Peru to argue that places where pre-Hispanic mining was performed were regarded as both ritually laden and dangerous. They suggest that these beliefs continued into the historical period, as evidenced in the maintenance of ancient place names or their translations in Spanish. As a mechanism for the transmission of social memory, toponyms can communicate information not only by the physical characteristics of certain spaces but also by the social consensus on particular attitudes toward such places.

In the final chapter, Jerry Moore offers a closing assessment of the different arguments presented by the individual contributors.

These chapters deal with theoretical and methodological concerns in anthropology and archaeology—including non-human and human agency, the development and maintenance of political and religious authority, ideology, cosmologies, and social memory—and their relationships with ritual action. By providing a diachronic and widely regional perspective on ritual in the Andes, this volume shows how ritual is both persistent and dynamic and also key in understanding many aspects of the formation, reproduction, and change of life in past Andean societies.

ACKNOWLEDGMENTS

This edited volume originated from the papers presented during the symposium Ritual Practice in the Andes, organized by the authors at the Society of American Archaeology Meeting in Memphis, Tennessee, in 2012. We are grateful to the symposium participants and the discussants Jerry Moore and Timothy Pauketat. We also thank the Stanford University Center for Latin American Studies and the Stanford Archaeology Center for their support in funding the initial development of this edited volume. We thank Nicco LaMattina for his help in preparing the manuscript. We thank two anonymous reviewers who provided helpful advice.

REFERENCES CITED

Abercrombie, T. A. 1998. *Pathways of Memory and Power: Ethnography and History among an Andean People*. Madison: University of Wisconsin Press.

Albarracin-Jordan, J., J. M. Capriles, and M. J. Miller. 2014. "Transformations in Ritual Practice and Social Interaction on the Tiwanaku Periphery." *Antiquity* 88 (341): 851–62. http://dx.doi.org/10.1017/S0003598X00050730.

Alberti, B., S. Fowles, M. Holbraad, Y. Marshall, and C. Witmore. 2011. "'Worlds Otherwise': Archaeology, Anthropology, and Ontological Difference." *Current Anthropology* 52 (6): 896–912. http://dx.doi.org/10.1086/662027.

Aldenderfer, M. 2011. "Envisioning a Pragmatic Approach to the Archaeology of Religion." *Archaeological Papers of the American Anthropological Association* 21 (1): 23–36. http://dx.doi.org/10.1111/j.1551-8248.2012.01035.x.

Allen, C. J. 1988. *The Hold Life Has: Coca and the Cultural Identity in an Andean Community*. Smithsonian Series in Ethnographic Inquiry. Washington, DC: Smithsonian Institution Press.

Anders, M. 1986. "Dual Organization and Calendars Inferred from the Planned Site of Azangaro: Wari Administrative Strategies." PhD dissertation, Department of Anthropology, Cornell University, Ithaca, NY.

Angelo, D. 2014. "Assembling Ritual, the Burden of the Everyday: An Exercise in Relational Ontology in Quebrada de Humahuaca, Argentina." *World Archaeology* 46 (2): 270–87. http://dx.doi.org/10.1080/00438243.2014.891948.

Arkush, E. 2005. "Inca Ceremonial Sites in the Southwest Titicaca Basin." In *Advances in the Archaeology of the Titicaca Basin*, ed. C. Stanish, A. Cohen, and M. Aldenderfer, 209–42. Los Angeles: Cotsen Institute of Archaeology, University of California.

Bastien, J. W. 1978. *Mountain of the Condor: Metaphor and Ritual in an Andean Ayllu*. Prospect Heights, NY: Waveland.

Bauer, B. S., and C. Stanish. 2001. *Ritual and Pilgrimage in the Ancient Andes: The Islands of the Sun and the Moon*. Austin: University of Texas Press.

Bell, C. M. 1992. *Ritual Theory, Ritual Practice*. New York: Oxford University Press.

Bell, C. M. 2007. "Response: Defining the Need for a Definition." In *The Archaeology of Ritual*, ed. E. Kyriakidis, 277–88. Los Angeles: Cotsen Institute of Archaeology, University of California.

Benson, E. P., and A. G. Cook, eds. 2001. *Ritual Sacrifice in Ancient Peru*. Austin: University of Texas Press.

Berggren, A., and L. N. Stutz. 2010. "From Spectator to Critic and Participant: A New Role for Archaeology in Ritual Studies." *Journal of Social Archaeology* 10 (2): 171–97. http://dx.doi.org/10.1177/1469605310365039.

Bolin, I. 1998. *Rituals of Respect: The Secret of Survival in the High Peruvian Andes*. Austin: University of Texas Press.

Bolton, R. 1979. "Guinea Pigs, Protein, and Ritual." *Ethnology* 18 (3): 229–52. http://dx.doi.org/10.2307/3773376.

Bourdieu, P. 1977. *Outline of a Theory of Practice*. Cambridge: Cambridge University Press. http://dx.doi.org/10.1017/CBO9780511812507.

Bradley, R. 2003. "A Life Less Ordinary: The Ritualization of the Domestic Sphere in Later Prehistoric Europe." *Cambridge Archaeological Journal* 13 (1): 5–23. http://dx.doi.org/10.1017/S0959774303000015.

Bray, T., ed. 2015. *The Archaeology of Wak'as: Exploration of the Sacred in the Pre-Columbian Andes*. Boulder: University Press of Colorado.

Cobo, B. 1997 [1653]. *Inca Religion and Customs*, 3rd ed. Trans. R. Hamilton. Austin: University of Texas Press.

Cutright, R. E., E. López-Hurtado, and A. J. Martin, eds. 2010. *Comparative Perspectives on the Archaeology of Coastal South America*. Pittsburgh: Center for Comparative Archaeology, University of Pittsburgh.

DeMarrais, E., L. J. Castillo, and T. Earle. 1996. "Ideology, Materialization, and Power Strategies." *Current Anthropology* 37 (1): 15–31. http://dx.doi.org/10.1086/204472.

Dillehay, T. D. 2004. "Social Landscape and Ritual Pause: Uncertainty and Integration in Formative Peru." *Journal of Social Archaeology* 4 (2): 239–68. http://dx.doi.org/10.1177/1469605304042396.

Flores Ochoa, J. 1977. "Aspectos magicos del pastoreo: Enqa, enqaychu, illa y khuya rumi." In *Pastores de Puna: Uywamichiq punarunakuna*, ed. J. Flores Ochoa, 211–37. Lima: Instituto de Estudios Peruanos.

Fogelin, L. 2007. "The Archaeology of Religious Ritual." *Annual Review of Anthropology* 36 (1): 55–71. http://dx.doi.org/10.1146/annurev.anthro.36.081406.094425.

Gamboa Velasquez, J. 2015. "Dedication and Termination Rituals in Southern Moche Public Architecture." *Latin American Antiquity* 26 (1): 87–105. http://dx.doi.org/10.7183/1045-6635.26.1.87.

Geertz, C. 1973. *The Interpretation of Cultures: Selected Essays*. New York: Basic Books.

Glowacki, M., and M. Malpass. 2003. "Water, Huacas, and Ancestor Worship: Traces of Sacred Wari Landscape." *Latin American Antiquity* 14 (4): 431–48. http://dx.doi.org/10.2307/3557577.

Gose, P. 1986. "Sacrifice and the Commodity Form in the Andes." *Man* 21 (2): 296–310. http://dx.doi.org/10.2307/2803161.

Handelman, D. 2004. "Introduction: Why Ritual in Its Own Right? How So?" In *Ritual in Its Own Right*, ed. D. Handelman and G. Lindquist, 1–32. New York: Berhahn Books.

Hastorf, C. 2007. "Archaeological Andean Rituals: Performance, Liturgy, and Meaning." In *The Archaeology of Ritual*, ed. E. Kyriakidis, 77–108. Los Angeles: Cotsen Institute of Archaeology, University of California.

Henare, A., M. Holbraad, and S. Wastell, eds. 2007. *Thinking through Things: Theorizing Artefacts Ethnographically*. London: Routledge.

Hodder, I. 2010. "Probing Religion at Çatalhöyük: An Interdisciplinary Experiment." In *Religion in the Emergence of Civilization: Çatalhöyük as a Case Study*, ed. I. Hodder, 1–31. Cambridge: Cambridge University Press. http://dx.doi.org/10.1017/CBO9780511761416.001.

Hodder, I., and C. Cessford. 2004. "Daily Practice and Social Memory at Çatalhöyük." *American Antiquity* 69 (1): 17–40. http://dx.doi.org/10.2307/4128346.

Hodder, I., and S. Hutson. 2003. *Reading the Past: Current Approaches to Interpretation in Archaeology*, 3rd ed. Cambridge: Cambridge University Press. http://dx.doi.org/10.1017/CBO9780511814211.

Houseman, M. 2004. "The Red and the Black: A Practical Experiment for Thinking about Ritual." In *Ritual in Its Own Right*, ed. D. Handelman and G. Lindquist, 75–97. New York: Berghahn Books. http://dx.doi.org/10.3167/015597704782352555.

Inomata, T., and L. A. Coben. 2006. *Archaeology of Performance: Theaters of Power, Community, and Politics*. Archaeology in Society Series. Lanham, MD: Altamira.

Insoll, T. 2004. *Archaeology, Ritual, Religion: Themes in Archaeology*. London: Routledge.

Isbell, B. J. 1978. *To Defend Ourselves: Ecology and Ritual in an Andean Village*. Austin: Institute of Latin American Studies, University of Texas Press.

Isbell, W. H., and A. Groleau. 2010. "The Wari Brewer Woman: Feasting, Gender, Offerings, and Memory." In *Inside Ancient Kitchens: New Perspectives in the Study of Daily Meals and Feasts*, ed. E. A. Klarich, 191–219. Boulder: University Press of Colorado.

Iteanu, A. 2004. "Partial Discontinuity: The Mark of Ritual." In *Ritual in Its Own Right*, ed. D. Handelman and G. Lindquist, 98–115. New York: Berghahn Books.

Izumi, S., and K. Terada, eds. 1972. *Andes 4: Excavations at Kotosh, Peru, 1963 and 1966*. Tokyo: University of Tokyo Press.

Jennings, J., and B. Bowser, eds. 2009. *Drink, Power, and Society in the Andes*. Gainesville: University Press of Florida. http://dx.doi.org/10.5744/florida/9780813033068.001.0001.

Kantner, J., and K. J. Vaughn. 2012. "Pilgrimage as Costly Signal: Religiously Motivated Cooperation in Chaco and Nasca." *Journal of Anthropological Archaeology* 31 (1): 66–82. http://dx.doi.org/10.1016/j.jaa.2011.10.003.

Klarich, E. A., ed. 2010. *Inside Ancient Kitchens: New Directions in the Study of Daily Meals and Feasts*. Boulder: University Press of Colorado.

Knobloch, P. J. 2000. "Wari Ritual Power at Conchopata: An Interpretation of Anadenanthera Colubrina Iconography." *Latin American Antiquity* 11 (4): 387–402. http://dx.doi.org/10.2307/972003.

Kuznar, L. 2001. "An Introduction to Andean Religious Ethnoarchaeology: Preliminary Results and Future Directions." In *Ethnoarchaeology of Andean South America: Contributions to Archaeological Method and Theory*, ed. L. Kuznar, 38–66. Ethnoarchaeological Series, vol. 4. Ann Arbor, MI: International Monographs in Prehistory.

Kyriakidis, E., ed. 2007. *The Archaeology of Ritual*. Los Angeles: Cotsen Institute of Archaeology, University of California.

MacCormack, S. 1991. *Religion in the Andes: Vision and Imagination in Early Colonial Peru*. Princeton, NJ: Princeton University Press.

Marcus, J. 2007. "Rethinking Ritual." In *The Archaeology of Ritual*, ed. E. Kyriakidis, 43–76. Los Angeles: Cotsen Institute of Archaeology, University of California.

Marcus, J., and K. Flannery. 2004. "The Coevolution of Ritual and Society: New 14 C Dates from Ancient Mexico." *Proceedings of the National Academy of Sciences of the United States of America* 101 (52): 18257–61. http://dx.doi.org/10.1073/pnas.0408551102.

Meddens, F., K. Willis, C. McEwan, and N. Branch, eds. 2014. *Inca Sacred Space: Landscape, Site, and Symbol in the Andes*. London: Archetype.

Moore, J. D. 1996. *Architecture and Power in the Ancient Andes: The Archaeology of Public Buildings*. New Studies in Archaeology. Cambridge: Cambridge University Press. http://dx.doi.org/10.1017/CBO9780511521201.

Moore, J. D. 2005. *Cultural Landscapes in the Ancient Andes: Archaeologies of Place*. Gainesville: University Press of Florida.

Moseley, M. 2001. *The Incas and Their Ancestors: The Archaeology of Peru*. Revised ed. New York: Thames and Hudson.

Murra, J. V. 1975. "El control vertical de un maximo de pisos ecologicos en la economia de las sociedades andina." *Historia Andina* 3: 59–115.

Nutini, H. G. 1988. *Todos los Santos in Rural Tlaxcala: A Syncretic, Expressive, and Symbolic Analysis of the Cult of the Dead*. Princeton, NJ: Princeton University Press.

Pauketat, T., L. Kelly, G. Fritz, N. Lopinot, S. Elias, and E. Hargrave. 2002. "The Residues of Feasting and Public Ritual at Early Cahokia." *American Antiquity* 67 (2): 257–79. http://dx.doi.org/10.2307/2694566.

Rappaport, R. A. 1999. *Ritual and Religion in the Making of Humanity*. Cambridge: Cambridge University Press. http://dx.doi.org/10.1017/CBO9780511814686.

Reinhard, J. 1985. "Sacred Mountains: An Ethno-Archaeological Study of High Andean Ruins." *Mountain Research and Development* 5 (4): 299–317. http://dx.doi.org/10.2307/3673292.

Renfrew, C. 2007. "The Archaeology of Ritual, of Cult, and of Religion." In *The Archaeology of Ritual*, ed. E. Kyriakidis, 109–22. Los Angeles: Cotsen Institute of Archaeology, University of California.

Rick, J. W. 2008. "Context, Construction, and Ritual in the Development of Authority at Chavín de Huántar." In *Chavín: Art, Architecture, and Culture*, ed. W. J. Conklin and J. Quilter, 3–34. Monograph 61. Los Angeles: Cotsen Institute of Archaeology, University of California.

Rosenfeld, S. A. 2012. "Animal Wealth and Local Power in the Huari Empire: Ñawpa Pacha." *Journal of Andean Archaeology* 32: 131–64.

Rostworowski de Diez Canseco, M. 1992. *Pachacamac y el señor de los milagros: Una trayectoria milenaria*. Lima: Instituto de Estudios Peruanos.

Rostworowski de Diez Canseco, M. 2001. *Historia del Tahuantinsuyu*. Lima: Instituto de Estudios Peruanos.

Sillar, B. 2004. "Acts of God and Active Material Culture: Agency and Commitment in the Andes." In *Agency Uncovered: Archaeological Perspectives on Social Agency, Power, and Being Human*, ed. A. Gardner, 153–89. London: UCL Press.

Swenson, E. R. 2011. "Stagecraft and the Politics of Spectacle in Ancient Peru." *Cambridge Archaeological Journal* 21 (2): 283–313. http://dx.doi.org/10.1017/S095977431100028X.

Swenson, E. R., and J. P. Warner. 2012. "Crucibles of Power: Forging Copper and Forging Subjects at the Moche Ceremonial Center of Huaca Colorada, Peru." *Journal of Anthropological Archaeology* 31 (3): 314–33. http://dx.doi.org/10.1016/j.jaa.2012.01.010.

Tantaleán, H., C. Stanish, A. Rodríguez, and K. Pérez. 2016. "The Final Days of Paracas in Cerro del Gentil, Chincha Valley, Peru." *PLOS ONE* 11 (5): e0153465. doi: 10.1371/journal.pone.0153465.

Tung, T. A. 2007. "Trauma and Violence in the Wari Empire of the Peruvian Andes: Warfare, Raids, and Ritual Fights." *American Journal of Physical Anthropology* 133 (3): 941–56. http://dx.doi.org/10.1002/ajpa.20565.

Turner, V. 1967. *The Forest of Symbols: Aspects of Ndembu Ritual*. Ithaca, NY: Cornell University Press.

Turner, V. 1969. *The Ritual Process: Structure and Anti-Structure*. Ithaca, NY: Cornell University Press.

Vaughn, K. J. 2004. "Crafts and the Materialization of Chiefly Power in Nasca." *Archaeological Papers of the American Anthropological Association* 14 (1): 113–30. http://dx.doi.org/10.1525/ap3a.2004.14.113.

Weismantel, M. J. 1988. *Food, Gender, and Poverty in the Ecuadorian Andes*. Philadelphia: University of Pennsylvania Press.

Williams, P. R., and D. Nash. 2006. "Sighting the Apu: A GIS Analysis of Wari Imperialism and the Worship of Mountain Peaks." *World Archaeology* 38 (3): 455–68. http://dx.doi.org/10.1080/00438240600813491.

2

The Nature of Ritual Space at Chavín de Huántar

John W. Rick

Chavín de Huántar is a well-known middle-late Formative (1200–500 BC) site located in the north-central sierra of Peru, recognized for its monumental construction that includes fully worked stone blocks of considerable size, extensive stone art that decorated many of its architectural contexts, and major use of underground space in the form of stone-lined galleries that are often labyrinth-like and run deep into the site's major platform mounds (figure 2.1). Although the term *castillo* is still used to refer to the site or some of its buildings (e.g., Quilter 2014:140), all current investigators consider the principal function of these monumental structures to be religious and often refer to the site as the temple(s) of Chavín (Burger 1992; Lumbreras 2007; Rick 2005). While rituals may occur in a variety of contexts, it seems obvious that religious contexts are likely to witness some degree of ritual.

Ritual itself is worthy of definition, not so much for detecting it in archaeological circumstances but to generate a context in which to think about it. Ritual includes the idea of action, as it usually consists of rites or ceremonies but adds the sense of repeated actions, done in a customary manner (Merriam-Webster, "Ritual"). Beyond this simple definition, ritual has been dealt with anthropologically in a literature impossible to summarize here, but Moore's (1996) definition of ritual architecture brings important elements to the fore. He agrees with Tambiah that ritual "is a culturally constructed system of symbolic communication" (ibid.:136,

DOI: 10.5876/9781607325963.c002

FIGURE 2.1. *Current interpretation of the architectural layout of Chavín de Huántar at about 600 BC cal. Art by Miguel Ortíz.*

citing Tambiah 1985:128). In application to most archaeological situations, however, Moore acknowledges that the symbolic meanings on an etic level will be difficult to recover. This definition leaves the archaeologist with the option of simply listing the traits or assemblages of traits found archaeologically or plunging into an interpretive depth that may or may not bear a resemblance to the original meanings understood by those involved in the ritual.

I propose a somewhat different perspective. Rituals may be a form of communication, but they are likely to have been carried out, consciously or customarily, according to the purposes of the various actors. This raises the issue of effectiveness in serving those purposes, and while feeling "symbolically communicated" may be one of those purposes, I suspect that more tangible outcomes were often at issue. Outcomes that can be obtained easily and reliably because of access, power, or other capability may not need ritual involvement. Similarly, impossible outcomes are unlikely to be pursued through ritual for any length of time because the rituals will be considered ineffective. But reasonably probable outcomes that are remote in time, space, or likelihood may be facilitated, perceptually or actually, by ritual—customary actions that are effective in obtaining outcomes over which the participants have little other controlling power. Needless to say, there may be multiple desired outcomes to rituals, especially those affecting or perceived to be affecting individuals in different roles. Thus, while communication is involved in ritual, the goals and perceptions vary according to situations and who is involved.

Chavín has long been seen as a religious center in which ceremonies occurred in various contexts involving audiences or participants. This defines a set of enactors, presumably based at Chavín, who designed and built the architecture and designed and carried out the rituals and another set of participants who observed or joined the rituals. The former have often been characterized as priests or religious leaders, while the latter are termed visitors, supplicants, or travelers. There may have been a role in the center for simple agrarian participants, but I have argued that the data and configuration of Chavín emphasize the presence of high-ranked individuals. What outcomes any of these involved parties would have sought is speculative, but the architectural contexts give hints about the strategy of the planners and the experience of the participants. This chapter reviews probable ritual contexts at Chavín de Huántar, including a number recently discovered, to update our vision of this key Andean site.

ARCHITECTURE

The architectural forms at Chavín help confirm both the site's probable religious function and the presence of ritual contexts. Plazas of various sizes, largely devoid of surface features indicating obvious non-ritual functions; staircases with fairly high steps made of cut stone transported significant distances; alignments of staircases representing likely procession-ways; and highly ornamented gateways are all highly compatible with generalized ideas of ritual practice. The dark, confusing, and extensive underground spaces, mysterious and unsettling to many visitors today, are difficult to see as contexts for any comfortable residential or materially productive activities; and the expense of their planning, construction, and maintenance is at odds with any attempt to place them in an energetically advantageous strategy of space use. Add to these the massive platform mounds capped by modest-sized but massive walled and symmetrically placed structures overlooking the plazas and accessways, and the scenario of ritual seems almost undeniable. Then the negative evidence—the lack of residential architecture in the site's monumental core,[1] the lack of occupation deposits with any apparent evidence of trash expected of residential function, and, perhaps tellingly, the complete lack of hearths suitable for residential cooking—is compatible with the assumption that the monumental center of Chavín functioned primarily as a religious center. Lack of evidence for storage of mundane materials, lack of any defensive strategy in the architecture, and the scarcity of generalized weaponry further distance us from alternative functions. Puzzling but perhaps compatible with these observations is the total lack thus far of interments of formally positioned, complete human remains, but the presence of non-articulated human bones—often broken, burned, or cut marked—in scattered locales suggests potential ritual activity resulting in the deposition of human remains (Lumbreras 2007:300). All of these are arguments that the monumental core of Chavín served primarily, if not exclusively, as a site of ideologically related activities. Moreover, others and I have argued that there seems to be consistency in the successive architectural forms and layouts that suggests a presence and continuity of a planning strategy over many centuries (Kembel 2008:78). I have argued that Chavín's configuration is a strategic attempt to create a physical context that would have generated desired psychological states in inductees and participants in the evident cult of Chavín (Rick 2005, 2006).

Thus, in a general sense, it is possible to argue for Chavín's core having served as a religious center, even if the heart of many of these arguments is to some degree the classic "if we can't otherwise identify the function, it must be religious/ceremonial/ideological." But the evidence can probably be seen as arguing that these are temples beyond a reasonable doubt. Turning to ritual, we face the necessity of populating the scene with specific contexts, actors, objects, activities, and intentionality on a far more explicit level. Aside from the inference of processions, what actual evidence is there for ritual activities in the center? Prior to the Proyecto de Investigaciones y Conservación de Chavín de Huántar (hereafter the Stanford Project), relatively few projects had either reached stratigraphic depths to observe Chavín period ceremonial remains, were working in appropriate locations, or had documented or published any relevant evidence. A notable exception was Lumbreras's excavation of the Ofrendas Gallery in 1966 and 1967, producing what he interprets as an extensive offering of highly elaborate pottery and other materials that served as a dedicatory offering for the adjacent Circular Plaza (Lumbreras 1993, 2007). The late site caretaker/curator Marino González Moreno cleared many key ritual locations in Chavín, but in spite of significant records of his work now being published (González Moreno 2012; Lumbreras and González Moreno 2012), it seems unlikely that data of the quality capable of inferring ritual behavior will emerge. Thus, we largely have conjectural contexts with little evidence of specific ritual activity.

This raises a particularly difficult issue for most ritual analysis, especially in formal settings such as ceremonial centers—the taphonomy of ritual evidence is often overlooked, and our most reasonable site formation models for intensively used and maintained ritual use surfaces will predict only rare and poorly preserved remnants of the actual activities. Chavín is no exception—our experience excavating over a wide range of Chavín surface contexts confirms that Chavín was maintained with an exceptional lack of accumulation of sediments or artifacts. Most deposits built up over likely ritual surfaces are identifiably post-Chavín in age, either from subsequent cultural periods or from post-Chavín erosional processes or events. While we attempt to intensify field methodologies to capture fugitive and small-scale data in such surface circumstances, overall the prospect of Pompeii-like fossilization of original surface materials in ritual-reflecting distribution is not promising. The Chavín Stanford Project has been able to identify discarded materials from the cleaning and reconstruction of ritual space and architecture (Mesía 2007), but behavioral inference from such materials will always be difficult at best. Chavín has the distinct advantage of cave-like underground contexts, in which at least some surface natural transformations of the archaeological record may be reduced (e.g., plowing, some forms of washing, heavy temperature swings) and dispersion contained. Other natural transformation, especially water transport in canals, and cultural transformations may be focused and extreme; in practical reality it seems that many of the galleries of Chavín were explored and largely cleared prior to the beginning of careful archaeological methodologies.

We are searching for the material correlates of ritual activity, which logically involve ritual material, its local distribution as relatable to human activity, the architectural and landscape contexts of those assemblages, and their greater pattern within a ceremonial core. At best we can hope for a certain percentage of the objects and patterns to be preserved and recoverable across time; many may have been eliminated, altered, reorganized, intermixed, and made otherwise difficult to use as evidence of ritual. Within Chavín, it is clear that many contexts have been altered or destroyed across time; the biggest factors are:

1. The inferred Chavín period maintenance of ritual areas, removing physical remnants of activities on a regular basis
2. Activities of immediately subsequent people who clearly dismantled and otherwise altered many contexts, particularly the more elaborate ceremonial ones
3. The long-term cultivation and animal husbandry still occurring on the site at the time of Julio C. Tello's early research in the early decades of the twentieth century (Tello 1960)
4. Clearing of sediments down to the highest recognized Chavín structures and surfaces, a mid-twentieth-century archaeological practice that took little care in detection and documentation, not to mention publication (Lumbreras and González Moreno 2012)

5. The erosion and displacement of structures and materials caused by the massive 1945 landslide (Indacochea and Iberico 1947; Turner, Knight, and Rick 1999), which impacted, scoured, and buried the site, injecting sediments under high pressure into even well-sealed underground spaces.

Thus, physical evidence of ritual activity on flat, unobstructed surfaces will be the least likely to have survived, having been easily cleaned, perforated through, swept away, or excavated out of existence. Contexts that accumulate sediment rapidly, such as sunken plaza floors and other basins, will have somewhat greater potential, as do intentionally sealed situations in which surfaces or structures were intentionally buried (see Contreras, this volume). Materials and contexts that are underground have much greater potential for preservation but are also foci of subsequent activity, at Chavín used for trash pits (or dumps) or post-Chavín interments or suffering intentional cleaning or looting. Ritual materials intentionally placed underground, such as offerings, have much greater potential for survival if not removed by looting. Perhaps the best situations that can be hoped for would be materials and contexts used for actual underground ritual activity, in which the chambers or other spaces will naturally contain the materials, where reduced light or access may limit the removal of materials, and where rapid sedimentation will tend to cover materials quickly.

MATERIAL EVIDENCE OF RITUAL AT CHAVÍN DE HUÁNTAR: RECENT FINDS

The strategy of this analysis will be to examine material finds in recent work at Chavín de Huántar by the Stanford Project, within general locational categories that consider the architectural and other contextual factors simultaneously.

Finds on Exterior Use Surfaces

A fair range of excavated areas falls within this category—notably, surfaces in the area of the Black-and-White Portal of Building A, the atrium of the Circular Plaza, the floor of the Circular Plaza, small surface areas to the west of Buildings A, B, and C (but within the core), surfaces to the north of Building C, and the edge of the monumental core in the Wacheqsa sector (figure 2.2). A complexity to consider is that many of these areas had multiple use surfaces in the Chavín period, as floors and buildings were superimposed over time. In most cases we only have the chance to see the latest Chavín surface, given our project policy of not removing or damaging Chavín period structures to

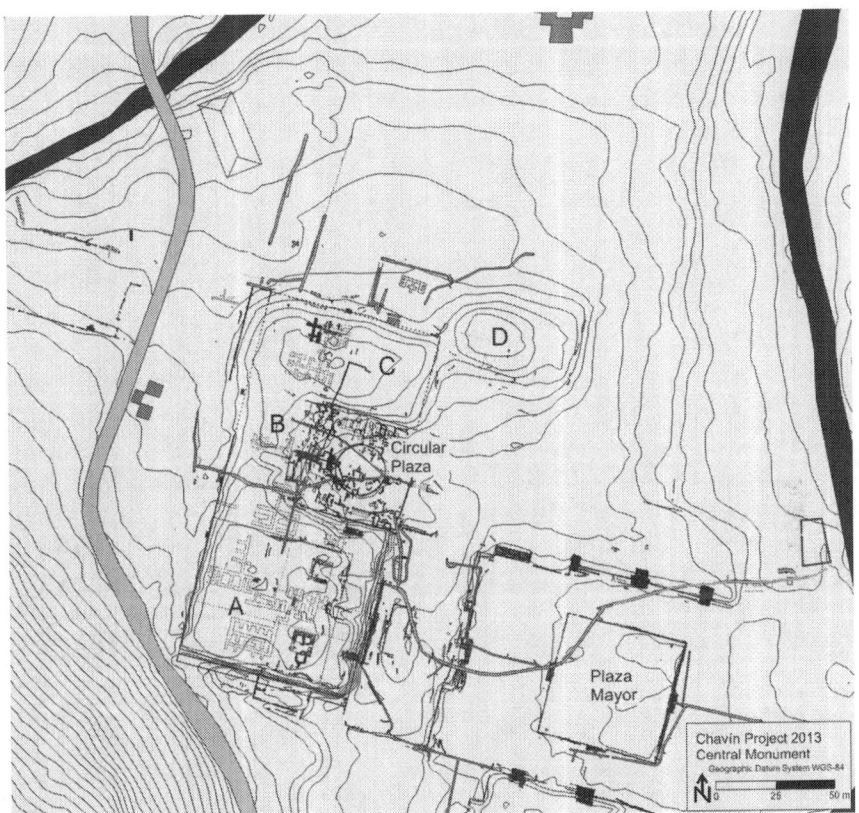

FIGURE 2.2. *Map of relevant parts of the monumental core of Chavín de Huántar, showing plazas, major buildings A–D, and locations mentioned in the text*

access underlying spaces. Although in many cases the preservation of these surfaces was adequate, very few materials were found on the surfaces, and there were few non-architectural indications of ritual arrangements. Materials in fills between Chavín surfaces are considered separately.

The most notable examples come from excavations to the north of Building C, where a complex arrangement of ceremonial architecture has been uncovered with some Chavín period use surfaces reasonably undisturbed. The central and perhaps dominant feature of this late Chavín (ca. 900–550 cal BC) arrangement is an otherwise unknown architectural form for the site—an elevated ramp leading to the facade of Building C. Lying between the balustrade walls of the ramp is an elongate flat surface bearing a small-dimension surface canal, which is draining toward the building rather than away from it.

The surface itself is well-defined, consisting of packed clay into which small fragments of material were embedded. The floor contents were primarily tiny but highly decorated Chavín black ware sherds, fragments of a variety of bone ornaments, and small fragments of turquoise and obsidian; it is unclear if the latter are broken ornaments or shatter from production. By a close examination, it has become obvious that obsidian was massively smashed and otherwise reduced and damaged. The abrupt angular fracture pattern and intense surface scratching on the very small obsidian fragments in a number of Building C ceremonial contexts suggest intentional destruction in what may have been sacrificial acts (figure 2.3). Overall, the material on this floor is small, broken, and detrital in character but consists of remnants of rare raw materials or highly worked items that would be consistent with showy ritual activity involving the intentional destruction of valued materials.

Another potentially parallel situation comes from the Circular Plaza, where an opportunity to excavate below the ca. 800 BC plaza floor revealed a flag-surfaced floor found about 2.5 m below. While the 2 m × 2 m area was insufficient to determine if this is a plaza floor, the area did reveal that a small-dimension canal, similar in size to the one mentioned above, was present on top of the flagstones and used them as the canal base. The floor was immediately overlain by typical layered stone and clay mortar fills but had been clean prior to the fill buildup.

Finds within Construction Fills

Chavín monumental construction "fills" generally consist of a formulaic combination of tempered clay mortar surrounding layered, highly selected quartzite blocks of elongate rectangular form, sometimes laid in courses that alternate orientation to provide an interlock between layers. On occasion we have penetrated this exceptionally stable core of construction and noted that within the massive clay mortar is a slight but consistent background of very small, often less than 1 cm pottery, obsidian, and marine shell fragments. The regularity of this presence likely represents some sort of background behavior regularly supplying this material to the construction process. A second fill content is the presence of camelid bones, usually found in small groups in limited fill areas, as if the remains of some camelid-related event that occurred at or near the time of the fill installation. Notable in these cases is that this occurs in fills of major buildings, as described, and in somewhat less organized fills used to build up terraces and some floor surfaces; also, the bones, often large fragments or complete bones, come from bony extremities

FIGURE 2.3. *Samples of smashed, hammered, and scratched obsidian angular debris illustrating intentional destruction of this material in a number of Building C contexts*

of camelids, which seem to be exceptionally large in size compared with modern llamas.

A quite different assemblage comes from clear concentrations within fills, representing materials deposited in high density within limited layers. Such a deposit was found in the West Field area (see Contreras, this volume, for a more detailed description of this sector) toward the top of a deep fill built up in a single event in late, possibly terminal, Chavín times (estimated on ceramic associations to 750–500 BC cal) to avoid the collapse of a massive facade of a West Field monumental building. This thin layer contained the fragmented remains of a very limited number of late Chavín vessels, with many fragments per vessel present. The pottery included polychrome pre-fire painted, post-fire resin-painted, and incised vessels with a decorative style unlikely to have come from the Chavín area, as well as Janabarroide[2] black polished circle-stamped vessels typical of Chavín and an oversized camelid ulna sculpted to provide a tray-like form. These objects and the surrounding soil were stained and at times saturated with a cherry-red mineral colorant that appears to be cinnabar, clearly an intentional scattering of concentrated pigment. The material was apparently deposited within a fill episode, but it is not certain whether this represents a use surface within that fill or simply materials deposited during continual filling.

A more ambiguous context comes from above the roof stone beams of lower Rocas Canal, just to the east of the north-flanking mound of the Plaza Mayor. Here, a highly localized and high-density concentration of Janabarroide sherds representing at least ten vessels was found, possibly a poorly defined pit fill or a deposit placed over the canal roof during a filling activity. Little other material was present, although a fair amount of charcoal was interspersed within the deposit. Most striking is that with very few exceptions, the hundreds of polished black potsherds were decorated only with circles, circle-dots, or concentric circle motifs—a very small subset of the Janabarroide design repertoire. We are not aware of any other sizable ceramic concentration at Chavín with anywhere close to this exclusivity of design, circles or otherwise. At the very least, this evidence indicates that pottery with certain designs was isolated for disposal and the pieces were probably used together, suggesting highly structured, likely ritual behavior (Rick 2014).

Finds within Pits or Cists

In Chavín it is rare to encounter pits dug from Chavín-era surfaces, a type of context that might have material remains that were cleaned and buried from ceremonial contexts or placed as small-scale caches or dedicatory offerings. I have previously observed the general lack of small-scale, informal, or otherwise modest offerings at Chavín (Rick 2006:210), while fairly clear offerings involve large amounts of material, exotic and probably valuable items of rare raw materials, and often a very specific range of objects, as in the case of the Ofrendas and Caracolas Galleries (Lumbreras 2007; Rick 2008:24–27).

A large conical pit of Chavín age was found in the West Field area, relatively near the major lower terrace. Although only partially excavated, since much lay beyond the excavation units undertaken, the pit was around 2.5 m in diameter and filled with fairly loose earth, complete and large fragments of camelid bones, large chunks of charcoal, and an unusual complex of Chavín pottery. Although new to us at the time, this pottery is clearly Chavín in form, often consisting of bottle forms, including some with small, spherical bodies and long, large-diameter tubular necks—often taller than the body itself by a considerable factor and often much heavier (figure 2.4). Other forms are present, but the distinctive characteristic is a fine, smooth finish on a battleship-gray

FIGURE 2.4. *Rare intact example of sacrifice ware found in a Building C subterranean canal below a vertical chimney, illustrating the striking form, fine but not highly polished surface treatment, and total lack of evident decoration typical of this category of ritual material*

ceramic that is not highly polished or decorated. Since this 2001 field season discovery, we have become accustomed to finding this ware in situations that seem to imply ritual, particularly sacrificial contexts. If accompanied by other ceramic forms, they are always among the most highly decorated of the Chavín pottery variants. In this pit, the pottery was found in distinctively large fragments—the breaks were fresh and sharp, and the vessels themselves showed little or no signs of wear, as if they arrived at this location brand-new and were broken by perhaps one simple, intentional act. The condition of this pottery seems similar to much larger sacrificial contexts associated with later Wari period sites (Cook 1984–1985; Isbell and Cook 2002) and may represent a less structured but still highly organized series of ritual acts, perhaps related to dedicatory or feasting behavior.

The large, square Plaza Mayor produced two likely ritual contexts that were located through two separate remote sensing efforts. In both cases resistive or dense anomalies were suggested starting just below the plaza surface and extending downward beyond the method's depth limitations at 2–4 m below surface. One, in the geometrical center of the plaza, proved to be a very large river boulder with signs of fire-reddening on its surface, resting within and on top of cultural deposits with varied characteristics (Rick 2008:17). To the west of the large boulder, which had been trimmed to accommodate it, we found a circular stone-lined pit covered with elongate stones. On top of the stone beams lay two *Spondylus* shell valves in closed position, full of a cherry-red powder that is likely to be cinnabar. Within the cist itself, neatly occupying the extent of the chamber, was a stone vessel with four short cylindrical feet. Low relief carving on the vessel's sides showed a continuous band of rhomboids. The vessel had originally contained pigments of various colors and a small series of poorly preserved beads of shell and soft stone. In the area of the cist we could discern the presence of a larger pit enclosing both the cist location and the huge boulder. A small air pocket was found under the boulder, sufficient to be sure that cultural material underlay it and to determine that another large rock of as-yet-unknown dimensions continues downward, within the area of the large encompassing pit. Excavation conditions and time did not permit further investigation of this feature.

A second geophysical anomaly was detected toward the northwest corner of the Plaza Mayor in 2009, which upon investigation proved to be a similarly huge river boulder again lying just below the original plaza floor and similarly burned on its surface, as evidenced by localized fire-reddening and heat spalling (figure 2.5). In this case, clear evidence was found of a pit, measuring approximately 3 m in diameter and closely enclosing the large boulder, which

FIGURE 2.5. *Exploration of deep pit below the floor of the Plaza Mayor, capped by a huge spalled and burned boulder. Pit extends at least 2 m below the base of the boulder; layers of plaza foundation construction including sizable boulders are visible in profile.*

extended downward for more than 3 m. Excavations around the boulder but within the pit found increasingly loose soil that eventually entered under the rock, but at a depth of greater than 4 m it became dangerous to work because of the overlying multi-ton boulder, and excavation was suspended. Little material of note came from the pit fill, but close to the maximum depth of our excavation we found a linear arrangement of five approximately 25 cm rounded stones of brilliant colors: red, mustard yellow, white, gray, and black.

In both of these cases, ritual activity is clearly indicated, but the activities remain enigmatic because of our incomplete knowledge of the very large pits' total contents and configuration.

Finds in Underground Contexts: Galleries

As most galleries were apparently cleaned out long ago, there are few opportunities to find intact deposits; one of the exceptions was the Ofrendas Gallery (figure 2.6), whose contents turned out to be surprisingly intact (Lumbreras 1993, 2007). Ofrendas suggests that some galleries may have functioned to receive offerings that were so extensive and covered so much floor area that it

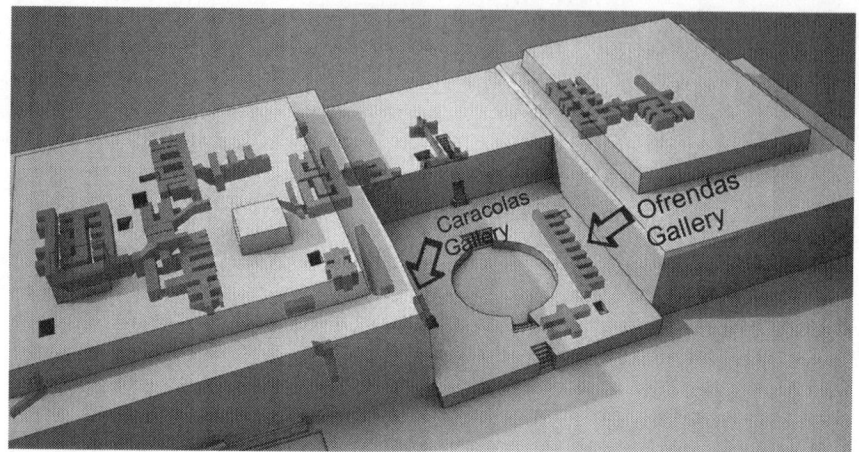

FIGURE 2.6. *Location of galleries mentioned in the text and general gallery distribution in Buildings A–C. Modified from graphics courtesy of the Rietberg Museum (Zurich, Switzerland), and ArcTron 3D.*

seems unlikely that the space could have been used subsequently for any other purpose involving human activity inside. The Lanzón Gallery, with its central idol and floor plan that seems to focus on this image, suggests that ritual involving repeated activity aimed at the Lanzón most easily explains the situation, and interpretations can easily include the possibility that the Lanzón functioned as an oracle or was otherwise consulted, viewed, or animated. Recent work by the acoustics team of the Stanford Project has shown that if the Lanzón spoke with the voice of a *pututu*, ducts leading out of the Lanzón Gallery would have enhanced and preferentially transmitted the native pututu frequencies for audibility outside the gallery, particularly in the Circular Plaza (Kolar et al. 2012). The Stanford Project has had the opportunity to work on three further cases of relatively intact gallery deposits.

The first was the Caracolas Gallery, the smallest of the galleries at barely more than 1 m × 6 m in size, which proved to contain twenty pututus or *Strombus galeatus* trumpets resting directly on the gallery floor plus fragments of many more instruments that had been broken up in the act of making small shell ornaments (Rick 2008:24–27). The gallery floor or near-floor sediments contained virtually nothing but these trumpets, and various contextual factors[3] argue that the horns were stored in a sacristy-like space, probably for use in the various ritual spaces— the Circular Plaza and Lanzón Gallery are just a few paces away. Storage of ritual instruments could have been a third primary function for the galleries.

Second was the Loco Gallery, where modest-sized excavations found that intact deposits and the gallery floor still existed in some areas, although areas of disturbance were present from small-scale looting. The relatively intact segments largely yielded clean floors, although one fragment of a slate plaque engraved with Chavín designs was found. This may be the best context of use for this fairly frequent class of decorated stone, whose original locus of use or display is otherwise unknown. The areas excavated thus far are passageway contexts rather than cells or rooms and were probably subject to frequent cleaning or at least movement of materials caused by the passing of feet. Thus, it is not surprising that in situ ritual materials or debris are not commonly found.

Finally, in Building C a gallery whose existence was mostly conjectural was discovered, opened, and conserved in 2012. One of a triad of linked galleries along with Loco and Mirador, the westernmost gallery has been dubbed the Capilla Gallery for the original chapel-museum that existed directly above it prior to the 1945 aluvión landslide. The gallery, a mirror image of the Mirador Gallery, suffered a major looting event, probably in the nineteenth century AD, but we have been able to locate significant segments of intact floor and carefully excavate the deposits immediately overlying it. Both Chavín period deposits and some materials suggesting post-Chavín activity are present in layers above the clear formal floor of the gallery. A second, precursor gallery immediately underlies the Capilla Gallery, still fully preserved to its full height except for the lack of roofing beams. The lower gallery was excavated down to its original floor in a very small area (approximately 1 m^2), which was found to have no cultural material whatsoever lying on it. The upper gallery floor, excavated to date over about 15 m^2, has produced a series of layers with cultural material, none in immediate contact with the floor but the lowest very close and apparently containing only Chavín period pottery and possibly of Chavín age. Notably, its primary content is the broken, intermixed, and disorganized bones of camelids and humans; neither is notably burned or with obvious cut marks. On occasion, human bones in anatomical positions (i.e., rib cage fragments) were found, and the human remains overall are predominantly from children.

UNDERGROUND CONTEXTS: CANALS

Investigations in Chavín's extensive underground water canal system, initially a mere component of our site conservation effort, have revealed a ritual world largely unknown before. This system did indeed serve to drain water from the overall monument area to the adjacent rivers, but many of its features and contents indicate a functionality that goes far beyond that of a mundane drainage system. First, as suspected previously (Contreras and Keefer 2009; Lumbreras, González, and Lietaer 1976), water was not only removed from the center but also brought to it. Supply canals have been identified, and one inevitable conclusion is that they were not primarily providing water for human consumption or aesthetic purposes but rather provisioning an active and recognized element that was fundamental to Chavín beliefs and ritual activity. The extension and complexity of this system are only beginning to be understood, and what is written here will probably be quickly outdated by further discoveries. Reasonably mature knowledge comes from the long-known Rocas Canal (originally termed a gallery [Lumbreras and Amat Olazabal 1965–66]), but it is easily separable as a canal system with little or nothing to do with the galleries (see figure 2.2). Our most recent work in the separate, previously unknown extensive canal systems around the north side of Building C has increased our knowledge of the diversity of activities involved with the canals, in part because of the canals' undisturbed contents.

Two initial points are important. First, the difference between underground canals and galleries is categorical, not a matter of degree. Galleries are almost always larger in cross-section; they are spacious enough to walk through comfortably, they always have prepared clay-gravel floors, the segments are leveled, any change in level is carried out with one or more formal stair steps, and they have horizontal ducts between segments or with the external world. Canals generally have flagstone floors, are often too small to walk through upright, always have measurable and usually uniform gradients, never have formal steps (except in descending staircase entrances into the canal), and ducting is in the form of vertical or inclined ventilators or input drains. Second, while galleries and canals are in some cases found reasonably close together, they almost never intersect, and their design and construction over time must have involved extensive planning to accommodate their use of common space with such hermetic separation, perhaps reflecting the risk of disastrous flooding of the gallery system.

From the first investigation of Chavín canals (Bustamante and Crousillat 1974) onward, it was clear that substantial quantities of elaborate Chavín-epoch materials were present in floor and near-floor sediments. At first it made sense to think that these contents were inadvertently washed in from outside or at most informal leavings, but it has become clear that perhaps the majority of Chavín material in the canals includes highly decorated pottery, large fragments of camelid bone representing relatively few animals, drug-related paraphernalia, or other categories of ritual material. Also, the condition of these materials is often pristine, with negligible evidence of water transport and often still bearing coatings of powdered colorants that would not have survived significant washing. Often, pottery sherds can be reassembled to reconstruct whole or near-whole vessels.

Rocas Canal

Rocas Canal remains the largest canal system at Chavín, and it basically drained the basin formed by Buildings A, B, C, and D and the north- and south-flanking mounds of the Plaza Mayor, as well as all three known sunken plazas. In 2011 we discovered that it passed completely underneath Building C; as of the date of writing, we have not found any upstream ends to the canal or its main branches. It seems likely that at least some upper parts of the canal took water from the Wacheqsa stream to also bring water into the canal, at least at certain times. The acoustic canal proposed by Lumbreras and colleagues (1976) is one such branch of Rocas and may represent a water supply brought in under a pressure head, allowing water to be elevated up into the major buildings in an otherwise downward trajectory. Elaborate vertical drains brought water down from building tops and plaza floors, usually through vertical drops that range from 2 m to as much as 8 m. The layout of the canal presents a fairly coherent, if extensive and complex, functional whole, but it has a wide variety of construction techniques, cross-sectional sizes, and other details that suggest some degree of modification and rebuilding over time. The canal has a fairly uniform gradient that smooths the vertical drops implied by the high buildings and major terraces and suggests a high degree of pre-planning. Most notably, as seen from the relatively final building plan of the late Chavín Black-and-White Phase, the canal has very little latitude in vertical or horizontal positioning to achieve the difficult function of draining the huge number of vertically spaced areas in one system. There can be little doubt that the basic layout of the canal was a nearly initial feature of the site, passing underneath major buildings and clearly predating them; yet the canal's positioning strategy corresponds to the site's final architectural design. Thus, the canal's planning was integral to that of the surface structures and the huge fills placed to shape Chavín's landscape, which suggests that its installation anticipated the building of structures hundreds of years later.[4]

Among the most notable aspects of the canal are the multiple formal entranceways into it (figure 2.7). These entranceways take the form of staircases and short gallery-like passages that occur, at times in pairs, in what seem to be strategic locations adjacent to plaza areas and, notably, at the joining of canal segments. While the staircases are not spacious in character, their dimensions

FIGURE 2.7. *Segment of Rocas Canal just west of the Circular Plaza, in original condition. Note the flagstone floor and formal staircase entrance. Canal continues to the left.*

and design go far beyond what would have been needed for simple maintenance access to the subsurface space. They are usually immediately upstream from canal segments that have yielded particularly rich concentrations of elaborate and ritually related materials. It seems very likely that these materials were introduced into the canal through the formal entrances, and their nature and state argue that they were broken and deposited in ritual acts that may have been sacrificial in character. In one clear case within the Circular Plaza, the subsidiary canal joining the main Rocas channel is in fact the abovementioned acoustic canal, which seems to be a water supply source that would have entered with extremely high energy and an angled immediate drop. If this were functioning simultaneously at the time of sacrifice, the water would have impressively swept away the broken offerings from the participants' view.

Canals in the Vicinity of Building C

Although still under investigation, a separate and apparently more spatially dense complex of canals has been discovered in a major esplanade area to the north of Building C. In an intensive sampling and area excavation effort, about 10 percent of this space of 80 m × 50 m has been excavated. Subsurface canals were found in all excavations that passed below Chavín use surfaces, with about 210 m of canals explored and excavated to date. Although perhaps to some degree interconnected, they represent six complex canal systems involving supply and drainage canals, clearly dating to more than one temporal phase of Chavín usage. Given sampling likelihoods, the canals known to date probably represent 10–20 percent of overall systems and a somewhat lesser percentage of total canal linear distance. Thus, this area is underlain by a dense network of canals completely inexplicable by any need for drainage function (figure 2.8). Only one short segment of one of the canals was known prior to 2011, when intensive work began in the area, and there is no evidence of post–Chavín period human activity or materials in these canals or any form of modern intrusion—unlike the Rocas system, which has both in many segments.

The canals are particularly useful for working with issues of canal function; their position rather near the Wacheqsa stream may help explain why there appears to be a particularly high density of canals in this area of the site. Supply canals, particularly those employing pressure heads to elevate water, would have been most easily built in this area of Chavín's monumental architecture. To date, it appears that the area north of Building C has a much higher frequency of canals than other known areas in Chavín, although canals are present in every sector where excavations have reached the necessary depth. This particularly great quantity of canals makes it obvious that they must not have been restricted to drainage functions. This in turn, given the contents of the canals, suggests that they represent a focus on water-related ritualism in this area of the site.

These canals repeat the same basic theme of the Rocas Canal—entranceways, sometimes paired; intersections of canals, frequently at staircase accesses; and clear concentrations of sacrificed elaborate, high-status materials in precisely these locations. A new theme, however, is the presence of very small-volume surface canals, either open or covered and just below ritual use surfaces. Most striking, these canals are frequently taking water toward Building C rather than away from it and are routed toward the base of the main Building C facade. After bringing water to these key areas, they seem to drop their water down to a lower canal level through short vertical chimneys. The water is then carried away from Building C (or the monumental core) toward the Mosna or Wacheqsa Rivers, often passing entranceway/canal juncture/sacrificial contexts (figure 2.9).

Three notable observations should be highlighted. First, at this early stage of revealing the canals, it is fair to say that water was probably running in

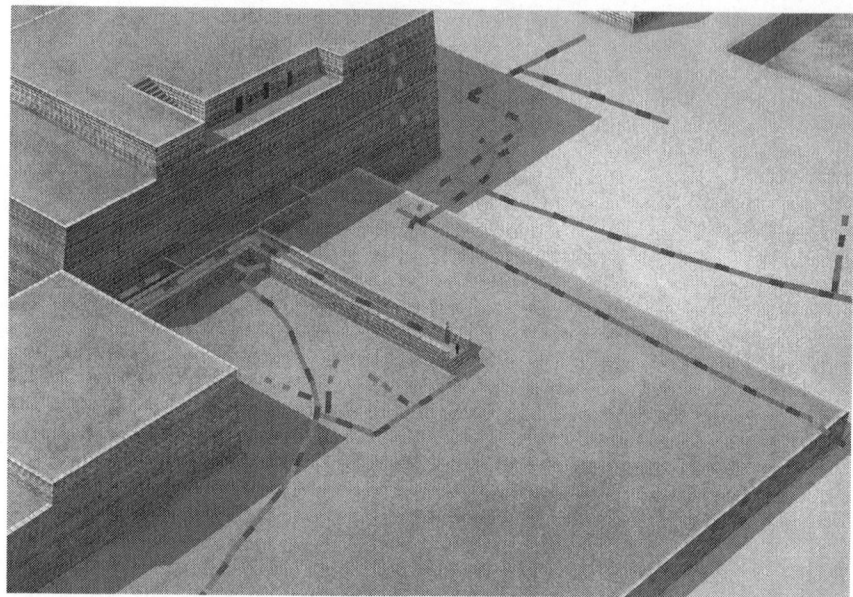

FIGURE 2.8. *Known canals in the north esplanade of Building C as of 2013. These systems represent a small percentage of the likely total of canals underlying Chavín surfaces in this area. Supply canals come from the top right area; drainage extends down to the Mosna and Wacheqsa Rivers to the north and east, respectively.*

many different directions at the surface and at different depths below it within any given period of canal use. Water was transported in and out of this sector, joined, split, crossed over or under other canals apparently in contemporary use, dropped out of sight, and raised to the surface; and it could potentially have had spring- or fountain-like features with water pushed upward under pressure.

Second, we can now start to more clearly recognize the pattern of canal junctures in which a larger principal or trunk low-slope canal is joined by a smaller-volume but rapidly descending high-energy tributary, which tends to be a supply canal rather than a receiver or drainage canal. Interestingly, these smaller canals always seem to enter the larger canals from the left side, looking downstream along the principal channel. In at least one case, the high-energy subsidiary approaches from the right side, crosses over, and then drops into the main canal, seeming to indicate special effort expended to achieve this right-side entrance. It is notable that this is the pattern of the meeting of the Mosna and Wacheqsa Rivers, which consists of a principal larger-volume and lower-energy channel (Mosna), with the lower-volume higher-energy Wacheqsa

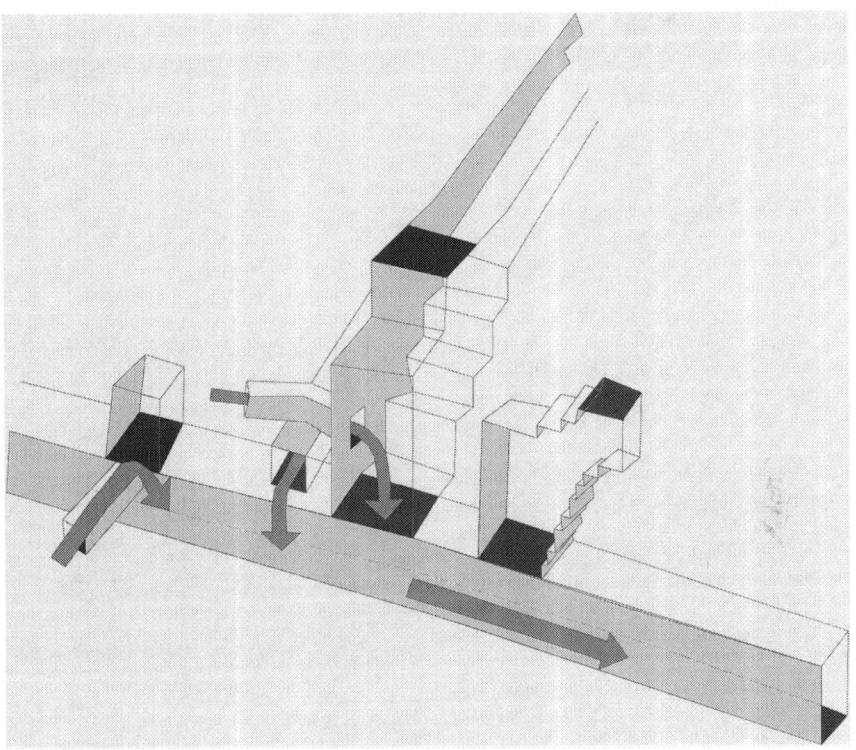

FIGURE 2.9. *Isometric drawing of Canal CE2 of the north esplanade of Building C, showing formal staircase entrances and secondary canal intersections. An important high-energy canal with fountain-like drop into the primary canal is indicated by the descending arrow.*

entering from the left side. This joining of the rivers is referred to locally as a *tinku* or *tinkuy*, terms of complex meaning in the Andes. Allen (1988) defines these terms primarily as the encounter, often violent, between watercourses or between people; Webb (2012) adds further complexity to the term that includes issues of complementary and opposing, even opposite forces or dualistic entities, their intermingling, and their sometimes turbulent coexistence. Structurally, the Chavín canal conjunctions could conceivably represent, on a small, controlled scale, the large tinku at which Chavín was built, in the similarly positioned pattern of unequal size and water energy.

Third, it is perhaps not surprising that such tinku-like features in the canals would be locations of sacrificial ritual activity. The finding of complete but smashed vessels and other materials similarly destroyed in the formal entranceways suggests that ritual participants are either inside the cramped canal itself or immediately outside. In either case, only a handful of individuals at a maximum could have witnessed or participated in these rituals, making them very restricted in character. Downstream in the canals below the tinku-like joining we frequently find an extended distribution of materials similar to those at the junction itself, suggesting that sacrificed materials were washed away by canal flow, perhaps intentionally. Because most canals are now known to have been supplied with water from the Wacheqsa stream, we can suggest the possibility that water flows were orchestrated with sacrifice actions and that the sweeping away of offerings, perhaps accompanied by water-generated sounds, may have been integral parts of Chavín canal-related ritual.

CONCLUSION

Although the amount of data related to ritual from Chavín de Huántar has greatly increased in the last two decades of research, even more important is the diversity of content, pattern, and location of the evidence (see Contreras, this volume). Whereas before it was possible to imagine a fairly monolithic ritual pattern of processions from lower to upper plazas and on into gallery settings of a simple, if hierarchical, religious leadership, this vision no longer comes close to encompass the range of activity that is evident.

First, the locations of ritual activity have increased notably. Broad new types of architectural contexts have been added, including elevated ramps, underground canals, sub-plaza locations, and contexts under construction. More important, most of these locations are not near the centerline of the U-shaped Chavín monumental layouts. In particular, investigations on the outside of the U-shaped enclosures have shown a wealth of evidence for ritual that suggests a locational diversity of concerted and systematic ritual at the site. It seems very likely that at least some of the diverse locations were in use contemporarily, indicating that a wide range of ritual activities took place, probably corresponding to calendric or cultic diversity.

Second, the material remains of the activities are also diverse, both within and between types of contexts. Categories such as shell, human and animal bone, obsidian and other semi-precious stone, and a diversity of ceramic wares and decorative types are differentially distributed in a way that argues for significant segregation of ritual materials, perhaps according to locational categories and, by extension, genres of ritual itself. Although beyond the bounds of this chapter, there is good evidence that at least some categories of ceramics are rarely found outside specific ritual settings, suggesting specialized production of materials for specific types of rituals.

The complexity we can begin to infer for Chavín ritual and its organization argues for the presence of either an extremely diverse yet highly structured central cult or, just as likely, the presence of more than one cult entity. The implication of multiple cults, should they become evident, is far from clear, but it suggests a sophistication and diversification beyond what I have previously conceived. While there is good evidence for artistic, technological, architectural, and craft traditions of long duration at Chavín, the growing multiplicity of these traditions uncovered over the course of decades of research and, apparently, centuries of Chavín period site use hints at organizational abilities greater than anticipated. In addition, a fair degree of uniqueness of the standout Chavín characteristics, compared with other contemporary Formative sites, suggests that local development and innovation were characteristic of this center, as I suspect they were of others. Far from contradicting my earlier ideas about interaction spheres in the Formative, this degree of distinction is probably the result of the conscious designing of cultic identities at each center, in awareness of those emerging across the Central Andes.

A few specific points about Chavín ritual are worth emphasizing in this context. It is clear that Chavín emphasized underground spaces, as has long been known for the gallery systems that in their multiplicity and sophistication seem to be one of the signatures of this center. The addition of underground canals into Chavín's panorama of ritual activities is important in a number of senses. It further emphasizes the use of highly restricted ritual spaces and the large proportion of evidence that suggests very small numbers of individuals were involved. At the same time, the canal systems are exceedingly complex in their multiplicity and interlinkage and hint at the local development, through innovation, of hydraulic knowledge that underwrote this system. The emphasis on water is not surprising, given later Andean developments, but it begins to put flesh on the bones of our knowledge of early water cults. Also, the canals of Chavín give surprising evidence of advance planning abilities—not only is there an intrinsic logic to the way the hydraulic systems work, but that logic, combined with the location of the canals over time, tells much about how later construction was anticipated by the canal system design. Canal systems in this case are far from poor, water-washed archaeological contexts but are actually excellent containers of data, less subject in many ways to destructive taphonomic processes than are many surface locations.

I feel that the conjunction of canal entrances, canal intersection, and material evidence of ritual activity provides a glimpse into some of the ritual concepts present in Chavín. Not just water but water acting in certain ways—joining forces, creating turbulence, even provoking the *huaicos* (massive, catastrophic landslides) and other land movement that are so apparent at Chavín. Recognizing the energy levels and the structure of drainage, the values and perils involved in natural world water distributions, and then replicating them under directly controllable circumstances in canals seems an almost predictable outcome and a great playing ground for a belief system.

Canals also emphasize, from the nature of their content, sacrificial acts that have become clear as a core of Chavín ritual. The systematic destruction of obsidian is emblematic of what is happening with other material categories more subject to destruction—for example, pottery, bone, coal. Rethinking many discoveries of ritually related materials now suggests to me that the many situations in which we have all or nearly all the pieces of heavily fragmented objects is a reflection of local sacrifice and deposition in a logic applied to many classes of material.

Canals such as those at Chavín focus our attention on water-related ritual, and in this sense we can return to the definition of ritual given at the beginning of this chapter. While it is difficult to address what the specific desired outcomes of Chavín ritual were—and the diversity of ritual evidence at Chavín suggests they were multiple—the site's context and setting can define some likely foci. Contreras (2007) and Contreras and Keefer (2009) have explored the relationships between natural water supply and the site's developed canal system. Similarly, they and others have emphasized the need for draining Chavín's many architectural features in this relatively rainy setting. Attention was paid to water, beyond a doubt, and Contreras's evaluation of environmental hazards and risks makes clear that in many senses water was a threat as well as undoubtedly a resource. Julio Vargas-Neumann, John Hurd, and I have further developed perceptions on the risks water represents to Chavín's construction and conservation, today and in the past (Rick, Hurd, and Vargas-Neumann 2012). I argue that controlling the challenge of these risks might have even been a measure of the competitive effectiveness of authorities in relation to natural forces. Lumbreras (2007:637–49) has emphasized Chavín's potential role in predicting water-driven climatic problems, both the provisioning of water to agricultural systems and the anomalous water situations that arise in El Niño climatic events. It is not unreasonable, although hardly proven, that Chavín might have been involved in prediction, detection, or even remediation of such climatologically driven issues.

The development of ritual within supply/drainage canals could certainly be related in many ways to issues of uncertainty in obtaining information, control, or desired results in a world of powerful water forces. First, what would have been better than to control the element—water—in a canal circumstance, showing cult dominance and control in obtaining obedience from a potentially destructive and limitedly predictable natural element? Second, divination, possibly using water pathways through multiple channels and water's acceptance/non-acceptance of sacrificed offerings, could have been a dynamic—and manipulable—ritual feature, with some apparent parallels known from Inka times. Third, of all the natural elements, water is the most observable, timely, and subject to priestly manipulation, perhaps in competition with fire—but perhaps even more predictable and controllable, especially in a canal setting. In sum, water could have been a condition, an outcome, a demonstration—all in the interest of showing control through ritual activity—of an important but capricious element, one capable of giving life but also of taking it away.

I want to add another very important, if somewhat obvious, observation about Formative ceremonial centers: their categorical difference from their hinterlands. The Formative period was definitely a time of change in almost every imaginable sense—major changes occurred in technology, organization, belief, interaction, scale, and probably subsistence; this in many ways is why we call it the Formative period. But change doesn't just happen, it comes from somewhere; where it came from was the regional centers. At Chavín, much of the development of technology—for example, ceramic, stone, bone, shell, acoustic, constructive, hydraulic developments—seems tightly linked to a driving need to innovate in ritual contexts, acts, and effects. But in the Chavín area at least, the hinterland is largely characterized by scattered, small-scale, modest dwellings and communities that seem largely to have remained much as they were over time. Perhaps they accepted or could gain access to certain new materials, ideas, or other aspects of life, but that access was limited; overall, they appear rather conservative and stable—the advent of the Formative probably had relatively little impact on the lifestyle in the hinterlands as opposed to the centers, which were likely a fountain of change, comparatively speaking.

As centers were the places of innovative change that promoted rituals emphasizing elites, they were also the primary drivers of social differentiation. These centers, as the most obvious contexts for the transfer of messages and ideas about such innovations, also spurred the increasing differentiation of elite versus rural traditional populations, but they needed ways to communicate and situate the very character of these changes. In a society that was undoubtedly conservative overall, innovation would not have been easily accepted or necessarily comprehended unless framed within a characterization—some sort of contextualizing that gave the change its meaning and valence (in a certain sense, "bundling" in the broader definition of Pauketat [2012]). It is logical that ritual would have played a significant role in this regard—a showcase for demonstrating, highlighting, making accessible or remote, controlling, classifying, ranking, and otherwise imposing structure and meaning to the material, behavior, and concepts that drove change in the Formative. A new social order was being installed, with all its beliefs, material correlates, and other components that made it a reality. Ritual may certainly have integrated participants, but it may equally have differentiated among them—either within the groups of participants or between participants and those not included in the ritual process.

ACKNOWLEDGMENTS

I would like to thank a few of the uncountable people and organizations that were helpful in this research. Major financial support for the work came from the Antamina Mining Corporation, Global Heritage Fund, the Historical Society (John Templeton Foundation), Fundacion Wiese, Stanford University, and the Harbor Lights Foundation. Permissions were granted by Peru's National Institute of Culture and later the Ministry of Culture. I thank Peruvian cultural officials at the local, regional, and national levels for their help with the fieldwork and paperwork. The Municipality of Chavín de Huántar has provided valuable assistance as well. My colleagues Luis G. Lumbreras, Rosa Mendoza de Rick, Daniel Contreras, Christian Mesia, Augusto Bazan, and Julio Vargas-Neumann have been instrumental in the development of both fieldwork and my thinking about Chavín. Any flaws in that process are my own.

NOTES

1. The *monumental core* refers to the area of monumental architecture at Chavín de Huántar, easily distinguished as the area that has platform buildings at least 5 m high.

2. Janabarroide refers to pottery with the generalized characteristics of the Jannabariu phase, as presented by Burger (1992); since no specific classes or types of pottery are delineated in his work, this term indicates pottery similar to the type illustrated for that phase. Approximate defining characteristics are stamped, modeled, and incised decoration on a predominantly polished blackware with a broad variety of forms present (see Rick et al. 2009:113 for a more complete description of and rationale for this ceramic class).

3. These include evidence that the trumpets may have been hung in bags from the walls of the gallery, the well-worn surfaces of many of the shells, and a short and immediately accessible entranceway convenient to the Circular Plaza atrium.

4. Although we do not have reliable dating for or necessarily know the earliest construction phase of Building B, it likely predates the beginning of the maximum-extension Black-and-White Phase construction (ca. 600 BC cal) by a minimum of 300 years, but the difference could be notably greater.

REFERENCES CITED

Allen, C. J. 1988. *The Hold Life Has: Coca and the Cultural Identity in an Andean Community.* Smithsonian Series in Ethnographic Inquiry. Washington, DC: Smithsonian Institution Press.

Burger, R. L. 1992. *Chavín and the Origins of Andean Civilization.* New York: Thames and Hudson.

Bustamante, J., and E. Crousillat. 1974. "Análisis Hidráulico del Sitio Arqueológico de Chavín de Huántar." Undergraduate thesis, National Engineering University, Lima, Peru.

Contreras, D. A. 2007. "Sociopolitical and Geomorphologic Dynamism at Chavín de Huántar, Peru." PhD dissertation, Department of Anthropological Sciences, Stanford University, Stanford, CA.

Contreras, D. A., and D. K. Keefer. 2009. "Implications of the Fluvial History of the Wacheqsa River for Hydrologic Engineering and Water Use at Chavín de Huántar, Peru." *Geoarchaeology: An International Journal* 24 (5): 589–618. http://dx.doi.org/10.1002/gea.20279.

Cook, A. G. 1984–1985. "The Middle Horizon Ceramic Offerings from Conchopata." *Ñawpa Pacha: Journal of Andean Archaeology* 22–23: 49–90.

González Moreno, M. 2012. *Chavín de Huántar: Diario de Campo de las Excavaciones de 1957 y 1958.* Lima: Instituto Andino de Estudios Arqueológico-Sociales.

Indacochea, G. A., and M. Iberico. 1947. "Aluvionamiento de Chavín de Huántar el 17 de Enero de 1945." *Boletín de la Sociedad Geológica del Perú* 20: 21–28.

Isbell, W., and A. Cook. 2002. "New Perspective on Conchopata and the Andean Middle Horizon." In *Andean Archaeology II: Art, Landscape, and Society*, ed. W. Isbell and H. Silverman, 249–305. New York: Kluwer Academic/Plenum. http://dx.doi.org/10.1007/978-1-4615-0597-6_11.

Kembel, S. R. 2008. "The Architecture at the Monumental Center of Chavín de Huántar: Sequence, Transformations, and Chronology." In *Chavín: Art, Architecture and Culture*, ed. W. J. Conklin and J. Quilter, 35–84. Monograph 61. Los Angeles: Cotsen Institute of Archaeology, University of California.

Kolar, M. A., J. W. Rick, P. R. Cook, and J. S. Abel. 2012. "Ancient Pututus Contextualized: Integrative Archaeoacoustics at Chavín de Huántar, Peru." In *Flower World—Music Archaeology of the Americas*, ed. A. A. Both and M. Stöckli, 23–53. Berlin: Ekho Verlag.

Lumbreras, L. G. 1993. "Chavín de Huántar: Excavaciones en la Galería de las Ofrendas." *Materialien zur Allgemeinen und Vergleichenden Archäologie* 51. Mainz am Rhein: P. von Zabern.

Lumbreras, L. G. 2007. *Chavín: Investigaciones Arqueológicas*. Lima: Universidad Alas Peruanas.

Lumbreras, L. G., and H. Amat Olazabal. 1965–66. "Informe Preliminar sobre las Galerias Interiores de Chavín (Primera Temporada de Trabajos)." *Revista del Museo Nacional* 34: 143–97.

Lumbreras, L. G., C. González, and B. Lietaer. 1976. *Acerca de la Función del Sistema Hidráulico de Chavín: Investigaciones de Campo*. Lima: Museo Nacional de Antropología y Arqueología.

Lumbreras, L. G., and M. González Moreno. 2012. *Chavín de Huántar: Los Descubrimientos Arqueológicos de Marino Gonzales Moreno*. Lima: Instituto Andino de Investigaciones Arqueológico-Sociales.

Mesía, C. 2007. "Intrasite Spatial Organization at Chavín de Huántar: Three-Dimensional Modeling, Stratigraphics, and Ceramics." PhD dissertation, Department of Anthropological Sciences, Stanford University, Stanford, CA.

Moore, J. D. 1996. *Architecture and Power in the Ancient Andes: The Archaeology of Public Buildings*. New Studies in Archaeology. Cambridge: Cambridge University Press. http://dx.doi.org/10.1017/CBO9780511521201.

Pauketat, T. R. 2012. "Bundles of/in/as Time." In *Big Histories, Human Lives: Tackling Problems of Scale in Archaeology*, ed. J. Robb and T. R. Pauketat, 35–56. Santa Fe, NM: School for Advanced Research Press.

Quilter, J. 2014. *The Ancient Central Andes*. New York: Routledge.

Rick, J. W. 2005. "The Evolution of Authority and Power at Chavín de Huántar, Peru." In *Foundations of Power in the Prehispanic Andes*, ed. K. J. Vaughn, D. Ogburn, and C. A. Conlee. Archeological Papers of the American Anthropological Association. Arlington, VA: American Anthropological Association. http://dx.doi.org/10.1525/ap3a.2005.14.071.

Rick, John W. 2006. "Un análisis de los centros ceremoniales del Período Formativo a partir de los estudios en Chavín de Huántar." *Boletín de Arqueología PUCP* (Lima) 10: 201–214.

Rick, J. W. 2008. "Context, Construction, and Ritual in the Development of Authority at Chavín de Huántar." In *Chavín: Art, Architecture, and Culture*, ed.

W. J. Conklin and J. Quilter, 3–34. Monograph 61. Los Angeles: Cotsen Institute of Archaeology, University of California.

Rick, J. W. 2014. "Cambio y Continuidad, Diversidad y Coherencia: Perspectivas sobre Variabilidad en Chavín de Huántar y el Período Formativo." In *El Centro Ceremonial Andino: Nuevas Perspectivas para los Períodos Arcaico y Formativo*, ed. Y. Seki. Senri Ethnological Studies 89. Osaka: National Museum of Ethnology.

Rick, J. W., J. Hurd, and J. Vargas-Neumann. 2012. "Chavín de Huántar, a Past Challenge to Nature, a Current Challenge to Archaeological Conservation." Paper Presented at the XI Conferencia Internacional sobre el Estudio y Conservación del Patrimonio Arquitectónico de Tierra: Terra 2012, Pontificia Universidad Católica del Perú, Lima.

Rick, J. W., C. Mesía, D. A. Contreras, S. Kembel, R. Rick, M. Sayre, and J. Wolf. 2009. "La Cronología de Chavín de Huántar y sus Implicancias para el Período Formativo." *Boletín de Arqueología PUCP* 13: 87–132.

Tambiah, S. J. 1985. *Culture, Thought, and Social Action*. Cambridge: Harvard University Press. http://dx.doi.org/10.4159/harvard.9780674433748.

Tello, J. C. 1960. *Chavín: Cultura Matriz de la Civilización Andina*. Lima: University of San Marcos.

Turner, R.J.W., R. J. Knight, and J. W. Rick. 1999. "Geological Landscape of the Pre-Inca Archaeological Site at Chavín de Huántar, Peru." *Current Research: Geological Survey of Canada* 1999-D: 47–56.

Webb, H. D. 2012. *Yanantin and Masintin in the Andean World*. Albuquerque: University of New Mexico Press.

3

Not Just a Pyramid Scheme?

Diversity in Ritual Architecture at Chavín de Huántar

Daniel A. Contreras

An excavation west of the monumental core of Chavín de Huántar in 2005 exposed a portion of a Mito-style structure (Contreras 2010), remarkably similar in its configuration to well-known examples from Kotosh and La Galgada (Bonnier 1997; Grieder et al. 1988; Izumi and Terada 1972a, 1972b). The presence of such a structure at Chavín de Huántar reinforces Chavín's links to other Central Andean centers, including some of its contemporaries as well as sites dating back to the early third millennium BCE. Moreover, while Bonnier suggests that the Mito Tradition spans the period 2500–1800 BCE in the Central Andean highlands (Bonnier 1997), this example from Chavín de Huántar suggests the persistence of the Mito Tradition as late as 800 BCE. At Chavín at least, this implies the coexistence of the Mito Tradition with those new ritual practices developing at the site during the middle to late Formative period (as early as 1000 BCE; see Rick et al. 2009).

I have discussed the regional implications of the presence of a Mito-style structure at Chavín elsewhere (Contreras 2010), and in this chapter I focus on the location and role of the structure in Chavín's array of ritual architecture. The place of this structure in the site geography, I argue here, can shed light on the sociopolitical underpinnings of the monumental ceremonial architecture at Chavín de Huántar. Reconceptualizing the site as at least somewhat decentralized in its arrangement of sacred space—rather than entirely focused on the central, oldest, and presumably sanctified entity of

DOI: 10.5876/9781607325963.c003

the Lanzón—suggests that the social sources of power and the political contributors to Chavín's existence may have been diverse. In other words, the political economy of the sacred was mapped onto the site's ritual architecture and may be read from it.

In considering Chavín's internal geography, I focus primarily on two areas: the monumental core and that portion of the protected area to the west of the modern road, referred to as the West Field (figure 3.1).

THE WEST FIELD

The area west of the road has been recognized as part of the archaeological site since at least as early as Julio C. Tello's work at the site in the 1940s (Tello 1960). No sign of the West Field appears in such early maps as those of Heinrich Witt (from his 1842 visit; 1992:ilustración 5), Ernst Middendorf (1974:75), Charles Wiener (from his 1880 publication; admittedly it is not detailed [1880:200]), or Wendell Bennett (from his 1938 excavations; 1944:72). None of these omissions need indicate that the researchers were unaware of the presence of Chavín-style megalithic architecture in the West Field, but they are certainly evidence of its de-emphasis. This was probably a result of both the lure of the then largely undescribed monumental core—with its massive in situ lithic sculptures (the Lanzón and at least one tenoned head), tantalizingly unknown galleries, and largely buried structures—and the presence of the small community of Raku in the West Field, documented by Hans Kinzl during his 1936 visit as part of the Austrian Anden-Expeditionen des Alpenvereins (see Diessl 2004:512; Kinzl and Scheider 1950) but later destroyed by the 1945 *aluvión* (Indacochea and Iberico 1947).

Tello's site map (1960:figure 4) does note a few features in the area west of the road, but he, too, understandably concentrated his attention on the monumental core. Luis G. Lumbreras provides similarly focused maps (e.g., Lumbreras 1989:20), although his collaborator, Amat, excavated in the West Field (Amat's results remain unpublished, but see Diessl 2004:509–16 for a capsule description). In their case the restricted site map thus obviously reflects a focus on the monumental core rather than ignorance of or lack of interest in the West Field. Ultimately, with the exception of Richard Burger's work in the 1970s (Burger 1982, 1984) and work by the Stanford Project beginning in 2000, archaeological attention has generally focused on the monumental core itself, probably reflecting traditional interest in the monumental at the expense of the domestic.

Surprisingly, in light of this general lack of concern for the area, even the archaeological remains visible on the surface are substantial. Two megalithic

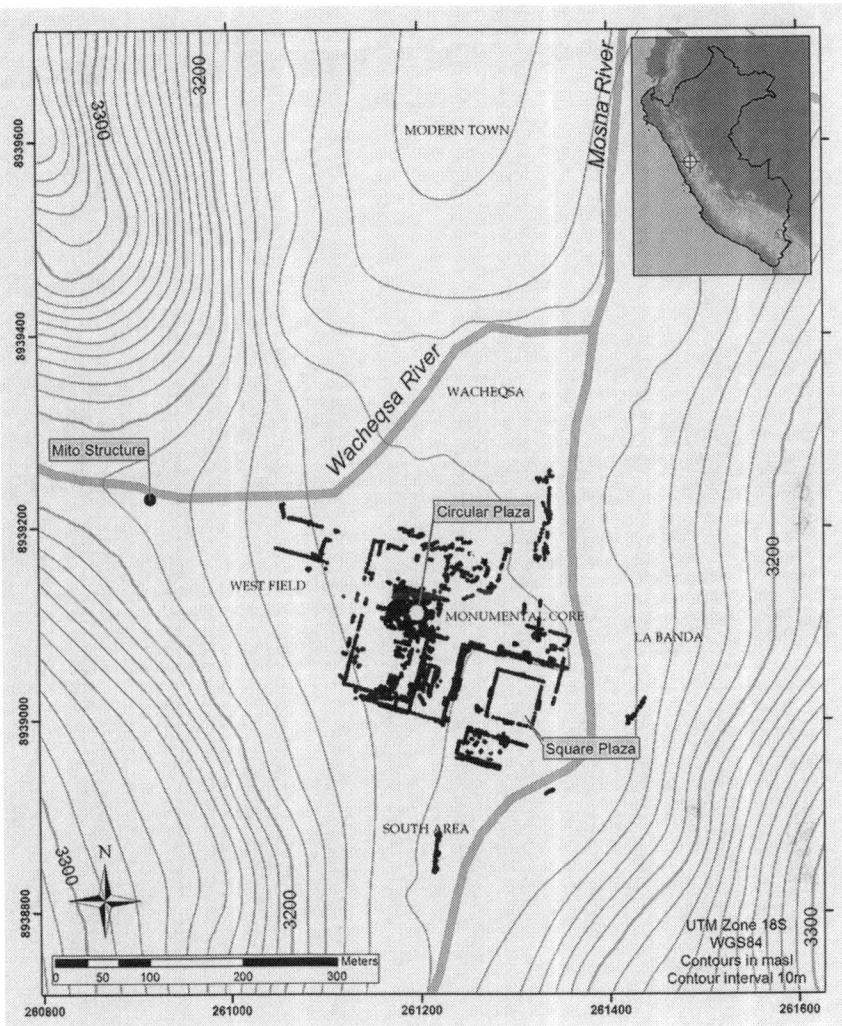

FIGURE 3.1. *Site sectors and major architectural features*

walls (apparently terrace facades), constructed of quartzite blocks in a style similar to that of the structures in the monumental core, are visible on the surface, as is one canal draining northward into the Río Wacheqsa (see figure 3.2). Until the construction in the 1970s of the road that currently separates the monumental core from the West Field, these east-west terraces were also associated with a north-south wall that was largely destroyed

FIGURE 3.2. *Visible architecture in the West Field*

by the road construction, suggesting a structure or structures in the West Field rather than simple megalithic terraces. This led Diessl—who stands out as the only researcher to make a point of including the West Field in his maps and reconstruction drawings—to describe a "West Temple" (Diessl 2004:510–16).

The history of archaeology in the West Field makes clear that the area—while recognized as containing archaeological remains—has generally been considered fairly marginal. The ceremonial core of the site has traditionally—if only implicitly—been defined by the Río Mosna to the east, the north edge of Structure D to the north, the south edge of Structure E to the south, and the west edge of Structures A, B, and C to the west (see figure 3.1).

This definition is at least in part a result of perceptions shaped by the local geomorphology. Colluvial and earth-flow deposition has obscured the West Field to a much greater degree than the monumental core, as I have discussed in detail elsewhere (Contreras 2007). The buried architecture is of similar style to, and appears to approach the scale of, the celebrated structures of the monumental core (see figure 3.2). The parallel upper and lower walls, both running east-west, are visible for stretches of 48 m and 37 m, respectively. Exploratory Stanford excavations carried out in 2000 and 2001 on the face of the visible terraces revealed deep Chavín deposits and suggested that the terrace walls continued downward for at least 2 m below the modern ground surface. Fragments of complementary north-south walls are also visible; like the longer east-west segments, these walls share the monument's architectural orientation (13° east of north; see Rick et al. 1998:197).

The combined implication of these observations appears to be that the constructions visible on the surface in the West Field are not simply terrace walls retaining slope sediments but rather platform faces backed by cultural fill. This inference is supported by the sectional exposure provided by the cut of the Río Wacheqsa, where at least one wall of similar scale is visible in profile to significant depth, and by a 2005 test excavation in the central-eastern area of the West Field (WF-09) that encountered almost entirely cultural fills to a depth of 6 m (see Contreras 2007:189–90). Moreover, the unexpected find in 2005 of a Mito-style structure (Unit WF-07; see figure 3.1 and Contreras 2010) at the far western extreme of the West Field, 300 m west of Structure A/B/C, suggests that the religious focus of the site may not have been strictly on the monumental core.

A MITO-STYLE STRUCTURE IN CHAVÍN'S WEST FIELD

The structure itself, excavated in 2005, is striking both for its similarity to the archetypal Mito structures from Kotosh (Bonnier 1997; Izumi and Terada 1972a, 1972b) and for its state of preservation. Although only the northeast quadrant of the structure was excavated, enough was exposed to clearly delimit a split-level room with a circular central hearth and north-facing entry (figure 3.3). Its full dimensions are estimated at approximately 3 m × 3 m; the entry opens ~21.3° east of north. My focus here, however, is not on the anatomy of this particular example of the Mito genre, except inasmuch as is necessary to identify it as such; a full description of the structure itself appears elsewhere (Contreras 2010).

The key features of the Mito Tradition, as defined by Elisabeth Bonnier, are the quadrangular room, central hearth, split-level floor, niches, and use of plaster (Bonnier 1997:137, figure 111). Bonnier's definition of the Mito Tradition drew primarily on the well-published examples from Kotosh; she also explicitly sought to differentiate the Mito Tradition as a specific subset of the more broadly inclusive Kotosh Religious Tradition defined by Burger and Salazar-Burger (1980). All of the elements she defined—with, arguably, the exception of the niches—are present in the Chavín example.

The Mito-style structure in the West Field, at the end of its use-life, was carefully interred with a massive sterile fill, and a sequence of stone-faced terraces was subsequently built over it, ascending the slope from north to south (figure 3.4; Contreras 2010:figure 10). These terraces and the associated series of

FIGURE 3.3. *West Field Mito structure*

floor deposits all contain diagnostic Chavín period Janabarroid ceramics and do not contain any identifiably later material. Associated radiocarbon dates confirm the contemporaneity of at least the earlier of these terraces (810–420 BCE) and the Mito-style structure (900–800 BCE) with the monumental core (900–500 BCE) (for a full discussion of the dating of the Mito structure, see Contreras 2010; for the architectural chronology of the monumental core, see Kembel 2008; Kembel and Haas 2013; Rick et al. 2009).

RITUAL DIVERSITY AT CHAVÍN

The contemporaneity of the Mito-style structure with the monumental ceremonial architecture of the site core makes it necessary to consider a role for this structure within the ritual life of Chavín. The broad consensus in the literature regarding Mito structures, at a variety of sites, is that they are foci of significant ritual activity (Bonnier 1997; Burger and Salazar-Burger 1986; Grieder and Bueno Mendoza 1985; Grieder et al. 1988; Onuki 1993; Pozorski and Pozorski 1996). At La Galgada, Grieder and Bueno Mendoza (1985) refer to the plastered rooms as "ritual chambers" and speculate about the fire-centered ceremonies they may have housed; Shady Solís and Machacuay have emphasized the centrality and ritual importance of one of the two Mito-style structures at Caral by terming it the "Altar del Fuego Sagrado"

FIGURE 3.4. *Stratigraphic context of the West Field Mito structure; note the layer of sterile fill sealing the structure, as well as the subsequent terraces*

(Shady Solís and Machacuay 2003). Bonnier (1997) even posits the existence of a "Mito religion."

Given this prevailing agreement regarding the significance of the architectural form, it seems appropriate to consider the Mito-style structure at Chavín as similarly important. Moreover, the combination of the substantial labor investment the structure represents and its careful interment through the deposition of a massive sterile fill of soil and rock (Contreras 2010:8–9) further emphasizes the importance of the structure. Such sealing recalls the "temple entombment" described by Matsuzawa at Kotosh, where superposition of Mito structures was the norm (Izumi and Terada 1972b:176; see also Onuki 1993), and the associated focus on renewal (see Onuki, this volume). It may also perhaps be conceptually linked to the ritual practice of sealed offerings at Chavín. While no other examples of sealed architectural features are known, the deposits of ceramics in the Ofrendas Gallery (Lumbreras 1993) and *Strombus* shell trumpets in the Caracoles Gallery (Rick 2008:24–27) may represent comparable practices.

In fact, the specifics of ritual activity at Chavín remain only tentatively understood. In contrast to the richly explicit iconographic and material record of ritual activity for such later Central Andean civilizations as the Moche, at Chavín, ritual activity must be inferred from the layout and character of architectural spaces, excavations of occasional offering deposits, and abstracted iconographic representations. A few aspects stand out: processions, offerings of valued and/or exotic material, and manipulation of water were all apparently important elements of Chavín's panoply of ritual activity (see Rick, this volume). Only the second of these—in the form of smashed obsidian fragments in the central hearth and fragments of anthracite mirror in the duct (see Contreras 2010:5–6)—can be associated with the Mito structure in the West Field, making this structure perhaps distinct in behavioral terms as well as spatial ones. As it can be discussed in somewhat more secure terms, I focus here on the latter: while, by analogy to such structures elsewhere and with reference to its careful interment, this Chavín period example of the Mito genre does appear to be a locus of important ceremonial activity, that activity is clearly spatially distinct from ritual in the site's monumental core, where the Lanzón monolith, the Circular Plaza, the Black-and-White Portal, and the Square Plaza have commonly been taken to comprise the ceremonial focus of the site.

SITUATING CHAVÍN RITUAL IN CENTRAL ANDEAN CONTEXT

As multiple researchers have suggested, Chavín represents an eclectic synthesis of preexisting Andean ritual traditions. Since Tello's time, archaeologists have recognized Chavín's iconographic links to both *selva* and *costa* (e.g., Lathrap 1971; Tello 1943), and its ritual architecture has often been tied to the U-shaped buildings and sunken circular plazas of the second millennium BCE on the Central Coast (Kembel 2001:226–30; Williams 1985). Burger has more recently rearticulated and clarified this argument for synthesis (Burger 1992, 1993), and Rick has reemphasized Chavín's adaptation of traditional elements of belief to a new context (Rick 2005:81, 2006a).

The presence of a Mito-style structure, apparently linked to antecedents in the Huallaga Valley and at other highland centers, reinforces this impression of ritual eclecticism and diversity. Chavín is not unique in this blending of elements, however. A similar juxtaposition of coastal (sunken plazas and large—though, interestingly, lacking the archetypal U-shape—structures) architectural elements with the characteristic structure of the apparently highland-centered Mito Tradition is present at Caral, where it has much greater antiquity (Shady Solís, Haas, and Creamer 2001; Shady Solís and Machacuay 2003), and may also be evident at El Paraíso (Guillen Hugo 2013). Mito-style structures themselves are proving to be remarkably widespread (Contreras 2010:figure 11),[1] and the tradition was apparently a long-lasting one (table 3.1).

The presence of a Mito-style structure at Chavín also reinforces the case for diversity in ritual practice by introducing a previously unknown element into the catalog of ceremonial architecture at the site. Kembel has argued that the earliest architectural forms at Chavín were rectangular, plastered chambers—including that which housed, or perhaps later came to house, the Lanzón—linked to (i.e., apparently derived from) the Kotosh Religious Tradition (Kembel 2001:226–27). The contemporaneous existence of a Mito-style chamber in the West Field does not speak directly to the derivation of these architectural forms from the Kotosh Religious Tradition, but it certainly bolsters the claim for strong links to that tradition. At Chavín, interestingly, there is no central hearth or central hearth analogue in either the Circular Plaza or the Square Plaza, and even the recognition of centrality in the latter (a construction offering [Rick, this volume]) was a hidden and singular, rather than communal or public and regular, event. However, the Lanzón originally occupied the central location in a rectangular chamber; Kembel explicitly characterizes this as an architectural analogue of the hearth in the ceremonial structures of the Kotosh Religious Tradition (Kembel 2001:227).

Connections to the Kotosh Religious Tradition, or more specifically the Mito Tradition, strengthen the argument for eclecticism at Chavín while also raising the possibility that ritual diversity may be indicated as much as

TABLE 3.1. Mito-style structures in the Central Andes and associated dates

Site	Locus	Interior Dimensions	Orientation	Associated Dates and/or Calibrated 95% Range of Associated ^{14}C Dates[a]	Associated ^{14}C Samples	Source
La Galgada	C-11:I-3 (Square Chamber)	2.9 m × 2.5 m	west	2470–2060 BCE	Tx-3167 (3820± 60), from adjacent chamber D-11:C-3	Grieder et al. 1988
Kotosh	ER-11 "Templo de los Nichitos"	7.5 m × 8 m	south	2000–1500 BC (Kotosh Mito phase dates)		Izumi and Terada 1972b
Kotosh	ER-19	7.5 m × 7 m	north	2000–1500 BC (Kotosh Mito phase dates)		Izumi and Terada 1972b
Kotosh	ER-23	6 m × 6 m	north	2000–1500 BC (Kotosh Mito phase dates)		Izumi and Terada 1972b
Kotosh	UR-22 "Templo de las Manos Cruzadas"	7 m × 7.5 m	south	2000–1500 BC (Kotosh Mito phase dates)		Izumi and Terada 1972b
Kotosh	ER-20	5 m × 4 m	north	2000–1500 BC (Kotosh Mito phase dates)		Izumi and Terada 1972b
Kotosh	ER-24	3.5 m × 3 m	north	2000–1500 BC (Kotosh Mito phase dates)		Izumi and Terada 1972b
Kotosh	ER-26	2.5 m × 2.5 m	north	3900 ± 900; 2000–1500 BC (Kotosh Mito phase dates)		Izumi and Terada 1972b
Kotosh	ER-28	3 m × 3 m	north	2000–1500 BC (Kotosh Mito phase dates)		Izumi and Terada 1972b

continued on next page

TABLE 3.1.—continued

Site	Locus	Interior Dimensions	Orientation	Associated Dates and/or Calibrated 95% Range of Associated 14C Dates[a]	Associated 14C Samples	Source
Kotosh	ER-27 "Templo Blanco"	3 m × 4 m (estimated)	north	2000–1500 BC (Kotosh Mito phase dates)		Izumi and Terada 1972b
Huaricoto[b]	Hearth XII			2875–2150 BCE	I-II,42 (3970 ± 110) (appears in Ziółkowski et al. n.d. with the number I-11142)	Burger and Salazar-Burger 1985
Huaricoto	Hearth XI			immediately postdates Hearth XII		Burger and Salazar-Burger 1985
Huaricoto	Hearth XIII			3310–2465 BCE	PUCP 3#3 (4210 ± 120)[c]	Burger and Salazar-Burger 1985
Huaricoto	Hearths IX, VIII, VII			Huaricoto phase (~1400–700 BCE)		Burger and Salazar-Burger 1985; Burger 1992
Huaricoto	Hearths IV, II, I	5.5 m diameter (Hearth IV); ~2 m × 2 m (Hearth II)		Capilla phase (~700–300 BCE)		Burger and Salazar-Burger 1985; Burger 1992
Caral	"Altar del Fuego Sagrado" (Templo Mayor)	2.81 m × 2.8 m	south	2400–1885 BCE	Beta-132593 and ISGS-4724 (3640 ± 50; 3730 ± 70); from "construction fill of atrium on top of Pirámide Mayor"	Shady Solís and Machacuay 2003; Shady Solís, Haas, and Creamer 2001

continued on next page

TABLE 3.1.—continued

Site	Locus	Interior Dimensions	Orientation	Associated Dates and/or Calibrated 95% Range of Associated ^{14}C Dates[a]	Associated ^{14}C Samples	Source
Caral	"Altar del Fuego Sagrado" (Templo de Anfiteatro)		west	Late Archaic (site date)		Shady Solis, Machacuay, and López 2003
El Silencio	Edificio Menor	3.3 m × 3.2 m	south	Late Preceramic		Montoya Vera 2007
El Silencio	Edificio Mayor	4.5 m × 5 m (1A) and 3.4 m × 4 m (1B)	south	Late Preceramic		Montoya Vera 2007
Keushu	Estructura EA-XII					Herrera 2010
Piruru	Templo P1	9 m × 9 m		2455–2020 BCE	GIF-7266 (3770 ± 60)	Bonnier and Rozenberg 1988; Bonnier 1997
Huacaloma	R-1	4.6 m × 3.2 m	northeast	early Huacaloma period (1500–255 BCE)[d]	TK-341a, TK-341b, y TK-409 (3080 ± 1130, 2710 ± 240, 2840 ± 90)	Terada and Onuki 1982
Shillacoto	S-R 7	12 m × 12 m	north	2000–1000 BC (Shillacoto Mito and Wairajirca phase dates)		Izumi, Cuculiza, and Kano 1972
Huaynuná		3.0 m × 2.5 m		2460–2060 BCE	UGa-5612 (3810 ± 50)	Pozorski and Pozorski 1996

continued on next page

TABLE 3.1.—continued

Site	Locus	Interior Dimensions	Orientation	Associated Dates and/or Calibrated 95% Range of Associated ¹⁴C Dates[a]	Associated ¹⁴C Samples	Source
Pampa de las Llamas-Moxeke		2.55 m × 2.45 m		1750–1435 BCE	UGa-5611 (3310 ± 70)	Pozorski and Pozorski 1996
Pampa de las Llamas-Moxeke		3.2 m diameter		3550–3150 BP (general site dates)		Pozorski and Pozorski 1996
Pampa de las Llamas-Moxeke		7.0 m × 7.0 m		3550–3150 BP (general site dates)		Pozorski and Pozorski 1996
Bahía Seca		4.32 m diameter		1685–1440 BCE	UGa-6023 (3280 ± 55)	Pozorski and Pozorski 1996
Taukachi-Konkán		3.5 m diameter		1500–1270 BCE	UGa-7038 (3120 ± 45)	Pozorski and Pozorski 1996
Taukachi-Konkán		4.0 m diameter		3530–3000 BP (general site dates)		Pozorski and Pozorski 1996
Taukachi-Konkán		3.0 m diameter		3530–3000 BP (general site dates)		Pozorski and Pozorski 1996
Huaricanga				2450–2330 BCE		Piscitelli 2012
Chavín de Huántar	WF-07	3.0 m × 3.0 m (estimated)	north	900–800 BCE[c]	AA69446 and AA69447 (2644 ± 45; 2712 ± 42)	Contreras 2010

continued on next page

TABLE 3.1.—continued

Site	Locus	Interior Dimensions	Orientation	Associated Dates and/or Calibrated 95% Range of Associated ¹⁴C Dates[a]	Associated ¹⁴C Samples	Source
El Paraíso		6.82 m × 8.04 m	northeast (44°)	Late Preceramic (3500–1800 BCE—general site dates)		Guillen Hugo 2013

Notes

a. When associated dates are single radiocarbon determinations or multiple dates whose relationship is clear, they have been calibrated in OxCal 4.2 (Bronk Ramsey 2009) using IntCal13 (Reimer et al. 2013; see Rick et al. 2009:90–95 and Ogburn 2012:223–225 for discussions of calibration curve selection in Peru). These probability ranges may represent, depending on the specific sample and context, either construction dates or use-dates; it is worth emphasizing that they represent irregularly distributed ranges of probability rather than lapses of time.

b. Hearth VIII at Huaricoto apparently comes the closest to the conventions of the Mito Tradition, with a split-level floor and sub-floor flue. Hearths at the site vary in their shapes, sizes, and features; while by definition they all belong to the Kotosh Religious Tradition, not all (if any) conform to the more narrowly defined norms of the Mito Tradition (see Contreras 2010).

c. This date appears in Ziółkowski et al. with the laboratory number PUCP-XXI, with a warning about that confusion (ANDES ¹⁴C: accessed 8 January 2017, http://andes-c14.arqueologia.pl/database/article/1799-pucp-xxi.html).

d. The imprecision of date TK-34 is such that it has not been included in the range.

e. Dates have been combined, as both samples are from a hearth deposit representing a single depositional event.

synthesis. Might Chavín have been a multiethnic or ecumenical ceremonial center? Certainly, nothing like enclaves of non-local residents have been found, but neither has anything other than a tiny fraction of the residential architecture at Chavín been explored. It may be that the diversity of ritual architecture—and, similarly, the diverse origins of materials and offerings at the site (Contreras 2011; Druc 2004; Lumbreras 1993; Lumbreras et al. 2003; Sayre, Miller, and Rosenfeld 2016)—is representative not just of pilgrimage but of a diversity of ceremonial practice. Heterarchy[2] may be reflected not just in the *number* of dispersed areas of ceremonial significance but also in the variety of practices apparently associated with those areas.

Heterarchical arrangements may have been typical of the Mito Tradition. At Kotosh, La Galgada, and Huaricoto, three of the sites key to defining the ritual tradition, multiple contemporaneous ceremonial chambers seem to have been the norm. However, at Huaricoto at least, the existence of multiple sacred hearths has been used to argue for their construction by diverse social entities (probably kin groups), using the modern *cargo* system as a model (Burger and Salazar-Burger 1986). Burger and Salazar-Burger contrast this situation with that at Kotosh, where they see, in the uniformity of construction, evidence for corporate organization of labor under a permanent authority: "The regularity and conservatism in the design of the Kotosh temples over several centuries, along with the standardized orientation of these buildings to the cardinal directions, is consistent with the notion that the undertakings were organized and directed by recognized leaders capable of subordinating the will of individual households in order to ensure the continuity of ritual patterns" (ibid.:77).

The former situation might be construed as heterarchical, but the latter clearly implies hierarchy. Onuki's suggestion (this volume) that the Mito Tradition was associated with a regional pattern in the Huallaga Basin of an evolution from ritual to ideology has a similar logic.

Where might Chavín—particularly in light of the new evidence provided by the excavation of a Mito-style structure—fall in such a typology? The dramatic diversity in ritual architecture at Chavín seems less to represent diverse means of—or capacities for—labor organization related to different components of the site than to reflect diverse ritual practices, as discussed below. The variability in ritual architecture at Chavín seems to be ordered rather than chaotic; at Huaricoto, it was the unordered variability that Burger and Salazar-Burger used to argue for diverse contributions of labor—and resulting architecture—without a central authority. They also argued that, relatively late in the Huaricoto sequence, the visible diversity came to consist not just of variations on the Kotosh Religious Tradition theme but also of variability in cult practice: "The Kotosh Religious Tradition was not disrupted at Huaricoto with the appearance of the alien Chavín cult. Instead, the two religious traditions coexisted in a syncretistic relationship" (Burger and Salazar-Burger 1980:27).

The eclecticism in ritual practice at Chavín, in contrast, appears to fit well within the model of site by design that Kembel and Rick (2004) outline. If Chavín was indeed actively seeking more followers and more effective means of social integration and establishment of authority, not to mention more effective means of influencing the natural world (Lumbreras 1989), then such an ecumenical, inclusive approach would make a great deal of sense. This is compatible with Kembel and Rick's model (2004) of Chavín as one ceremonial center among many, competing widely with its contemporaries for adherents.

Such intra-site heterogeneity also complicates a model positing a trajectory of increased sociopolitical differentiation—reinforced and legitimized by ritual—during the middle and late Formative period (~1500–500 BCE). Moore (among others; see, for instance, Lumbreras 1989; Rick 2006b) describes the developmental changes of that time period explicitly in terms of ritual practice and legitimized hierarchy: "In a sharp departure from previous patterns, the Formative period was marked by the development of public vs. private religion, by an increasing social distance between participants and observers in public ceremony, and the development of complex social institutions that relied on the legitimacy imparted by highly visible, public ritual" (Moore 1996:226).

The persistence of the Mito Tradition alongside these later developments—not, apparently, as a marginalized survivor among a population resisting the changes but rather incorporated into institutionalized ceremonial practices—suggests that the change was perhaps not so abrupt. Moreover, those developing the rituals associated with sociopolitical difference found it either necessary or expedient to appeal to ancient practices (by the time the Mito-style chamber in the West Field was abandoned, the Mito Tradition had an antiquity of nearly two millennia).

The question of the continuity of the Mito Tradition is complex. Even if the radiocarbon dates from the West Field Mito-style structure represent terminal dates and we liberally estimate the use-life of the structure at a century, there remains a gap of at least 800 years between the latest of the Mito chamber dates Bonnier considers and this appearance of the type at Chavín. While architectural and ceremonial archaism or revival cannot be ruled out, the simplest explanation would seem to be that the Mito Tradition persisted through the beginnings of the Early Horizon. If that is the case, more research is very much needed to shed light on how and where the tradition survived the intervening centuries. Of course, inasmuch as the Mito-style chamber at Chavín may also be described as belonging to the broader category of the Kotosh Religious Tradition, its existence also reinforces Burger and Salazar-Burger's (1985:118) contention that that tradition persisted into the Early Horizon.

READING RITUAL ARCHITECTURE AT CHAVÍN

The Lanzón itself, and more broadly the galleries, structures, and plazas that surround it, has generally been understood as the focus of the site. Rowe posited that the Lanzón "was probably the principal cult object of the original temple at Chavín" (Rowe 1967:75), while Kembel (2001, 2008) argues that the Lanzón is associated with the oldest area of monumental architecture (the NEA)[3] and that the design of subsequent architecture in the area went to great lengths to maintain access to that ancient sacred focus (Kembel's emphasis on the continued importance of the icon is in contrast to Rowe's argument that the Lanzón declined in importance over time). Rowe's contention was a result of his architectural chronology, with its shift in emphasis over time from Old Temple to New Temple, while Rick and Kembel (Kembel 2001, 2008; Rick et al. 1998) emphasize the contemporaneity of the Circular Plaza and the Square Plaza.

This centrality of the Lanzón and the Circular Plaza, coupled with the apparent importance of the Square Plaza and the supposed bounded-ness of the monumental core, is suggestive of the sort of "concentric cline of the sacred" proposed by Kolata (1996) for Tiwanaku. At Tiwanaku, Kolata argues, the ceremonial architecture recapitulates a social order, in the process legitimizing that order by aligning it with sacred principles. The result was that progress "toward the civic-ceremonial core of the city . . . entailed passage across a nested, hierarchical series of socially and ritually distinct spaces" (ibid.:230). This architectural and civic layout mirrored, reinforced, and legitimized conceptions of both cosmic and social order.

The possibility that a similar cline may have existed at Chavín is implicit in arguments for the centrality of the Lanzón (and the NEA complex). The contrast between the open spaces of the plazas and the smaller, restricted-access spaces of the galleries offers a similar argument for a relatively linear gradient, a progression from the relatively open and publicly visible plaza spaces to the restricted-access and private galleries. The primacy of the latter is suggested both directly—by their housing of such features as the Lanzón—and theoretically—by the model of ritual practice elaborated by Rick and Kembel (Kembel and Rick 2004; Rick 2005, 2006a, 2008). Rick highlights the centrality of the gallery spaces in his argument for the nature of Chavín ritual practice: "If they were indeed creating a convincing system based on elaborate and impressive ritual action within a created architectural world, they would have faced intrinsic limitations. If the effects of contexts and ritual are related to the intimacy and exclusivity of the experience, then the groups gaining experience must necessarily be limited in size . . . to be truly convincing, Chavín needed to work in small settings for the most effective rituals" (Rick 2006a:110).

The presence of a contemporary ceremonially important feature—the Mito-style structure—well outside the monumental core (~300 m to the west) suggests a contrasting interpretation. If a concentric cline focused on a central area reflects and reinforces hierarchy, then a dispersed and diverse array of ritually significant areas may conversely be indicative of pluralism and heterarchy.

Inasmuch as political economy can be read from ritual geography, the coexistence of a Mito-style structure in the West Field with the NEA complex (and the Square Plaza and the many galleries) suggests just such a heterarchical arrangement by providing an indication of multiple ceremonial foci. Chavín displays not a concentric cline of the sacred so much as a dispersed array of sacred foci (as might also be suggested, even within the ceremonial core, by the number and heterogeneity of the galleries, as well as by the diversity and spatial dispersion of identifiable locations of ritual activity; see Rick, this volume).[4]

Plurality and heterarchy are suggested not just by the spatial dispersion of ritual foci but also by their inferred use. Although an argument can be made for the increasingly restricted character of access to the spaces within the monumental core (i.e., from the large Square Plaza to the smaller Circular Plaza to still smaller interior galleries; see Burger 1992:179; Rick 2006b:207, 2008:20–24), it is also possible to focus on the difficulty of stitching the entire architectural complex of the monumental core into one processional sequence.

The corpus of lithic art (e.g., on cornice fragments from Structure A [Rick 2008] and on the plaques of the Circular Plaza [Lumbreras 1977]) testifies to the importance of processions at the site. Moore, reviewing the architectural evidence for the use of plazas in the prehispanic Andes, infers an important role for processions, describing "constructed spaces . . . arranged actually to disrupt visual impact" (Moore 1996:224)—that is, spaces designed to be experienced rather than viewed. Rick's recent characterization of Chavín's architectural spaces recalls this focus on procession: "The architectural placement of individuals in sunken plazas, where much of the outside world is blocked . . . or in underground galleries in which all the external world is annulled, would be a way of definitively altering situational experience" (Rick 2006a, 110).

TABLE 3.2. Estimated areas and capacities of selected ritual spaces at Chavín

	Area (m^2)	Capacity (at 0.46 m^2/person)	Capacity (at 2 m^2/person)
Square Plaza	2,401	5,220	1,200
Circular Plaza	284	617	142
Inner Lanzón Gallery	7	15	3
Mito structure	9	20	4

The contrasting sizes of the spaces involved limit the potential numbers of participants in any ritual activity. These range from the Square Plaza, which might have accommodated as many as approximately 5,200 participants,[5] to the Circular Plaza, which could have held ~600, while the internal spaces would have been limited to only handfuls of participants. Open-air ceremony might have been witnessed by much larger numbers in the spaces surrounding the plazas, but activity in interior spaces would have necessarily been much more limited (e.g., to approximately 15 people in the inner portion of the Lanzón Gallery and not more than 2–4 in the canal entries). The West Field Mito structure, though it may not have been the only one, is similar to the gallery spaces—able to accommodate only 20 persons in relatively intimate activities. The narrow entry steps suggest the ability to tightly restrict access.

Evidence for *where* processions would have taken place is ambiguous. The progression described above—from public plazas to private galleries—combined with the identification of the NEA Complex and Structure A as sacred foci may be an indication of the directionality of processions. It may be telling, moreover, that the figures sculpted in relief on the plaques surrounding the Circular Plaza are all processing—converging, if a mirror-image southern arc is inferred to match the partially preserved northern one—on the stair that leads to the Lanzón Gallery. Such an argument for directionality and the cline of the sacred it implies, however, is complicated by the fact that there is not *one* clear processional pathway through the site.

In fact, as Rick (2006b, 2008) has pointed out, two obvious paths exist: (1) through the Plaza Mayor from east to west, ascending the Black-and-White Staircase, crossing the Plaza Menor, and reaching the Black-and-White Portal; and (2) through the Plaza Mayor from east to west, across the Plaza Mayor terrace to the northwest, up the Middendorf Staircase, through the Circular Plaza Atrium and its approach, into the Circular Plaza, and up the Structure B staircase to enter the Lanzón/Laberintos Gallery complex (figure 3.5; also Rick 2006b:207–9, 2008:23–24). The existence of these paths in parallel rather

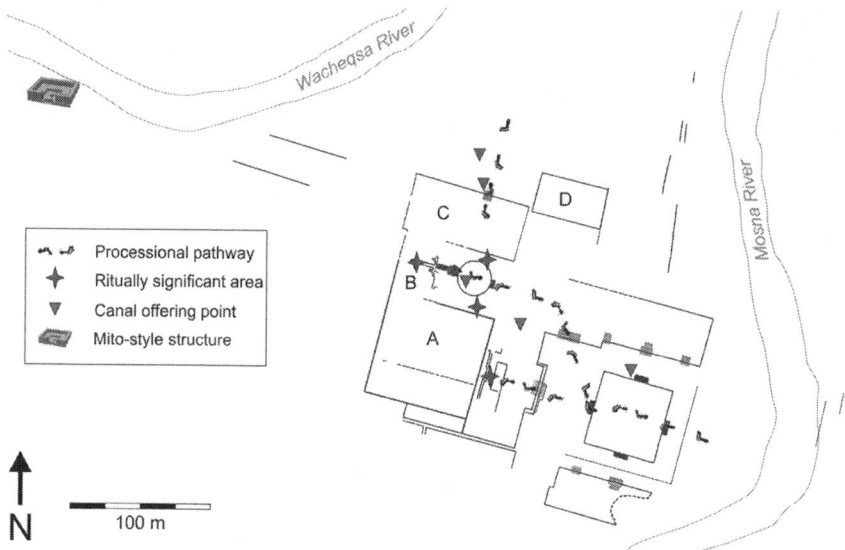

FIGURE 3.5. *Hypothesized processional pathways through the monument, a selection of ritually significant locations (e.g., the Lanzón and Ofrendas Galleries), and a selection of canal access ways where evidence for ritual activity has been found. For a more comprehensive discussion of ritual spaces in the monumental core, see Rick, this volume. Note that the Mito-style structure in the West Field is intended to illustrate location only and is not to scale.*

than in sequence may have been a significant contributor to Rowe's definition of Old and New Temples. Rowe postulated worship of distinct deities in the north and south wings of the site, by which he meant the smaller U-shaped complex composed of part of Structure A and Structures B and C, and the larger U-shaped complex composed of Structures E, A, and F; he saw the latter largely supplanting the former over time (Rowe 1967). Kembel's (2001, 2008) demonstration of the contemporaneity of the Old and New Temples thus begs the question of why multiple processional paths should coexist.

The presence of a Mito-style structure in the West Field suggests an answer: rather than a holy-of-holies on which the site was focused, there existed multiple ritual foci. Moreover, the coexistence of the NEA complex and the Black-and-White Portal, as well as the profusion of galleries (see Kembel 2008:figure 2.9), argues for a dispersal of ritual significance among several loci. Furthermore, the record of diversity of ritual foci continues to increase, as recent work by the Stanford Project has demonstrated that subsurface canals outside of the major structures were locations of ritual practice. Ritual activity focused on these subsurface canals included both access to them through formal entryways and the deposition of artifact offerings (pot-smashes) through small vertical shafts. In addition, recent excavation has revealed a major staircase on the north side of Structure C, indicating a third likely processional path and suggesting that processions were not necessarily limited to the interior of the site's U-shape (see Rick, this volume).

CONCLUSION

The evidence discussed here for ritual practice at Chavín raises questions about the nature and function of the site as a ritual center, suggesting heterarchical as well as hierarchical patterns. Ritual activity of various kinds taking place in diverse locations throughout the site, as well as a diversity of potential pathways for publicly visible procession (both internal and external to the site's U-shape), suggest a site that was a hive of ritual activity—various practices in various places, perhaps occurring simultaneously, perhaps each at its distinct time.

The multiple sacred foci, profusion of galleries and plazas, and absence of a strict processional or increasingly restricted-access sequence might be seen as difficult to reconcile with Kembel and Rick's arguments for the importance and centrality of deliberate, top-down, and long-term planning at the site. Can a model of Chavín as *designed* (Kembel and Rick 2004:64–68; Rick 2005:78–80)—implying a hierarchical, top-down approach to its construction and a central authority—be reconciled with a diversity of ritual practice that suggests heterarchy?

A distinction between heterarchy and egalitarianism is vital—heterarchy may incorporate a significant degree of sociopolitical differentiation even while it implies social tension that mandates against strict ordering. The implication is of inclusiveness but not independence, of diverse ritual practices subsumed to the authority of the polity, of heterarchy nested within hierarchy. This suggests an avenue for further research at Chavín and indeed into the sociopolitical processes of the Formative period more generally: how did ceremonial centers both incorporate diverse ritual practices (implying perhaps diverse practitioners, or adherents and pilgrims attentive to some aspects of centers but not others) and maintain (or develop) a centralized authority that could command tribute and was capable of strategic and long-term planning?

The existence of a Mito-style structure at Chavín does not necessarily call into question the importance of procession or restriction of access in ritual practice at the site, but the presence of ceremonial architecture in an otherwise relatively marginal area suggests that ritual space was diverse rather than singular and that authority at Chavín was perhaps heterarchical as well as hierarchical. The Mito structure in the West Field—almost literally in the shadow of the temple complex, certainly sanctioned and included rather than in any way clandestine—suggests that ritual practice at Chavín was at least inclusive and perhaps actively syncretic.

ACKNOWLEDGMENTS

The excavation of the Mito-style structure at Chavín was funded by a National Science Foundation Doctoral Dissertation Improvement Grant (#0532350), with additional support from a Stanford School of Humanities and Sciences Graduate Research Opportunity Grant, an Amherst College Memorial Fellowship, and the Lynford Family Foundation. The work was carried out as part of the Stanford Project directed by John Rick, thanks to the permission of the Peruvian Instituto Nacional de Cultura. My fieldwork was carried out with the invaluable help of Parker van Valkenburgh, Verónica Castro Neves, and Jose Luis Nuñez; priceless logistical support came from Maria Mendoza, Christian Mesia, and the people of the town of Chavín.

NOTES

1. The map does not include Mito-style structures recently described at Huaricanga in the Fortaleza Valley (Piscitelli 2012), Qeushu in the lower Callejón de Conchucos (Herrera 2010), or El Paraíso in the Chillón Valley (Guillen Hugo 2013). For an updated version, see Contreras (2016:figure 9).

2. Heterarchy refers to a situation wherein the individuals or groups involved are either unranked or have rankings that are fluid rather than fixed, changing depending on context (Crumley 1995).

3. The NEA designation refers to the northeastern portion of Structure A, which is among the oldest pieces in the construction sequence that Kembel was able to identify. I here refer to the Lanzón and the gallery that houses it, in combination with the Circular Plaza, as the NEA Complex; this elides significant architectural change over time but emphasizes the persistent ceremonial focus on this area.

4. Moreover, the small scale of the excavations in the West Field bears emphasizing—only just under 18 m^2 were excavated, and only about 6 m^2 of that reached the level of the Mito-style structure. Stratigraphic evidence from the river cut a scant 5 m to the north demonstrates that construction at the level of the chamber—and

below—extended at least that far, but we simply have no idea about the horizontal extent of construction related to this feature. The substantial later deposits may hide an array of contemporary Mito-style structures, as at Kotosh, or this example may be solitary.

5. Using the most liberal of Moore's (1996) estimates for architectural capacities—0.46 m²/person. For areas and more conservative calculations, see table 3.2.

REFERENCES CITED

Bennett, W. C. 1944. *The North Highlands of Peru: Excavations in the Callejón de Huaylas and at Chavín de Huántar*. Anthropological Papers of the American Museum of Natural History Vol. 39. New York: American Museum of Natural History.

Bonnier, E. 1997. "Preceramic Architecture in the Andes: The Mito Tradition." *Archaeologica Peruana* 2: 120–44.

Bonnier, E., and C. Rozenberg. 1988. "Del Santuario al Caserío: Acerca de la Neolitización en la Cordillera de los Andes Centrales." *Bulletin de l'Institut Français d'Études Andines* 17: 1–12.

Bronk Ramsey, C. 2009. "Bayesian Analysis of Radiocarbon Dates." *Radiocarbon* 51 (1): 337–60. http://dx.doi.org/10.1017/S0033822200033865.

Burger, R. L. 1982. "'Pojoc and Waman Wain: Two Early Horizon Villages in the Chavín Heartland." *Ñawpa Pacha: Journal of Andean Archaeology* 20 (1): 3–40. http://dx.doi.org/10.1179/naw.1982.20.1.002.

Burger, R. L. 1984. *The Prehistoric Occupation of Chavín de Huántar, Peru*. Berkeley: University of California Press.

Burger, R. L. 1992. *Chavín and the Origins of Andean Civilization*. New York: Thames and Hudson.

Burger, R. L. 1993. "The Chavín Horizon: Stylistic Chimera or Socioeconomic Metamorphosis?" In *Latin American Horizons*, ed. D. S. Rice, 41–82. Washington, DC: Dumbarton Oaks.

Burger, R. L., and L. Salazar-Burger. 1980. "Ritual and Religion at Huaricoto." *Archaeology* 33 (6): 26–32.

Burger, R. L., and L. Salazar-Burger. 1985. "The Early Ceremonial Center of Huaricoto." In *Early Ceremonial Architecture in the Andes: A Conference at Dumbarton Oaks, 8th to 10th October 1982*, ed. C. Donnan, 111–35. Washington, DC: Dumbarton Oaks.

Burger, R. L., and L. Salazar-Burger. 1986. "Early Organizational Diversity in the Peruvian Highlands: Huaricoto and Kotosh." In *Andean Archaeology: Papers in Memory of Clifford Evans*, ed. R. Matos Mendieta, S. A. Turpin, and H. H. Eling

Jr., 65–82. Monograph 27. Los Angeles: Institute of Archaeology, University of California.

Contreras, D. A. 2007. "Sociopolitical and Geomorphologic Dynamism at Chavín de Huántar, Peru." PhD dissertation, Department of Anthropological Sciences, Stanford University, Stanford, CA.

Contreras, D. A. 2010. "A Mito-Style Structure at Chavín de Huántar: Dating and Implications." *Latin American Antiquity* 21 (1): 3–21. http://dx.doi.org/10.7183/1045-6635.21.1.3.

Contreras, D. A. 2011. "How Far to Conchucos? A GIS Approach to Assessing the Implications of Exotic Materials at Chavín de Huántar." *World Archaeology* 43 (3): 380–97. http://dx.doi.org/10.1080/00438243.2011.605841.

Contreras, D. A. 2016. "La Incorporación de la Tradición Mito en el Ámbito Ritual de Chavín de Huántar." In *Arqueología de la Sierra de Ancash 2: Ensayos y Reportes*, ed. B. Ibarra, 21–44. Lima: Instituto de Estudios Huarinos.

Crumley, C. L. 1995. "Heterarchy and the Analysis of Complex Societies." *Archaeological Papers of the American Anthropological Association* 6 (1): 1–5. http://dx.doi.org/10.1525/ap3a.1995.6.1.1.

Diessl, W. 2004. *Huantar, San Marcos, Chavín: Sitios Arqueológicos en la Sierra de Ancash*. Lima: Instituto Cultural Runa.

Druc, I. C. 2004. "Ceramic Diversity in Chavín de Huántar, Peru." *Latin American Antiquity* 15 (3): 344–63. http://dx.doi.org/10.2307/4141578.

Grieder, T., and A. Bueno Mendoza. 1985. "Ceremonial Architecture at La Galgada." In *Early Ceremonial Architecture in the Andes: A Conference at Dumbarton Oaks, 8th to 10th October 1982*, ed. C. Donnan, 93–110. Washington, DC: Dumbarton Oaks.

Grieder, T., A. Bueno Mendoza, C. Earl Smith Jr., and R. M. Malina. 1988. *La Galgada, Peru: A Preceramic Culture in Transition*. Austin: University of Texas Press.

Guillen Hugo, M. A. 2013. *Templo del Fuego y la Tradición Mito en el Paraíso*. Accessed 8 January 2017. http://paraisoarqueologico.wordpress.com/2013/02/09/templo-del-fuego-y-la-tradicion-mito-en-el-paraiso/.

Herrera, A. 2010. "Informe Final de Labores del Proyecto de Investigación Arqueológico Wanduy, Temporada 2008." Informe presentado al Instituto Nacional de Cultura, Lima.

Indacochea, G. A., and M. Iberico. 1947. "Aluvionamiento de Chavín de Huántar el 17 de Enero de 1945." *Boletín de la Sociedad Geológica del Perú* 20: 21–28.

Izumi, S., P. J. Cuculiza, and C. Kano. 1972. *Excavations at Shillacoto, Huanuco, Peru*. Bulletin 3. Tokyo: University Museum, University of Tokyo.

Izumi, S., and K. Terada, eds. 1972a. *Andes 4: Excavations at Kotosh, Peru, 1963 and 1966*. Tokyo: University of Tokyo Press.

Izumi, S., and K. Terada, eds. 1972b. *Excavations at Kotosh, Peru: A Report on the Third and Fourth Expeditions.* Tokyo: University of Tokyo Press.

Kembel, S. R. 2001. "Architectural Sequence and Chronology at Chavín de Huántar, Perú." PhD dissertation, Department of Anthropological Sciences, Stanford University, Stanford, CA.

Kembel, S. R. 2008. "The Architecture at the Monumental Center of Chavín de Huántar: Sequence, Transformations, and Chronology." In *Chavín: Art, Architecture, and Culture,* ed. W. J. Conklin and J. Quilter, 35–84. Monograph 61. Los Angeles: Cotsen Institute of Archaeology, University of California.

Kembel, S. R., and H. Haas. 2013. "Radiocarbon Dates from the Monumental Architecture at Chavín de Huántar, Perú." *Journal of Archaeological Method and Theory* 22 (2): 345–427. http://dx.doi.org/10.1007/s10816-013-9180-9.

Kembel, S. R., and J. W. Rick. 2004. "Building Authority at Chavín de Huántar: Models of Social Organization and Development in the Initial Period and Early Horizon." In *Andean Archaeology,* ed. H. Silverman, 51–76. Malden, MA: Blackwell.

Kinzl, H., and E. Scheider. 1950. *Cordillera Blanca (Perú).* Innsbruck: Universitats-Verlag Wagner.

Kolata, A. 1996. "Mimesis and Monumentalism in Native Andean Cities." *RES: Anthropology and Aesthetics* 29 (1): 223–36.

Lathrap, D. W. 1971. "The Tropical Forest and the Cultural Context of Chavín." In *Dumbarton Oaks Conference on Chavín,* ed. E. P. Benson, 73–100. Washington, DC: Dumbarton Oaks.

Lumbreras, L. G. 1977. "Excavaciones en el Templo Antiguo de Chavín (Sector R); Informe de la Sexta Campaña." *Ñawpa Pacha: Journal of Andean Archaeology* 15 (1): 1–38. http://dx.doi.org/10.1179/naw.1977.15.1.001.

Lumbreras, L. G. 1989. *Chavín de Huántar en el Nacimiento de la Civilización Andina.* Lima: Instituto Andino de Estudios Arqueologicos.

Lumbreras, L. G. 1993. *Chavín de Huántar: Excavaciones en la Galería de las Ofrendas.* Materialien zur Allgemeinen und Vergleichenden Archäologie, Bd. 51. Mainz am Rhein: P. von Zabern.

Lumbreras, L. G., R. Gebhard, W. Häusler, F. Kauffmann-Doig, J. Riederer, G. Sieben, and U. Wagner. 2003. "Mössbauer Study of Ceramic Finds from the Galería de las Ofrendas, Chavín de Huántar." *Hyperfine Interactions* 150 (1–4): 51–72. http://dx.doi.org/10.1023/B:HYPE.0000007214.89534.37.

Middendorf, E. W. 1974. *Peru: Observaciones y Estudios del País y sus Habitantes Durante una Permanencia de 25 Años.* Lima: Universidad Nacional Mayor de San Marcos.

Montoya Vera, M. 2007. "Arquitectura de la 'Tradición Mito' en el Valle Medio del Santa: Sitio 'El Silencio.'" *Bulletin de l'Institut Français d'Études Andines* 36 (2): 199–220. http://dx.doi.org/10.4000/bifea.3795.

Moore, J. D. 1996. *Architecture and Power in the Ancient Andes: The Archaeology of Public Buildings*. New Studies in Archaeology. Cambridge: Cambridge University Press. http://dx.doi.org/10.1017/CBO9780511521201.

Ogburn, D. 2012. "Reconceiving the Chronology of Inca Imperial Expansion." *Radiocarbon* 54 (2): 219–37. http://dx.doi.org/10.1017/S0033822200046944.

Onuki, Y. 1993. "Las Actividades Ceremoniales Tempranas en la Cuenca del Alto Huallaga y Algunos Problemas Generales." In *El Mundo Ceremonial Andino*, ed. L. Millones and Y. Onuki, 69–96. Senri Ethnological Studies 37. Osaka: National Museum of Ethnology.

Piscitelli, M. 2012. *Ritual Is Power: An Exploration of Ceremonial Architecture at Huaricanga*. Accessed 8 January 2017. http://diggingperu.wordpress.com/context/huaricanga/.

Pozorski, T., and S. Pozorski. 1996. "Ventilated Hearth Structures in the Casma Valley, Peru." *Latin American Antiquity* 7 (4): 341–53. http://dx.doi.org/10.2307/972263.

Reimer, P. J., E. Bard, A. Bayliss, J. W. Beck, P. G. Blackwell, C. B. Ramsey, C. E. Buck, H. Cheng, R. L. Edwards, M. Friedrich et al. 2013. "IntCal13 and Marine13 Radiocarbon Age Calibration Curves 0–50,000 Years Cal BP." *Radiocarbon* 55 (4): 1869–87. http://dx.doi.org/10.2458/azu_js_rc.55.16947.

Rick, J. W. 2005. "The Evolution of Authority and Power at Chavín de Huántar, Peru." In *Foundations of Power in the Prehispanic Andes*, ed. K. J. Vaughn, D. Ogburn, and C. A. Conlee, 71–89. Archeological Papers of the American Anthropological Association. Arlington, VA: American Anthropological Association. http://dx.doi.org/10.1525/ap3a.2005.14.071.

Rick, J. W. 2006a. "Chavín de Huántar: Evidence for an Evolved Shamanism." In *Mesas and Cosmologies in the Central Andes*, ed. D. Sharon, 101–12. San Diego Museum Papers 44. San Diego: San Diego Museum of Man.

Rick, J. W. 2006b. "Un Análisis de los Centros Ceremoniales del Período Formativo a Partir de los Estudios en Chavín de Huántar." *Boletín de Arqueología PUCP* 10: 201–14.

Rick, J. W. 2008. "Context, Construction, and Ritual in the Development of Authority at Chavín de Huántar." In *Chavín: Art, Architecture, and Culture*, ed. W. J. Conklin and J. Quilter, 3–34. Monograph 61. Los Angeles: Cotsen Institute of Archaeology, University of California.

Rick, J. W., S. Kembel, R. Rick, and J. A. Kembel. 1998. "La Arquitectura del Complejo Ceremonial de Chavín de Huántar: Documentación Tridimensional y sus Implicancias." *Boletín de Arqueología PUCP* 2: 181–214.

Rick, J. W., C. Mesía, D. A. Contreras, S. Kembel, R. Rick, M. Sayre, and J. Wolf. 2009. "La Cronología de Chavín de Huántar y sus Implicancias para el Período Formativo." *Boletín de Arqueología PUCP* 13: 87–132.

Rowe, J. H. 1967. "Form and Meaning in Chavín Art." In *Peruvian Archaeology: Selected Readings*, ed. J. H. Rowe and D. Menzel, 72–103. Palo Alto: Peek.

Sayre, M., M. J. Miller, and S. A. Rosenfeld. 2016. "Isotopic Evidence for the Trade and Production of Exotic Marine Mammal Bone Artifacts at Chavín de Huántar." *Archaeological and Anthropological Sciences* 8 (2): 403–417.

Shady Solís, R., J. Haas, and W. Creamer. 2001. "Dating Caral, a Preceramic Site in the Supe Valley on the Central Coast of Peru." *Science* 292 (5517): 723–26.

Shady Solís, R., and M. Machacuay. 2003. "El Altar del Fuego Sagrado del Templo Mayor de la Ciudad Sagrada de Caral-Supe." In *La Ciudad Sagrada de Caral-Supe: Los Orígenes de la Civilización Andina y la Formación del Estado Prístino en el Antiguo Perú*, ed. R. Shady and C. Leyva, 169–85. Lima: Instituto Nacional de Cultura.

Shady Solís, R., M. Machacuay, and S. López. 2003. "Recuperando la Historia del Altar del Fuego Sagrado." In *La Ciudad Sagrada de Caral-Supe: Los Orígenes de la Civilización Andina y la Formación del Estado Prístino en el Antiguo Perú*, ed. R. Shady Solís and C. Leyva, 237–54. Lima: Instituto Nacional de Cultura.

Tello, J. C. 1943. "Discovery of the Chavín Culture in Perú." *American Antiquity* 9 (1): 135–60. http://dx.doi.org/10.2307/275457.

Tello, J. C. 1960. *Chavín Cultura Matriz de la Civilización Andina*. Lima: University of San Marcos.

Terada, K., and Y. Onuki, eds. 1982. *Excavations at Huacaloma in the Cajamarca Valley, Peru, 1979*. Tokyo: University of Tokyo Press.

Wiener, C. 1880. *Pérou et Bolivie: Récit de Voyage Suivi d'études Aarchéologiques et Ethnographiques et de Notes sur L'écriture et les Langues des Populations Indiennes*. Paris: Libraire Hachette.

Williams, C. 1985. "A Scheme for the Early Monumental Architecture of the Central Coast of Peru." In *Early Ceremonial Architecture in the Andes: A Conference at Dumbarton Oaks, 26 and 27 October 1982*, ed. C. Donnan, 227–40. Washington, DC: Dumbarton Oaks.

Witt, H. 1992. *Diario 1824–1890: Un Testimio Personal Sobre el Peru del Siglo XIX*. Lima: Banco Mercantil.

Ziółkowski, M. S., M. F. Pazdur, A. Krzanowski, and A. Michczyński. n.d. *Radiocarbon Database for Bolivia, Ecuador, and Peru*. Accessed 8 January 2017. http://andes-c14.arqueologia.pl/component/content/article/9-uncategorised/72-overview.html.

4

From Ritual to Ideology

Ritual Activity and Artistic Representations in the Northern Highlands of Peru in the Formative Period

Yoshio Onuki

The Formative period of Andean civilization is a complicated process of interaction among, and vicissitudes of, many local cultures that occupied different ecological niches in the coastal lowlands as well as in the highlands. Although it is true that religion, ritual, cosmology, and ideology played a very important role in this process, it has been difficult to understand their roles in a more detailed way. At many Andean centers, including the Mito Tradition phase at Kotosh and the later site of Kuntur Wasi, dismantling one ceremonial structure and building a new one on top of it was a careful and recurrent activity. Here I present a hypothesis that involves the ideology of temple renovation as a prime mover of social development in the Formative period. Such ideology was the result of a long sociocultural process starting in the late Archaic period/initial Formative period, possibly related to Amazonian mythology and the transformative power of slash-and-burn agriculture practiced in the rainforest.

KOTOSH AND OTHER SITES IN THE UPPER HUALLAGA BASIN

In the 1960s, several sites were excavated around Huánuco city located in the Upper Huallaga Basin (Peru) with the principal objective to clarify the sociocultural process before and after the so-called Chavín culture (Izumi and Sono 1963; Izumi and Terada 1972).

DOI: 10.5876/9781607325963.c004

The intensive excavations were carried out in three seasons at the site of Kotosh, which produced new data for the Andean archaeology of those days. I choose three points from those results that I think are worth mentioning here. One is the establishment of a chronology of the Formative period around Huánuco, which begins with the Kotosh Mito phase, which is preceramic, and then continues through two phases of pre-Chavín pottery. The Kotosh Chavín phase follows, which gives way to the Kotosh Sajarapatac phase with the characteristics of the White-on-Red pottery style (figure 4.1). The second contribution was the discovery of two pre-Chavín phases with pottery, the Kotosh Wairajirca phase and the Kotosh Kotosh phase, and the third was the discovery of a series of preceramic constructions, the most salient of which was the Temple of the Crossed Hands. These three points were corroborated through excavations at other sites such as Shillacoto, Paucarbamba, Wairajirca, and Sajarapatac, all in the same Upper Huallaga Basin.

MITO PHASE CEREMONIAL ARCHITECTURE AT KOTOSH

Kotosh is located 1,950 meters above sea level (masl) and about 5 km west of Huánuco city on the right bank of the Higueras River, a tributary of the Huallaga River. The entire valley bottom and its immediate lower parts of the surrounding slopes belong to the *yunga* zone of Pulgar Vidal's (1967) scheme. This zone is below 2,400 masl, warm and dry throughout the year with a small amount of precipitation during the winter, and it is suited for growing many crops and fruits. This important ecological zone is located in both the coastal valleys and the highlands.

Temple of the Crossed Hands

The excavations revealed that the preceramic ceremonial architecture was a three-terrace complex. The first terrace, that is, the topmost terrace, has been lost because of looting activity, probably during the colonial period. The Temple of the Crossed Hands was unearthed on the second terrace in a fairly good state of preservation (figure 4.2). Widening the excavation area for this temple, we found that another similar structure had been laid just above the temple. We named this new one the Temple of the Small Niches. So here, we distinguished two sub-phases.

Many traces of similar structures appeared on the third terrace to the north of the second one, and the excavations made clear that there was a third sub-phase, namely, the sub-phase of the White Temple, which had at least two

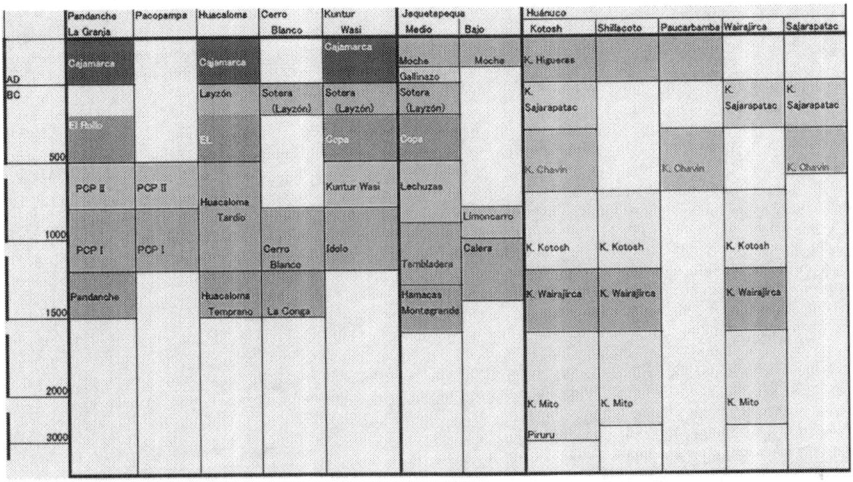

FIGURE 4.1. *Chronological chart for some excavated sites in the northern highlands*

contiguous rooms. Consequently, the Mito phase is divided into three sub-phases (figure 4.3).

In the first sub-phase the White Temple was constructed on the third, or lowest, terrace. At least two rooms form this temple: one, ER-28, is 4 m × 4 m with a narrow entrance in the center of the north wall, and only half of the other room, ER-27, was excavated. The wall thickness is 60–70 cm, and every face and the surface of the floor are thickly coated with fine clay finished in white. A two-level floor with a circular hearth in the center and small niches on the interior faces are characteristic of the walls. In one niche, several unbaked clay objects were found: two figurines, a gourd-like object, a discoidal one, and a tiny bowl.

If this temple complex was built on the three-tier massive platform, then there must have been some structure on the second terrace that was buried under the Temple of the Crossed Hands. A small test pit was dug from the floor of this temple, and a well-coated floor was detected under the layers of ash and soil. This means the Temple of the Crossed Hands was built after another, previous structure built on the second terrace and contemporaneous with the White Temple was buried.

The Temple of the Crossed Hands (UR-22) was found in an excellent condition of preservation (see figure 4.3). The outer dimension is 9.50 m × 9.30 m, and the walls are 2.39–2.85 m high. The wall is about 1 m thick. In the interior, large and small niches are arranged symmetrically; the largest on the

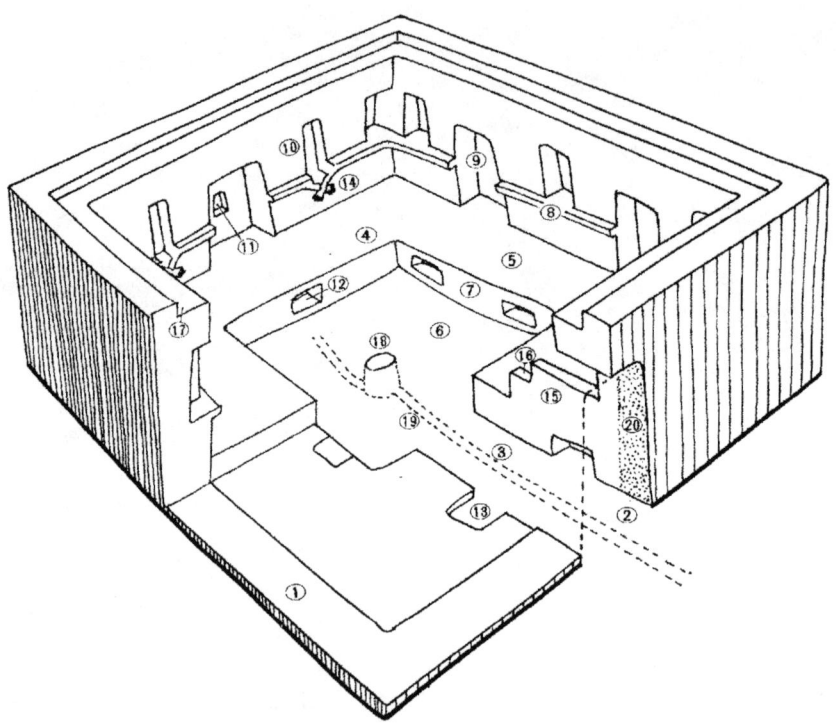

(1) main wall
(2) entrance
(3) entryway
(4) split-level construction
(5) upper-level floor
(6) lower-level floor
(7) perimeter wall
(8) stringcourse
(9) large niche
(10) niche
(11) niche-within-a-niche
(12) samll niche at the perimeter wall
(13) niche in the flanking wall of the entryway
(14) relief depicting crossed hands
(15) flanking wall
(16) incut of the flanking wall
(17) incut margin of the main wall
(18) hearth
(19) flue
(20) red pigment applied to the outer half of the end of the wall at the entrance

FIGURE 4.2. *Temple of the Crossed Hands at Kotosh*

north wall is impressive, with a small niche on each side, and the high reliefs of crossed hands were attached on the wall face below these two niches. The whole interior from the floor to the walls was plastered in creamy white. It seems that the outside was painted red.

FIGURE 4.3. *Several temples of the Kotosh Mito phase, showing the trace of renovation*

The floor is a split-level structure, *pericaust* (lower floor) and *epicaust* (upper floor) according to the terminology used by Bonnier (1997), and a hearth 40 cm in diameter was found in the center of the lower floor. The difference between the two floor levels is 40–50 cm. Beneath the floor, two ventilating ducts were prepared, running from the hearth to the north and south.

When observing the overlapping of these buildings, it is clear that after some time passed, this temple together with the rooms on the third terrace were buried or destroyed. A new temple, the Temple of the Small Niches, was built just above the fill of the Temple of the Crossed Hands.

Temple of the Small Niches

The excavation of this temple revealed the details of its ritualized construction process. In the beginning fine black sand was piled to cover the two reliefs of crossed hands; the sand ultimately formed a cone. Slightly later, the entrance was filled with cobblestones and clay mortar. The logs used for the roof were removed. A huge amount of cobblestone filled the inner space of the temple as well as the outside in the space between the walls and newly built retaining walls that surrounded the west and north sides of the temple. These stones were fairly large, able to be carried two or three at a time by one person, and they had smooth and clean surfaces without any dirt or stains.

Reddish-brown clay was piled thick to prepare the floor of a new temple (the Small Niches). A stone-lined hearth was turned into this reddish-brown soil, and two flues (ducts) were set and connected to the hearth. All of these were covered with soil, and then a row of stones was laid around the area to form the perimeter walls that were to divide the pericaust from the epicaust. A fairly large amount of ash and small pieces of charcoal were spread in the area defined for the pericaust. Again, a sufficient quantity of soil was brought and carefully piled to prepare the split-level floor, together with the construction of perimeter walls with small niches, as well as the four outer, thick walls. The creamy-white plaster was put all over the surface and floor, and the Temple of the Small Niches was complete. Bonnier (1997) suggested that the red soil on the floor was important to this process of demolishing an old temple and rebuilding a new one, but I posit instead that the scattering of ash below the pericaust was much more significant, since the ash scattering appeared to have been limited to the area surrounded by the stone alignment for the pericaust.

This phenomenon of scattered ash below the pericaust floor is repeated in every room of the Kotosh Mito phase. Although we did not excavate below the Temple of the Crossed Hands, a small test pit showed a layer of ash below the floor (we found a deer antler in the ash), and there was a well-plastered floor at a deeper level.

INTERPRETING THE MITO TEMPLES AT KOTOSH

We do not know how to interpret the meaning of the crossed hands. Viewed from the entrance, the left one is thicker than the right-side one. We can only suggest that perhaps the pair may represent the masculine and the feminine, a kind of dualism, but we cannot go further yet. In contrast, the ash below the floor, together with the act of renovation, tells us much more. Two characteristics of the ceremonial architecture of the Kotosh Mito phase are worth emphasizing. One is what I once called "renovation of temple" (Onuki 1993, 1994b). The overlapping of temple structures during the Mito phase can be divided into three sub-phases, and, as Bonnier (1997) pointed out, there were minor renovations during these sub-phases. Through renovation, some structures were buried completely and the other ones destroyed; only the floors were left. The careful covering of the reliefs of the hands led Izumi and Matsuzawa (1967) to coin the term *temple entombment* for this act of burying the temples. This term has become popular in various archaeological publications.

I would rather emphasize the aim of the burying, however. The question is, why did the temples have to be buried? Since there is no regularity in the manner of burying—with many destroyed and some buried without damage—and since the new ones were built in a uniform and ritual manner, it is obvious that old temples were destroyed and buried so new ones might be built on the newly prepared platforms. The basic concept is the temple renovation. We do not know what cosmology was behind this temple renovation, but similar activities are found in the preceramic public architectures at Caral (Shady Solís 2005; Shady Solís and Leyva 2003) and in much later sites such as Huacaloma of the Formative period in Cajamarca (Terada and Onuki 1982, 1985) and Huaca de la Luna of Moche culture. Beyond the Central Andes we see many other cases in Mesoamerica, such as Teotihuacan and Copan.

The second characteristic is also related to renovation: the preparation of a hearth and spread of ash at the beginning of construction of a temple. The old temple was abandoned, and the new temple emerges on the surface of ash. The renovation means the rebirth of the temple, and it comes out of ash. The process is reminiscent of slash-and-burn agriculture, a common agricultural technique in the tropical rainforest in which a new field is opened and the fallen trees are burned to ash. New plants come out of the soil that contains the ash. After some time, the field is abandoned and a new field is prepared; thus, the same process is repeated.

Not only the ash and hearth but also the subterranean flues are reminiscent of myths told in northwestern Amazonia.

M5 *He* Anaconda

Then he [*He* Anaconda] told his son to light a fire and burn him on it so that there would be more *He*. His son lit a fire, dragged *He* Anaconda round and round the house and then out of the front door on to the plaza. There he put him on a big fire till he burned to ashes.

In the place where the fire had been, tobacco, caraiuru, fish-poison, calaloo, and a paxiuba palm grew up, first tobacco and then the palm.

From the place where *He* Anaconda was burned, the people came and obtained all kinds of magic substance used in shamanism.

M6 B Manioc-Stick Anaconda Burns Himself

Manioc-stick Anaconda was angry with himself. He put snuff in his mouth and then took it out and put it in a little heap on the ground. It began to burn and a spark landed on his neck.

Manioc-stick Anaconda burned and everything round him caught fire. The whole land was white from the ash of the fire.

His soul left his body and became another man, also Manioc-stick Anaconda. He was a man like us.

Manioc-stick Anaconda's shadow lay on the ground burned to ash. From the charcoal on the ground grew up manioc, all the manioc there is today[:] green calaloo (*Phytolacca* sp.), red calaloo (*Phyto*. Sp.), various fungi, fish-poison. (Hugh-Jones 1979:284, 293–94)

These myths make it tempting to interpret the flues in the ash layer under the floor as references to the anaconda or serpent.

Anthropologists commonly conceptualize the cosmology of a given society through analysis of ritual, myth, and exogenic explanations made by local people. Many societies have no theory or philosophy about human existence in the universe, explicitly and "logically" told. We must abstract it from ritual performances on various occasions and from what the people say. Archaeologists do the same through analysis of what remains in a site.

Temple renovation is observed not only at Kotosh but also at Caral, La Galgada, and other sites, as well as at Huacaloma in the Cajamarca Basin and many Formative sites. Although we do not know much about subsistence at these sites, a few known cultigens (e.g., manioc) originate from the tropical environment. Given the potential links outlined above, the relation of the temple renovation with cultigens from the tropical forest may prove a fruitful topic for further research.

ANOTHER STYLE OF RENOVATION: EXCAVATIONS AT KUNTUR WASI

In 1979 we began excavations at the large and complex site of Huacaloma in the Cajamarca Basin (figure 4.4). The chronology for the Formative period

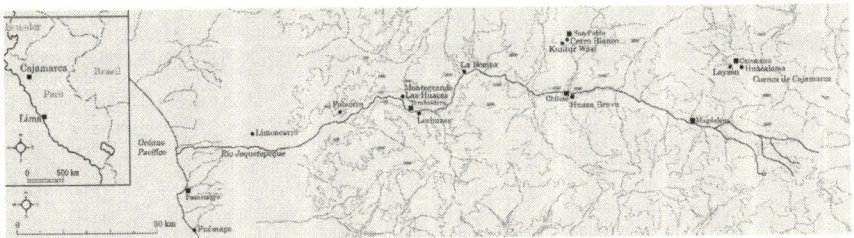

FIGURE 4.4. *Location of some Formative sites in the Jequetepeque and Cajamarca Valleys*

has four phases, beginning with the Early Huacaloma and continuing through the Late Huacaloma and EL before ending with the Layzón phase (see figure 4.1).[1] It was during the excavations at Huacaloma that the idea of temple renovation began to take shape, since the repetition of construction of large-scale retaining walls was noticed for the Late Huacaloma phase. While the pottery from that phase shares some traits with the so-called Cupisnique-style pottery, we have not been able to define a phase as definitely Cupisnique, which is different from the Kotosh Chavín phase in Huánuco (Onuki 1994a; Onuki and Inokuchi 2011).

The absence of a definite phase of Cupisnique-related culture in the Cajamarca Basin but its presence at Kuntur Wasi, which lies just on the other side of the mountains from Cajamarca, eventually led us to initiate the Kuntur Wasi project in 1988. Prior to Kuntur Wasi, a small-scale excavation had been carried out at the site of Cerro Blanco, about 1 km northeast of Kuntur Wasi. A comparison of stratigraphy among these three sites revealed a very interesting fact.

As mentioned, the chronology for the Formative period at Huacaloma is the Early Huacaloma, Late Huacaloma, EL, and Layzón. At Cerro Blanco, the first two phases shared almost the same characteristics with Huacaloma, but then there was a lapse in occupation; reoccupation began in the Sotera phase, equivalent to the Layzón phase in Cajamarca. The first occupation at Kuntur Wasi began in the Idolo phase, equivalent to the Cerro Blanco and Late Huacaloma phases, and the next occupation was the Kuntur Wasi phase, which was accompanied by a drastic change in ceremonial architecture as a whole. In the subsequent Copa phase the same pattern of ceremonial architecture continued, but there was a noticeable change in pottery style. After the Copa phase, the ceremonial structures of the Sotera phase completely destroyed those of the previous phase. The Kuntur Wasi phase pottery had many characteristics of the Cupisnique style, which had been observed rather

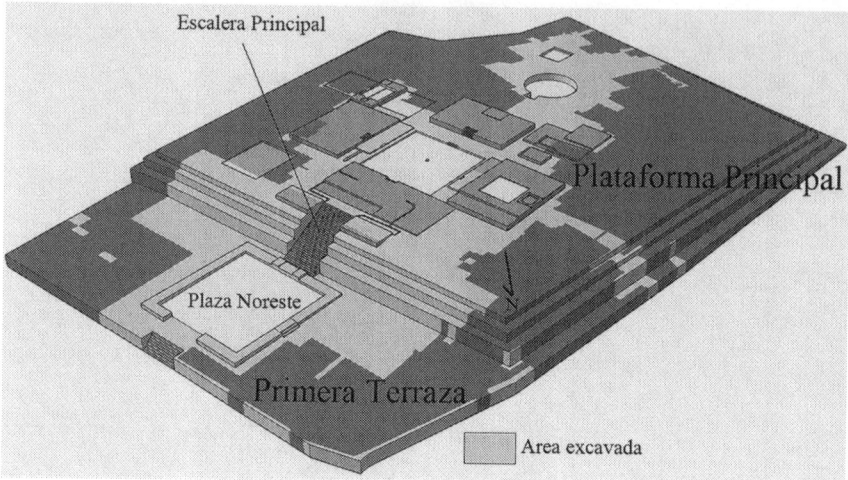

FIGURE 4.5. *Plan of the temple of the Kuntur Wasi phase*

sporadically in the Cerro Blanco and Late Huacaloma phases. The EL phase shares the principal characteristics of pottery with the Copa phase, but both the Kuntur Wasi phase and the Copa phase were definitely absent at Cerro Blanco, a neighboring site very close to Kuntur Wasi.

The architectural plan of the Kuntur Wasi phase is summarized in figure 4.5:

1. The entire complex is composed of terraced platforms, with the highest terrace the topmost platform (the Principal Platform) upon which the most important architecture was built.
2. On the Principal Platform are arranged a U-shaped complex with three platforms and a sunken square court. This occupies the northern half of the top of the platform where several stone sculptures were unearthed.
3. The square sunken court has four staircases, one each in the center of each side, and each has a stone sculpture set firmly on the fourth, highest step. Two of these were excavated in 1946 and had been considered to be lintels.
4. Five special tombs were found below the floor of the Central Platform of the U-shape. Four were associated with cinnabar, Cupisnique-style pottery, and gold objects such as crowns, nose ornaments, ear ornaments, and pendants.
5. There was a circular sunken court and a series of platforms on the southern half of the Principal Platform. Special tombs with gold objects were found below the floor of the platforms outside the circular court.

6. Subterranean canals ran below the platforms and sunken courts, with outlets in the retaining walls of the four sides of the Principal Platform.

The most unexpected discovery in the excavations at Kuntur Wasi was a series of exceptionally well-prepared tombs associated with elaborate gold objects. The tombs with gold were found in both the Kuntur Wasi and Copa phases. Some gold pieces have very figurative designs, tempting us to conjecture about their meanings or the underlying cosmology. Although we observe the renovation of buildings or temples during the Idolo phase, the phase of the first occupation at the hill of Kuntur Wasi, the new temples of the second phase (the Kuntur Wasi phase) were the result of a rather violent destruction and building with a completely distinct idea of what constituted a ceremonial center.

RITUAL AT KUNTUR WASI

The Serpent-Coiled Eye and the Square Eye

One notable trait in the figurative representations at Kuntur Wasi is manifested in the eyes observed in stone sculptures and a gold object (figure 4.6). One eye is round, and a serpent coils it with its tail; the other one is square or rectangular with the pupil looking up. This set of eyes is represented on the face of the stone sculpture discovered in 1946 (figure 4.7). It was found by accident during agricultural cultivation, and we do not know its original position. One side represents a standing figure with a large feline face that has that set of eyes. The figure grabs a small human head with sharp claws and stands upright with crossed legs. The other side also represents a standing figure, but it has two round eyes, and the face lacks a jaw. It holds a long lance or stick with a triangular sharp point. Two serpents emanate from its two round eyes toward both sides of the face.

The set of two eyes is represented in a peculiar manner in the four stone sculptures set in the staircases of the Central Plaza (the square sunken court). Here, coming from the main stairway of the Principal Platform, one faces the Plaza and the Central Platform beyond, and then one sees the stone set on the southern staircase of the Central Plaza. This stone represents a feline face or two feline profiles facing each other, and the eyes are square. The other three stones have the feline face first, but all of them have serpent-coiled eyes. It is obvious that these four stones represent the dualism of eyes as opposition. The standing figure can therefore be considered the representation of the integration of two opposite principles into one.

FIGURE 4.6. *Gold nose ornament of the monster face with two different eyes*

In 1989, when we found one stone on the stairway on the east side of the Central Plaza, we thought there would be another stone on the opposite side with the representation of square eyes. In 1990, however, the excavation revealed the stairway and the stone on it, but the stone had round eyes coiled by a serpent tail. This set of four stone sculptures in the Central Plaza, then, is not symmetrically arranged. The arrangement is of one stone with square eyes opposed to three stones with round eyes.

The four sculptures with two distinctive eyes share a characteristic form of mouth that is rhomboidal and seems to be an outlet for a canal. A very interesting stirrup-spout bottle, said to be from the North Coast Cupisnique culture, is exhibited in the National Museum of Anthropology, Archaeology, and History in Lima. It is polished black, representing in its body a feline face with an eye coiled by a serpent tail and another square eye, and the feline face

FIGURE 4.7. *Stone sculpture with two different eyes*

has a mouth that consists of a short, square tube. This representation has the same characteristics as the four stones in the Central Plaza of Kuntur Wasi. This pottery and the four stones apparently had some meaning related to water.

Another sculpture found in the fill of the Central Plaza was present during the Copa phase in some structure on the eastern platform of the U-shape. It represents a human face without any mythical elements except a serpent design hanging below the jaw. The noticeable trait is that the mouth has a hole cut deep into the interior. Although the original position is unknown, this sculpture also must have had some meaning related to water.

A Gold Ornament with the Motif of Twins and a Monster

One tomb under the Central Platform was for an old man buried with a gold crown, a pair of ear ornaments of rectangular plates, and two nose ornaments (the term *mouth mask* can also be used). At first these objects, except the crown, were considered to be pectorals, but the similarity to the nose ornaments attached to the gold masks of the Calima culture of Colombia changed our interpretation to that of a nose ornament and led us to interpret the two rectangular objects as ear ornaments. These and the Calima nose pendants share the same structural characteristics. The form is the shape of the letter H. The horizontal bar of the H is wide, and a feline-like face is expressed in *repoussé*. The four extremities of the H end in the shape of a human or animal face; while the lower two are in a normal position, the upper two are in the reverse position, looking up.

We do not know why this similarity occurs. Except for one H-shaped gold object possessed by Enrico Poli, which is apparently a nose ornament, there are no other examples of this type of nose pendant reported in Peru or outside Calima. Furthermore, there is a time lag of at least 500 years between Kuntur Wasi and the Calima culture.

This *repoussé* design represents a fierce monster in the center (figure 4.8). Two arms and legs come out of the monster and end in sharp claws. Two small human figures with feline profiles sit on the monster's knees, and the two claws grab the small figures on the back. The figures are small and naked, and they lack teeth, which leads us to posit that they are either two children, brothers, or twins and to consider myths about the twins and a monster, jaguar, toad, and so on. The theme is about the twins as culture heroes. There is a tale from the Canta province in the Peruvian highlands about Pachamama's son and daughter, the twins, and a savage Wacon, and it is a variant of the twins and monster theme. A legend from the Marañon River in the highlands is about a monstrous old woman named Achucay and twins, and a legend from Huamachuco tells a story of the Wachemines tribe; a girl of the tribe bore twins who acted as culture heroes when they grew up (Agustinos 1952).

The wide distribution of this theme in the tropical lowlands from Venezuela through Colombia and Ecuador to Peru on the east side of the Andean mountains, as presented by Carrión Cachot (1959), may lead us to suppose that the prototype of this theme may have been among the incipient agriculturalists in the tropical lowlands of northwestern South America.

The Gold Crown of Twelve Hanging Faces

The crown has the design of two rows of hexagonal frames, like windows, with human faces hanging in them. The style of hexagonal meshes apparently

FIGURE 4.8. *Gold nose ornament of the monster and twins*

represents a woven basket. If this motif is one of heads in a basket, we are reminded of a stone plate introduced by Burger and Salazar-Burger (1982), which depicts in relief a feline-face spider carrying a bag with heads. A spider grabs a head by the hair. Apparently, this design refers to a headhunting, probably for sacrifice and offerings, and the executioner is identified with a spider. Later examples of this spider as headhunter are well-known to us in the wall decorations at Huaca de la Luna and El Brujo, as well as from the gold bells found on Sipán and Chimu pottery from the Casma Valley (Carrión Cachot 1959).

While there is no evidence related to a spider, the motif of heads in a basket or bag is found in Cupisnique pottery. It seems probable that many of those bottles came from the Cupisnique culture of the Jequetepeque Valley. The head in the hexagonal frame is a motif found in the incised designs on the pottery vessels of the Late Huacaloma phase in the Cajamarca Basin and in the Pacopampa I phase (1200–800 BC) at Pacopampa. This motif is fairly common in the pottery of the early Formative period in the northern highlands, especially in the pottery of, so to speak, the Pacopampa-Huacaloma style. This style was found at Cerro Blanco and also at Kuntur Wasi, called the Cerro Blanco phase and the Idolo phase, respectively; at Kuntur Wasi it preceded the occupation by the Cupisnique-related Kuntur Wasi phase. There is a group of pottery found in the middle Jequetepeque Valley, sometimes called Tembladera style, which features the frequent use of post-fire painting that is much more common in the Pacopampa-Huacaloma style and less common, even rare, in the Cupisnique style of the North Coast.

With respect to the relationship of Kuntur Wasi with the Cupisnique style, a human figure with a feline face is worth noting. Its form, size, and appearance made the local people working in the excavations call it "Idolo" (idol), which in turn made us denominate the associated architectural phase the Idolo phase. This idol was made of unbaked clay, to be attached to the wall of a room; therefore, it was part of a wall decoration. It represents a feline-faced standing figure, about 73.5 cm high, 21 cm wide, and 10 cm thick. All of the surface is painted: the top of the head is pink, the head and body are red with cinnabar, a narrow headband and a waist belt are yellow, the eyes are black, and a big necklace is green with pulverized malachite. The square eyes are eccentric with upturned pupils, and the mouth shows the teeth and fangs with squared, not pointed, tips (figure 4.9). Stylistically, it can be called Cupisnique, and Bischoff points out the similarity to the decorative relief at Huaca de los Reyes (Bischof 1998:66).

Nevertheless, Kuntur Wasi was a recipient of Cupisnique traits, as was Chavín de Huántar, as Pozorski pointed out more than thirty years ago: "The type site of Chavin de Huantar cannot be viewed as a purely 'Chavin' site, and certainly not as the source for all related architectural, iconographic, and ceramic elements. Instead, Chavin de Huantar is a blending of elements from the coast, the highlands, and the tropical forest and was apparently a receiver, not a sender, of what have come to be called 'Chavin' traits" (Pozorski 1983:36).

The pottery of the Idolo phase, as stated before, is almost identical to that of the Cerro Blanco phase as well as to the Pacopampa-Huacaloma style. However, the representation of feline-man is not found in the pottery. The relationship between Tembladera and Cupisnique must be clarified to resolve the dynamic process between the highlands and the coast during the early Formative period.

FROM RITUAL TO IDEOLOGY

In the area of Huánuco from Kotosh down to Wairajirca, we detected at least five sites located about 5 km from one another. From west to east these sites are Kotosh, Shillacoto, Jancao, Warampayloma, and Wairajirca. The sites

FIGURE 4.9. *"Idol" figure of earth for a wall relief of the Idolo phase*

of Kotosh, Shillacoto, and Wairajirca were excavated, and all of them have three stratigraphic phases: the Kotosh Mito, Kotosh Wairajirca, and Kotosh Kotosh phases. All of them also had ceremonial architecture during the Kotosh Mito phase. It seems possible that the other two sites, unexcavated as of yet, have the same kind of buildings in the Kotosh Mito phase strata. It is clear, therefore, that each settlement had a similar kind of ceremonial or public building, sharing with each other the same ritual tradition. Burger and Salazar-Burger (1980) call this the Kotosh Religious Tradition, and Bonnier (1997) terms it the Mito Tradition.

The small size of the architecture at Wairajirca suggests that the building was constructed with a small amount of labor. If there was a small village of about twenty or thirty households, the labor of the inhabitants may have been enough to construct the building on the stone-faced platform. It can be said, consequently, that the ritual was of a smaller scale than that at Kotosh or Shillacoto. The sizes of the building were different according to population size or some other factors in each settlement or village.

The renovation of temples may have begun as ritual. The cosmology behind the ritual may have been parallel to slash-and-burn agriculture, as stated above, but the ritual was practiced within the village. The importance of the ritual, whatever the scale of participants, is that the place where the ritual was performed had to be renewed periodically. This ritual was deeply set in the society as custom. Nobody asked why or for what purpose the ritual was performed, but all the people knew well what to do.

With the passage of time, however, social conditions can change. For example, we might consider an increase or decrease in the population or changes in agricultural production or in the relationship with neighboring villages. Such changes in the society influence the ritual performance, and the change in ritual creates a need for explanation. This interactive process between society and cosmology causes ritual to become more complicated and sophisticated over time. The relationship or competition with neighboring villages also reinforces this process of sophistication. Thus, it may have begun as a somewhat simple ritual. A small place was prepared for the ritual, with the idea that the place would be renewed after some time. The next renovation was elaborated on a slightly larger scale, or better, than the previous place. The social and cultural effects of this renovation can be summarized as follows.

This renovation had an important effect, setting in train a series of other activities, although the residents may have been unaware of this at the time. Temple construction required the accumulation of food and drink, which stimulated the search for more productive cultigens and technologies. Enlarging a temple required a greater labor force, accelerating population growth. A larger population required increased food production and more efficient systems of social control. To justify the renovation, the temple had to provide its congregation with a more refined and sophisticated cosmology and rituals, together with their material representations. Thus, temple renovation, even though it began on a small scale, triggered a series of technological, social, and cultural innovations. As a result, communities that practiced it became more open to innovation, more productive, and more efficient (Onuki 2002:65).

So far as this ritual activity can be performed within a village or in a much smaller social group, it is justified by custom, but when the renovation demands a concentration and control of labor because of the enhanced scale of building, the ritual performance needs to be reinforced by explicative cosmology. By then, the justification must have been refined on the basis of sophistication of the cosmology. In response to the complicated procedure of ritual, there must have been a growing group of people specialized in ritual, cosmology, and social control, at least in labor allocation. When this group justifies itself, its ritual activity, and its control of labor with cosmology in a convincingly explanatory form, such a cosmologically justified explanation can be called ideology. Temple renovation was possible without ideology in the Upper Huallaga Basin, at least during the Kotosh Mito phase, but I am not sure if it was possible to continue the work of renovating much larger temples, such as those at Caral, without ideology.

There are few visible representations of a cosmological or mythical concept among the preceramic public constructions. The figurative representations in relief or mural painting are abundant in the large-scale architecture from the earliest ceramic phase. Although the renovation continued on a larger scale, it had already surpassed the limit a village-sized community could support. It is highly possible that some elite group directed the construction by organizing the laborers and sustaining them on food produced within a well-planned economic system.

At Huacaloma, the earliest settled life with pottery began in the Early Huacaloma phase, and almost identical pottery is found at Pandanche near Pacopampa, Cerro Blanco near Kuntur Wasi, and the middle valley of Jequetepeque in such sites as Montegrande, La Bomba, and Las Huacas, excavated by Tellenbach (1986), Seki (1997), and Tsurumi (2008), respectively. Although elevated platforms with niches and courts were found at Montegrande, and they are considered to have had some public function, no visual or figurative representation of symbolic meaning such as wall painting or relief was found.

At Huacaloma, it is during the Late Huacaloma phase that the colorful wall painting and reliefs were abundant in the buildings on a large platform 130 m × 115 m and 8 m high. Although there were some contemporaneous sites in the Cajamarca Basin, Huacaloma surpassed others in the scale of construction, gorgeousness of decoration, and rich variety of pottery. Furthermore, a new site was chosen for a new ceremonial center of a completely new building plan. It is at Layzón where the wide extension of bedrock was cut and modified into six terraces. The presence of powerful control can be supposed behind this scene of construction, together with active and persuasive force elaborated on the base of traditional cosmology. It can be said that ideology played an important driving role in the construction of such a huge center.

During the Early Huacaloma phase, each village seems to have had its own ritual building, and there is no marked difference among the contemporaneous sites. In the Late Huacaloma phase, however, no other site is comparable to Huacaloma in size except the bedrock terraces of Layzón. This means that one or a few centers began to concentrate the power of influence over other, smaller settlements, and the polychromatic mural painting and reliefs led the people to convince themselves that the task demanded by the center had been fulfilled. It can be said, therefore, that the magnificence of "temples" and visual representation became the main means of ideological expression.

The same trend from ritual to ideology can be observed at Kuntur Wasi. The hill of Kuntur Wasi, left unoccupied during the La Conga phase, shared the same pottery style with Montegrande in the Jequetepeque Valley and the Early Huacaloma phase in the Cajamarca Basin. At the Cerro Blanco site itself, no trace of large ceremonial building was detected through excavations.

Kuntur Wasi was exploited for the first time during the Idolo phase. Platforms and courts, thickly plastered in white, were built on the summit area. One room was decorated with a relief of mud/clay representing a standing human figure with feline characteristics such as a fanged mouth and eccentric eyes. Then, the next Kuntur Wasi phase brought about profound change in the entire plan and structure of the center. Beside the decoration of the architecture, stone sculptures were placed in various positions so that each sculpture, together with its representation, might have had a special meaning by itself as well as in relation to others. It is highly possible that the stone sculpture led to consolidation of the ideological image. While wall paintings and clay reliefs are easily perishable and destroyed at every moment of renovation, stone sculpture continues to exist in a concrete form, fixing the image and its meaning.

CONCLUSION

Since the time of Julio C. Tello, the Tello Obelisk from Chavín de Huántar has been interpreted as a representation of caimans that did not live in the nearby river or even in the upper Marañón. Lathrap (1973) identified tropical plants on the obelisk: manioc, achira, gourd, and *ají*. Cordy-Collins (1977) saw hallucinogenic plants, also of origin in the tropical environment. If the linkage with the tropical environment existed during the late Archaic period, as seemingly suggested at Kotosh and Caral, the representation of tropical plants on the Tello Obelisk had roots in much earlier times.

After observing the distribution of stone mortars and taking into consideration the use of hallucinogenic plants, Zeidler (1988) proposed the "pre-Chavín Tropical Forest/Highland sphere" or simply "pre-Chavín interaction sphere." In the last two decades, little attention has been paid to this idea, but new data from Kuntur Wasi and the Cajamarca region suggest that it is time to reconsider it.

This long-term continuity in the Central Andes may be founded, at least in part, on shared ideas about the importance of temple renovation, which in turn may be related to broadly distributed cosmology related to slash-and-burn cultivation in tropical forest environments. Somewhere and sometime, when an idea of renovation of ritual places was firmly set, the construction of a small building began. The ritual was carried out as a public but modest activity within a small settlement or community. However, the requirement of renovation after a certain time generated accelerating change in various aspects of culture, such as technology, social organization, and religion or cosmology. Competition among the settlements or villages, or among certain social groups responsible for taking charge of the ritual, may have played a role in accelerating the process of enlargement and sophistication, and eventually a kind of massive public building worth calling a temple was constructed. The renovation of the temple, together with competition for prestige, ignited a process of ever-increasing activities, such as population growth, technological improvement of food production, planning of architecture and labor investment, and sophistication of religious concepts and ritual itself, together with ritual paraphernalia. In this process ideology was formed on the basis of cosmology, and elites began to manipulate it to lead society (Onuki 2008). Together with ideological refinement, the artistic representation accelerated its elaboration not only in architecture and its decoration but also in pottery, gold, and other materials. In some cases this ritual of temple renovation resembles the slash-and-burn agriculture practiced in the tropical lowlands. The question of whether the idea that a new temple must be constructed above the ash layer is ubiquitous and still needs to be investigated.

NOTE

1. EL is the name of a phase between the Late Huacaloma and the Layzón phases. At first it temporally meant Enigmatic Layers as well as Early Layzón because we could not define its own special characteristics as an independent phase. Now it is clear that it is an independent phase, but the name EL remains.

REFERENCES CITED

Agustinos. 1952 [1557]. "Religión en Huamachuco." In *Las pequenos grandes obras de historia americana*, ed. Francisco Loayza. Series 1, vol. 17. Lima: Miranda.

Bischof, H. 1998. "El Período Inicial, el Horizonte Temprano, el Estilo Chavín y la Realidad del Proceso Formativo en los Andes Centrales." In *I Encuentro Internacional de Peruanistas: Estado de los Estudios Histórico-Sociales sobre el Perú a Fines del Siglo XX 1*, 57–70. Lima: Universidad de Lima / Oficina Regional de Cultura para América Latina y el Caribe, UNESCO / Fondo de Cultura Económica.

Bonnier, E. 1997. "Preceramic Architecture in the Andes: The Mito Tradition." *Archaeologica Peruana* 2: 120–44.

Burger, R. L., and L. Salazar-Burger. 1980. "Ritual and Religion at Huaricoto." *Archaeology* 33 (6): 26–32.

Burger, R. L., and L. Salazar-Burger. 1982. "La Araña en la Iconografía del Horizonte Temprano en la Costa Norte del Perú." *Beiträge zur Allgemeinen und Vergleichenden Archäologie* 4: 213–53.

Carrión Cachot, R. 1959. *La Religión en el Antiguo Perú: Norte y Centro de la Costa*. Lima: Período Post-Clásico.

Cordy-Collins, A. 1977. "Chavín Art: Its Shamanistic/Hallucinogenic Origins." In *Pre-Columbian Art History: Selected Readings*, ed. A. Cordy-Collins and J. Stern, 353–62. Palo Alto: Peek.

Hugh-Jones, S. 1979. *The Palm and the Pleiades: Initiation and Cosmology in Northwest Amazonia*. Cambridge: Cambridge University Press.

Izumi, S., and T. Matsuzawa. 1967. "Early Preceramic Cultist Culture of the Central Andes: The Kotosh Mito Phase." [In Japanese] *Latin American Studies* 8: 39–69.

Izumi, S., and T. Sono, eds. 1963. *Andes 2: Excavations at Kotosh, Peru, 1960*. Tokyo: Kadokawa Shoten.

Izumi, S., and K. Terada, eds. 1972. *Andes 4: Excavations at Kotosh, Peru, 1963 and 1966*. Tokyo: University of Tokyo Press.

Lathrap, D. W. 1973. "Gifts of the Cayman: Some Thoughts on the Subsistence Basis of Chavín." In *Variation in Anthropology*, ed. D. W. Lathrap and J. Douglas, 81–105. Urbana: Illinois Archaeological Survey.

Onuki, Y. 1993. "Las Actividades Ceremoniales Tempranas en la Cuenca del Alto Huallaga y Algunos Problemas Generales." In *El Mundo Ceremonial Andino*, ed. L. Millones and Y. Onuki, 69–96. Senri Ethnological Studies 37. Osaka: National Museum of Ethnology.

Onuki, Y. 1994a. *Kuntur Wasi y Cerro Blanco: Dos Sitios del Formativo en el Norte del Perú*. Tokyo: Hokusensha.

Onuki, Y. 1994b. "Las Actividades Ceremoniales Tempranas en la Cuenca del Alto Huallaga y Algunos Problemas Generales." In *El Mundo Ceremonial Andino*, ed. L. Millones and Y. Onuki, 71–95. Lima: Editorial Horizonte.

Onuki, Y. 2002. "Japanese Research on Andean Prehistory." *Japanese Review of Cultural Anthropology* 3: 57–78.

Onuki, Y. 2008. "Los Líderes del Templo Kuntur Wasi." In *Señores de los Reinos de la Luna*, ed. K. Makowski, 254–57. Lima: Banco de Crédito del Perú.

Onuki, Y., and K. Inokuchi. 2011. *Gemelos Prístinos: El Tesoro del Templo de Kuntur Wasi*. Lima: Fondo Editorial del Congreso del Perú.

Pozorski, T. 1983. "The Caballo Muerto Complex and Its Place in the Andean Chronological Sequence." Carnegie Museum of Natural History, Pittsburgh. *Annals of the Carnegie Museum* 52: 1–40.

Pulgar Vidal, J. 1967. *Geografía del Perú*. Lima: Ocho Regiones Naturales del Perú.

Seki, Y. 1997. "Excavaciones en el Sitio La Bomba, Valle Medio de Jequetepeque, Cajamarca." *Boletín de Arqueología PUCP* 1: 115–36.

Shady Solís, R. 2005. *La Civilización de Caral-Supe: 5000 Años de Identidad Cultural en el Perú*. Lima: Instituto Nacional de Cultura.

Shady Solís, R., and C. Leyva, eds. 2003. *La Ciudad Sagrada de Caral-Supe*. Lima: Instituto Nacional de Cultura.

Tellenbach, M. 1986. *Las Excavaciones en el Asentamiento Formativo de Montegrande, Valle de Jequetepeque en el Norte del Perú*. Materialien zur Allgemeine und Vergleichenden Archäeologie 39. München: Verlag C.H. Beck.

Terada, K., and Y. Onuki. 1985. *The Formative Period in the Cajamarca Basin, Peru: Excavations at Huacaloma and Layzón, 1982*. Tokyo: University of Tokyo Press.

Terada, K., and Y. Onuki, eds. 1982. *Excavations at Huacaloma in the Cajamarca Valley, Peru, 1979*. Tokyo: University of Tokyo Press.

Tsurumi, E. 2008. "La Secuencia Cronológica de los Centros Ceremoniales de la Pampa de las Hamacas y Tembladera, Valle Medio de Jequetepeque." *Boletín de Arqueología PUCP* 12: 141–69.

Zeidler, J. A. 1988. "Feline Imagery, Stone Mortars, and Formative Period Interaction Spheres in the Northern Andean Area." *Journal of Latin American Lore* 14: 243–83.

5

Architecture and Ritual Practices at Huaca A of Pampa de las Llamas–Moxeke

Rafael Vega-Centeno Sara-Lafosse

This chapter explores the spatial organization of a major mound from Pampa de las Llamas–Moxeke known as Huaca A, as a means to examine the sociopolitical dynamics manifested in specific human practices such as ritual performances. Pampa de las Llamas–Moxeke is a large architectural complex located in the lower Casma Valley that was built and occupied during the early Formative period (1800–1200 BC) of the Central Andes.

The architectural design of Huaca A was analyzed through Gamma Analysis (Hillier and Hanson 1984) to determine its spatial structure and evaluate different possible movements, according to the arrangements of rooms and corridors. In the Gamma Analysis approach, architectural space establishes boundaries that generate discontinuous sets of spatial units or cells; the connection of these sets requires a complex system of controlled permeabilities (ibid.:144–46).

Following specific graphic conventions, Gamma Analysis reveals different structural arrangements, understandable in terms of asymmetry and distributedness. These variables might indicate, on one hand, the degree of hierarchy in the organization of spatial units and, on the other hand, how centralized or exclusive are the routes that connect the spatial units within a building (ibid.:147–55). The results of Gamma Analysis in Huaca A reveal a highly centralized but weakly hierarchical spatial structure. Such a structure and its inferred possibilities of movement suggest the existence of a large-scale social entity, such as a regional system, in which

DOI: 10.5876/9781607325963.c005

several smaller units (communities or lineages) were allowed to participate in ritual activities at the Huaca A summit.

This scenario of congregating social units under a larger entity has not been reported for the organization of other early buildings. Thus, it can provide new insights for discussion of the nature of early Formative period societies in the Central Andes.

The analysis of Huaca A is preceded by a review of the theoretical discussion of the social significance of ritual and its archaeological study, as well as of the debate over the development of social complexity in the early Formative period of the Central Andes.

RITUAL IN SOCIETY

The social significance of ritual was outlined in the beginning of the twentieth century by Durkheim (1995 [1912]:532), who defined it as a mode of action that recreates society. In a similar direction, more recently Rappaport (1999:27, 30) noted that the ritual recreation of society was manifested in the construction of conventional orders invested with morality, which compel participants to accept a "social contract," often established within a singular time frame invested with eternity. Furthermore, ritual is currently recognized as a powerful means to mobilize and congregate collective entities, which develop through ideas of membership but also of dependence on the social group (Kertzer 1988:82). In addition, ritual can conjure feelings of solidarity and conviction even in social groups that, as a result of inequalities or competing agendas, lack consensus (ibid.:78–79).

The effectiveness of ritual in shaping and reshaping social relations and power positions lies in its communicative power, as rituals are displayed and received through schemes of perception deeply rooted in material conditions of existence (Bourdieu 1977:116). However, the communication of messages cannot be fully understood without taking into account the nature of participation in rituals. Ritual does not describe actions or phenomena but constitutes an action and puts something into practice (Connerton 1989:57–58). This action (unlike performances, which involve actors and audiences) implies that all participants are, albeit in different ways, performers.

Indeed, it is through this active participation that individuals and groups not only transmit messages about themselves but also transmit themselves in those messages. Moreover, in ritual, the transmitters of messages are often the most important receivers of those messages. Through ritual participation individuals and groups transcend their private selves and enter into a public, canonical order, where they might acquire a social category that will frame their own private process (Rappaport 1999:51, 106).

Rappaport noted that ritual participants, while becoming both transmitters and receivers, are fused with the messages displayed in ritual. As a consequence there is an intrinsic acceptance of such messages by those who participate in it—although acceptance does not necessarily mean belief or total compliance. Therefore, ritual becomes a fundamental act of acceptance of certain messages and in that way forms the basis for a public order (ibid.:119, 122–23).

Several authors have noted that the extraordinary time signaled by ritual implies a de-structuration of social structure or organization, as well as a dilution of social identities. This state is what Victor Turner defined as the experience of *communitas*. According to Turner (1969:95–96), most rituals include a stage defined as liminality, which implies the detachment of daily existence and the creation of common bonds by participants. In a liminal state social structure and organization are ignored, and an undifferentiated community (i.e., communitas) is generated. Rappaport adds that the experiencing of communitas alters not only society but also consciousness, with the inhibition of rationality and an increase in emotional aspects. Consequently, communitas also becomes a state of mind in which canonical messages are transmitted (Rappaport 1999:219–22).

Thus, the social significance of ritual is explained by its capacity to transmit persuasively several meanings that reinforce social and political relations. Such a capacity lies in the performative nature of ritual, which merges convention with behavior. In this way ritual presents the conventional and its morality as factual and, consequently, as a natural phenomena.

RITUAL, ARCHAEOLOGY, AND ARCHITECTURE

Within the archaeological record, "ritual function" is commonly applied to contexts that are difficult or impossible to explain. This negative definition makes many scholars doubt the validity of interpreting ritual functions. To address these doubts, it is necessary to construct a behavioral definition of ritual and its material correlates.

Several authors have stressed the need to unpack the religion-and-ritual phenomenon and address ritual as a social practice with its own dynamics and cross-cultural regularities (Kertzer 1988:2; Walker 1995:67). Thus, as a social practice ritual can be defined as a set of formalized, standardized, repetitive, and sequentially ordered acts (e.g., movements, gestures, and postures) and utterances through which meaningful information is transmitted and communicated among its participants (Connerton 1989:44; Kertzer 1988:9; Rappaport 1999:3, 24).

These utterances and acts in ritual are highly formalized and even stereotyped (Kertzer 1988:9) as a means to ensure that performances will be conducted in a correct way (Rappaport 1999:115–16). Utterances and acts have differentiated roles in the transmission of messages. While utterances transmit canonical messages, physical displays often signal the participation and acceptance of such messages (ibid.:152). I have proposed that the utterances and physical acts, as well as their interactions, generate eight categories of ritual behavior: congregation, code reciting, musical display, simulation, physiological exercises, consumption (of both intoxicating and edible substances), offering, and competition (Vega-Centeno 2005:50–55; 2006).

Congregation is probably the most socially weighted category of ritual behavior. It implies the displacement and meeting of participants in the space for ritual, including long walks and processions. The activities involved in this category are particularly significant, as rituals are concerned not only with the performances conducted within the ritual space but also with the way participants engage with that space. Thus, congregation acts provide meaningful information about the participants of ritual, as one can observe the rhythm of displacements, their directionality, the pathways and entryways participants need to pass through, and finally, the positions they take and locations they occupy immediately before the beginning of the activities within the ritual space. As mentioned, the ritual sphere is often marked by the dilution of social structure through the experience of communitas (Turner 1969:95–96); such a structure is often reinforced immediately before or after entering into the communitas state. Consequently, congregation acts are particularly informative on the nature of the social structure of the participant group.

Messages related to congregation are strongly related to architectural design, as architectural units potentially carry meanings and provide specific cues and signs for those who experience them (Moore 1996; Rappaport 1999:20, 106). Consequently, through its ability to transmit meaningful information on congregation acts, architectural design might orient the displacement and distribution of participants within the ritual space. As a result, the size and configuration of spatial units might indicate the number of allowed participants. Similarly, the use of architectural features for internal divisions, such as benches, ramps, or steps, might indicate the spatial distribution of participants within spaces. Finally, the number, location, and characteristics of entryways might reflect and orient the frequency, intensity, and amount of simultaneous movements, as well as their required sequences within the overall ritual space. In sum, architectural space might reflect the way people are spatially organized (and thus socially structured) for their participation in ritual. These characteristics explain why architectural designs of ritual spaces are often highly patterned and formalized, as they are responsible for transmitting correctly the meaningful messages of congregational behaviors and activities (see Chicoine et al., this volume).

Ritual spaces are usually identified by different names in the archaeological literature. They can be defined as "public architecture," "monumental architecture," or "religious architecture." I suggest that these definitions outline different characteristics that are usually related to ritual spaces. The notion of "public" refers to spaces whose construction and related uses are beyond the household sphere. The idea of "monumental" addresses the scale, quality, and durability of the built space. Finally, the concept of "religious" notes the usual concerns and commitments that motivated the construction and use of ritual spaces (Abraham, this volume). These definitions, however, do not address the specific functional or behavioral dimensions of an architectural unit. According to their function, the built ritual spaces could be labeled "ritual architecture" or "ceremonial architecture." Nevertheless, a careful analysis of the architectural design is necessary to apply this definition to any architectural unit.

Architectural designs always have a spatial dimension, which can be understood as a structure in which spatial units are differentiated, distributed, and interrelated through a given access system. Hillier and Hanson (1984) have proposed a methodological approach known as syntactic organization to understand the spatial structure of such designs. Gamma Analysis reduces the structure of buildings into basic spatial units (cells) and the connections between them. The spatial arrangements are translated into graphs, on which spatial units are represented by circles, and their connections, or permeabilities, are represented by lines.

These graphics reveal different structural arrangements, which can be understood on the basis of two variables: (1) symmetry/asymmetry and (2) distributedness/non-distributedness. The degree of symmetry or asymmetry is related to the number of spatial units and the number of levels in which these units are organized. A highly asymmetrical structure might include several levels in which a limited number of spatial units are organized. In contrast, a highly symmetrical structure will include few levels for numerous spatial units sharing the same spatial restrictions. As a result, this variable indicates the degree of hierarchy in the organization of spatial units in terms of the distance between them and the outer space. In contrast, the degree of distributedness or non-distributedness is related to the number of spatial units and the number of permeabilities among them. A high distributed structure tends to include multiple pathways that inter-communicate the spatial units, while a low distributed structure includes a limited (even a single) pathway for the connection of spatial units. As a result this variable demonstrates how some access routes can be more central or exclusive than others (Hillier and Hanson 1984:147–55). Both variables can be measured through specific procedures. The first one can be quantified through an index of relative asymmetry (RA), defined as follows:

$$RA = \frac{2(MD-1)}{K-2}$$

Where MD is the mean depth (calculated after adding the number of spatial units weighted by their depth level) and K is the number of spatial units or cells in the structure. The second variable is quantified through an index of relative ringiness (RR). This index denotes how, when there is more than one pathway connecting two units, the second pathway must be represented by an encircling ring. Consequently, the number of rings over the maximum possible straight lines will reveal how distributed the spatial organization is. The RR is defined as follows:

$$RR = \frac{r}{2p-5}$$

Where r is the number of distinct rings identified in the structure and p is the number of unit cells of the structure (ibid.:108–9, 152). Especially for understanding congregation acts, the measurement of degrees of hierarchy and centralization in the spatial structure of buildings becomes particularly insightful for the study of ritual spaces.

As previously stated, liturgical orders regulate congregation activities by transmitting canonical messages that indicate correct displacements, entries, and positioning. In addition, the conduct of those acts by participants is a source of self-referential messages, as they can be related or differentiated as a result of their displacement routes or their capacity to pass through certain spaces. These differentiations often reveal diverse social states or conditions (either situational or structural). Consequently, the definition of boundaries and regulated access systems within a ritual space may reflect and also reinforce self-referential messages about social personae and their relations, defining how differentiated or undifferentiated their participation is. Following these considerations, the outlined Gamma Analyses reveal the existence of both vertical and horizontal spatial differences, thus providing a unique means of evaluating how social differentiations might have been outlined through architectural design during ritual acts of congregation.

SOCIAL ORGANIZATION AND RITUAL ARCHITECTURE IN THE ANDEAN FORMATIVE PERIOD

Several lines of evidence demonstrate the development of social complexity during the Andean Formative period (ca. 1800–200 BC). Research at several sites has revealed populations that show internal differences in the quality and location of their dwellings (Burger and Salazar-Burger 1992:125–26; Pozorski and Pozorski 1989; Siveroni 2006:126–36), as well as differences in the elaboration of and investment in mortuary practices (Larco Hoyle 1941:193–203; Onuki 1994:15–19). Unfortunately, current data are too scarce to attain a comprehensive view of these phenomena for the entire period.

The most studied manifestation of "sociopolitical complexity" for the Formative period has been what is commonly called "public architecture." This emphasis on architectural data can be explained by the conspicuous presence of impressive and elaborate buildings throughout the Central Andes. Archaeologists often define public buildings as religious architecture and interpret their presence as the manifestation of a theocratic social class that concentrated astronomical knowledge and ritual paraphernalia (e.g., Lumbreras 1987). Even without this kind of interpretation, several authors have outlined the need for a centralized decision-making entity to have overseen the construction of such buildings (Haas 1987:32; Lanning 1967:94; Pozorski 1987:23). Alternatively, Burger argues that early public buildings were the product of weakly stratified societies in which communal ideology was more important than individual differentiation (Burger 1992:54–55).

Beyond the competing explanations for monumental architecture, one of the most significant problems is the limited information on the architectural design of Formative period buildings. It is common, for example, to find descriptions of Formative buildings already defined as "platform mounds" or "open areas" based on surface records or limited excavations that do not account for the true architectural design. A satisfactory record of an architectural design should provide the complete configuration of architectural units, including the number and size of spaces and access systems.

As a consequence, significant dimensions of social and political organization cannot be addressed from an archaeological perspective and remain ignored or mentioned only in tentative or speculative ways. Reliable data

FIGURE 5.1. *Air photo of Pampa de las Llamas–Moxeke (source: Esri, Digital Globe)*

on the architectural design of a public building would allow researchers to investigate human interactions involved in the building's use and their organizational implications. Fortunately, such information is provided by the excavators of Huaca A, a building at the site of Pampa de las Llamas–Moxeke in the southern branch of the Casma Valley (Pozorski and Pozorski 1986, 1987, 1991, 1992:855, 1994).

PAMPA DE LAS LLAMAS–MOXEKE AND HUACA A

The site of Pampa de las Llamas–Moxeke consists of an architectural complex (figure 5.1) oriented along a southwest-northeast axis that is dominated by two major buildings: Moxeke at the southwestern end and Huaca A at the northeastern end. Several open spaces or "plazas" are aligned between these mounds. In addition, around seventy smaller platform mounds are aligned along the northwestern and southeastern sides of the complex. Finally, clusters of domestic structures have been recorded on the east side of the complex. Pozorski and Pozorski reported nine radiocarbon dates that place Pampa de las Llamas–Moxeke in the early Formative period, between 1800 and 1200 BC (Pozorski and Pozorski 1987:10–11).

Archaeologists consider Pampa de las Llamas–Moxeke to be the center of a polity that spread throughout the Casma branch of the Casma Valley (Wilson 1994:192–94) because of its large size and the absence of competing sites of the same scale in the surrounding area. In addition, the excavators reported significant inequalities among residential units, evidenced by the differences in size, construction materials, and differentiated access ways to more "domestic-like" ritual structures (Pozorski and Pozorski 1986:393–96, 1992:857–58).

Pampa de las Llamas–Moxeke also displays evidence of internal social differentiation based on the variations in architecture and restricted accesses. However, how was this society articulated or integrated? Pozorski and Pozorski noted the presence of the two main buildings (Moxeke and Huaca A) as clear manifestations of an authoritative body that integrated Pampa de las Llamas–Moxeke's inhabitants and possibly other surrounding sites (Pozorski and Pozorski 1987:32–34, 1992:853). The authors, however, proposed that the mounds had different functions. While Moxeke was designed to be a religious building, Huaca A became an administrative one. Together, they embodied a highly centralized state-like polity (Pozorski 1987:34, Pozorski and Pozorski 1992:853). This statement is based mainly on the differences observed between Moxeke and Huaca A: while Moxeke is seen as a U-shaped mound, Huaca A has a "peculiar multi-room organization" at the summit that provided storage functions (Pozorski and Pozorski 1986:386–93, 397–98) (figure 5.2).

The Function of Huaca A

The proposed storage use of Huaca A rooms can be assessed on the basis of the summit's spatial organization, as well as the reported associated artifacts and figurative features. For example, controlling the spread of pests and decay would have been better accomplished with numerous small spaces. To facilitate administration, storerooms should have been of uniform size. Nevertheless, the supposed storage rooms of Huaca A present considerable variability in size; some are large rooms with additional elements such as niches, which are more suited for display than storage purposes. In addition, the access system between the various rooms is variable, which implies that some rooms have restricted accessibility. Many of the rooms, for example, can only be reached by passing through other rooms. While the rooms could have functioned as storage, this theory does not account for the differences in room accessibility. Why are some rooms more restricted than others? I suggest we consider the limited accessibility as a meaningful cue for people's movement throughout the summit spatial organization.

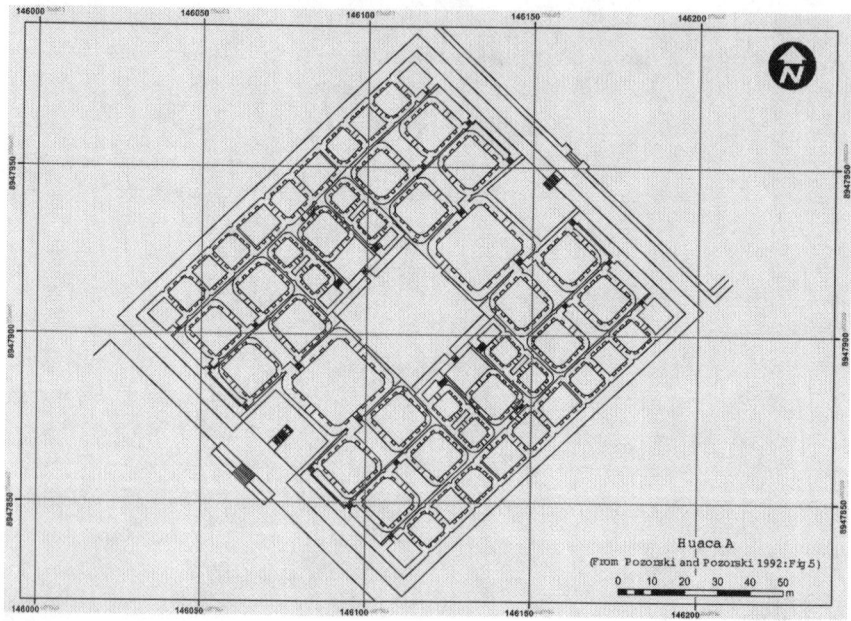

FIGURE 5.2. *Plan of Huaca A (redrawn by A. Tranlavina, from Pozorski and Pozorski 1992:figure 5)*

The consideration of a more "secular nature" of Huaca A in contrast to Moxeke has also been stated on the basis of the location and configuration of associated friezes (Pozorski and Pozorski 1992). While the friezes from both mounds appear thematically different, both are incomplete records of iconographic compositions (Pozorski and Pozorski 1986:388–89, 1994:58–59; Tello and Mejía Xesspe 1956:60–64). Moreover, the published reports are the product of excavations in specific places and do not demonstrate conclusively the absence of friezes in other areas (e.g., the indoor atriums of Moxeke or the outdoor platform walls of Huaca A).

The inferred administrative function was also based on the massive presence of rodent bones and traces of pollen. Both lines of evidence suggest but do not prove that these rooms were used for storage. At Huaca A, pollen identification has been qualitative in nature (Ugent, Pozorski, and Pozorski 1983), with no comparison samples from other contexts. Hence, it still needs to be ascertained whether there is a particular pattern of pollen deposition in the Huaca A rooms in contrast to other areas within the site. Second, although the gathering of rodent colonies in the rooms can be explained by the accumulation of foodstuffs during the building's use-life, it could also have happened after abandonment. Even if one accepts that these rooms were used for storage, foodstuffs were not the only items found during excavations. A jet mirror, a wooden figurine, and turquoise beads were also recovered (Pozorski and Pozorski 1986:387), which suggests that the rooms could have stored ritual paraphernalia (Burger 1992:84). Hence, the potential distribution of the stored goods should be discussed. Were they transported to distant places, or were they consumed within the Huaca A summit? If the second scenario is correct, how were they consumed or used?

While acknowledging the possible storage function of the Huaca A rooms, the activities conducted within the summit spaces should be evaluated in the context of (1) a highly formalized architectural design that influenced the displacement and organization of the activity participants, (2) the presence of iconographic devices, and (3) the presence of artifacts with symbolic value—that is, mirrors, figurines, turquoise beads—along with the inferred foodstuffs. I consider that this design and features reveal that the summit organization was conceived to cope with the requirements of a ritual order. In short, activities might have involved significant dimensions of social life far beyond administrative purposes.

Architectural Design and Ritual at Huaca A

To test the possible functional properties of Huaca A's architectural design and its relation to ritual performances, a definition of the different kind of spaces is required. Then, an analysis of the spatial organization will be conducted, complemented by considerations of how the defined architectural spaces might have been experienced. The spatial units found at the summit of Huaca A (figure 5.3) include:

1. CORRIDORS: Defined as spaces that are located between rooms and open areas in the mound's summit. We also find stairs that connect parts of corridors placed at different summit levels.
2. OPEN SPACES: Usually labeled as atriums or plazas, they are unroofed areas that connect with rooms, platforms, and other enclosed spaces.
3. ROOMS: Square units with one or two entryways and rounded corners, which vary in size from 20 m × 20 m to 8 m × 8 m. The walls are between 4 m and 7 m high and show niches in the upper parts.

Generally, the first two kinds of spaces have intermediate functions of connecting and isolating rooms. To fully understand the relations among these

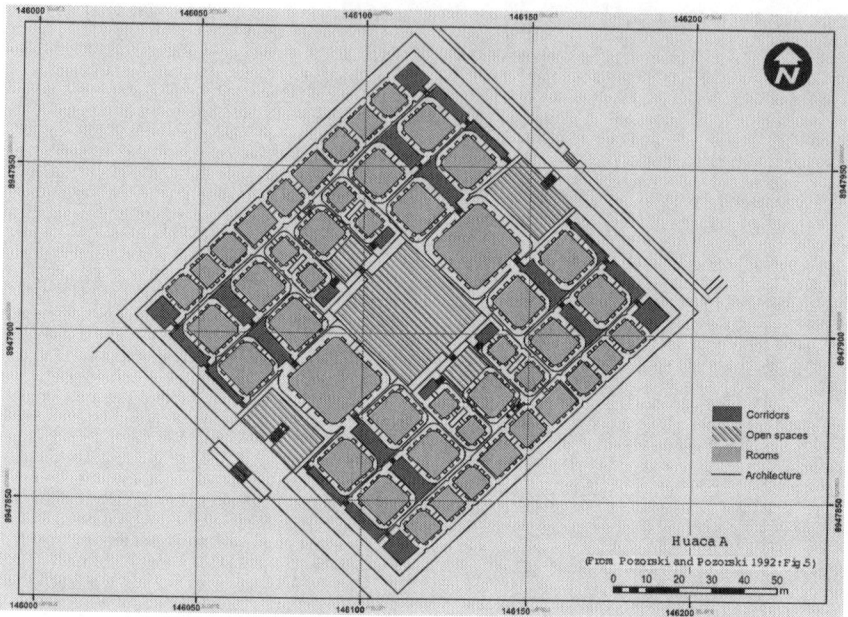

FIGURE 5.3. *Plan of Huaca A indicating corridors, open spaces and rooms (redrawn by A. Tranlavina, from Pozorski and Pozorski 1992:figure 5)*

features, it is important to observe the possible circuits or movements the architecture allows in the summit (figure 5.4):

1. After reaching the summit, from the outer atriums: movement can be through lateral corridors, toward a set of three aligned and interconnected rooms, or toward a large central room.
2. From the central room: movement can be through lateral corridors, toward a set of four rooms arranged at both sides of the corridor, or toward the plaza.
3. From the plaza: movement can be toward the lateral atriums.
4. From the lateral atriums: movement can be to two lateral and interconnected rooms or to a larger central room with three aligned back rooms.

Within the general design, there seems to be a basic unit consisting of an atrium, central rooms, and lateral rooms that adapts to spatial restrictions (figure 5.5).

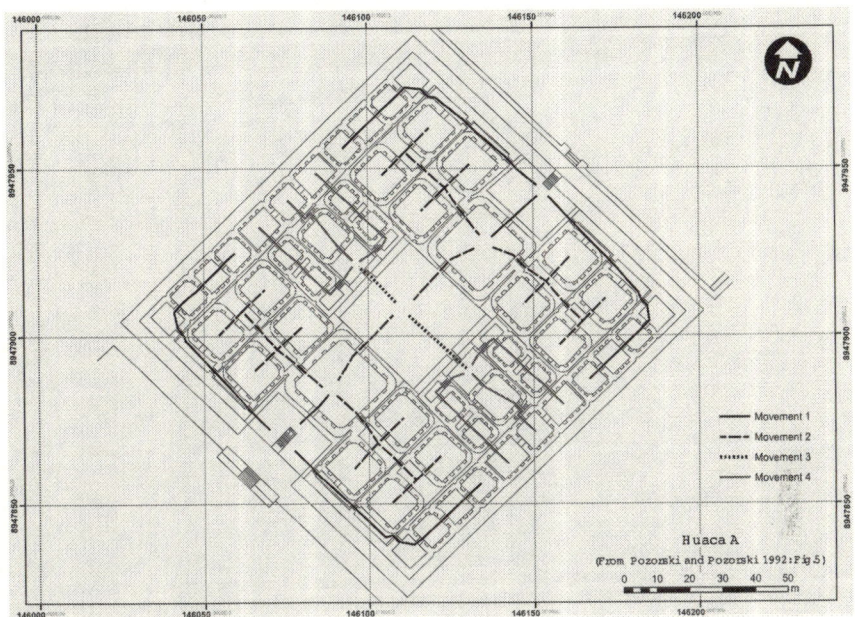

FIGURE 5.4. *Plan of Huaca A indicating possible movements (redrawn by A. Tranlavina, from Pozorski and Pozorski 1992:figure 5)*

Pozorski and Pozorski have recorded this type of architecture as a repetitive pattern in several buildings at the Pampa de las Llamas–Moxeke site, which they labeled "Intermediate Architecture" (Pozorski and Pozorski 1989:26–27). This architectural pattern is composed of a platform and a central room, often accompanied by two lateral rooms and a central atrium, which gives the entire summit a U-shaped form. This pattern has also been identified at Moxeke, which the Pozorskis labeled as having a U-shaped architectural mound (Pozorski and Pozorski 1987:34). Tello and Mejía Xesspe (1956:67) published a map of Moxeke's summit that depicts the presence of several rooms, which appear to have been arranged by two large U-shaped platforms, thus defining two hierarchical levels.

Similar arrangements were reported for other architectural complexes, such as the earliest building of Cerro Sechin (Maldonado 1992:77) and Bahía Seca (Pozorski and Pozorski 1992:848). These and other sites configure a well-defined architectural pattern for public buildings on the southern North Coast (Vega-Centeno 1995, 1999), and the summit configuration of Huaca A appears to be a development of this basic pattern.

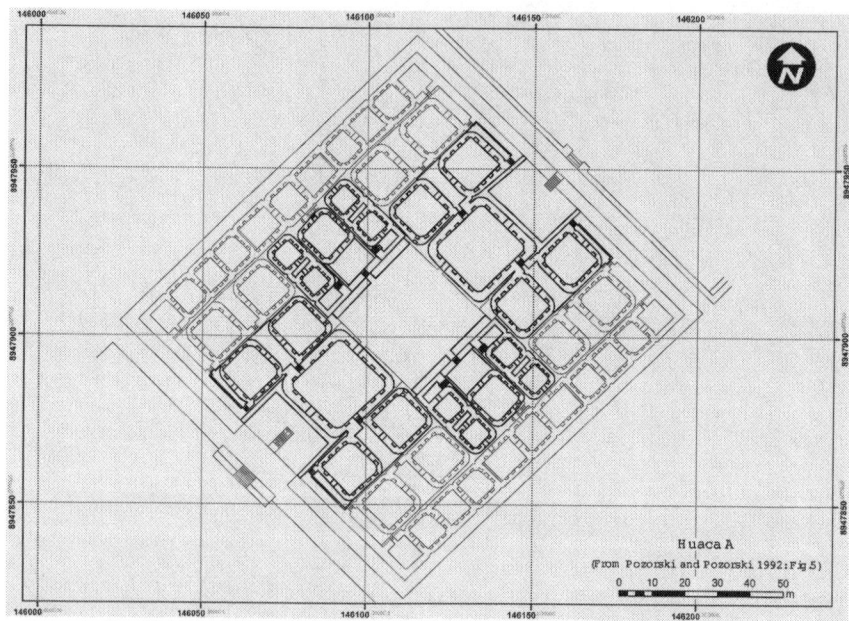

FIGURE 5.5. *Atrium U-shape forms at Huaca A (redrawn by A. Tranlavina, from Pozorski and Pozorski 1992:figure 5)*

Spatial Structure at Huaca A

To analyze the spatial structure of the Huaca A summit, a Gamma Analysis was conducted (Hillier and Hanson 1984:147–55). Gamma Analysis depicts spaces as circles and access systems as connecting lines. This graphic convention goes beyond visual examination, providing a quantifiable basis for effective comparison among different spatial units. In the case of Huaca A, there were a total of seventy-five spatial units among the rooms and open areas. The analysis also reveals a spatial organization that outlines a dual arrangement of rooms, previously noted by the Pozorskis (1989) (figure 5.6). Furthermore, it shows that this dual organization is repeated at different levels, showing a careful arrangement of spaces into paired clusters.

It is significant that the spatial organization of Huaca A has a very low RA (0.095) (table 5.1), which suggests that the design emphasizes symmetry and horizontality rather than asymmetry and hierarchy in the spatial organization. The RR index, which reveals the degree of alternative pathways within the structure, is also extremely low (0.0068), indicating a highly centralized access system.

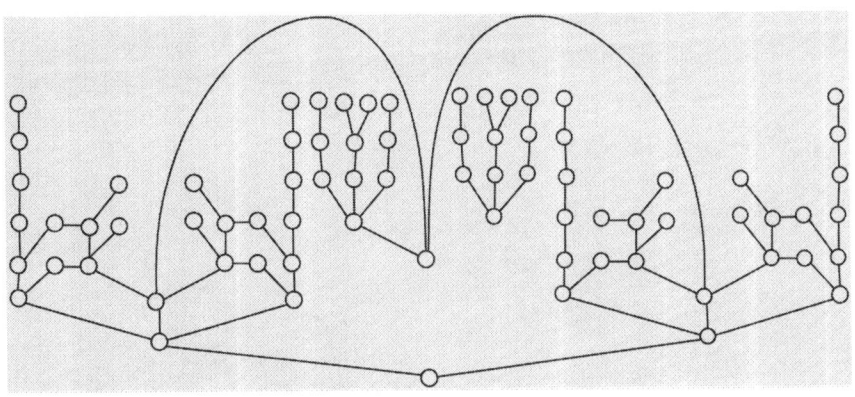

FIGURE 5.6. *Diagram of Gamma Analysis*

TABLE 5.1. Gamma Analysis results

Depth Levels	Spatial Units per Level
Carrier	1
1	2
2	6
3	13
4	18
5	14
6	10
7	12
Total spatial units	76
Mean depth	4.52
Rings	10
Relative asymmetry	0.095
Relative ringiness	0.0068

Spaces and Displacements: Experiencing Huaca A Architecture

The design of Huaca A enabled a visual contrast between open and closed spaces enhanced by the combination of narrow corridors that lead to a medium-sized or large room, atrium, or plaza. Thus, the final destinations, which are the rooms or set of rooms, might have been perceived as remote spaces.

The rooms also generate a distinct visual impact. First, the walls are unusually tall (4–7 m) and have niches, features that allow the deposition of goods in a visible location. In that sense they reinforce the visual dimension of the room design. Thus, individuals performing an activity in a room may have passed through several intermediate narrow spaces, with the corresponding experience

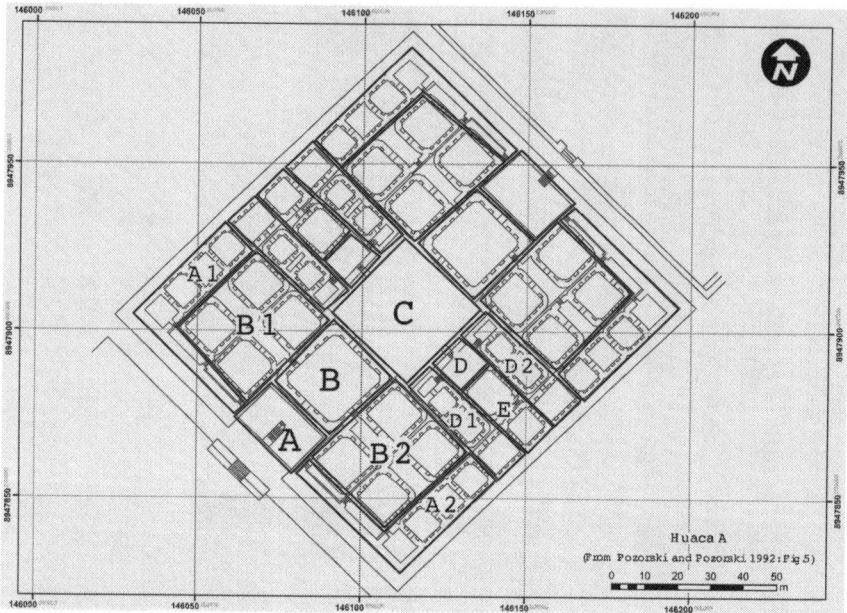

FIGURE 5.7. *Plan of Huaca A and possible organization of groups within rooms (redrawn by A. Tranlavina, from Pozorski and Pozorski 1992:figure 5)*

of isolation and difficult access. In addition, within the room individuals experienced the visual impact of a large space in which several elements may have been placed in the walls' niches. Whatever the activities performed in the rooms, visual performance characteristics may have played an important role.

While the rooms vary in size, the most important feature is that they all share the same design and inner components (e.g., high walls and niches). Thus, it is reasonable to suggest that these rooms were designed to conduct similar activities. Hence, the disparity in room size relates to the number of people able to congregate in the room. It is therefore important to evaluate how people moved and organized themselves throughout and within the rooms (figure 5.7).

According to the spatial units' dimensions and the access pattern, the summit allowed the access of a certain group of people (Group A). From the atrium this group could have divided into two groups (Groups A1 and A2) to reach the three aligned lateral rooms. The same re-gathered group or another group or sub-group (Group B) could have reached the large central room. From this room, the group could have subdivided into two groups (B1 and B2), and each of them could have also subdivided according to the existing rooms, becoming eight subgroups that might have performed similar kinds of activities in the same number of rooms. Afterward, the same group or a smaller one (Group C) could have passed to the inner plaza. From this position an even smaller group (Group D) could have reached the inner atrium and divided to get into the smaller lateral rooms (Groups D1 and D2) and return to the atrium, while a final group (Group E) could have reached the central and back rooms. Notably, this performance could have been done by two different and equivalent groups of individuals, arriving at the summit by the two stairways.

Ritual, Design, and Social Dynamics

On the basis of the observations and analysis of the spatial structure and possibilities of displacement at Huaca A, some inferences about the social and political characteristics of its participants can be made.

First, the design of the Huaca A summit suggests the existence of two equivalent social units that, while performing similar activities, may have had a symmetrical relationship. These units could be subdivided into two, then also be divided into four sub-units. Each resultant group of eight sub-units had the same level of access to an autonomous space for ritual activities. However, there seems to have been a smaller group in each larger social unit that was allowed to reach the inner, less accessible spaces. This smaller group was again subdivided into two sub-units.

What kind of social units participated in the activities at Huaca A? To answer this question, we must return to the basic architectural units identified for the Early Formative sites of the Casma region. As mentioned, they were composed of an atrium, a rear room, and two lateral rooms, depicting a U-shaped organization. This design suggests a social entity that could split into two groups after reaching the atrium to get into the lateral rooms. This kind of organization seems to correspond to a social unit of a communal nature, which organized ritual participation in moieties beyond a lineage or familiar range. This kind of organization has been proposed for architectural units of the late Archaic period, such as Cerro Lampay (Vega-Centeno 2005:330–38).

If the described units represent communal groups, Huaca A definitely represents a larger social unit with a regional range. This interpretation is reinforced by the absence of similar structures in the southern branch of the Casma Valley (Wilson 1994:192–94). Nonetheless, the settlement layout of Pampa de las Llamas–Moxeke, with the simultaneous presence of buildings that represent both communal and regional entities, seems to imply a set of relationships that are more complex than a mere two-level hierarchy. Such complexity is also revealed at the Huaca A summit.

As we have seen, the spatial organization of Huaca A presents a low degree of asymmetry but a high degree of centralization. It also includes several rooms for similar activities in which the social groups were dispersed and clustered in different moments. In this way the horizontal differentiations revealed by the design suggest that participants came from sixteen social units organized into two moieties, while the vertical differentiations suggests that a sub-group of these sixteen units (a sub-group or representative of each one?) could only have reached the outer area.

In this context the access system seems to correspond to a highly centralized liturgical program that enhanced the large-scale institution that congregated the constituent social units. By its devices and structure, the spatial organization of Huaca A appears to be a "sociopolitical map," a physical representation of a regional polity and its constituent social units. From outside, the building displays the idea of a central entity, whereas the summit organization materializes a scenario of sub-units with autonomous spaces. This contrast suggests that the development of centralized institutions by no means implied the canceling of smaller representations during ritual acts.

CONCLUSION: SOCIOPOLITICAL ORGANIZATION DURING THE FORMATIVE PERIOD

The preceding analysis has demonstrated that the access devices and spatial units of the Huaca A summit were designed to organize congregation acts of a large social unit with a dual division that also involved sixteen basic social units that appeared to be supporters of the larger entity. Although I suggested that Huaca A's design might be considered a sociopolitical map, the extrapolation of such a model to a real sociopolitical scenario requires caution. The spatial organization of Huaca A might have represented a sociopolitical reality, but it might also have expressed an ideal that may or may not have corresponded exactly to the sociopolitical reality at Pampa de las Llamas–Moxeke.

To further the evaluation of the sociopolitical characterization of this entity, Huaca A (or Moxeke) designs should be compared with the general distribution and configuration of intermediate architecture within Pampa de las Llamas–Moxeke and neighboring sites. In addition, the range of the Pampa de las Llamas–Moxeke polity and its sphere of influence should be assessed to evaluate the number of social units involved in its region. Additional research would clarify the nature of Pampa de las Llamas–Moxeke society. Nevertheless, the results of the Huaca A design analysis show how the development of a regional system is much more complex than a simple or mechanical process of power concentration or wealth accumulation. It surely involved the development of power relationships and sociopolitical representations (like those materialized in the spatial organization of a ritual building) in which hierarchy, autonomy, membership, and subordination could be constantly developed, assured, or negotiated.

REFERENCES CITED

Burger, R. L. 1992. *Chavín and the Origins of Andean Civilization*. New York: Thames and Hudson.

Burger, R. L., and L. Salazar-Burger. 1992. "La Segunda Temporada de Investigaciones en Cardal, Valle de Lurín, 1987." In *Estudios de Arqueología Peruana*, ed. D. Bonavía, 123–47. Lima: Fomciencias.

Bourdieu, P. 1977. *Outline of a Theory of Practice*. Cambridge: Cambridge University Press. http://dx.doi.org/10.1017/CBO9780511812507.

Connerton, P. 1989. *How Societies Remember*. Cambridge: Cambridge University Press. http://dx.doi.org/10.1017/CBO9780511628061.

Durkheim, É. 1995 [1912]. *The Elementary Forms of Religious Life*. New York: Free Press.

Haas, J. 1987. "The Exercise of Power in Early Andean State Development." In *The Origins and Development of the Andean State*, ed. J. Haas, S. Pozorski, and T. Pozorski, 31–35. Cambridge: Cambridge University Press.

Hillier, B., and J. Hanson. 1984. *The Social Logic of Space*. Cambridge: Cambridge University Press. http://dx.doi.org/10.1017/CBO9780511597237.

Kertzer, D. I. 1988. *Ritual, Politics, and Power*. New Haven, CT: Yale University Press.

Lanning, E. P. 1967. *Peru before the Incas*. Englewood Cliffs, NJ: Prentice Hall.

Larco Hoyle, R. 1941. *Los Cupisniques*. Lima: La Crónica y Variedades.

Lumbreras, L. G. 1987. "Childe and the Urban Revolution: The Central Andean Experience." In *Studies in the Neolithic and Urban Revolutions*, ed. L. Manzanilla, 327–44. BAR International Series 349. Oxford: British Archaeological Reports.

Maldonado, E. 1992. *Arqueología de Cerro Sechín*. Tomo I: *Arquitectura*. Lima: Pontificia Universidad Católica del Perú.

Moore, J. D. 1996. *Architecture and Power in the Ancient Andes: The Archaeology of Public Buildings*. New Studies in Archaeology. Cambridge: Cambridge University Press. http://dx.doi.org/10.1017/CBO9780511521201.

Onuki, Y., ed. 1994. *Kuntur Wasi y Cerro Blanco: Dos Sitios del Formativo en el Norte del Perú*. Tokyo: Hokusensha.

Pozorski, S. 1987. "Theocracy vs. Militarism: The Significance of the Casma Valley in Understanding Early State Formation." In *The Origins and Development of the Andean State*, ed. J. Haas, S. Pozorski, and T. Pozorski, 15–30. Cambridge: Cambridge University Press.

Pozorski, S., and T. Pozorski. 1986. "Recent Excavations at Pampa de las Llamas–Moxeke, a Complex Initial Period Site in Peru." *Journal of Field Archaeology* 13 (4): 381–401.

Pozorski, S., and T. Pozorski. 1987. *Early Settlement and Subsistence in the Casma Valley, Peru*. Iowa City: University of Iowa Press.

Pozorski, S., and T. Pozorski. 1989. "Planificación Urbana Prehistórica en Pampa de las Llamas–Moxeke, Valle de Casma." *Boletín de Lima* 66: 19–30.

Pozorski, S., and T. Pozorski. 1991. "Storage, Access Control, and Bureaucratic Proliferation: Understanding the Initial Period (1800–900 BC) Economy at Pampa de las Llamas–Moxeque, Casma Valley, Peru." *Research in Economic Anthropology* 13: 341–71.

Pozorski, S., and T. Pozorski. 1992. "Early Civilization in the Casma Valley, Peru." *Antiquity* 66 (253): 845–70. http://dx.doi.org/10.1017/S0003598X00044781.

Pozorski, T., and S. Pozorski. 1994. "Sociedades Complejas Tempranas y el Universo Ceremonial en la Costa Nor-Peruana." In *El Mundo Ceremonial Andino*, ed. L. Millones and Y. Onuki, 47–70. Lima: Horizonte.

Rappaport, R. A. 1999. *Ritual and Religion in the Making of Humanity*. Cambridge: Cambridge University Press. http://dx.doi.org/10.1017/CBO9780511814686.

Siveroni, V. 2006. "Mi Casa es tu Templo: Una Visión Alternativa de la Arquitectura de la Tradición Kotosh." *Arqueología y Sociedad* 17: 121–48.

Tello, J. C., and T. Mejía Xesspe. 1956. *Arqueología del Valle de Casma*. Lima: Universidad Nacional Mayor de San Marcos.

Turner, V. 1969. *The Ritual Process: Structure and Anti-Structure*. Ithaca, NY: Cornell University Press.

Ugent, D., S. Pozorski, and T. Pozorski. 1983. "Restos Arqueológicos de Tubérculos de Papas y Camotes en el Valle de Casma en el Perú." *Boletín de Lima* 5 (25): 28–48.

Vega-Centeno, R. 1995. "Arquitectura Monumental y Arte Figurativo del Formativo Temprano en la Costa Nor-Central del Perú: Una Aproximación a la Definición de Unidades Cronológicas." Tesis de Licenciatura, Facultad de Letras y Ciencias Humanas, Pontificia Universidad Católica del Perú, San Miguel, Lima.

Vega-Centeno, R. 1999. "Punkurí en el Contexto del Formativo Temprano de la Costa Nor-Central del Perú." *Gaceta Arqueológica Andina* 25: 5–21.

Vega-Centeno, R. 2005. "Ritual and Architecture in a Context of Emergent Complexity: A Perspective from Cerro Lampay, a Late Archaic Site in the Central Andes." PhD dissertation, Department of Anthropology, University of Arizona, Tucson.

Vega-Centeno, R. 2006. "El Estudio Arqueológico del Ritual." *Investigaciones Sociales* 16: 171–92.

Walker, W. H. 1995. "Ceremonial Trash?" In *Expanding Archaeology*, ed. J. M. Skibo, W. H. Walker, and A. E. Nielsen, 67–79. Salt Lake City: University of Utah Press.

Wilson, D. J. 1994. "Prehispanic Settlement Patterns in the Casma Valley, North Coast of Peru: Preliminary Results to Date." *Journal of the Steward Anthropological Society* 23 (1–2): 189–227.

6

Territoriality, Monumentality, and Religion in Formative Period Nepeña, Coastal Ancash

David Chicoine, Hugo Ikehara, Koichiro Shibata, and Matthew Helmer

This chapter takes a regional and comparative approach to explore variations in religious constructions and their visual perception in the Nepeña Valley, coastal Ancash, Peru. Like other contributors to this volume, we are interested in the perception of religiously significant places, landscapes, and monuments (Nielsen, Angiorama, and Ávila, this volume; Van Gijseghem and Whalen, this volume). More specifically, we evaluate the level of sociopolitical variability between local communities as viewed through the design of public monuments, their visual impact, and placement within the Nepeña landscape. Recent field research in the region suggests the development of polities and communities with different levels of sociopolitical integration based on settlement patterns and the distribution of ceramic styles (Ikehara and Chicoine 2011). These developments coincide with the abandonment of Chavín- and Cupisnique-related religious centers on the north and central coastal regions of Peru at the end of the middle Formative period (Kaulicke 1998, 2010; Onuki 1994; Rick et al. 2011; Shibata 2010). Indeed, the following late Formative period (ca. 800 BC) marked the emergence of a multitude of settlements varying in scale, size, and integration, which were occupied for several generations.

We investigate architectural monumentality and focus on the visual properties of religious buildings throughout the Nepeña Valley. Visibility corresponds to variables of display, exclusivity, and secrecy. We seek to answer the following questions: are ritual practices

DOI: 10.5876/9781607325963.c006

broadcasted to large numbers of people with the idea of propagating canonic messages? Or, in contrast, are ritual practices rather exclusive events mainly aimed directly at participants? Can we detect sociopolitical interaction, integration, or competition through the design and placement of public monuments within the region? Addressing these questions using a valley-wide case study will allow a better understanding of power, religion, and politics during the Formative period.

RELIGIOUS AUTHORITY, MONUMENTALITY, AND SOCIOPOLITICAL INTEGRATION

Our objective in this chapter is to reconstruct and contrast patterns of ritual practices through their materialization in built settings. We are particularly interested in considering the relationships among the scales of ritual practice, integration, and spectacle, including modes of religious authority, social control, and elite strategies. By studying the design of religious monuments, our research has the potential to shed light on the diverse nature of authority during the Formative period. We suggest no clear division between religious ceremonies and public events. Hence, we interpret the design, use, abandonment, and renovation of ritual settings as potent political actions. Not only do public rituals have the capacity to transcend daily experiences, they represent ideal moments to affirm, negotiate, resist, or reaffirm relations of power (Swenson 2011; Tambiah 1985). Hence, the study of ritual practices, and their variability across time and space, allows for comparisons of varying modes of political authority, from centralized state-sponsored festivals to small household shrine offerings and communal ancestor worship (see Fernandini and Ruales, this volume). While the study of the internal spatial syntax of ceremonial structures can bring insights into sociopolitical organizations (see Vega-Centeno Sara-Lafosse, this volume), here we focus on the visibility and perception of religious monuments at the regional level. Using Geographic Information Systems (GIS), we reconstruct landscapes of ritual practices within a small valley of coastal Ancash and monitor their changes during the transition from the middle through the late and final Formative, a time of major sociopolitical reorganization.

THE FORMATIVE PERIOD IN NEPEÑA

Andean archaeologists have traditionally conceptualized the late and final Formative (i.e., Early Horizon) to be contemporaneous with the spread of Chavín religious imagery (Patterson 1971; Willey 1951). Although recent research has questioned the chronological placement of Chavín and its associated ceremonial centers (Burger 1981, 2008; Burger and Salazar-Burger 2008; Rick 2008; Rick et al. 2011), most scholars still agree that there was a brief period during which many distant communities exchanged objects, ideas, and possibly people (Burger 1992, 2008; Druc 1998; Lumbreras 1993; Onuki 1994; Shibata 2010). In Nepeña, relationships between Chavín de Huantar and local populations remain unclear (Shibata 2010:306). However, excavations have revealed a style of monumental architecture and public visual art that shows symbolic and stylistic similarities with Chavín- and Cupisnique-related religious ideologies. Rather than a period of uncontested integration, it appears that the late and final Formative were times of great ritual diversity. Chavín was only part of a very complex series of related developments that included regional and interregional changes that intertwined different styles of architectural design, religious ideology, and public art. Furthermore, recent work at Chavín itself emphasizes the diversity of ceremonial buildings and ritual practices at the highland center (see Contreras, this volume; Rick, this volume). Our chapter sheds light on Nepeña's geopolitics and cultural diversity in light of new research done since 2002.

Between 2002 and 2005, excavations were carried out at the archaeological sites of Cerro Blanco and Huaca Partida. The data acquired from these excavations helped construct a chronological sequence specific to Formative Nepeña (Shibata 2010, 2011) (table 6.1). The sequence is divided into four phases based on changes in ceramic styles, architecture, visual arts, and radiocarbon dates: (1) Huambocayán (1500–1100 cal BC), corresponding to the earliest ceramic assemblage so far confirmed in the valley; (2) Cerro Blanco (1100–800 cal BC), named after and related to the eponymous site where Tello (1939, 1943) excavated famous feline murals and corresponding to recently discovered colossal friezes at Huaca Partida; (3) Nepeña (800–450 cal BC), when Cerro Blanco and Huaca Partida witnessed large-scale megalithic renovations that covered earlier architecture and friezes; and (4) Samanco (450–150 cal BC), a time when monumental constructions were abandoned at both sites.

In the lower valley, perhaps one of the most salient cultural transformations during the Formative was the abandonment of Cerro Blanco and Huaca Partida and the subsequent relocation of public activities at Caylán and other associated complexes. While more information is needed on the religious significance and ritual behaviors associated with the abandonment of the middle Formative temples (see Capriata Estrada and López-Hurtado, this volume; Edwards, this volume), this shift was linked to economic innovations, including the increasing use of maize. At the same time, changes in religious iconographies and visual arts hint at a major reorganization of ritual life. For

TABLE 6.1. Chronological table for the Formative period in Nepeña

			Lower Valley Sites					Middle Valley Sites				Approximate Correspondence with the Chronological Frame of:		
	Uncalibrated BC	Cal BC	Samanco	Huambacho	Caylán	Huaca Partida	Cerro Blanco	Virahuanca Bajo	Paredones	Kushipampa	Huancarpón	Burger 1992	Kaulicke 1998	Onuki 2001
Samanco phase	500–250	450–150										Early Horizon	Final Formative	Late Formative
Nepeña phase	700–500	800–450											Late Formative	
Cerro Blanco phase	1000–700	1100–800										Initial period	Middle Formative	Middle Formative
Huambocayán phase	1300–1000	1500–1100											Early Formative	Early Formative

Credit: Koichiro Shibata

a. Monumental architecture—benched plazas and colonnaded patios with geometric clay friezes.
b. Reutilization of the former megalithic platform.
c. Monumental architecture—terraced solid platform with megalithic retaining wall.
d. Monumental architecture—terraced solid platform with polychrome Cupisnique/Chavín-related clay friezes.
e. Occupation without architectural evidence.
f. Monumental architecture—multiple connected plazas enclosed by outer wall.
g. Virahuanca Bajo, Paredones, and Huancarpón have not been excavated, so their chronological position is speculative.
h. Monumental architecture—multiple connected plazas enclosed by megalithic outer wall.

example, imagery and architecture often associated with highland Chavín and coastal Cupisnique were apparently rejected or avoided by late and final Formative groups at Caylán, Huambacho, and Samanco. Transformations in public visual arts likely paralleled profound shifts in religious ideologies (see Onuki, this volume). In Nepeña, the religious messages broadcasted from the late Formative onward appear to focus less on supernatural beings and more on generic metaphysical ideas portrayed through geometric designs (Chicoine 2006; Chicoine and Ikehara 2010). At the same time, patterns of foodways and ritual feasting lend weight to the importance of commensal politics in the competition for supporters (Chicoine 2011; Ikehara and Shibata 2008). Yet we know little about the use of religious monuments in the negotiation of political authority during that critical transition.

Since Tello's work, systematic surface survey and excavation projects have brought renewed interest in Nepeña. Based on results from his surface surveys, Proulx (1968, 1973, 1982) suggested a territorial divide between the upper and lower sections of the valley during the Early Intermediate Period (ca. cal AD 1–800). Here, the exclusive distribution of Moche and Recuay styles of ceramics in the lower and upper valleys, respectively, is interpreted as the existence of two independent yet contiguous polities. Our combined research suggests that the division between the Moro Pocket in the upper reaches of the valley and the lower portions west of Moro existed perhaps as early as the late Formative (Ikehara and Chicoine 2011; see also Daggett 1983). The division was created based on settlement patterns, ceramic styles, and monumental architecture. In this chapter we also investigate cultural diversity in Formative Nepeña by focusing on forms of public monuments and religious practices.

Our exploration of public monuments employs two methods to look at complementary scales of analysis. First, we analyze the visibility of Formative period public buildings in the Nepeña Valley. Second, we evaluate the visibility and organization of religious structures in the settlements with the objective of defining how they structured ritual experiences through their use during ritualized gatherings, as suggested by Moore (1996b). Our goal is to weigh the extent to which religious structures acted as binding social agents at the regional level through their permanence and centrality. Moreover, this information is used to infer the degree of political integration of different communities.

FORMATIVE PERIOD MONUMENTS IN NEPEÑA

Our sample includes nine sites located in the upper and lower valley whose occupations span the middle to final Formative, or from the Cerro Blanco to

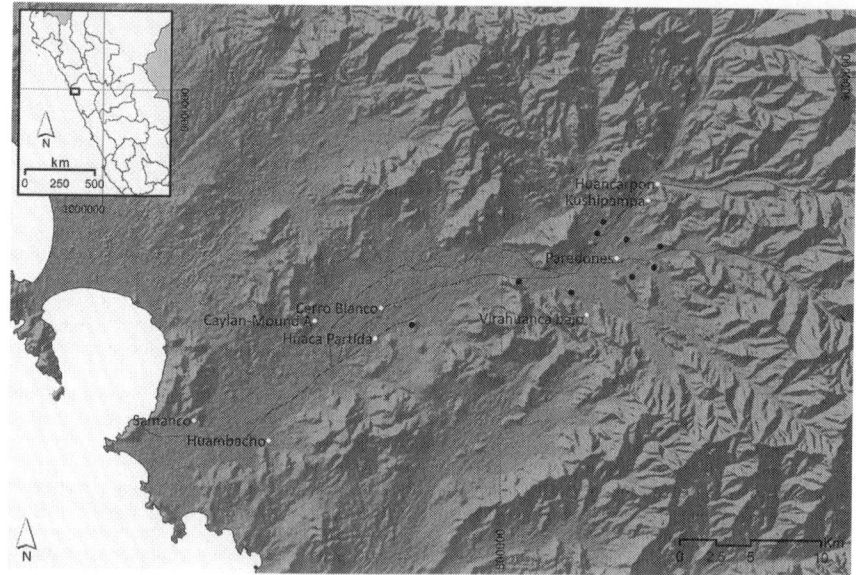

FIGURE 6.1. *Map of the Nepeña Valley showing the location of the Formative period sites mentioned in the text (white dots) and other Formative sites with significant monumental architecture (black dots)*

the Samanco phase (figure 6.1). Here we provide a brief description of each site and its major public monument(s). The ceremonial center of Cerro Blanco (1100–450 cal BC) is located on the north bank of the Nepeña River, 20 km inland from the coastline (145 meters above sea level [masl]). The architecture of the site comprises three artificial mounds that form a U-shaped configuration that encloses a possible central plaza (figure 6.2). The central mound, or "Main Platform," measures 115 m by 85 m at its base and 15 m in height.

Though excavations revealed part of the Cerro Blanco phase architecture in all mounds including the polychrome feline iconography discovered by Tello (1943; see MAAUNMSM 2005), only the Main Platform of the Nepeña phase can be analyzed here. Constructed of large cut stones, the megalithic retaining walls are quite distinct from the earlier phase in which only small stones and adobes were employed. So far, no ritual imagery has been registered from this architectural context.

The ceremonial center of Huaca Partida (1100–450 cal BC) is located on the southern margin of the river (130 masl), approximately 2 km southwest of Cerro Blanco. In contrast to the U-shape of Cerro Blanco, Huaca Partida consists of a large rectangular platform, 10 m high (see figure 6.2). The Cerro

FIGURE 6.2. *Photograph of Cerro Blanco de Nepeña: (A) an east-to-west view of the site of Cerro Blanco, (B) the polychrome clay frieze with eccentric eye motive discovered by Tello—Cerro Blanco phase and (x) south mound, (y) central mound, or Main Platform, and (z) north mound; photograph of Huaca Partida showing (C) an east-to-west view of the site, (D) the bichrome high-relief clay carving of a feline motive (the pole measures 2 m)—Cerro Blanco phase.* Courtesy, *Koichiro Shibata.*

Blanco phase component at Huaca Partida has the earliest monumental architecture analyzed in this chapter. Huaca Partida consists of two rectangular rooms with a colonnaded atrium between the rooms. This ritual complex is located on top of a large terraced platform. The exterior side of the rooms, frontal columns, and the platform's retaining walls are ornamented with incised polychrome paintings, polychrome paintings, and bichrome high-relief clay carvings, respectively. The Nepeña phase at Huaca Partida witnessed a substantial change in many facets of the material culture. Similar to Cerro Blanco, the site was converted into a large megalithic construction, with only a few simple religious images carved in stone.

Caylán (800–1 cal BC), with its dense nucleus of stonewall enclosures of more than 50 ha, is the largest settlement in the Nepeña Valley (Chicoine and Ikehara 2010, 2014). The complex lies on a pampa (130 masl), tucked between the V-shaped hills of Cerro Caylán 15 km from the coast. The urban core of

FIGURE 6.3. *Photographs of Caylán's urban complex, showing (A) the dense nucleation of enclosure compounds and the location of Mound-A (white arrow), (B) the geometric clay and stone friezes adorning the facades of Mound-A, and (C) a trench excavation realized in 2010. Courtesy, David Chicoine.*

the site is composed of more than forty compounds, each of which is organized around a monumental benched plaza, a series of colonnaded patios, and smaller roofed areas. A number of low mounds dot the site core and complement some of the benched plazas. The plazas display ornate clay friezes and decorated rectangular pillars. These spaces appear to have played a critical role in public gatherings and ritual performance (Helmer, Chicoine, and Ikehara 2012). Excavations of associated refuse indicate that music performance and food consumption were likely activities during ritual gatherings. Access to plaza spaces was tightly controlled through sophisticated systems of corridors, baffled entryways, and door locks. The wall and column friezes display intricate geometric designs that emphasized the interplay of light, shadow, and movement of geometric forms.

While a significant portion of Caylán ritual life was located inside architectural walls provided by the enclosed plaza architecture, architects and builders also invested in the construction of a mound, which today stands more than 10 m above ground level (figure 6.3). This Main Mound (Mound-A) measures 50 m wide at its base, and the summit contains a series of colonnaded patios accessed through an elaborate system of zigzagging corridors and staircases. The clearing of the southern facade in 2010 indicates that terrace levels were decorated with wall friezes analogous in design and iconography to the art in the plaza. In contrast, the mound architecture and its friezes are clearly designed to be seen by a larger number of people spread over a much broader geographic distance. Mound-A at Caylán is included in our analysis.

The site of Huambacho (800–200 cal BC) is located on the southern margin of the river, 8 km from the coast (65 masl). We estimate that the original extension of the site spanned 12 ha. Based on the architectural features and material culture found during excavations, Huambacho appears to be a small elite center associated with the larger settlement of Caylán (Chicoine 2006). Huambacho originally had two enclosures on the valley floor; however, only one stands today (Main Compound). As at Caylán, entrances are constructed in a zigzagging fashion, and their access is indirect. The Main Compound is subdivided into two distinct spaces, each dominated by a benched plaza. Plazas are associated with the use of complexes of raised colonnaded patio rooms. The raised areas had facades decorated with geometric clay friezes. In our analysis we consider the Huaca-A Complex located in the northeast portion of the Main Compound.

Samanco (ca. 800–1 cal BC) is similar to Huambacho and Caylán in architectural design and material assemblage. It is located 3 km from the coast (40 masl) and is the closest major Formative settlement to the Pacific Ocean. The site contains six separate enclosure compound areas totaling hundreds of agglutinated rectangular rooms, including plazas, colonnaded patios, corrals, and smaller domestic structures (Helmer and Chicoine 2015). Samanco is nestled within ravines and hillsides along the northern margin of the Nepeña River, near the Bahía de Samanco. The center is approximately 30 ha in extent, with a 17 ha dense architectural core. Samanco contrasts with Huambacho and Caylán through its extensive use of terracing above the pampa and into the hillsides, with a general separation of 25 m in elevation between lower and upper structures. Although fieldwork in 2012 and 2013 failed to document representational art, the presence of a monumental plaza hints at the existence of ceremonial settings.

Samanco has one major plaza (Plaza Mayor) measuring approximately 50 m by 30 m, with wide terraced platform benches on three sides and two terraced open courtyards. The Plaza Mayor is located at the uppermost extent of the site (70 masl), abutting the hillsides on top of a series of terraces. In contrast to plazas at Huambacho and Caylán, which are embedded in walled compounds, Samanco's Plaza Mayor is larger and located in a more open space. The Plaza Mayor was chosen for our comparative analysis because of its centrality and the absence of mounds at Samanco. Based on architectural features and ceramic styles, Samanco's Plaza Mayor likely corresponds to the Nepeña and Samanco phases.

The upper section of the valley is characterized by a widening of the arable plain. This area is enclosed within ridges and hills where river tributaries intersect. It is commonly known as the "Moro Pocket." Based on survey data (Daggett 1984, 1987; Proulx 1968, 1973, 1985), this area witnessed a particularly dense occupation during the final Formative, or Samanco phase. We interpret upper valley centers as competing political entities (Ikehara and Chicoine 2011). Their rivalry may have included vectors of violence, exchange, and possibly an eventual sociopolitical integration (ibid.).

A sample of four centers was chosen from the Moro area. Surface ceramics suggest a main occupation during the final Formative (450–150 cal BC). Two sites, Kushipampa and Paredones, share a similar architectural style known as "megalithic architecture" (Daggett 1983; Ikehara 2010) (figure 6.4). They differ in their location, however. While Kushipampa (25 ha) was built over an alluvial terrace at 600 masl in a narrow section of the valley, Paredones (21 ha) was placed at a lower elevation (430 masl) in the middle of the valley floor, at a more central location compared to other upper valley sites. Both sites have an orthogonal arrangement. It is clear that the layout was the result of subsequent divisions of the space defined by the outer walls. Perimeter walls are as high as 4 m. In this sense the design is similar to the way lower valley sites, such as Caylán, were built. Here, the difference resides in the absence of large, replicated compounds.

At both Kushipampa and Paredones, multiple contiguous plazas indicate the potential flow of people during ceremonies. The most private areas were dominated by low-lying platforms (4 to 5 m) supported by megalithic walls filled with cobbles. Their exact function and use cannot be determined at this time. During excavations in 2009 the platforms yielded no activity remains, and their walls bear no evidence of elaborate decoration. The sophisticated finish of the megalithic rocks, especially in the doorways and corners, points toward their use without any further surface treatment. Finally, at Kushipampa, a medium-size village has been identified next to the monumental core (Ikehara 2010).

Some features, including megalithic corners and shared ceramic styles, suggest a strong connection among Kushipampa, Paredones, and the site of Huancarpón (20 ha). The linear arrangement of mounds and plazas distinguishes Huancarpón, as it resembles earlier traditions from the Casma Valley

FIGURE 6.4. *Photographs of Kushipampa showing (A) a northwest-to-southeast view of the ceremonial complex with indication of the location of the mounds, (B) view of the masonry of the mounds after excavations in 2008, (C) view of a megalithic doorway after excavations in 2008, and (D) detail of the finishing of the megalithic rocks used in corners of the structures.* Courtesy, *Hugo Ikehara.*

(see Pozorski and Pozorski 1987). The mounds at Huancarpón are at least 10 m higher than the plazas, and they are composed of several superimposed platforms. Excavations have yet to be carried out at the site, and our surface observations noted that the walls did not have any murals.

Another distinctive feature of Huancarpón is the existence of defensive features, including walls that encircle the monumental core and moats that interrupt the connection between plazas and mounds (Daggett 1984; Proulx 1985). While neighboring Kushipampa is located on an alluvial terrace overlooking the valley floor, Huancarpón is placed on an adjacent terrace at 660 masl, separated by a dry ravine but one that oversees most of the intersection of the Salitre and Jimbe Rivers and their respective valley floors.

Finally, the fourth example from the upper valley, Virahuanca Bajo, is located in an alluvial fan (400 masl) at the edge of the valley floor. The site shows a contrasting architectural layout in comparison to typical ridge-top complexes. Virahuanca Bajo comprises three aligned low-lying mounds (up to 2 m high) located within a massive open space retained by a perimeter wall approximately 1.5 m in height. This structure is surrounded by other, smaller enclosures and some terraces in the adjacent hills. The area where this architecture is present covers approximately 45 ha, but Daggett (1983, 1984) considers that the Virahuanca Bajo monument forms part of the same complex with the habitation areas and mounds located north of it, covering more than 100 ha. No mural decoration or megalithic architecture features have been recorded from surface survey.

Together, these sites represent most of the Formative building traditions in Nepeña. These traditions include early pyramid temples with familiar feline murals in the case of Huaca Partida and Cerro Blanco; megalithic complexes such as Paredones, Huancarpón, and Kushipampa, the last two with attached villages; dense enclosure compounds reminiscent of later coastal groups, seen at Caylán, Huambacho, and Samanco; and finally, minimalist monumental architecture with low-density occupations such as Virahuanca Bajo. In the following section we evaluate Nepeña's Formative landscape through the modeling of visual experiences.

METHODS AND ANALYSES

Our method is inspired by Moore's work on the archaeology of monuments in the Andes (Moore 1996a, 1996b). As pointed out by Moore (1996b:98), there is a "direct relationship between a monument's design and its communicative potential, and thus its ability to serve as a marker of social cohesion." Borrowing from Higuchi's (1983) study of Japanese landscapes, Moore's methodology considers the design and visual impact of mound construction in the Andes. More specifically, Moore uses "angles of incidence," which refer to the inclination of the slope of a particular structure where surfaces perpendicular to the viewer (more than 30°) tend to be more easily perceived and have a stronger visual impact than those with more gentle (less than 15°) or frontal (15°–30°) views (ibid.). Through the analysis of seventeen monuments from eleven sites, Moore (1996b) evaluates a series of variables including the angles of incidence of a monument, its associated landscaping, and visual impact from different locations.

As pointed out by Higuchi (1983:32–35) and Moore (1996b:106), the visual impact of a monument is related to the different points of view adopted by visitors: as a visitor approaches a structure, the person experiences different perceptions as the monument fills visual thresholds. More significant, the progressive visual perception of a monument at 18°, 27°, and 45° of vision above the horizontal eye line informs on how a particular building was meant to impact viewers. Were monuments designed to be experienced visually from far away, or was their visibility limited to select groups of nearby viewers? Was a religious building arranged to provide similar views (i.e., isovistas) to people living in different sectors of a settlement or accessing a structure from specific points (e.g., ramps, staircases)?

Moore's analysis is enlightening as it reveals the existence of distinct traditions of mound building in coastal Peru. For example, Manchay mounds from the Formative period in the Central Coast are more visually impressive when experienced directly in front of the monument, while much larger Sechín mounds in the Casma Valley have more visual impact from afar (ibid.:118; see Burger and Salazar-Burger 2008). Clearly, some buildings' monumentality was meant to be shared between viewers across different locations, while others were less visible and designed to impress select individuals with privileged access to ritual spaces. Our study uses this methodology to explore variability in religious architecture in the Nepeña Valley during the Formative period and considers the locations of the various public monuments regionally. We consider the design of religious monuments as a tool of religious proselytizing by evaluating for whom and from where the monuments were visible. Was a building mainly designed and located to be visible from far away and to act as a form of external communicative agent, or was it laid out to be experienced by local settlement dwellers, or both? Were structures strategically placed in the landscape to maintain a visual connection with supporters but to also be seen by potentially competing factions? These data have the potential to inform on the scale of religio-political integration through time and space.

We compare the placement of the different Formative monuments to evaluate the geographic areas from which they are visible. For that purpose we employ the ArcMAP viewshed tool over a Digital Elevation Model (DEM) obtained from ASTER satellite with a 30 m resolution. A viewshed analysis of a site provides a raster image in which each cell has a value of 0 or 1, not visible or visible, of the location's visibility from a vantage point (Conolly and Lake 2006). A combined viewshed provides a value that corresponds to the number of selected points from which the location is visible. Simplifying the analysis, we are basically assuming that the other way is equivalent, so the combined viewshed analysis corresponds to how many monuments under study can be visible from a specific location. Such information is recorded as a value for each of the raster cells. In this analysis we use as an offset value the approximate height of the monument but not a specific height for the observer.

We assume that if a monument were conceived to be visually prominent for a population living in a specific area, its location will benefit such visibility. Were monuments designed to be watched only by people living nearby or also by people living farther away? We assess this question by exploring the relationship between the visibility of the surrounding area and the space beyond it. These circular areas were defined by two arbitrary radiuses: 7 km and 10 km starting from each monument. Our field observations noted the monuments were difficult to see beyond a 10 km radius because of cloudiness, topography, and the limited width of the valley. Consequently, a 7 km radius defines a circle that is roughly half the area of a 10 km radius. Then we use the ratio of the total visibility under 7 km and 10 km, respectively. If visibility between the two areas is equally distributed, the ratio is expected to be 0.5. Otherwise, if a preference for the adjacent land was preferred, the ratio will be closer to 1. Finally, if the monument was intended only for the more distant population, the ratio must be closer to 0.

Religious Buildings, Visual Arts, and Isovistas

The analysis of angles of incidence reveals significant patterns and allows for a tripartite classification of the Formative period monuments in Nepeña (figures 6.5, 6.6). The angle of incidence for each building was obtained measuring, in profile sketches, the angle between the ground and the line connecting the top of the highest structure and the lowest point of the base. A first category (Class 1) includes Samanco, Cerro Blanco (Nepeña phase), and the west section of Huancarpón. Class 1 buildings display gentle angles of incidence between 11° and 12°. A second group (Class 2) includes Huaca Partida's mound during both phases as well as Huambacho, where monuments have frontal angles of incidence between 24° and 26°. Finally, as part of Class 3, Caylán's Mound-A, Huancarpón's west view, Paredones, Virahuanca Bajo, and Kushipampa show perpendicular angles of incidence of more than 30°. It is significant that these last three have indeed nearly 90° slopes. The structures are solid mounds with almost perpendicular retaining walls.

Class 1 buildings, with gentle angles of incidence between 11° and 12°, are interpreted as having little visual impact. Here, the main architectural feature, an enclosed public space, is similar to many of the benched plazas at Huambacho and Caylán. It was not designed for outsiders but for internal audience members and ritual participants. The emphasis on internal decorations and platform benches facing the inner patio at these three sites reinforces this interpretation. During the Nepeña phase, the front-facing view of

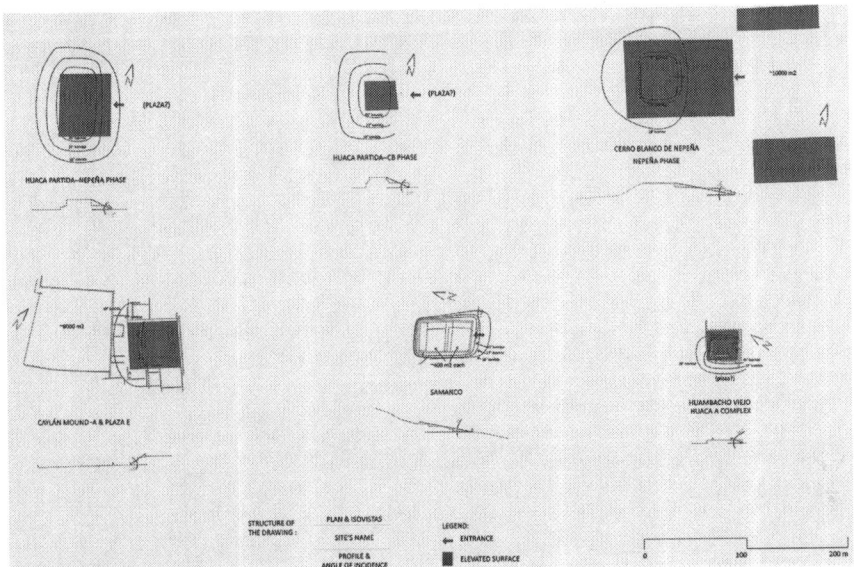

FIGURE 6.5. *Results of visual impact (angles of incidence) and isovistas with schematic representation of structures for Huaca Partida (Cerro Blanco and Nepeña phases), Cerro Blanco (Nepeña phase), Caylán (Mound-A), Samanco, and Huambacho's Main Platform Complex. For Caylán, Samanco, and Huambacho, there are large areas of architectural remains not represented in this image.* Courtesy, Hugo Ikehara.

Cerro Blanco's inner patio can be characterized similarly. Viewed from the sides or the back, the building had a greater visual impact than from the base of the mound (18° isovista). This condition may be related to ritual processions coming from a central plaza (surrounded by two low mounds), going up to the wide lower platform, and then confronting the upper mound built with megaliths and an impressive stone lintel. The spaces are distributed in a linear axis and become gradually smaller, thus creating a spatial mechanism for segregating people during rituals. While large portions of the public were aware of the structures, only a few could access the base of the upper building where details can be appreciated (45° isovista) or the top of it by a narrow corridor in an L or S shape. Our last example of a low angle of incidence pertains to the west-to-east view of Huancarpón. In this monument the westernmost mound blocks the view of the buildings to the east, creating a clear view of only one mound from the residential sector. An observer from the adjacent village would not be aware of the complexity of the monumental sector until the person stood on top of the mound. Indeed, the mound summit is the

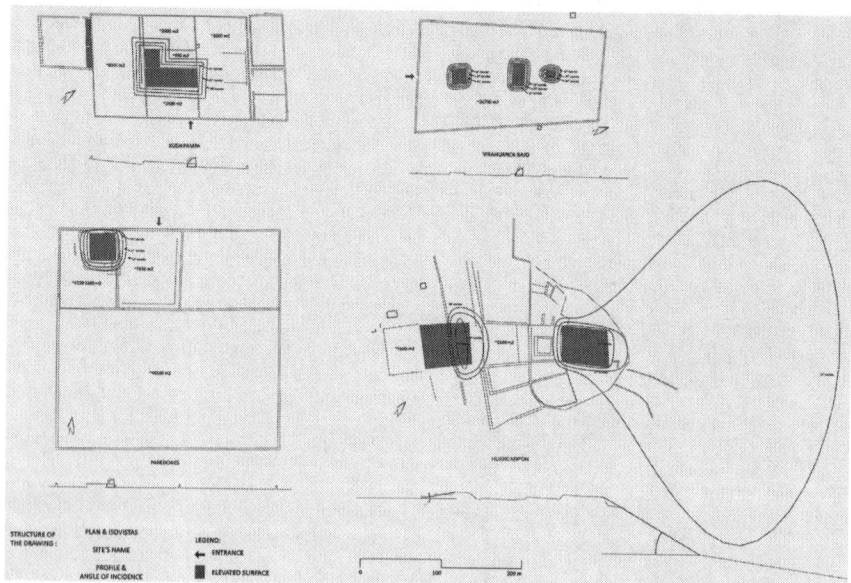

FIGURE 6.6. *Results of visual impact (angles of incidence) and isovistas with schematic representation of structures for Kushipampa, Virahuanca Bajo, Paredones, and Huancarpón. For Kushipampa, Virahuanca Bajo, and Huancarpón, there are large areas of architectural remains not represented in this image.* Courtesy, *Hugo Ikehara.*

only area from which the entire monumental sector can be appreciated, and vice-versa (18° and 27° isovistas). This contrasts with the east-to-west view of the site explained below.

Class 2, with angles of incidence between 24° and 26°, includes monuments with slightly stronger higher visual effects. In the case of Huambacho, visual impact is hampered by the presence of enclosed compounds and roofed areas. In this way the raised mound and its decorated walls were only visible to select individuals who had privileged access to the ritual precinct. The Huambacho case is hence similar to what we observe at Samanco. In contrast, Huaca Partida, during both the Cerro Blanco and Nepeña phases, clearly had more visibility. Furthermore, at least during the Cerro Blanco phase, the monumentality of the structure was complemented by vivid mural imagery on the sides and frontal facade. The isovistas indicate that both buildings were designed to be visible from afar. Meanwhile, architectural details and visual arts were meant to be recognized and fully appreciated by people walking at the foot of the monuments. The Cerro Blanco phase's wall carvings of felines, as well as the lateral polychrome friezes, may have been appreciated in this way. The analysis of the symbolic content of the visual arts associated with each ceremonial structure is beyond the scope of this chapter, but major differences existed in the religious messages broadcasted between the Middle and late/final Formative.

The results may indicate that Class 3 constructions were designed to have the highest visibility and therefore visual impact when confronted by an audience. However, all the cases are mounds built inside or surrounded by a walled enclosure. The lowest angle of vision (isovista 18°) falls inside an enclosed space in all cases. This is a significant contrast, since monuments cannot be clearly noticed from a distance. Viewers have to enter and go through different spaces until they are confronted by such buildings. With one exception, Virahuanca Bajo, monuments of the third category display hierarchical spaces connected by different plazas, patios, and corridors. Similar to those described by Moore (1996b:118) for the Late Intermediate Period (cal AD 1000–1470), these monuments consist of spaces that may have served to segregate people during rituals. By contrast, the view of the easternmost mound at Huancarpón has a high visual impact because of both the shape of the building and the adjacent natural slope. Consequently, the mound is highly visible from far away. It stands out as the most visually prominent example in our sample. At Huancarpón, the processional character of ritual activities is emphasized by the linear aspect of the site layout.

In summary, the analysis of the angles of incidence, isovistas, and surrounding architecture indicates that ritual performance and monument prominence varied from community to community in Nepeña during the first millennium BC. Some monuments were built to emphasize visibility and appreciation for their construction (e.g., Huaca Partida, Huancarpón east view). Others were designed to limit visual impact to surrounding populations (e.g., Cerro Blanco [Nepeña phase] and Samanco). And some monuments were built in such a way that a strong visual impact was partially obscured by adjacent rooms, walls, and corridors (e.g., Huambacho, Caylán, Paredones, Kushipampa, Virahuanca Bajo). Some ritual spaces were built to guide processional ceremonies (e.g., Huancarpón and Cerro Blanco [Nepeña phase]), while others had a spatial arrangement that segregated groups into hierarchically distributed spaces (e.g., Caylán, Kushipampa). Finally, while some buildings were designed to aggregate people in wide-open spaces (e.g., Paredones, Kushipampa, Huaca Partida, Cerro Blanco [Nepeña phase]), others emphasized spatial seclusion and fragmentation (e.g., Huambacho, Caylán, Samanco).

Monument Visibility, Territoriality, and Religio-Political Organization

A total of eleven structures from nine sites are considered in this analysis. Results (see table 6.2, figures 6.7, 6.8) indicate clear variability in the patterns of visibility of Formative period centers. At one end of the spectrum, Caylán's Mound-A and Huaca Partida, especially in the Nepeña phase, are located in areas of high visibility, even from afar. Indeed, the ratios of 0.60 and 0.62, respectively, mean that between 38 percent and 40 percent of the surrounding areas from where the sites and their main monuments are visible are farther than 7 km.

At the other end of the spectrum, the site of Samanco (0.98) was mainly visible to local people while at the same time almost invisible to viewers located beyond the 7 km threshold. Here, we must caution that the location of the settlement near the littoral zone limits the amount of space from where people can stand to look at monuments. Also, Samanco is the only site in our sample bounded on three sides by hills. This is potentially related to defensive concerns by settlement planners.

Overall, the majority of sites included in our analysis have between 60 percent and 79 percent of their visibility areas within 7 km. This is significant for several reasons. First, it suggests that most sites and their associated monuments were designed and built to enhance social cohesion at the local level. This is particularly significant for the upper valley communities, where no site appears more visible than the others beyond the threshold of 7 km. Second, it reinforces the relationship between Caylán and Huaca Partida as centers with monuments designed to broadcast messages beyond their respective immediate vicinity during the Nepeña phase. Caylán and Huaca Partida were competing for supporters through the manipulation of public monuments. This is evidenced by the sharp contrast between the ideological messages and their likely opposing religious views of the world (Shibata 2014). A look at visibility maps for the upper and lower sections of the valley strengthens these two points.

It appears that the Caylán, Huambacho, and Samanco communities, who shared similar forms of ritual structures and religious imageries, maintained strong ties through mutually complementary visibility of the entire lower valley (overlapping of 7%) (see table 6.3, figure 6.7). At the same time, a comparison of the combined visibility of the monuments at Caylán and Huaca Partida with that at Cerro Blanco indicates a significant overlap (51%). Considering the marked contrast in the forms of religious structures and ritual paraphernalia between Caylán and Huaca Partida, these two centers can be interpreted as indicating the existence of competing communities. Finally, in the upper

TABLE 6.2. Total area from which the monuments are visible under the two proposed thresholds for analysis (7.07 km and 10 km)

Site/Monument	Land Area (km²) with Visibility of the Monument		Ratio A/B
	A: r = 7.07 km	B: r = 10 km	
Samanco	16.07	16.43	0.98
Huambacho	32.48	42.15	0.77
Caylán Mound-A	34.02	56.35	0.60
Huaca Partida	32.02	51.53	0.62
Cerro Blanco	56.77	78.84	0.72
Virahuanca Bajo	17.72	27.49	0.64
Paredones	36.27	49.88	0.73
Kushipampa	27.94	41.65	0.67
Huancarpón	22.30	28.12	0.79

Credit: Hugo Ikehara

valley, the sample of four centers shows moderate overlapping viewsheds (34%), describing a similar competitive political landscape as that in the lower valley (see figure 6.8). For the upper valley, the cases under study represent a limited sample of a larger site population. Considering the remaining potential ceremonial centers located close to each other, the relatively small Moro Pocket probably displays a higher degree of visual overlap than our data suggest.

CONCLUSION

In this chapter we have developed a comparative approach to investigate the design, perception, and visibility of public religious monuments in the Nepeña Valley during the Formative period. By building on Moore's study of isovistas and the use of monumentality as a religio-political strategy of authority, we have demonstrated that leaders, architects, and builders in Nepeña were using ceremonial monuments as tools for multiple purposes, including social control, political integration, and inter-communal competition. In addition, we have used GIS to quantify the visibility of ceremonial buildings on the Nepeña landscape. Overall, our contribution highlights the complexity of the geopolitical strategy in Nepeña, especially through the demise of the Chavín- and Cupisnique-related imageries during the Cerro Blanco phase and into the Nepeña and Samanco phases. The study echoes other contributions in this volume and emphasizes the value of ritual settings and religious monuments

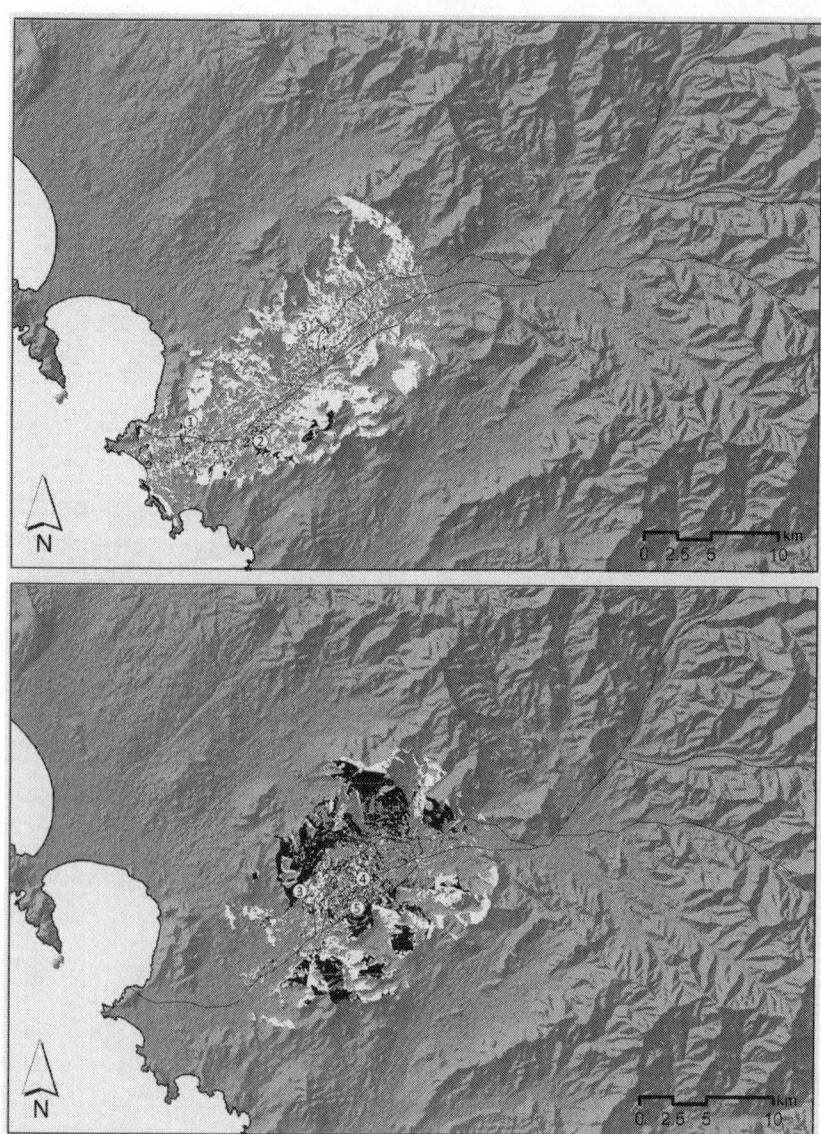

FIGURE 6.7. *Maps showing the combined visibility from/of the monuments at (*top*) Samanco, Huambacho, and Caylán's Mound-A (1, 2, and 3, respectively) and (*bottom*) Caylán's Mound-A, Cerro Blanco, and Huaca Partida (3, 4, and 5, respectively). Topography is represented in gray tones, surface area from where only one monument is visible is indicated in white, and area from where more than one monument is visible is indicated in black.* Courtesy, *Hugo Ikehara.*

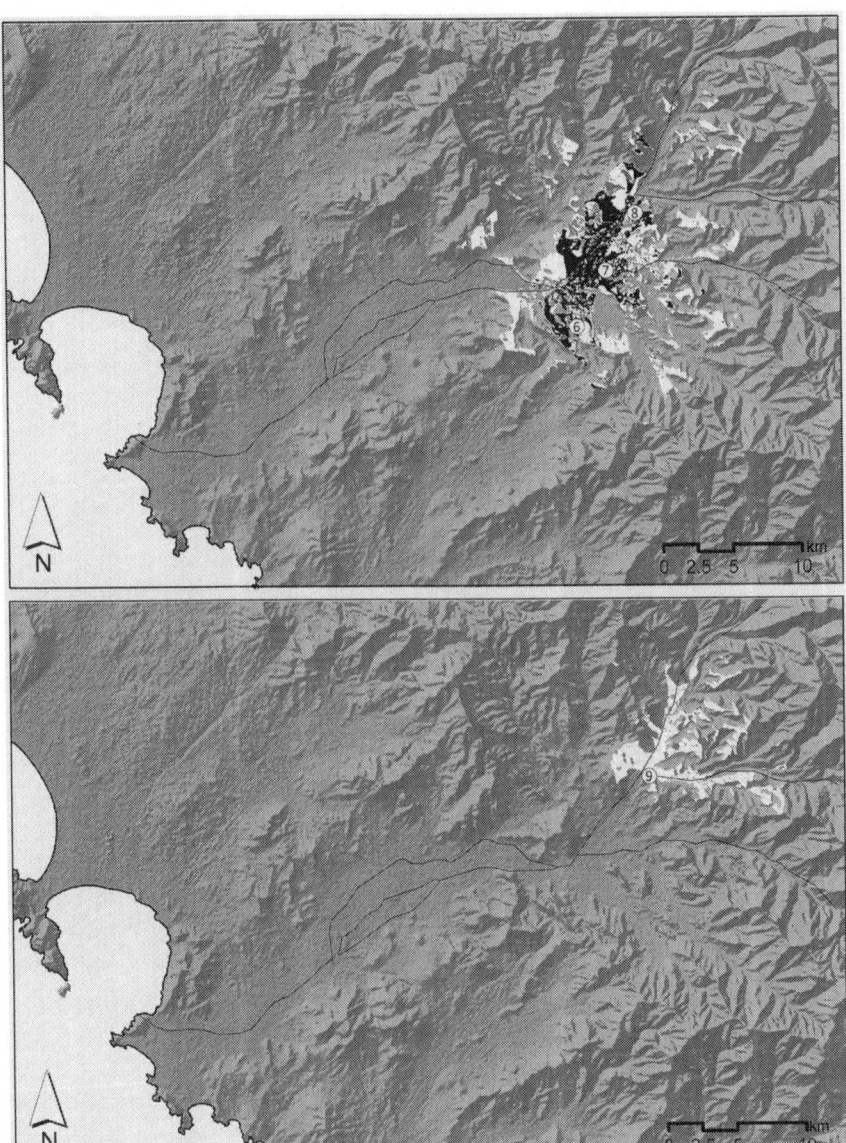

FIGURE 6.8. *Maps showing the combined visibility from/of the monuments at (top) Virahuanca Bajo, Paredones, and Kushipampa (6, 7, and 8, respectively) and (bottom) Huancarpón (9). Topography is represented in gray tones, land from where only one monument is visible is indicated in white, and land from where more than one monument is visible is indicated in black.* Courtesy, *Hugo Ikehara.*

TABLE 6.3. Results of GIS analysis of multiple visibilities of monuments in different cases. Case 1 includes Samanco, Huambacho, and Caylán Mound-A; Case 2 includes Caylán Mound-A, Cerro Blanco, and Huaca Partida; and Case 3 includes Virahuanca Bajo, Paredones, and Kushipampa. The numbers represent percentages.

# of Visible Monuments	Case 1	Case 2	Case 3
1	0.92	0.49	0.66
2	0.08	0.35	0.24
3	0.00	0.16	0.09
Total	1	1	1
% overlapping	7	51	34

Credit: Hugo Ikehara

as active social and political agents (Abraham; Contreras; Rick; Vega-Centeno Sara-Lafosse, this volume).

In the lower Nepeña Valley, the integration of most of the plain's communities is evidenced during the Cerro Blanco phase and potentially the Huambocayán phase as seen through the construction of Punkurí. During that time groups coalesced at elaborate mound centers (e.g., Cerro Blanco, Huaca Partida) where platform structures were decorated with colorful friezes depicting supernatural beings. The analysis of isovistas indicates that the buildings of this architectural style were designed to impress large audiences and viewers located beyond the immediate architectural precinct. Evidently, religio-political leaders went to great lengths to reach believers and ritual participants beyond the immediate vicinity of the ceremonial complex.

During the ninth and eighth centuries BC, Nepeña communities underwent major transformations, including settlement and shifts in farming practices, building traditions, and religious messages. While the cause for these changes remains unclear, it is apparent that some groups, possibly dissidents from the large religio-political agglomerations, resettled on the valley margins and used strikingly different ideas of community planning, space, and ritual life. Innovations are particularly salient at the level of ceremonial architecture and public monuments. Isovistas indicate a marked concern toward increased control and exclusivity over ritual spaces and performances. Clearly, the design of the public monuments (e.g., Caylán's Mound-A, Kushipampa, Samanco's Plaza Mayor) was tailored toward smaller groups of ritual participants who had access to the buildings' most sacred spaces.

Our GIS analysis of combined viewsheds from which a group of monuments can be seen further adds to these observations by informing on the regional context in which each building was placed and designed to be seen by ritual participants and competitors. Three striking observations can be made based on the GIS analysis. First, the overlap in Cerro Blanco's, Huaca Partida's, and Caylán's visibilities suggests that the sites were competing for supporters, most likely at the end of the Cerro Blanco phase and the beginning of the Nepeña phase. This interpretation is supported by the markedly contrasting religious iconographies and ritual practices documented at Cerro Blanco/Huaca Partida and Caylán. Further, Caylán is currently interpreted as the primary center of complex regional polity that developed during the Nepeña phase until the end of the Samanco phase and beyond. Second, our GIS analysis indicates that the Caylán, Huambacho, and Samanco visual areas complement each other, with minimum overlapping and covering a maximum of territory, reinforcing their integration into a single political entity. Third, the upper valley (or Moro Pocket) represents a completely independent system that contrasts in terms of both settlement pattern and monumental architecture. Here, sites were exclusively located on mountain ridge tops, with monuments meant to be visible to neighboring viewers. At the same time, our viewshed analysis indicates that Huancarpón stood as a center independent from the Kushipampa, Paredones, and Virahuanca Bajo geopolitical system. Huancarpón appears to have been tailored to the needs of communities closer to the Jimbe drainage, beyond the Moro Pocket and the Loco and Salitre tributaries.

Our combined research on the Formative period in Nepeña brings new and significant insights into the diversity and complexity of ritual practice and its materialization during that crucial time frame (see also Contreras, this volume). In this chapter we have adopted a perceptual and geographic approach to understand the design and impact of religious buildings in the life of human communities in ancient Peru. Religious practices and their associated monuments, because of their power over collective actions and memories, are especially attractive tools for social control and political integration. Here, we have demonstrated that multiple strategies were at play in Nepeña. Through the close examination of architectural designs and patterns of monumental visibility, this chapter exemplifies the need to study ritual practices and their associated sociopolitical meanings in the development of complex societies in the ancient Andes.

REFERENCES CITED

Burger, R. L. 1981. "The Radiocarbon Evidence of the Temporal Priority of Chavín de Huántar." *American Antiquity* 46 (3): 592–601. http://dx.doi.org/10.2307/280603.

Burger, R. L. 1992. *Chavín and the Origins of Andean Civilization.* New York: Thames and Hudson.

Burger, R. L. 2008. "Chavín de Huántar and Its Sphere of Influence." In *Handbook of South American Archaeology*, ed. H. Silverman and W. Isbell, 681–703. New York: Springer. http://dx.doi.org/10.1007/978-0-387-74907-5_35.

Burger, R. L., and L. Salazar-Burger. 2008. "The Manchay Culture and the Coastal Inspiration for Highland Chavín Civilization." In *Chavín: Art, Architecture, and Culture*, ed. W. J. Conklin and J. Quilter, 85–105. Monograph 61. Los Angeles: Cotsen Institute of Archaeology, University of California.

Chicoine, D. 2006. "Early Horizon Architecture at Huambacho, Nepeña Valley, Peru." *Journal of Field Archaeology* 31 (1): 1–22. http://dx.doi.org/10.1179/009346906791072070.

Chicoine, D. 2011. "Feasting Landscapes and Political Economy at the Early Horizon Center of Huambacho, Nepeña Valley, Peru." *Journal of Anthropological Archaeology* 30 (3): 432–53. http://dx.doi.org/10.1016/j.jaa.2011.06.003.

Chicoine, D., and H. Ikehara. 2010. "Nuevas evidencias sobre el Período Formativo del valle de Nepeña: Resultados preliminares de la primera temporada de investigaciones en Caylán." *Boletín de Arqueología PUCP* 12: 349–70.

Chicoine, D., and H. Ikehara. 2014. "Ancient Urban Life in the Nepeña Valley, North-Central Coast of Peru: Investigations at the Early Horizon Center of Caylán." *Journal of Field Archaeology* 39 (4): 336–52. http://dx.doi.org/10.1179/0093469014Z.00000000094.

Conolly, J., and M. Lake. 2006. *Geographic Information Systems in Archaeology.* Cambridge Manuals in Archaeology. Cambridge: Cambridge University Press. http://dx.doi.org/10.1017/CBO9780511807459.

Daggett, R. E. 1983. "Megalithic Sites in the Nepeña Valley, Peru." In *Investigations of the Andean Past*, ed. D. H. Sandweiss, 75–97. Ithaca, NY: Cornell University Latin American Studies Program.

Daggett, R. E. 1984. "The Early Horizon Occupation of the Nepeña Valley, North Central Coast of Peru." PhD dissertation, Department of Anthropology, University of Massachusetts, Amherst.

Daggett, R. E. 1987. "Toward the Development of the State on the North Central Coast of Peru." In *The Origins and Development of the Andean State*, ed. H. Haas, S. Pozorski, and T. Pozorski, 70–82. Cambridge: Cambridge University Press.

Druc, I. C. 1998. *Ceramic Production and Distribution in the Chavín Sphere of Influence.* Bar International Series 731. Oxford: British Archaeological Reports.

Helmer, M. and D. Chicoine. 2015. "Seaside Life in Early Horizon Peru: Preliminary Insights from Samanco, Nepeña Valley." *Journal of Field Archaeology* 40 (6): 626–43.

Helmer, M., D. Chicoine, and H. Ikehara. 2012. "Plaza Life and Public Performance at the Early Horizon Center of Caylán, Nepeña Valley, Peru." *Ñawpa Pacha: Journal of Andean Archaeology* 32 (1): 85–114.

Higuchi, T. 1983. *The Visual and Spatial Structure of Landscape*. Cambridge, MA: MIT Press.

Ikehara, H. 2010. "Kushipampa: El final del Período Formativo en el valle de Nepeña." *Boletín de Arqueología PUCP* 12: 371–404.

Ikehara, H., and D. Chicoine. 2011. "Hacia una revaluación de Salinar a partir de la evidencia del Formativo Final en Nepeña, costa de Ancash." In *Arqueología de la Costa de Ancash*, ed. M. Giersz and I. Ghezzi, 153–84. ANDES Boletín del Centro de Estudios Precolombinos de la Universidad de Varsovia 8. Warsaw and Lima: Centro de Estudios Precolombinos de la Universidad de Varsovia / Institut Français d'Études Andines. http://dx.doi.org/10.4000/books.ifea.7367.

Ikehara, H., and K. Shibata. 2008. "Festines e integración social en el Período Formativo: Nuevas evidencias de Cerro Blanco, valle bajo de Nepeña." *Boletín de Arqueología PUCP* 9: 123–59.

Kaulicke, P., ed. 1998. *Perspectivas Regionales del Período Formativo en el Perú*. Boletín de Arqueología PUCP 2. Lima: Pontificia Universidad Católica del Perú.

Kaulicke, P., ed. 2010. *Las cronologías del Formativo 50 años de investigaciones japonesas en perspectiva*. Lima: Fondo Editorial de la Pontificia Universidad Católica del Perú.

Lumbreras, L. G. 1993. *Chavín de Huántar: excavaciones en la Galería de las Ofrendas*. Materialien zur allgemeinen und vergleichenden Archäologie, bd. 51. P. Mainz am Rhein: von Zabern.

MAAUNMSM. 2005. *Arqueología del Valle de Nepeña: Excavaciones en Cerro Blanco y Punkurí*. Lima: Museo de Arqueología y Antropología, Universidad Nacional Mayor de San Marcos (MAAUNMSM).

Moore, J. D. 1996a. "The Archaeology of Plazas and the Proxemics of Ritual: Three Andean Traditions." *American Anthropologist* 98 (4): 789–802. http://dx.doi.org/10.1525/aa.1996.98.4.02a00090.

Moore, J. D. 1996b. *Architecture and Power in the Ancient Andes: The Archaeology of Public Buildings*. New Studies in Archaeology. Cambridge: Cambridge University Press. http://dx.doi.org/10.1017/CBO9780511521201.

Onuki, Y. 1994. "Las actividades ceremoniales tempranas en la cuenca del alto Huallaga y algunos problemas generales." In *El Mundo Ceremonial Andino*, ed. L. Millones and Y. Onuki, 71–95. Lima: Editorial Horizonte.

Onuki, Y. 2001. "Una perspectiva del Período Formativo en la sierra norte del Perú." In *Historia de la Cultura Peruana*, vol. 1, 103–26. Lima: Fondo Editorial del Congreso del Perú.

Patterson, T. C. 1971. "Chavín: An Interpretation of Its Spread and Influence." In *Dumbarton Oaks Conference on Chavín*, ed. E. P. Benson, 29–48. Washington, DC: Dumbarton Oaks.

Pozorski, S., and T. Pozorski. 1987. *Early Settlement and Subsistence in the Casma Valley, Peru*. Iowa City: University of Iowa Press.

Proulx, D. A. 1968. *An Archaeological Survey of the Nepeña Valley, Peru*. Department of Anthropology Research Report 2. Amherst: University of Massachusetts.

Proulx, D. A. 1973. *Archaeological Investigations in the Nepeña Valley, Peru*. Department of Anthropology Research Report 13. Amherst: University of Massachusetts.

Proulx, D. A. 1982. "Territoriality in the Early Intermediate Period: The Case of Moche and Recuay." *Ñawpa Pacha: Journal of Andean Archaeology* 20 (1): 83–96. http://dx.doi.org/10.1179/naw.1982.20.1.005.

Proulx, D. A. 1985. *An Analysis of the Early Cultural Sequence in the Nepeña Valley, Peru*. Department of Anthropology Research Report 25. Amherst: University of Massachusetts.

Rick, J. W. 2008. "Context, Construction, and Ritual in the Development of Authority at Chavín de Huántar." In *Chavín: Art, Architecture, and Culture*, ed. W. J. Conklin and J. Quilter, 3–34. Monograph 61. Los Angeles: Cotsen Institute of Archaeology, University of California.

Rick, J. W., C. Mesía, D. A. Contreras, S. Kembel, R. Rick, M. Sayre, and J. Wolf. 2011. "La cronología de Chavín de Huántar y sus implicancias para el Período Formativo." *Boletín de Arqueología PUCP* 13: 87–132.

Shibata, K. 2010. "Cerro Blanco de Nepeña dentro de la dinámica interactiva del Período Formativo." *Boletín de Arqueología PUCP* 12: 287–315.

Shibata, K. 2011. "Cronología, relaciones interregionales y organización social en el Formativo: esencia y perspectiva del valle bajo de Nepeña." In *Arqueología de la Costa de Ancash*, ed. M. Giersz and I. Ghezzi, 113–34. ANDES Boletín del Centro de Estudios Precolombinos de la Universidad de Varsovia 8. Warsaw and Lima: Centro de Estudios Precolombinos de la Universidad de Varsovia / Institut Français d'Études Andines. http://dx.doi.org/10.4000/books.ifea.7365.

Shibata, K. 2014. "Centros de 'Reorganización costeña' durante el Formativo Tardío—un ensayo sobre la competencia faccional en el valle bajo de Nepeña, costa nor-central peruana." *Senri Ethnological Studies* 89: 245–60.

Swenson, E. R. 2011. "Stagecraft and the Politics of Spectacle in Ancient Peru." *Cambridge Archaeological Journal* 21 (2): 283–313. http://dx.doi.org/10.1017/S095977431100028X.

Tambiah, S. J. 1985. *Culture, Thought, and Social Action*. Cambridge, MA: Harvard University Press. http://dx.doi.org/10.4159/harvard.9780674433748.

Tello, J. C. 1939. "Sobre el descubrimiento de la cultura Chavín del Perú." *Proceedings of the 27th International Congress of Americanists* 1: 231–52.

Tello, J. C. 1943. "Discovery of the Chavín Culture in Perú." *American Antiquity* 9 (1): 135–60. http://dx.doi.org/10.2307/275457.

Willey, G. R. 1951. "The Chavín Problem: A Review and Critique." *Southwestern Journal of Anthropology* 7 (2): 103–44. http://dx.doi.org/10.1086/soutjanth.7.2.3 628619.

7

Ritual Practice at the End of Empire

Evidence of an Abandonment Ceremony from Pataraya, a Wari Outpost on the South Coast of Peru

Matthew J. Edwards

This chapter reports on evidence for the planned abandonment of Pataraya, a small Wari installation in the Nasca Valley of the south coast of Peru, at around AD 950, just as the Wari Empire itself began to collapse. Pataraya encompasses a well-planned architectural core built in the repetitive, rectilinear style typical of provincial Wari administrative buildings. Several complimentary lines of evidence suggest a detailed, if not particularly elaborate, sequence of closing rituals. They consist of burned offerings, smashed pottery, and obstructed passageways in addition to evidence for intentional, though shallow, burial of many of the site's internal spaces. Because Pataraya's controlled pattern of access limits travel within the enclosure, the obstructed passageways suggest that these events occurred sequentially. Such a processional ceremony may reflect culturally constructed concepts of how living and ritual spaces should be abandoned and suggests that while the Wari collapse generally may have been attended by increased violence, vandalism, and ecological calamities, Pataraya was simply carefully abandoned and then quietly forgotten. Therefore, the mechanics of the procession itself contributed to the archaeological detection of this rather specific rite, as opposed to simply noting potential ritualized behavior when more mundane explanations fall short.

Ritual is a term used frequently in the social sciences, and it is often employed to describe a wide range of human activities, from the relatively quotidian to the

DOI: 10.5876/9781607325963.c007

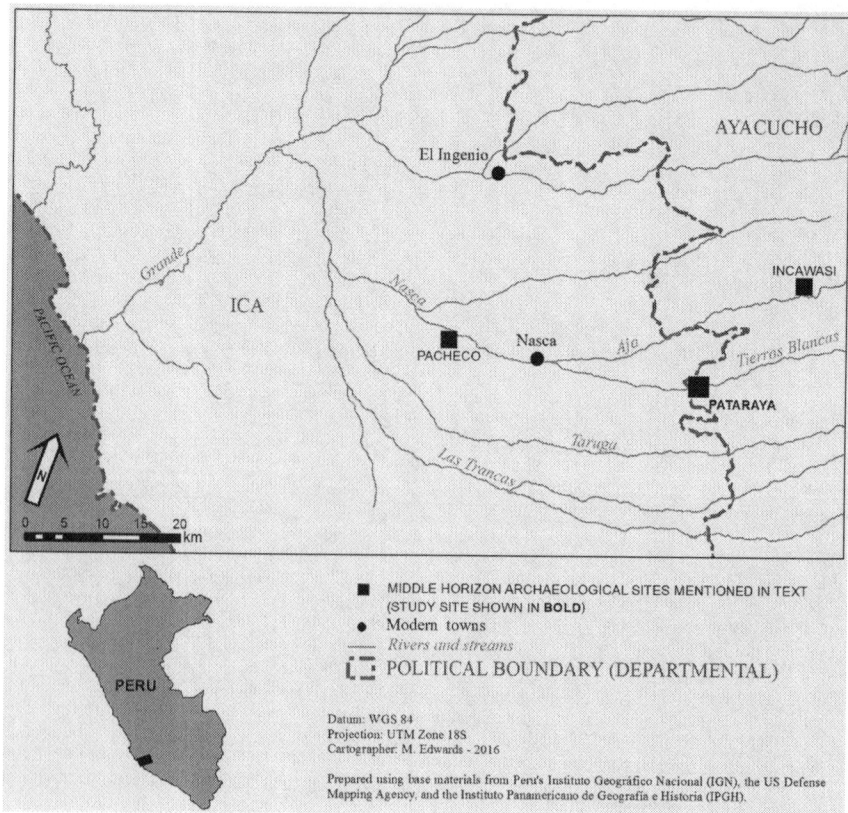

FIGURE 7.1. *Location map*

highly ceremonial, so it is worthwhile to state upfront how the term is used in this chapter (Bradley 2005:3–10; Insoll 2004:10). Although it is generally accepted that ritual activities and performances can play a role in virtually all aspects of life, this chapter differs from most of the contributions to this volume by emphasizing the role of rituals associated with the state as a tool of governance over their role as "the behavioral aspect of religion" (Nielsen, Angiorama, and Avila, this volume). This is not always an easy—or even necessary—distinction to make, as most pre-modern (and many modern) states were probably built, to one degree or another, on concepts of divine right. In this sense, then, the politics at play in state rites have many of the same dynamics as religious rituals—this similarity is perhaps the source for many archaeologists' preference of the term *ideology* over *religion* (Insoll 2004:2).

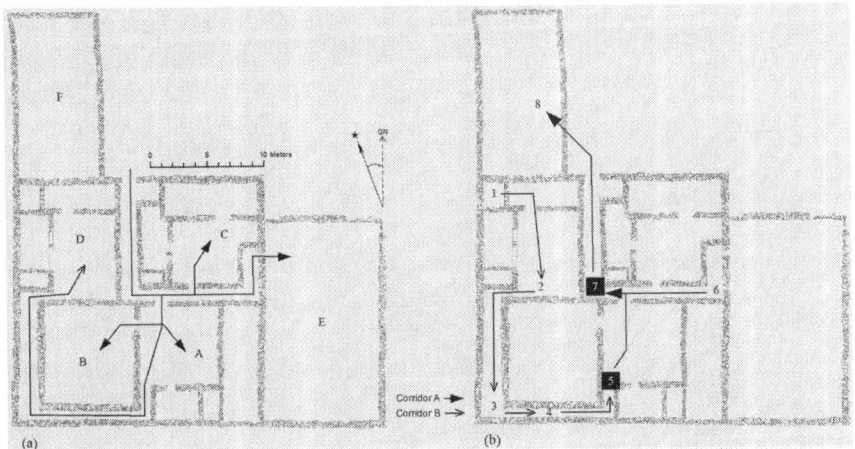

FIGURE 7.2. *Access and circulation within the Pataraya enclosure (a) between major use areas during occupation and (b) during abandonment activities described in the chapter*

These dynamics can be explored from a number of perspectives (Dietler 2001:69–75). Traditionally, religion—and, by extension, ideology—has been viewed in light of its integrative and social reproductive functions (Durkheim 2001 [1912]:313–14; Turner 1967:30). The principal critique of this view has come largely from materialists, especially those with Marxist leanings, who tend to view ideology as a tool of the powerful to mystify and obfuscate unequal social relations (Althusser 1971:133; Marx and Engels 1999:58–59). Interestingly, despite the obvious differences in these two perspectives, both see ideology as a largely conservative force that emphasizes and reproduces cultural and social norms (Weber 1999:120–22). Most current researchers, however, view ideology and its attendant rituals as both reproductive and transformative (see, e.g., Dietler 2001:71; Gose 1994:254; Insoll 2004:81).

In this view the transformative aspect of ritual lies in an expanded understanding of Marx's insight: that ritual offers the potential for manipulation to meet political ends (ibid.:54; Patterson 2004:66). However, in this more nuanced perspective, different classes, factions, and individuals all have the ability, to a greater or lesser extent, to manipulate shared ideas (Dietler 2001:72). The analysis presented in this chapter also emphasizes the emotionality of ritual and its ability to express an idealized sense of how the world ought to be, even as that ideal is filtered through the specific political, economic, and even psychological needs and aspirations of its participants (Gose 1994:4; Turner 1967:54). This emotive component of ritual can also be linked to the governmental goals of the state (see Stepputat 2004:258 for a modern example).

With these ideas in mind, this chapter reports on a series of features encountered during excavations at the archaeological site of Pataraya that likely represent the remains of a highly ritualized abandonment ceremony (also see Edwards 2010:448–58). The site is located along the Tierras Blancas River, one of two tributaries forming the Nasca River, at an elevation of about 1,300 m (figure 7.1). Pataraya is located in an ecologically transitional zone on the western face of the Andes mountains, roughly halfway between the coastal plain of Nasca and the highland peaks, plains, and valleys of Ayacucho. Though small, Pataraya encompasses a well-planned architectural core that consists of a walled enclosure organized by the regular division of interior space into more or less square patios surrounded by long, narrow rooms and corridors (figure 7.2). This distinctive architectural style is repeated at contemporaneous archaeological sites throughout the Andes and is, alongside distinctive portable artifacts, diagnostic of Wari culture. Although the site also includes agricultural, mortuary, and road segments, the main enclosure was the locus of the activities discussed here. Absolute dates recovered from such sites across the Andes have situated the Wari phenomenon within a period from around AD 650 to 1000 (Finucane et al. 2007:582–87; Tung 2007:263–64). ^{14}C dates from Pataraya match this span well, ranging from ca. cal AD 670–990 (yrs ± 2σ; see Edwards 2010:205–7; Edwards and Schreiber 2014:224–26). The site was the focus of archaeological research into the Wari occupation of the mid- to upper Nasca drainage that included extensive excavation at Pataraya, survey of the upper valley, and more limited excavation at other Middle Horizon sites discovered during the survey.

ARCHAEOLOGICAL CONTEXT

Pacific coastline topography of south coastal Peru's Ica province has resulted in a drainage pattern for the Río Grande de Nasca Basin that is unique in the Central Andes. Impeded in their journey to the ocean by an ancient coastal range, the basin's rivers merge on the desert coastal plain to form a single stream before emptying into the ocean (Garayar et al. 2003:127–30). As a result, and unlike the North and Central Coasts where human occupation spreads out along the littoral as well as along the river valleys, settlement in the Río Grande de Nasca Basin is focused well inland of the shoreline and nearer the Andean slope. A general pattern of decreasing discharge from north to south is observed for the rivers of the basin, resulting from smaller headwaters

TABLE 7.1. Major use areas during occupation, keyed to figure 7.2(a)

A	Food preparation
B	Commensal politics
C	Administrative activities
D	Residential area
E	Secondary deposits
F	Work area

TABLE 7.2. Abandonment features and activities, keyed to figure 7.2(b)

1	Cache/offering placed/commemorated
2	Offering burned/vessels smashed
3	Offering burned
4	Vessels smashed
5	Passageway blocked
6	Vessels smashed/offering burned
7	Passageway blocked
8	Commemoration/vessels smashed

and fewer tributaries for the southern streams (ONERN 1971:265). The northern rivers—Grande, Palpa, Viscas, and Ingenio—tend to flow year-round, whereas the southern Aja, Tierras Blancas, Taruga, and Trancas have low water volumes and intermittent flow. Farming and permanent settlement of the middle stretches of these valleys is made possible by an ancient system of filtration gallery aqueducts, knows as *puquios*, that were likely first built during the mid- to late Early Intermediate Period (after ca. AD 450) (Schreiber and Lancho Rojas 1995:250). In contrast, river water is generally available in the upper portions of these valleys above about 1,200 meters above sea level (masl).

The Río Grande de Nasca Basin is well-known to archaeologists as the home of the Nasca culture (ca. AD 1–650). Although Nasca was interpreted as a pristine state by early researchers, current evidence suggests a loose confederation of chiefdoms, with regional integration between valleys focused on a shared ideological universe during earlier times that appears to have shifted toward increased competition, strife, and even warfare during the Middle and Late Nasca phases (Schreiber 1998:263; Silverman and Proulx 2002:253; Vaughn 2009:3–5). Nasca religion and ideology is expressed archaeologically in the ruins of important ceremonial sites like Cahuachi, the lines and geoglyphs the

Nasca etched onto the desert plain, and their elaborate ceramics—decorated with complex designs executed in a rich color palette made from mineral pigments (Vaughn et al. 2007:18). The latter influenced the development of Wari culture in the highlands, and a close technological and iconographic relationship between Nasca and Wari ceramics has been recognized since the early days of Wari scholarship (Knobloch 1991:248–50; Menzel 1964:9–10).

Pataraya is not the only Wari site in the Nasca drainage. The much-better-known site Pacheco is located along the Nasca River about 30 km to the west and downstream of Pataraya on the coastal plain. Unfortunately, that site, which was excavated in the 1930s and yielded many of the diagnostic ceramics that led to the early identification of Wari styles, has been almost completely destroyed by modern agricultural activity (ibid.:23–25; Schreiber 1999:168–69). We also recorded another site, known as Incawasi, during project surveys of the high-elevation headwaters of the Nasca River's other main tributary, the Aja—about 20 km northeast of Pataraya (Edwards and Schreiber 2014:226–28; Schreiber and Edwards 2010:161). In addition to this presence in Nasca, Wari architecture and artifacts are found throughout Peru. This observation led the period of Wari influence in the Andes to be demarcated in the standard Andean chronology, one of New World archaeology's oldest, as the Middle Horizon—even before the site of Huari, the namesake for the stylistic horizon, was identified as the center of diffusion for Middle Horizon cultural markers (Isbell and McEwan 1991:6–7). While Wari sites in the Huamanga Basin of northern Ayacucho, such as Huari itself, have earlier antecedents, Wari sites outside the core are intrusive, unlike anything preceding them in their respective regions, leading most scholars working at these sites to interpret them as administrative outposts of an expansionist state centered in Ayacucho (e.g., ibid.; Lumbreras 1974; Menzel 1964, among others). Such is certainly the case for Pataraya, which was planned and built all at once on previously unoccupied land and inhabited by ethnically foreign residents for virtually the entire span of Wari dominance in Nasca and the Andes, then abandoned as that dominance waned and the Wari system collapsed (see Santley, Yarborough, and Hall 1987 for a discussion of such ethnic enclaves). The events at the moment of this abandonment are the subject of the remainder of this chapter.

ARCHAEOLOGY OF PATARAYA

Wari Pataraya consists of a main enclosure that measures roughly 20 m on a side and is defined by a double-faced, rubble-filled masonry wall with two additional rectangular enclosures appended to it (see figure 7.2). The square space inscribed by the enclosure wall is divided into four quadrants that themselves are subdivided into patios surrounded on their perimeters by long, narrow rooms called galleries—some of which are further subdivided to form smaller rooms—and corridors. Analysis of wall joining patterns indicates that the site was built according to a preconceived plan in which the square outer enclosure wall was built first, then it was divided into four quadrants, and, finally, each of these quadrants was subdivided into patio groups. Two rectangular constructions were added to the main block and match its orientation: a large enclosure abutting the structure to the east and another, smaller one to the north. Construction technique for the larger eastern addition is as robust as the main enclosure, and it is also incorporated into the site's overall system of communication, whereas the smaller addition has low walls and is the only sector that can be entered without first passing through the main enclosure's single entrance.

To evaluate the strength of the inferences made here, it is important to highlight two salient points about site formation: stratigraphic deposition and spatial organization, paying attention to the "taphonomy of ritual evidence" (Rick, this volume). Because of its location on an arid valley bench above the narrow Tierras Blancas River, soil formation at the site is practically nonexistent, as are disturbances from vegetation and burrowing animals. The resulting stratigraphic sequence is therefore relatively simple, consisting of the natural basal layer that underlies the landform, the cultural strata, and a post-abandonment cap of wind-deposited sediments. Except in midden, the cultural strata consist of thin layers of artifacts, features, and, in some places, soot atop prepared floors and sub-floors. A thin layer of sand, which appears to have been taken from the nearby river, covers the occupation level inside Pataraya's architectural core and marks a clear cessation of Middle Horizon cultural activity at the site. Because all the evidence for cultural activity at the site is compressed into a thin artifact-bearing stratum, inferences about the sequence of events attending abandonment depend largely on Pataraya's architectural plan and, specifically, the consequences of that plan for communication between sectors of the site.

As mentioned, Pataraya's architectural plan closely follows the tenets of the Wari architectural canon, and excavations at other Wari sites have demonstrated a profound concern with controlled and restricted access by Wari architects and builders (Spickard 1983:139–40). Because a large percentage of Pataraya's living surface could be exposed as a result of the enclosure's relatively small size, we have a complete understanding of access into and communication within the enclosure—a prerequisite for effective access analysis (Cutting 2003:5). The main enclosure at Pataraya has a single entrance located along the north wall (see figure 7.2; table 7.1). Entering the enclosure, the visitor travels south along a walled corridor (Corridor A) toward a blind corner before making a 90° left turn to the east. After this turn an entrance into Patio Group A opens on the right; a little further along, another entrance into Patio Group C opens on the left. From here, Patio Group A serves as a node for access to the rest of the main enclosure. Patio B can be entered using a doorway in the wall that separates the two adjoining sectors. In the southwest corner of Patio Group A is another doorway. This one enters Corridor B, formed by the space between the main enclosure wall and the wall that encloses Patio B. A visitor walking this corridor travels almost 50 m around the perimeter of Patio B, making three blind turns, before entering Patio Group D. For the purposes of this chapter, the most important point of this discussion is that this pattern of access allows extremely limited choices for travel within the site (for a more in-depth discussion, see Edwards 2013:568–74). Specifically, from Patio Group D, in space syntax terms the "deepest" part of the site, one can only exit the enclosure by passing through Corridor B, Patio Group A, and Corridor A (see discussions in Hillier, Hanson, and Graham 1987:364–65; Stockett 2005:389; Vega-Centeno Sara-Lafosse, this volume, for more information on space syntax analyses).

Use of Space at Pataraya during the Middle Horizon

Use of space within the enclosure is highly segregated, matching the hierarchical system of internal communication just described (see figure 7.2). Excavations in Patio A and the galleries of the southeast quadrant revealed the site's only evidence for extensive cooking and food preparation, as indicated by a thick secondary deposit of domestic and cooking fire refuse in the east gallery, a kitchen and food storage area or granary in the south gallery, and an area for milling grains found in the corner of the patio formed by the two galleries. A large groundstone slab, or *batán*, found here is the only one recorded at the site, further indicating centralized food production (see Goldstein 2008:39; Nash 2002:51). There is also evidence that guinea pigs, or *cuy*, a common source of animal protein and fat in the Andes, were raised in Patio Group A as evidenced by apparent pens and an abundance of coprolite in flotation samples (Andrews 1972:129; Rosenfeld 2008:128).

The most substantial and dense site furniture was found in the northern gallery of Patio Group C, located immediately across from Patio Group A in the northeast quadrant of the enclosure. This furniture consists of two freestanding platforms on one end of the gallery and a substantial bench on the other.

Artifacts and macrobotanical remains recovered here, while similar to those found in Patio Group A, suggest a different function for Patio Group C and its two galleries. Food remains were recovered here, as were sherds from serving vessels, but evidence of food preparation is absent. Broken but largely complete decorated vessels recovered from wall rubble suggest that they rested in niches. In addition to food remains and culinary equipment, spindle whorls (though not as many as in Patio Group A) and a comparatively high density of lithic debitage found in the patio suggest that domestic activities occurred here as well, but the focus may have been related to other activities including administrative duties, as evidenced by the elaborate furnishings of the north gallery.

The northwest quadrant of the enclosure—Patio Group D and its two galleries—can be considered the most remote area of the site (see figure 7.2). Although somewhat impacted by a brief reoccupation of the space that occurred during the Late Intermediate Period, the site's best-preserved and most elaborate artifacts were recovered here. Most of these artifacts were recovered from a cache of decorated serving vessels, described in more detail below, found in a small room at the east end of the north gallery. Other richly decorated vessels were recovered from disturbed contexts in the main gallery and from wall fall, again suggesting the presence of niches. Unlike the other patio groups just discussed, this area has no furniture and very little evidence of domestic activity other than spinning, which appears to have been a nearly ubiquitous activity at the site (Edwards, Fernandini Parodi, and Alexandrino Ocaña 2008:91). Other than these materials and the intrusive reoccupation of this sector of the site, the area is devoid of artifacts or features, suggesting a residential area—an interpretation echoed by its extremely private setting within the communicational configuration of the site.

The southwest sector of the site, Patio B, has a unique architectural plan in addition to its specialized function. Organized as a single patio rather than a patio group, the interstitial area between the patio and Pataraya's perimeter wall that forms the gallery rooms of the other three sectors is instead used to create a narrow and circuitous corridor providing access to Patio Group D. The space also encloses a white, hard plaster floor that, other than the ubiquitous thin layer of sand used to bury the site at abandonment, was left to the archaeological record virtually spotless. A thick layer of clean fill raises and levels the surface of the plaster floor in what appears to have been a low spot in the original construction surface. The cloth-wrapped skeleton of a juvenile camelid was found below the fill in a shallow pit excavated into the subsoil—similar offerings have been documented in other Wari contexts (see, e.g., Cook 2001:147; Finucane 2005:14). These details, alongside the patio's proximity to the kitchen area of Patio A, suggest an area dedicated to commensal activity in which special ceremonies, rituals, parties, feasts, and other politically important activities—probably involving visitors to the site—occurred (Bray 2003:1–2; Dietler 2001:66–67; Jennings and Bowser 2009:4–9).

Excavations in the two rectangular additions appended to the main square recovered only generalized, secondary deposits of refuse—presumably originating in the main areas of the complex—from the more substantial of the two additions (E). However, a number of unique features were uncovered in the center of sector F, the low-walled rectangular addition that extends to the north. These features consist of two conjoined and well-built cylindrical stone masonry structures and a stone-lined channel to the south. While the channel has not yet been fully explored, this collection of features appears to have formed a drainage or water distribution and storage system. Artifact deposits suggest that the area was also used for various chores and industries, perhaps focused on those that require more space and open air than would have been available inside the enclosure. Most notable is chipped stone tool manufacture, which, while lightly ubiquitous throughout the site, may have been particularly concentrated in this area. A square stone-lined bin filled with obsidian waste flakes was found near the end of the field season, which could have been a receptacle for the hazardous remnant shards of volcanic glass.

Features Related to Pataraya's Abandonment

Ten features were recorded throughout the main enclosure that are stratigraphically contemporaneous with each other and with the thin cap of clean river sand that represents the last Middle Horizon cultural stratum at the site (see figure 7.2; table 7.2). Two of these are large stones, measuring approximately 0.6 m^3 and weighing ca. 50 kg, obstructing Corridors A and B. As discussed, these corridors provide all of the communication between sectors of the main enclosure. Because of the fact that once Corridor B was blocked, Patio Group D could no longer be entered, and once Corridor A was blocked, the entire enclosure was inaccessible, the placement of these obstructions suggests timing and directionality for the inferred events signaled by the remaining eight features. The first of these was also arguably the most dramatic find at the site, a cache of nine whole ceramic vessels carefully placed upside down atop the prepared floor of a small room in the farthest northwest corner of Patio Group D and buried in a matrix of white river sand and *Spondylus* (sp.) shell artifacts. Eight of the nine vessels are fine Wari or local Middle Horizon (Loro) styles; the remaining vessel is a miniature cooking pot. *Spondylus* shell is native to the warm Pacific Ocean waters off modern-day Ecuador and is known as a valuable trade item throughout most of Andean prehistory (Paulsen 1974:603–5).

Diagonally opposite the cache, against the wall in the southwest corner of Patio Group D, we found a pair of features consisting of a small charcoal/ash stain and a complete but smashed Wari-style ceramic jar. The ash feature appears to have been created by a single, small, low-intensity fire likely used to burn some kind of small offering, as modern Andeans are known to do historically and ethnographically with coca leaves, llama fat, corn, and similar items (Sillar 2009:374). Another smashed serving vessel/burned offering feature pairing was found alongside the edges of Corridor B. The offering was burned in the extreme southwest corner of the enclosure with the smashed vessel, a fine Wari-style cup, a few meters to the east along the passageway. A third smashed serving vessel/burned offering feature pairing was identified in the southeast corner of Corridor A. Finally, a great deal of smashed decorated pottery was found just outside the main enclosure in sector F, the low-walled rectilinear yard to the left of the entrance into the compound.

A thin layer of clean white river sand was also found covering most of the site's abandoned surfaces, including the features just described. There is no discernible stratigraphic break between this deposit and the surfaces it covers; nor is there any indication that the sediment was deposited by natural means. A stratum of naturally deposited aeolian sediment that is clearly different in color and composition from the river sand covering the abandoned living surfaces generally caps the entire site, including the modern surface of the landform outside the structure. While areas inside and outside the structure are subject to the same post-abandonment deposition processes, mainly aeolian, the river sand was documented only inside the structure (see Gay 1999:281). The nearest source for the sand is the Tierras Blancas River bed, located 250 m away in a relatively steeply scored channel—suggesting that the sand was carried manually to the site.

Radiocarbon samples recovered from the site demonstrate that Pataraya's abandonment is roughly co-terminus with generally accepted dates for the collapse of the Wari Empire. The latest radiocarbon sample recovered from Middle Horizon contexts at the site dates to cal AD 922 (median at 2σ, range is cal AD 807–990 [93.4%], µ = cal AD 912).[1] A clear cessation of significant cultural activity is evident after this date. While circumstantial, the close correlation between the latest dates from Pataraya and our best estimates for the collapse of the Wari Empire suggests that Pataraya's abandonment was directly related to the demise of Wari power in the Andes generally and in Nasca in particular.

DISCUSSION

This pattern of burned offerings, smashed pottery, intentional burial, and obstructed passageways appears to represent the final activities at the site as it was being abandoned, no later than AD 950 or so (see Capriata Estrada and López-Hurtado, this volume, for an interesting discussion of the relationship between terminal rituals involving intentional destruction and site abandonment). Evidence from throughout the Andes suggests that the Wari Empire had begun to show signs of stress by this time and had completely collapsed by the end of the eleventh century (Finucane et al. 2007:591). Because all communication within the site was afforded by a limited number of corridors and entryways, the placement of the offerings and obstructions suggests a sequential order to the events reported here, possibly indicating a procession of some kind (also see Chicoine et al., this volume). I posit that the hypothetical ritual described in the remainder of this chapter is a good inference from the available data.

In this scenario the performers of this final ritual at Patarayacarefully placed intact ceramic vessels on the floor of the remote room in the northwest corner of the enclosure and buried them in selected sand and *Spondylus* shell. They then burned an offering and smashed a large decorated jar, possibly containing a ceremonially important liquid such as corn beer, near the doorway into Corridor B before leaving Patio Group D. When they reached the southwest corner of the corridor, another offering was burned and, a few steps away, another vessel, this time a decorated bowl, was sacrificed. The performers then exited the corridor and blocked further entry by placing a large stone to obstruct passage—while too small to effectively prevent reentry, its placement would have communicated the area's closure to ceremony participants. A final offering was burned in the southeast corner of Corridor A, and yet more vessels were smashed. The performers then left the site for good by way of Corridor A and the enclosure's main entrance, again obstructing the route as they left. Finally, the last Wari inhabitants of Pataraya may have gathered outside the enclosure for a final round of corn beer served in the smashed vessels found there. Burial of the site's living surfaces in a thin layer of sand would also have accompanied this ritual performance. Such burial may express an attitude toward cleanliness related to culturally constructed concepts of how living and ritual spaces should be appropriately abandoned (Fernandini and Ruales, this volume). More labor-intensive efforts to bury sites at abandonment have been documented or can be suggested at other Wari sites (e.g., McEwan 2005:53; Williams and Nash 2002). However, at Pataraya, a smaller resident population may have engaged in an effort that was more symbolic than actual—with the thin layer of sand standing in for a more formal and adequate burial. Similarly, the stones obstructing the corridors, which are not terribly large, were perhaps placed to stand in for the more formal closures of doorways and access routes seen at other Wari sites.[2]

CONCLUSION

Returning to the place where this chapter started, these final ritual performances at Pataraya fit into a wider anthropological understanding of ritual generally and the political transformations of Andean prehistory specifically. I conclude by briefly discussing them in terms of their political context, their participants, and the meaning they held for those participants. Although Pataraya was very likely abandoned as a consequence of the Wari Empire's fading power and influence as it neared political collapse, the occupants of Pataraya do not seem to have been confronting those challenges, whatever they were, directly. While evidence from Wari sites in other regions suggests increased violence, vandalism, and ecological calamities, Pataraya appears to have been carefully abandoned and then quietly forgotten (cf. Arkush 2006:307; Tung 2008:115; Williams 2002:372). Pataraya is not the only Wari site to have been abandoned in this fashion, suggesting that the Wari collapse was not necessarily spectacular or sudden and may have been preceded by a period of strategic retreat (McEwan 2005:53; Moseley et al. 2005:17271; Williams and Nash 2002). Indeed, Pataraya's Wari residents may have believed they were leaving Nasca for a greater good. Given this wider political context and the nature of the archaeological data, the ceremony described here was probably a largely private affair, conducted by *and* for the site's ethnically Wari occupants. Echoes of similar ritual abandonments have been described at other known Wari sites, which suggests there was a Wari style or practice of closing sites. This is perhaps analogous to the lowering and folding of a country's flag before its embassy is closed today. During such an increasingly uncertain time for their empire, such traditions may have been particularly meaningful to the Wari at Pataraya as they prepared to leave Nasca for the last time.

ACKNOWLEDGMENTS

Thanks first and foremost to Katharina Schreiber, principal investigator for the project, and to the National Science Foundation (award no. 0612728). All work carried out in Peru was conducted under permits authorized by the Instituto Nacional de Cultura (INC) in Lima and supervised by the INC office in Ayacucho. Ana Cecilia Mauricio is thanked for her professionalism and expertise as project co-director during the excavations at Pataraya. Francesca Fernandini, Grace Alexandrino, Andrés Cuentas, Franco Mora, and Steve Wirtz helped with the excavations; and Patricia Chirinos Ogata served as laboratory director in Nasca. I would especially like to thank Victor Cantoral Alvarez, Gumercindo Sarmiento, and the rest of the residents of Ronquillo for their assistance in the field and their hospitality during our stay. Also, thanks to the editors of this volume, Stefanie Bautista and Silvana Rosenfeld, for organizing such an interesting symposium and for their hard work in preparing this volume, as well as to the discussant, Jerry Moore, and to two anonymous reviewers for their insightful comments.

NOTES

1. Dates were calibrated using OxCal v.4.1 (Bronk Ramsey 2009) and the IntCal04 calibration curve (Reimer et al. 2004).

2. See Moseley et al. (2005:17271) for discussion of a similar abandonment ceremony at Cerro Baúl, a contemporary Wari site located in the Moquegua Valley 500 km to the south.

REFERENCES CITED

Althusser, L. 1971. "Ideology and Ideological State Apparatuses (Notes towards an Investigation)." In *Lenin and Philosophy and Other Essays*, ed. L. Althusser, 127–76. New York: Monthly Review Press.

Andrews, D. H. 1972. "On the Ethnozoology of the Guinea Pig." *Ñawpa Pacha: Journal of Andean Archaeology* 10–12 (1): 129–34. http://dx.doi.org/10.1179/naw.1972.10-12.1.007.

Arkush, E. 2006. "Collapse, Conflict, Conquest: The Transformation of Warfare in the Late Prehispanic Andean Highlands." In *The Archaeology of Warfare: Prehistories of Raiding and Conquest*, ed. E. Arkush and M. W. Allen, 286–335. Gainesville: University Press of Florida.

Bradley, R. 2005. *Ritual and Domestic Life in Prehistoric Europe*. London: Routledge.

Bray, T. L. 2003. "The Commensal Politics of Early States and Empires." In *The Archaeology and Politics of Food and Feasting in Early States and Empires*, ed. T. L. Bray, 1–13. New York: Kluwer Academic/Plenum. http://dx.doi.org/10.1007/978-0-306-48246-5_1.

Bronk Ramsey, C. 2009. "Bayesian Analysis of Radiocarbon Dates." *Radiocarbon* 51 (1): 337–60. http://dx.doi.org/10.1017/S0033822200033865.

Cook, A. G. 2001. "Huari D-Shaped Structures, Sacrificial Offerings, and Divine Rulership." In *Ritual Sacrifice in Ancient Peru*, ed. E. P. Benson and A. G. Cook, 137–63. Austin: University of Texas Press.

Cutting, M. 2003. "The Use of Spatial Analysis to Study Prehistoric Settlement Architecture." *Oxford Journal of Archaeology* 22 (1): 1–21. http://dx.doi.org/10.1111/1468-0092.00001.

Dietler, M. 2001. "Theorizing the Feast: Rituals of Consumption, Commensal Politics, and Power in African Contexts." In *Feasts: Archaeological and Ethnographic Perspectives on Food, Politics, and Power*, ed. M. Dietler and B. Hayden, 65–114. Washington, DC: Smithsonian Institution Press.

Durkheim, É. 2001 [1912]. *The Elementary Forms of Religious Life*. New York: Oxford University Press.

Edwards, M. J. 2010. "Archaeological Investigations at Pataraya: A Wari Outpost in the Nasca Valley of Southern Peru." PhD dissertation, Department of Anthropology, University of California, Santa Barbara.

Edwards, M. J. 2013. "The Configuration of Built Space at Pataraya and Wari Provincial Administration in Nasca." *Journal of Anthropological Archaeology* 32 (4): 565–76. http://dx.doi.org/10.1016/j.jaa.2013.09.004.

Edwards, M. J., F. Fernandini Parodi, and G. A. Ocaña. 2008. "Decorated Spindle Whorls from Middle Horizon Pataraya." *Ñawpa Pacha: Journal of Andean Archaeology* 29 (1): 87–100. http://dx.doi.org/10.1179/naw.2008.29.1.002.

Edwards, M. J., and K. Schreiber. 2014. "Pataraya: The Archaeology of a Wari Outpost in Nasca." *Latin American Antiquity* 25 (2): 215–33. http://dx.doi.org/10.7183/1045-6635.25.2.215.

Finucane, B. C. 2005. "Isotopes and Animal Management at Conchopata, Peru." MA thesis, Research Laboratory for Archaeology and the History of Art, Oxford University, Oxford, England.

Finucane, B. C., J. E. Valdez, I. P. Calderon, C. V. Pomacanchari, L. M. Valdez, and T. O'Connell. 2007. "The End of Empire: New Radiocarbon Dates from the Ayacucho Valley, Peru, and Their Implications for the Collapse of the Wari State." *Radiocarbon* 49 (2): 579–92. http://dx.doi.org/10.1017/S003382220004248X.

Garayar, C., W. H. Wust, G. Coronado, and M. de Coronado Muñoz. 2003. *Atlas departamental del Perú: Imagen geográfica, estadística, histórica y cultural*. Lima: Publicada por el diario La República, en coedición con Peisa.

Gay, S. P., Jr. 1999. "Observations Regarding the Movement of Barchan Sand Dunes in the Nazca to Tanaca Area of Southern Peru." *Geomorphology* 27 (3–4): 279–93. http://dx.doi.org/10.1016/S0169-555X(98)00084-1.

Goldstein, R. C. 2008. "Hearths, Grinding Stones, and Households: Rethinking Domestic Economy in the Andes." In *Gender, Households, and Society: Unraveling the Threads of the Past and the Present*, ed. C. Robin and E. M. Brumfiel, 37–48. Archeological Papers of the American Anthropological Association, vol. 18. Washington, DC: American Anthropological Association. http://dx.doi.org/10.1111/j.1551-8248.2008.00003.x.

Gose, P. 1994. *Deathly Waters and Hungry Mountains: Agrarian Ritual and Class Formation in an Andean Town*. Toronto: University of Toronto Press.

Hillier, B., J. Hanson, and H. Graham. 1987. "Ideas Are in Things: An Application of the Space Syntax Method to Discovering House Genotypes." *Environment and Planning: B, Planning and Design* 14 (4): 363–85. http://dx.doi.org/10.1068/b140363.

Insoll, T. 2004. *Archaeology, Ritual, Religion: Themes in Archaeology*. London: Routledge.

Isbell, W., and G. F. McEwan. 1991. "A History of Huari Studies and Introduction to Current Interpretations." In *Huari Administrative Structure: Prehistoric Monumental Architecture and State Government*, ed. W. Isbell and G. F. McEwan, 1–17. Washington, DC: Dumbarton Oaks.

Jennings, J., and B. Bowser. 2009. "Drink, Power, and Society in the Andes: An Introduction." In *Drink, Power, and Society in the Andes*, ed. J. Jennings and B. Bowser, 1–27. Gainesville: University Press of Florida. http://dx.doi.org/10.5744/florida/9780813033068.003.0001.

Knobloch, P. J. 1991. "Stylistic Date of Ceramics from the Huari Centers." In *Huari Administrative Structure: Prehistoric Monumental Architecture and State Government*, ed. W. Isbell and G. F. McEwan, 247–58. Washington, DC: Dumbarton Oaks.

Lumbreras, L. G. 1974. *The Peoples and Cultures of Ancient Peru*. Washington, DC: Smithsonian Institution Press.

Marx, K., and F. Engels. 1999. "Feuerbach: Opposition of the Materialist and Idealist Outlook." In *Anthropological Theory: An Introductory History*, ed. R. J. McGee and R. L. Warms, 53–66. Mountain View, CA: Mayfield.

McEwan, G. F. 2005. "Excavations at Pikillacta." In *Pikillacta: The Wari Empire in Cuzco*, ed. G. F. McEwan, 29–62. Iowa City: University of Iowa Press.

Menzel, D. 1964. "Style and Time in the Middle Horizon." *Ñawpa Pacha: Journal of Andean Archaeology* 2 (1): 1–105. http://dx.doi.org/10.1179/naw.1964.2.1.001.

Moseley, M., D. J. Nash, P. R. Williams, S. D. deFrance, A. Miranda, and M. Ruales. 2005. "Burning Down the Brewery: Establishing and Evacuating an Ancient Imperial Colony at Cerro Baul, Peru." *Proceedings of the National Academy of Sciences of the United States of America* 102 (48): 17264–71. http://dx.doi.org/10.1073/pnas.0508673102.

Nash, D. 2002. "The Archaeology of Space: Places of Power in the Wari Empire." PhD dissertation, Department of Anthropology, University of Florida, Gainesville.

Oficina Nacional de Evaluación de Recursos Naturales (ONERN). 1971. *Inventario, evaluacion y uso racional de los recursos naturales de la costa: Cuenca del rio Grande.* Lima: Nazca.

Patterson, T. C. 2004. "Social Archaeology and Marxist Social Thought." In *A Companion to Social Archaeology*, ed. L. Meskell and R. Preucel, 66–81. Oxford: Blackwell.

Paulsen, A. C. 1974. "The Thorny Oyster and the Voice of God: Spondylus and Strombus in Andean Prehistory." *American Antiquity* 39 (4): 597–607. http://dx.doi.org/10.2307/278907.

Reimer, P. J., M.G.L. Baillie, E. Bard, A. Bayliss, J. W. Beck, C.J.H. Bertrand, P. G. Blackwell, C. E. Buck, G. S. Burr, K. B. Cutler et al. 2004. "IntCal04 Terrestrial Radiocarbon Age Calibration, 0–26 cal kyr BP." *Radiocarbon* 46 (3): 1029–58. http://dx.doi.org/10.1017/S0033822200032999.

Rosenfeld, S. A. 2008. "Delicious Guinea Pigs: Seasonality Studies and the Use of Fat in the Pre-Columbian Andean Diet." *Quaternary International* 180 (1): 127–34. http://dx.doi.org/10.1016/j.quaint.2007.08.011.

Santley, R. S., C. Yarborough, and B. Hall. 1987. "Enclaves, Ethnicity, and the Archaeological Record at Matacapan." In *Ethnicity and Culture: Proceedings of the Eighteenth Annual Conference of the Archaeological Association of the University of Calgary*, ed. R. Auger, M. F. Glass, S. MacEachern, and P. H. McCartney, 85–100. Calgary: University of Calgary Archaeological Association.

Schreiber, K. 1998. "Afterword: Nasca Research since 1926." In *The Archaeology and Pottery of Nazca, Peru: Alfred Kroeber's 1926 Expedition*, ed. P. Carmichael, 261–70. Walnut Creek, CA: Altamira.

Schreiber, K. 1999. "Regional Approaches to the Study of Prehistoric Empires: Examples from Ayacucho and Nasca, Peru." In *Settlement Pattern Studies in the Americas: Fifty Years since Virú*, ed. B. R. Billman and G. M. Feinman, 160–71. Washington, DC: Smithsonian Institution Press.

Schreiber, K., and M. J. Edwards. 2010. "Los centros administrativos huari y las manifestaciones físicas del poder imperial." In *Señores de los Imperios del Sol*, ed. K. Makowski, 152–61. Lima: Banco de Crédito del Perú.

Schreiber, K., and J. Lancho Rojas. 1995. "The Puquios of Nasca." *Latin American Antiquity* 6 (3): 229–54. http://dx.doi.org/10.2307/971674.

Sillar, B. 2009. "The Social Agency of Things? Animism and Materiality in the Andes." *Cambridge Archaeological Journal* 19 (3): 367–77. http://dx.doi.org/10.1017/S0959774309000559.

Silverman, H., and D. A. Proulx. 2002. *The Nasca*. Oxford: Wiley-Blackwell. http://dx.doi.org/10.1002/9780470693384.

Spickard, L. E. 1983. "The Development of Huari Administrative Architecture." In *Investigations of the Andean Past*, ed. D. H. Sandweiss, 136–60. Ithaca, NY: Cornell University Press.

Stepputat, F. 2004. "Marching for Progress: Rituals of Citizenship, State, and Belonging in a High Andes District." *Bulletin of Latin American Research* 23 (2): 244–59. http://dx.doi.org/10.1111/j.1470-9856.2004.00107.x.

Stockett, M. K. 2005. "Approaching Social Practice through Access Analysis at Las Canoas, Honduras." *Latin American Antiquity* 16 (4): 385–407. http://dx.doi.org/10.2307/30042506.

Tung, T. A. 2007. "The Village of Beringa at the Periphery of the Wari Empire: A Site Overview and New Radiocarbon Dates." *Andean Past* 8: 253–86.

Tung, T. A. 2008. "Violence after Imperial Collapse: A Study of Cranial Trauma among Late Intermediate Period Burials from the Former Huari Capital, Ayacucho, Peru." *Ñawpa Pacha: Journal of Andean Archaeology* 29 (1): 101–17. http://dx.doi.org/10.1179/naw.2008.29.1.003.

Turner, V. 1967. *The Forest of Symbols: Aspects of Ndembu Ritual*. Ithaca, NY: Cornell University Press.

Vaughn, K. J. 2009. *The Ancient Andean Village: Marcaya in Prehispanic Nasca*. Tucson: University of Arizona Press.

Vaughn, K. J., M. L. Grados, J. W. Eerkens, and M. J. Edwards. 2007. "Hematite Mining in the Ancient Americas: Mina Primavera, a 2,000 Year Old Peruvian Mine." *JOM* 59 (12): 16–20. http://dx.doi.org/10.1007/s11837-007-0145-x.

Weber, M. 1999. "Class, Status, Party." In *Anthropological Theory: An Introductory History*, ed. R. Jon McGee and R. L. Warms, 117–29. Mountain View, CA: Mayfield.

Williams, P. R. 2002. "Rethinking Disaster-Induced Collapse in the Demise of the Andean Highland States: Wari and Tiwanaku." *World Archaeology* 33 (3): 361–74. http://dx.doi.org/10.1080/0043824012010742 2.

Williams, P. R., and D. J. Nash. 2002. "Imperial Interaction in the Andes: Wari and Tiwanaku at Cerro Baúl." In *Andean Archaeology I*, ed. W. Isbell and H. Silverman, 243–65. New York: Plenum. http://dx.doi.org/10.1007/978-1-4615-0639-3_8.

8

From the Domestic to the Formal

A View of Daily and Ceremonial Practices from Cerro de Oro during the Early Middle Horizon

Francesca Fernandini and Mario Ruales

Ritual and everyday practices in the modern Andes maintain permeable boundaries, showing a recursive relationship between the extraordinary and the mundane (Insoll 2004). Every day, quotidian activities such as starting a workday in the agricultural fields may involve simple, almost systematic ceremonies, while important religious and calendar dates deserve more elaborate services. The study of this varied spectrum of cultural practices allows us to understand how rituals, regardless of their scale, produce and reproduce social dispositions within a society (Bourdieu 1977).

Throughout this chapter we intend to move beyond the dualistic distinctions that segregate ritual and domestic as two apparently incommensurable realms of social life (Angelo 2014) by exploring ritual as a relational practice. In doing so, we propose that ritual practices are better understood from a multi-scalar approach that emphasizes the way meanings, social rules, and relations are embedded within the recurrent practices that produce and reproduce their material habitus (Bourdieu 1977; Hodder and Cessford 2004). In this way the nature of ritual can be seen as a process in which repetitive actions socialize people into particular dispositions; in turn, these dispositions establish a recursive relationship with rituals in which social meaning is produced and reformulated through repetition.

This study focuses on the multiple facets of ritual practices at Cerro de Oro in an attempt to explore how everyday mundane practices, such as disposal

DOI: 10.5876/9781607325963.c008

activities, as well as sacred ceremonies, such as large-scale closure practices and intrusive burials, form part of the ritual spectrum. Following this line of argument, emphasis is placed on how the recurrence of these practices defines ritual as a relational process that produces and reproduces social meanings throughout time.

Cerro de Oro, located in the Lower Cañete Valley, is a large monumental settlement that presents continuous occupation from the end of the Early Intermediate Period (EIP) (AD 500–600) to Early Republican times (AD 1540–1600) (Fernandini 2015; Rostworowski de Diez Canseco 2004; Ruales 2000). Its denser occupation is associated with a continuous period between the end of the EIP and the start of the Middle Horizon (MH) (AD 500–800), a period that has been labeled the *Cerro de Oro occupation* (Fernandini 2015; Fernandini and Alexandrino 2016). The architectural and cultural contexts of Cerro de Oro are concentrated over a large mound that spans 145 ha (figures 8.1, 8.2). The majority of Cerro de Oro occupation contexts are located toward the south and northeast sections of the mound, while the Late Intermediate Period (LIP) (AD 1000–1475) and Late Horizon (AD 1476–1534) contexts are located more in the north and northwest sections. Moreover, a late period intrusive cemetery area intrudes the *Cerro de Oro occupation* contexts in the south.

Though many archaeologists recognize Cerro de Oro as an important settlement for the development of social complexity on the Peruvian South Coast (Engel 2010; Kroeber 1937; Menzel 1964; Ruales 2000; Stumer 1971), Cerro de Oro has been markedly underrepresented in academic research. During the early twentieth century, archaeologists such as Tello in 1923 (Kroeber 1937; Stumer 1971; Tello 1923) and Wallace in 1958–59 (Wallace 1963) performed sporadic excavations at the site without proper documentation and with limited publications. It was not until the early twenty-first century that investigations continued at Cerro de Oro with the Proyecto de Investigación Arqueológica Cerro de Oro (PIACO), led by Ruales (2000), focusing mainly on the Southwest Area of the settlement (ibid.). Following this investigation, Fernandini (2013, 2014) led the Proyecto Arqueológico Cerro de Oro (PACO) between 2012 and 2015, which centered on the Southeast Area (Southeast Plain and Southeast Ravine; see figure 8.2). Both PIACO and PACO documented EIP and MH (*Cerro de Oro occupation*) contexts, showing a continuous occupation between these periods. This continuous occupation was characterized by a sequence of floors that extend from the modern surface to bedrock.

The *Cerro de Oro*[1] occupation revealed a series of changes in the artifact assemblage as well as in the usage of space. Architecturally, this occupation demonstrated a radical increase in monumentality and settlement size. Numerous

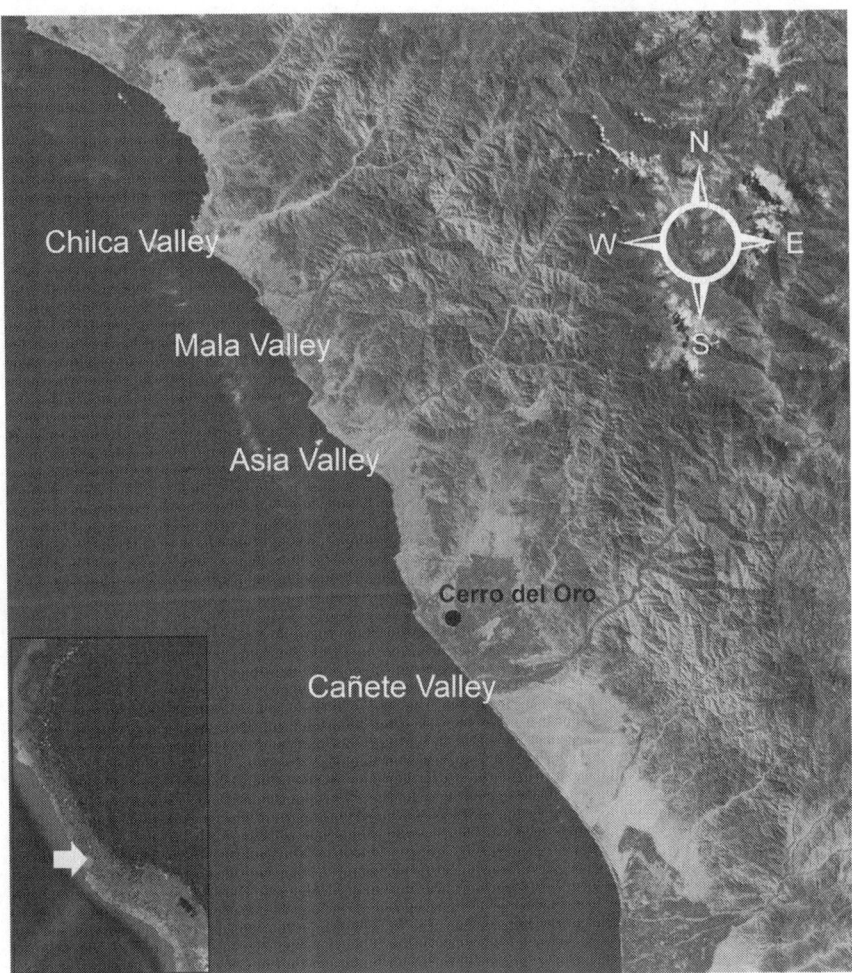

FIGURE 8.1. *Map showing the location of Cerro de Oro and neighboring valleys*

compounds, platforms, and monumental structures were constructed following a recurrent 240° orientation on east-west walls and a 60° orientation on north-south walls with relatively regular sizes and shapes of adobe (ca. 10–15 cm × 10 cm × 3.5 cm), covering an area of approximately 80 ha. Most of these walls were stuccoed, while several were painted white and yellow and included numerous friezes (Ruales 2000). As a way to clarify the spatial configuration of Cerro de Oro, the settlement has been divided into different sectors and areas within those sectors. This study focuses on the South Sector, mainly on

FIGURE 8.2. *Map of Cerro de Oro showing SW Area (PIACO) and SE Area (SE Plain and SE Ravine) (PACO)*

the excavations performed by Ruales on one of the compounds in the SW Area and on the research conducted by Fernandini on two compounds in the SE Plain and three platforms from the SE Ravine.

Research performed in these areas has brought light to some of the activities that took place in different spaces of the settlement. For instance, evidence from excavations has shown a marked difference between activities that took place in the compounds of the SE Plain and those performed in the platforms of the SE Ravine. This evidence shows that while the SE Ravine was associated mainly with food processing, cooking, and disposal activities, the compounds on the SE Plain point to storage and communal gathering and eating.

Likewise, the ceramic assemblage pertaining to the *Cerro de Oro occupation* shows a very standardized process of ceramic production in which paste composition seems to present very small variations. However, as the spatial configuration of the settlement was reshaped, a series of ceramic innovations also changed the ceramic repertoire. These innovations are reflected in the introduction of foreign designs and a new shape: the *colador* (sieve). New designs seem to have been introduced as a process of hybridization in which local ceramics were blended with elements from Nasca-, Chakipampa-, Lima-, Estrella-, and possibly Cajamarca-style traditions. This process seems to have been a local response to the highly interactive social context that characterized

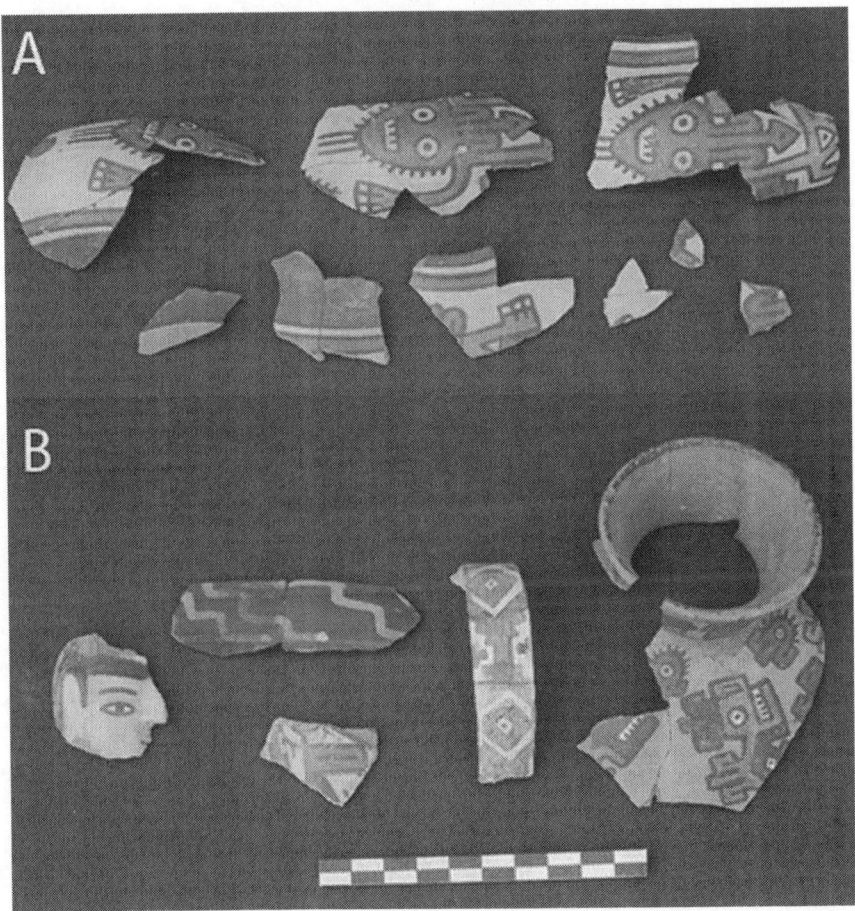

FIGURE 8.3A, 8.3B. *Fragments from bowl showing the different blends of Middle Horizon 1 styles*

the South-Central, Central, and South Coast during this time, showing that Cerro de Oro was part of its cultural milieu (figure 8.3). Moreover, coladores are elaborate vessels with thin walls and fine pastes that always present some type of decoration. Microbotanical evidence from residue analysis shows the remains of non-local beans,[2] reflecting the idea that these vessels could have been involved in the production of an important drink or food.

Situating Cerro de Oro within its cultural and geographic setting shows that it was the largest settlement in the Lower Cañete Valley during the end of the EIP and the start of the MH (Chavez 2006; Ruales 2000). During

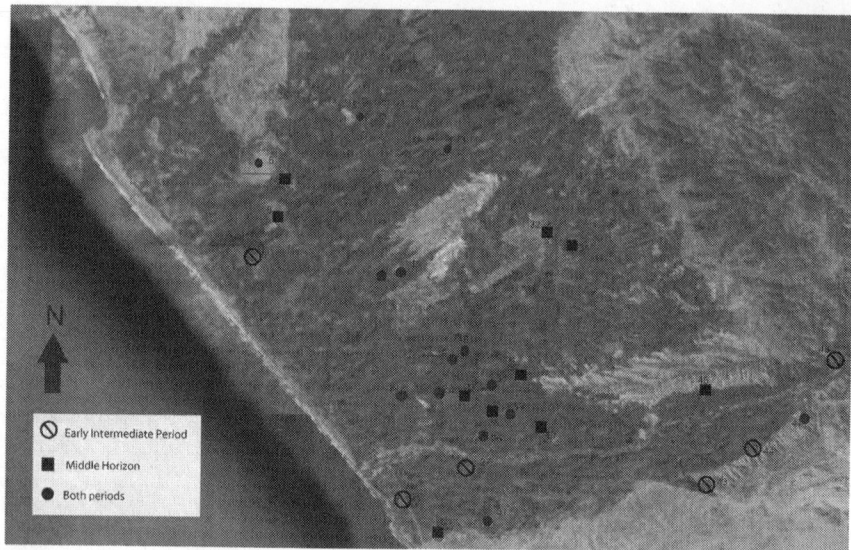

FIGURE 8.4. *Prehispanic settlements in the Lower Cañete Valley. Adapted from Chavez 2006.*

this time there seems to have been an increase in the number of settlements located 5 km or more from the Cañete River, with Cerro de Oro 13 km from the river (figure 8.4). This change in the area's settlement pattern has been interpreted in association with an expansion of the canal system, allowing for the enlargement of the agricultural frontier and the positioning of new settlements. Given that Cerro de Oro was the largest site and was the farthest from the river, it is possible that it could have been the prime mover behind hydraulic investments.

Neighboring valleys also experienced drastic changes in material culture during the end of the EIP and start of the MH, which seem to be associated with Cerro de Oro. Prior to this period, the Cañete, Asia, and Mala Valleys showed a cultural affiliation or unity reflected in a similar material culture as well as mortuary and settlement patterns (Ángeles Falcón 2009; Gabe 2000). During the end of the EIP and start of the MH, these inter-valley affinities became more noticeable, with Cerro de Oro playing a pivotal social and possibly political role. Ruales (2000) argues Cerro de Oro played this role given that it was the only monumental settlement in the Mala, Asia, and Cañete region that had a dominant presence in the landscape because of its location on a high mound and its highly visible painted walls. Also, the population size of the *Cerro de Oro occupation*, calculated based on the number of domestic structures at Cerro de Oro and compared with evidence recorded through surveys conducted on the Asia and Mala Valleys (Ángeles Falcón 2009), seems to have greatly surpassed that of any neighboring valley. While a ceramic production center has yet to be recorded at the site, excavations by PACO yielded large amounts of ceramics that repeatedly show the same type of decorations, colors, and shapes. Based on this evidence, we suggest that Cerro de Oro maintained control of ceramic production and distribution; however, only further research will clarify this phenomenon. Furthermore, Ruales's (2000) finding of a *kipu* in a context associated with the main platform at Cerro de Oro hints at a complex management of resources at the site.

Excavations at Cerro de Oro have shown that the presence of Cerro de Oro–style ceramics was recurrently associated with the construction of high walls and platforms and the reorganization of internal divisions. Likewise, the shift toward monumentality and possible mass production of ceramics was also reflected in the Cañete and Asia Valleys through an increase in population, as revealed by a rise in the number and size of sites (Ángeles Falcón 2009; Chavez 2006) (figure 8.4). Moreover, the Asia Valley presents evidence for a hiatus in the use of the main funerary and ceremonial space, Huaca Malena. This site was used from the EIP through MH 2 (AD 800–1000), until the Cerro de Oro political organization declined (Ángeles Falcón 2009; Ángeles Falcón and Pozzi-Escot 2000). Therefore, we suggest that Cerro de Oro grew as a political center, with its presence resonating in the surrounding settlements.

Thus, we argue that from the end of the EIP and beginning of the MH, Cerro de Oro housed a ruling group that foresaw the enlargement of the settlement's size and appearance and the increase in ceramic production and that, to some extent, influenced the populations from the Cañete and neighboring valleys. Cerro de Oro appears to have been a short-lived but well-organized political center that exerted an important influence within the Mala-Asia-Cañete cultural unit. This influence has been recognized mainly through the recurrence of settlement patterns and funerary and ceremonial practices in contemporary contexts in these valleys (Ángeles Falcón 2009).

RITUAL PRACTICES AT CERRO DE ORO

Everyday Domestic Practices

Cerro de Oro's urban-like characteristics and possible mass production of ceramics reveal a complex settlement in which people were organized in a physically controlled landscape that reproduced hierarchical structures through the maintenance of a systematically planned environment and a consistent material culture. In this context evidence for homogeneous ritual practices in different sectors of the site reflects a systematic organization of ceremonialism. From excavations carried out by PIACO and PACO, it seems that these ceremonies ranged from regularly occurring small-scale rituals to closure or single-use ceremonies.

A particular practice that has drawn our attention is the recurrent presence of pits on cultural floors associated with cooking or disposal spaces, which have been interpreted as part of a quotidian ritual practice. Ruales (2001) recorded this type of practice in a compound located in the SW Area of the settlement, while Fernandini (2015) encountered it in the domestic platforms of the SE Ravine. Although Ruales recorded the majority of these pits in Late Intermediate Period (ca. AD 1000–1300) contexts, a significant amount of them are clearly associated with *Cerro de Oro occupation* contexts based on their stratigraphic location and the presence of Cerro de Oro ceramics.

The *Cerro de Oro occupation* contexts excavated revealed a pattern in which materials seem to have been selected and placed intentionally in different pits. We suggest that a type of organized disposal practice was performed using specially selected material such as partial/complete animals, decorated sherds, musical instruments, and frieze fragments, among others. For example, Unit 11 presents a series of pits with different combinations of organic materials (e.g., human hair and a fish head). Unit 9 presents a pit with partial adobe bricks, organic remains, and an *ocarina* (a type of whistle). Unit 5 includes twelve pits filled with soil, clumps of clayish soil, fragments of white plaster, and a piece of cloth with dark resin attached to it. Early stratigraphic layers from Unit 18 reveal a pit that contained a complete pelican, while a later context in Unit 23 shows a pit containing an adult guinea pig (*cuy*) and a bag with unidentified non-organic white powder. Most noteworthy is a large burning area in Unit 6, which shows successive burning events evidenced by seven different pits or hearths (Ruales 2000). The events are labeled A–G based on their stratigraphic location, with A the most recent finding. This context is particularly interesting since the contents of each layer tentatively show the remains of a large meal. Table 8.1 provides a description of these contexts. All of these contexts seem to be intrinsically associated with the presence of cooking and storage areas, establishing a particular link among unconsumed, consumed, and disposed food. Likewise, the stratigraphic record shows that this organized disposal practice was recurrent throughout the *Cerro de Oro occupation*. Moreover, the size of these contexts seems to reveal that while some of these pits show the remains of small meals, others

TABLE 8.1. Stratigraphy of the burned contexts at Cerro de Oro

Layer	Description
A	Charcoal, partially burned shell, ceramics, and camelid bones
B	Very dense fill of ceramics, including the face of a figurine
C	Small amounts of charcoal and a large concentration of organic remains, mollusks, and the remains of small animals
D	Large quantities of feathers, mollusks, and organic remains
E	Shells, small animal remains, different vegetal remains, and ceramic fragments
F	Small quantities of organic remains, which include hair, fiber strings, and ceramic fragments
G	Small amounts of organic remains and some ceramic fragments
H	Earth-packed floor that had three pits, one with ceramic fragments and one with organic remains; the other one was empty

reflect large meals possibly associated with communal gatherings or feasts (Fernandini 2015).

Fernandini (2013) excavated a similar context on a domestic platform in the SE Ravine (see figure 8.2) in which six different pits intruded into a thick clay floor. These pits included small amounts of organic materials, clumps of soil, and some ceramic fragments. Based on their paste and iconographic attributes, these ceramic fragments have been cataloged as Cerro de Oro fine-ware. The sherds recovered from these pits were the most finely decorated ceramics from this platform. Similar to the contexts excavated by Ruales described above, these pits were in close proximity to a delimited burning area that showed successive burning events.

The persistent practice of excavating pits close to cooking areas and filling them with different materials has been interpreted as part of a quotidian ceremonial practice. We suggest that this practice formed part of a routinized domestic activity in which embedded meanings regarding the use of space and the social practice of food consumption were recurrently reproduced in different areas of the settlement. The rituality of this seemingly anodyne practice is seen in its repetition and consistency throughout space, reflecting how dispositions are socialized and internalized through the involvement of people in the reproduction of their habitus (Bourdieu 1977).

Moreover, the quantity of pits increases depending on the size of the cooking space, with large contexts such as those recorded for Unit 6 tentatively suggesting communal feasting events. If this context in fact does represent a communal event, then the quotidian domestic practice of pit disposal grows in scale, becoming ingrained within a larger ritual practice. In this way the scale of the ritual grows, yet the nature of the practice remains the same: always establishing an inextricable relation between food and its disposal in a recurrent and significant way. The recurrence of pits associated with possible cooking areas has also been recorded in archaeological sites other than Cerro de Oro. At Conchopata, an important Wari center in the Ayacucho heartland, similar contexts were recorded in several domestic structures. Ochatoma Paravicino and Cabrera (2000) distinguished the placement of cuys with worked *Spondylus* shells in small pits within cooking or storage areas as a type of ritual offering at the site. In addition, they reported a series of pits inside a patio closely associated with the cooking area that were filled with burned human and camelid bones, small figurines, obsidian knifes, and ceramic fragments. Rosenfeld (2012) also reported the presence of a complete young camelid and thirty-two complete cuys in a floor intrusion inside a cooking area in Conchopata. Conchopata is also characterized by the presence of large-scale and recurrent ritual ceremonies that involved sacrificing large ceramic vessels as well as people within the sacred D-shaped temple as part of the religious program (Isbell 2000). The presence of these two types of practices in this important settlement is an example of the broad spectrum of ritual that ranges from small-scale domestic practices to large-scale ceremonies.

Closure and Abandonment Practices

While the domestic practices mentioned above demonstrate evidence for quotidian ceremonialism at Cerro de Oro, both Ruales (2001) and Fernandini (2015) recorded archaeological evidence that reveals other types of ritual practices. This second set of practices points to a ritual event that was recurrently recorded in different areas of the settlement, seemingly embedded within the process of its abandonment.

Sealing practices are unique events that "prepare" spaces for their abandonment or reuse. The practices described below show how Cerro de Oro people selected certain spaces of the settlement to perform a series of actions categorized as a "closure practice." This preparation seems to have had the intent of producing a deliberate, targeted, and systematic act whose main objective was to prevent the further use of that specific space (sensu Capriata Estrada and López-Hurtado, this volume).

Based on stratigraphic analysis, it seems that the end of the early MH occupation at the site was marked by an intensive pluvial event. Evidence for this climatic event has been recorded in different contexts of the SW and SE Areas.

TABLE 8.2. Stratigraphic sequence for Unit 22W at Cerro de Oro

Layer	Description
A	LIP material culture
B	LIP material culture
C	Associated with dismantling of walls
D	Semi-compact layer with large amounts of human coprolites
E	Thin layer of sand and debris with no cultural material
F	Laminated clayish soil with no cultural material (40 cm)
G	Cerro de Oro (Early MH) material culture

Based on Ruales 2001.

In the SW Area this evidence has been found mainly in Unit 22W, where the tops of the northwest and southeast walls had signs of water erosion and their lateral surfaces showed signs of water runoff. Table 8.2 describes the sequence of layers evidencing this major climatic event.

Similarly, evidence for the atypical presence of water runoff on adobe architecture has been found in the west sector of the compound, in Units 1, 12, and 23. These units had a very fine-grained and compact clayish layer (20 cm thick) over the structure's occupation floor. These sediments had been deposited through a filtration process, evidencing the presence of large quantities of water. Coincidently, evidence for this pluvial event could only be found in contexts that were not part of the access routes leading to the lower part of the settlement. This lower part has been associated with the more consistent LIP occupation that reused earlier adobes in the construction of new structural elements, such as rooms and ramps. Based on this evidence, it can be argued that later occupations might have altered the evidence of water erosion.

Similar environmental phenomena have also been recorded in contemporaneous settlements throughout the Peruvian central and North Coast. For example, research at Cajamarquilla has demonstrated that settlement construction was intrinsically related to an increment in water availability in the Huaycoloro or the Jicamarca Quebrada (Mogrovejo and Makowski 1999). During excavations within Sector I of the Julio C. Tello architectonic complex, Segura and Mogrovejo recorded a stratigraphic hiatus similar to the one recorded at Cerro de Oro (Mogrovejo and Llanos 2000). This hiatus showed clear signs of flooding temporally associated with Middle Horizon 1–style ceramics such as Chakipampa. Consequently, Narváez Luna attests the presence of a layer composed of sandy silt covering a cultural layer with ceramic remains pertaining to MH 1A, such as Lima 8 or 9 (Narváez Luna 2006), which he found while investigating a different sector (XI) of the Tello complex. Tentatively, it seems that these authors date these events sometime between MH 1A and 1B (AD 550–700). Similarly, recurrent flooding events reveal an extremely wet period at Huaca 20 in Complejo Maranga that led to the temporary abandonment of part of the settlement around AD 600 (Mac Kay 2007). According to Mauricio (2011), the stratigraphic record shows clear evidence for high precipitation rates that created flood deposits and aeolian sand accumulation. Furthermore, Franco and Paredes (2000) present evidence for similar contemporaneous events in Pachacamac, where they recorded thick muddy layers over EIP occupational floors. We have interpreted the architectural modifications that occurred on top of these muddy layers as a shift in cultural tradition and propose that these "heavy rains" marked the transition between the EIP Lima occupation and the posterior Wari associated evidence.

Additional evidence for a wetter than usual period between the EIP and the MH has been recorded in several other archaeological sites along the North Coast, such as Alto Piura, Pampa Grande, and Huacas de Moche (Dillehay and Kolata 2004; Kaulicke 1993; Shimada et al. 1991; Uceda and Canziani 1993), which further supports the hypothesis for an unstable climate between the end of the EIP and the start of the MH. Moreover, paleoenvironmental records from the Quelccaya ice cap, located in the southeastern Peruvian Andes, reveal a particularly wet year in AD 572 followed by a wet period between AD 602 and 635 (Kaulicke 2000; Shimada et al. 1991; Thompson, Mosley-Thompson, and Morales Arnao 1984).

We see the evidence for this atypical environmental event as a temporal marker that divided the activities associated with the abandonment of the settlement from the actual occupation of these buildings. Within the events that preceded the abandonment of the settlement, we recorded the recurrent practice of dismantling architecture, filling previously used areas with the dismounted materials as well as with other elements, and placing deceased individuals on top of this fill (table 8.3). While excavating the compounds placed on the main platform in the SW Area, Ruales revealed the recurrence of this type of fill, with examples ranging in size from 160 cm to 50 cm. These fills were composed of organic material, complete and partial adobes, broken decorated vessels, and a higher than usual amount of decorated ceramic fragments. One of these contexts included the remains of two friezes (one black and white and the other black and pale orange), while two other similar contexts had clay blocks with leaf imprints interpreted as roof remains. These fill contexts were constantly associated with dismounted architecture, particularly

TABLE 8.3. Schematic description of occupations at Cerro de Oro

Period	Description
Late Horizon	Tapial architecture in N sector, reoccupation of MH architecture for funerary purposes
Late Intermediate Period	
Late Middle Horizon	Intrusive architecture and tomb
Early Middle Horizon	Abandonment
Early Middle Horizon Early Intermediate Period	Multi-step closure event: dismantling of walls, fill, intrusive tombs
	Pluvial event
	Offerings in pits
	Internal divisions of space within compounds, Cerro de Oro–style ceramics
	Monumental architecture forming architectural compounds, geometric decorations on ceramics
Late Formative?	Conical adobes

of thick, tall, slipped walls. Stratigraphic analysis shows that the fills were created concurrent with the dismantling and burial of preexisting structures but before the placement of deceased individuals.

The funerary contexts intruding these fill contexts had similar funerary structures, while age, sex, and associations varied in each case. For instance, on the headway of the main perimeter wall of the compound, Ruales recorded five intrusive tombs that ran parallel to this wall. All of these contexts included a rectangular or square adobe funerary structure with variable sizes that ranged from 1 m × 1 m to 70 cm × 50 cm. Inside these structures, individuals were placed in a fetal position with their heads close to their knees and oriented toward the northeast. In one case, the individual had been tied with a thin fiber rope, a diagnostic practice found in the Nasca Valley associated with Middle Horizon tombs (Silverman and Proulx 2002).

Further evidence for the dismantling of architecture, the preparation of a closure fill, and the placement of a funerary context (table 8.4) was recorded by Fernandini in different places within the SE Area, mainly the SE Plain and the SE Ravine (see figure 8.2). In the SE Plain, Fernandini (2013, 2014) recorded a fill composed of approximately 2 m of broken adobe, organic material, textile fragments, and thousands of decorated and undecorated ceramic vessels, all pertaining to the final phase of the *Cerro de Oro occupation* (Fernandini 2015; Rodriguez 2015). Within this fill, two intrusive funerary contexts, CF06 and

TABLE 8.4. Description of the funerary contexts (CF = Contexto Funerario) at Cerro de Oro

CF	Associations	Unit	Individuals	Observations
1	Various textiles, a clay figurine, *Spondylus* beads, and early Middle Horizon ceramics	22	1	
2	No associations	22	1	
3	Fiber sewing kit, a clay figurine, and a small cotton bag	22 Ext.	0	
4	Gourd with three carved bone figurines and a *Spondylus* shell inside, a *Spondylus* bead tied to a thread, a carved figurine, chaquira beads, a small tapestry with red, yellow, and black designs of waves and concentric circles, and a group of plain bags tied to each other	23	2	Tied bags are common at Cerro de Oro and appear to be restricted to the Early Middle Horizon Period. Bags are usually found inside funerary bundles between wrapping textiles.
5	Fiber sewing kit, a fiber bag, and part of a sandal close to the fiber bag	11	1	
6	Gourd, maize cobs sewn onto the funerary bundle	D1	1	Unidentified metal object placed above the skull
7	Maize cobs sewn onto the funerary bundle	D1	1	This funerary bundle was recorded below CF06 and had no adobe structure.

CF07, were placed in the corner of a compound. CF06 was a funerary bundle placed in a structure identical to the ones recorded by PIACO. CF07 was a funerary bundle placed directly underneath CF06 and did not present a structure. X-rays performed on these funerary bundles have revealed that the individuals had modified elongated craniums. Likewise, CF06 revealed an unidentified metal object approximately 10 cm × 10 cm, recorded above the skull.

Moreover, a similar context was recorded in the SE Ravine, yet this closure practice was not intended to prepare a compound for abandonment; rather, it was oriented toward the sealing of a domestic platform where food was processed and disposed of. Similar to the other contexts, this closure practice was located close to structural walls. The fill recorded was 60 cm thick, covering an area of 12 m², and was composed of a series of complete and partial adobes and high quantities of organic materials such as cotton, corn, beans, human hair, and isolated adult and infant bones, including mandibles, crania, femurs, and humeri. Over 3,000 ceramic fragments that included partial remains of at least six highly decorated vessels and hundreds of textile fragments had been included in this fill. The textiles showed a wide range of techniques, such as tapestry, sewing parts together, double fabric, and embroidery, among others. Intrusive to this context was a partially complete individual with its cranium, both femurs, and one humerus intact. The individual was found associated with several plain ceramic fragments and an embroidered double fabric band. This funerary context had no architecture; while no evidence of modern disturbance was recorded, it is not clear if the human remains were placed while the flesh was present or when only bones were placed as an offering. Very close to this context, part of a leg and paw of a small dog was placed over a textile fragment.

Taking this evidence as a whole, it seems that the dismantling of architecture, the preparation of the fill, and the placement of intrusive funerary contexts alongside walls demonstrate evidence of a methodically planned closure ritual. The ritual practice of preparing these spaces for their abandonment seems to have occurred only once yet was recurrently evidenced in different areas of the settlement. Moreover, based on the particular contexts in which they were recorded, it seems that the scale of these practices also varied from context to context. While complete individuals placed in funerary adobe structures were recorded within compounds, a partially complete individual placed directly into the closure fill was recorded in the domestic area of the SE Ravine. This evidence points to a practice that seems to have varied regarding the place in which it was performed, showing that greater investment in funerary structures and in the size of the fill was made in compounds, while the ritual was reproduced at a smaller scale within the domestic SE Ravine.

This varied set of closure rituals shows that while this type of practice may have varied in size and place, its ritual nature is attested in the recurrence as a social practice that represented the actions of a community. In a way, the presence of this closure ritual in different parts of the settlement can be extrapolated as a settlement-wide process that prepared the settlement and particularly the community for the abandonment of their homes.

Post-Abandonment

After the structures pertaining to the *Cerro de Oro occupation* were abandoned, a series of post-abandoned events was recorded in selected compounds within the Cerro de Oro hill. Post-abandonment events at Cerro de Oro are characterized by the construction of rectangular rooms that intrude into the *Cerro de Oro occupation*. The floors of these rooms were found 2.5–3 m below the surface. While some of the rooms lacked diagnostic material culture, the act of constructing intrusive rooms seems to have been a recurrent practice evidenced in different parts of the settlement. In the SW Area, PIACO recorded several rooms with offerings, while PACO recorded three in the SE Plain, located in the SE Area of the settlement.

PIACO recorded rooms composed of four walls without any opening for an access way. Most of these rooms had tall walls and were similar in size, approximately 1.80 m × 1.20 m. The walls were mud-slipped and in some cases painted white. While most of the rooms lacked diagnostic material culture, two of them included offerings inside. The first of these rooms was painted white and contained a camelid burial. The camelid was complete, but its cranium had been removed and placed backward and its legs had been switched, placing the anterior legs in the posterior position and vice versa. The second room contained a textile bundle with attached metal plaques, which was placed intruding into the pluvial layer mentioned above. The rest of the rooms were excavated right next to this one, yet the only remains found in the rooms were filled with only soil and partial adobe bricks. While no evidence of funerary remains was found in these rooms, they seem to have been contemporaneous with funerary-related intrusions in the SE Plain.

The rooms excavated by PACO in the SE Plain were located within one compound associated with the *Cerro de Oro occupation*. Three rooms were labeled A, C, and G based on the project's labeling of internal divisions within compounds. The dimensions of these rooms were Room A, 120 cm × 80 cm; Room C, 255 cm × 1.75 cm; and Room G, 100 cm × 130 cm. Similar to the rooms recorded by PIACO, these rooms also intruded into the *Cerro de Oro occupation*'s sequence, had mud-slipped walls, and were located approximately 3 m below the surface. Yet unlike the rooms excavated by PIACO, these rooms had entranceways on the northeast wall as well as a series of niches. The entrances for the three rooms were sealed with a layer of adobe constructed in a less polished manner, contrasting with the fine finishing of the rest of the room. The entrance for Room C was directly connected to three steps that descended from the top of the walls (40 cm below the modern surface). This characteristic seems to point to recurrent reentering before its closure. Furthermore, while Rooms C and G were found empty, they record evidence that shows that they were once used as a funerary chamber (Fernandini 2015), while Room A did present a complex funerary context (figure 8.5).

Among the evidence for their use as funerary chambers is the fact that all of these rooms included a series of offerings directly associated with their entrances. The offering associated with Room A was a deceased child

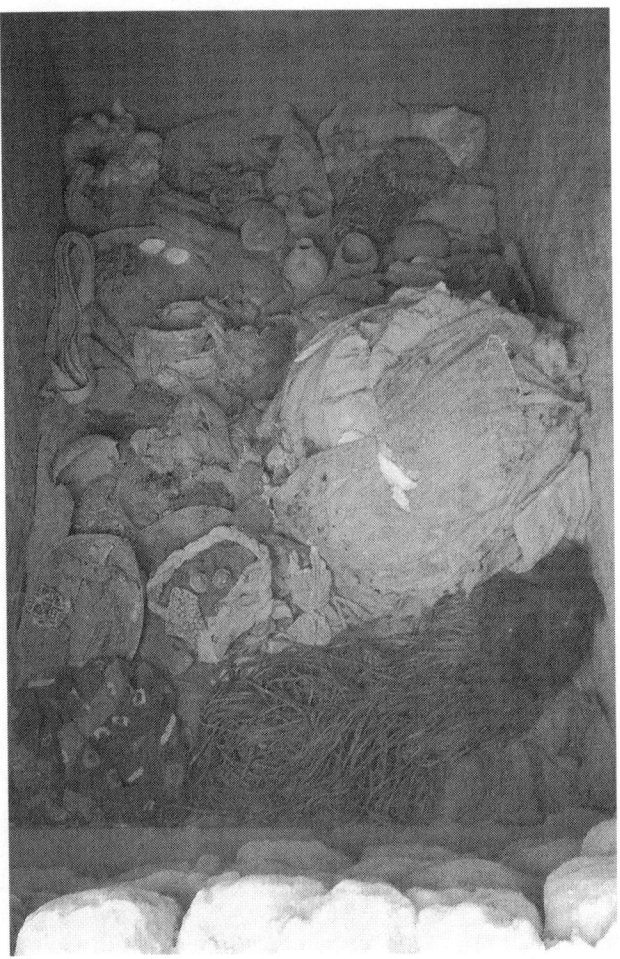

FIGURE 8.5. *Remains inside Room A*

approximately 9–10 years of age (Boza, personal communication, 2013) placed in front of the room's entrance, on top of a *Cerro de Oro* occupational floor that had been broken during construction of the room. The offering for Room C consisted of a spinster's spade, a metal ax, and a knitted bag filled with forty camelid gallstones. Finally, the offering for Room G was a young camelid placed directly on top of the bedrock in front of the entrance. Further evidence for the use of these chambers as funerary structures is found in the presence of small fragments of tapestries similar to those found associated with the funerary bundle in Room A. It seems that at some point in time these contexts were intruded and their contexts removed, leaving only traces of their remains in Rooms C and G and leaving a false bundle in Room A.

When we performed excavations in Room A, the bundle we recorded only contained soil, yet a reconstruction process performed after analyzing the context in the lab has shown that this bundle originally contained an individual (the imprints of its head and the remains from tissue decomposition are clear in the textiles used to wrap him or her). This individual was wrapped in a bundle with twenty-nine textiles; the final layer was an *unku* (tunic). Moreover, based on the analysis of the associated remains found in the context, we propose that this bundle had a false head, a turban, and a wig. In association with this bundle were over 200 objects, most of them placed in reed baskets.

The most noteworthy funerary associations were (figure 8.6):

A four-point hat made using knotted technique (figure 8.6a)

A square hat made using knotted technique (figure 8.6b)

A braided wig made of human hair (figure 8.6c)

A pair of wooden ear pieces showing an anthropomorphic figure (figure 8.6d)

A pair of miniature leather sandals (figure 8.6e)

A wooden feline figurine (figure 8.6f)

A tie-dye textile (figure 8.6g)

Based on the materials associated with the funerary context in Room A and the textile fragments from Rooms C and G, we have interpreted these rooms as belonging to the later part of the Middle Horizon, or MH2, and the objects particularly associated with Wari society. While only contexts in the SE Plain present clear diagnostic material culture, the similarity in construction techniques and their stratigraphic location with contexts in the SW Area signal all of these contexts as pertaining to this period.

Moreover, evidence for intrusive funerary contexts has also been recorded in the nearby Huaca Malena (Ángeles Falcón and Pozzi-Escot 2000), as well as several examples from the Central Coast (Flores Espinoza 2005, 2013). All of these burials also intruded into abandoned settlements and present Wari-affiliated elements. Thus, the recurrence of these contexts points to the repetitive practice of intruding previous settlements to place their deceased. The common denominator within this recurrent practice is that all of these intrusive burials present Wari elements—some exclusively (as was the case at Cerro

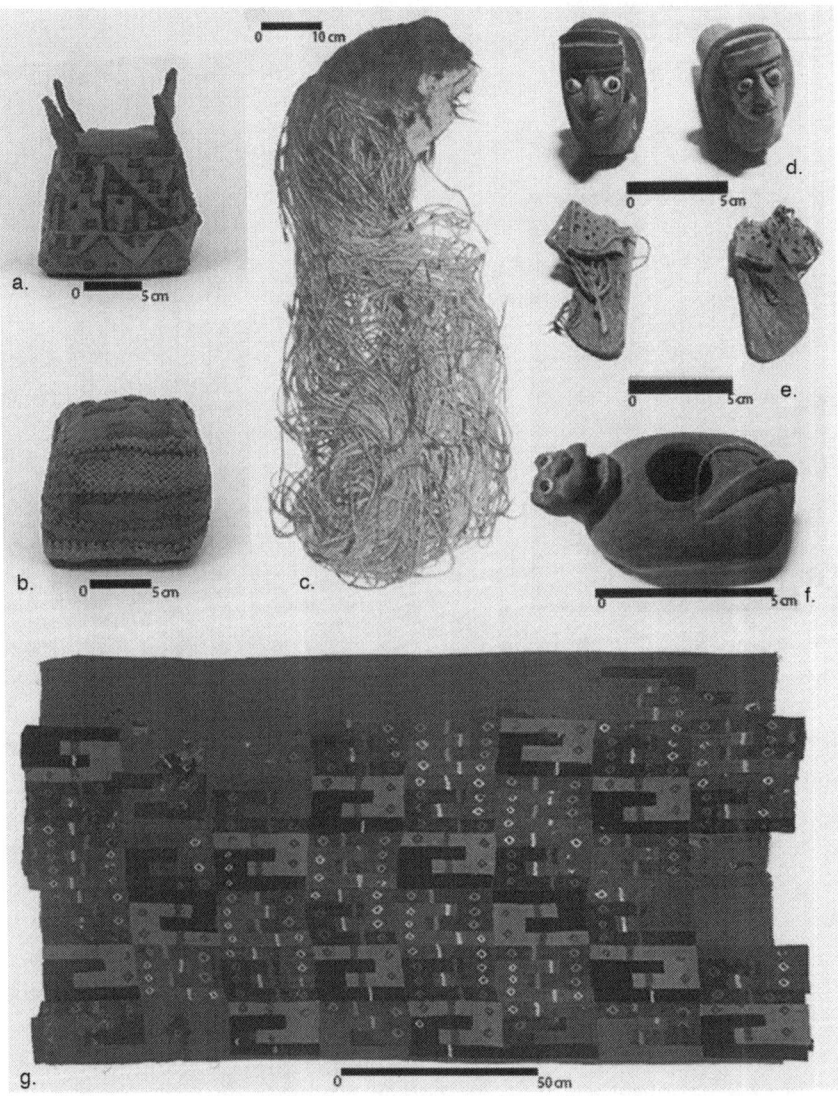

FIGURE 8.6. *Composition of funerary associations found inside Room A at Cerro de Oro*

de Oro) and others within a wider range of foreign and local objects (as is the case at Huaca Malena [Ángeles Falcón and Pozzi-Escot 2000]).

Given that residential settlements for this period do not show evidence of Wari presence, we propose that this practice of using abandoned settlements to inter the dead with foreign emblematic objects can be considered a local attempt to reappropriate abandoned yet once-important settlements. Thus, this repetitive practice would be revealing a local reformulation of the social landscape. In this context the ritualistic nature of these practices can be seen in their recurrence throughout the area, showing that certain ritual dispositions can be shared and reproduced within larger contexts. In this sense, as this practice is reproduced in different areas of the South-Central and Central Coast, the dispositions of a regional shared ritual practice seem to have been reformulated within particular historical trajectories.

DISCUSSION

This study has focused on describing and analyzing a different set of practices with the objective of showing the permeable boundaries between the mundane and the eventful. While moving away from the dualistic perspective that segregates ritual from daily activities, we have presented a series of examples in which the nature of ritual is centered in the way social dispositions and meanings are embedded within repetitive practices.

In this way we have shown how the recurrent disposal of elements in a selective way can be considered a ritual practice in which individuals are socialized into a practice particularly linked to the consumption and disposal of food. Moreover, this simple yet meaningful practice of disposing has been recorded in different scales, from disposing the refuse of small-scale meals to discarding the remains from repetitive communal gatherings. However, the contexts show that regardless of the size, the rituality of the practice is evidenced in its repetitive nature as a disposition that becomes embedded in the way people do things throughout time, thus ritualizing everyday social action.

Moreover, evidence associated with closure practices shows that this was a ritual process, which seems to have been performed as a way to prepare the settlement for its abandonment. While this practice seems to have selected only particular spaces for sealing and invested more in compounds than in domestic platforms, the practice in itself seems to have involved the community in a consistent process of abandonment. This process prepared both the settlement and the community for abandonment. In this sense the ritualistic nature of this practice is evidenced in the way these repetitive actions instilled a particular reality into the population, integrating them in the process of reproducing the closing of a life cycle.

Finally, the final set of ritual practices focuses on the intrusive placement of burials dressed with foreign objects in the abandoned settlement Cerro de Oro. These burials were placed with a clear notion of where previous rooms within the compound were located, establishing a possible connection between the present action and the building's past. Moreover, this practice has also been recorded in other settlements on the South-Central and Central Coasts, reflecting that it was a seemingly shared practice. We propose that this recurrent practice reflects the ritual appropriation of abandoned settlements by local populations. Following this line, this recurrent ritual can be seen as an example for the large-scale reproduction of social dispositions through the enactment of a shared practice.

In sum, evidence from Cerro de Oro has been used to present a multi-scalar approach that understands ritual practices through the repetitive actions that produce and reproduce social practices within a community. This view explores the ways rituals socialize people into particular dispositions. These dispositions can range from a community´s reproduction of meanings established by the link between people, food and disposal practices, involved in the abandonment of their homes, to the shared practice of reappropriating abandoned settlements.

CONCLUSION

In conclusion, this chapter has attempted to explore the wide spectrum of ritual practices that took place in the settlement Cerro de Oro. This multi-scalar analysis has shown that the nature of ritual does not lie in the scale of the practice or in the role of its actors; rather, it can be found in the way its occurrence and recurrence instills a series of social meanings among the people who participate in the rituals. In this sense, analyzing rituals through their practice allows us to grasp often elusive meanings regarding a society's social orderings and actions.

In this way the analysis of ritual practices at Cerro de Oro has allowed us to introduce ourselves into the social context of the settlement, where we can follow the ways people produced and reproduced their own social dispositions through their participation. Thus, an exploration of the way people related to food and its disposal, how they internalized their own process of abandonment or the shared processes that occurred after abandonment can lead to an understanding of how people were involved in these practices. Thus, a focus on the ritualized actions people do every day and their involvement in grand ritual ceremonies allows us to enter the realm of the archaeologically intangible.

NOTES

1. Cerro de Oro is used to refer to the site, while *Cerro de Oro* is used to refer to the Middle Horizon occupation.

2. One colador had remains of *Erythrina edulis* (*mompas* bean). The tree that grows these beans is typical of the tropical Andes located over 1,000 km north of Cerro de Oro.

REFERENCES CITED

Ángeles Falcón, R. 2009. "El estilo Cerro del Oro del Horizonte Medio en el valle de Asia." *Revista Chilena de Antropología* 20: 77–112.

Ángeles Falcón, R., and D. Pozzi-Escot. 2000. "Textiles del Horizonte Medio: Las evidencias de Huaca Malena, valle de Asia." *Boletín de Arqueología PUCP* 4: 401–24.

Angelo, D. 2014. "Assembling Ritual, the Burden of the Everyday: An Exercise in Relational Ontology in Quebrada de Humahuaca, Argentina." *World Archaeology* 46 (2): 270–87. http://dx.doi.org/10.1080/00438243.2014.891948.

Bourdieu, P. 1977. *Outline of a Theory of Practice*. Cambridge: Cambridge University Press. http://dx.doi.org/10.1017/CBO9780511812507.

Chavez, C. 2006. *Patrones de Asentamientos Prehispánico en el Valle Bajo de Cañete*. Ayacucho, Perú: Departamento de Ciencias Sociales, Universidad Nacional San Cristobal de Huamanga.

Dillehay, T., and A. Kolata. 2004. "Long-Term Human Response to Uncertain Environmental Conditions in the Andes." *Proceedings of the National Academy of Sciences of the United States of America* 101 (12): 4325–30. http://dx.doi.org/10.1073/pnas.0400538101.

Engel, P. 2010. *Arqueología Inédita de la Costa Peruana*. Lima: Asamblea Nacional de Rectores.

Fernandini, F. 2013. *Informe Final del Proyecto de Investigación Arqueológica Cerro de Oro*. Lima: Ministerio de Cultura.

Fernandini, F. 2014. *Informe Final del Proyecto de Investigación Arqueológica Cerro de Oro*. Lima: Ministerio de Cultura.

Fernandini, F. 2015. "Beyond the Empire: Living in Cerro de Oro." PhD dissertation, Department of Anthropology, Stanford University, Stanford, CA.

Fernandini, F., and G. Alexandrino, eds. 2016. *Cerro de Oro: desarrollo local, cambio y continuidad durante el Período Intermedio Temprano y el Horizonte Medio*, vol. 9. Lima: Boletín del Centro de Estudios Precolombinos de la Universidad de Varsovia.

Flores Espinoza, I. 2005. *Pucllana: Esplendor de la Culture Lima*. Lima: Instituto Nacional de Cultura.

Flores Espinoza, I. 2013. *Wari en Pucllana: la tumba de un sacerdote.* Lima: Ministerio de Cultura.

Franco, R., and P. Paredes. 2000. "El Templo Viejo de Pachacamac: Nuevos Aportes al Estudio del Horizonte Medio." Huari y Tiwanaku: Modelos vs. Evidencias, part 1. *Boletín de Arqueología* 4: 607–30.

Gabe, C. 2000. *Investigaciones arqueológicas en Cerro Salazar, Mala: Serie de Investigaciones CEAMA, 1.* Lima: Editorial Alfagraf S.A.

Hodder, I., and C. Cessford. 2004. "Daily Practice and Social Memory at Çatalhöyük." *American Antiquity* 69 (1): 17–40. http://dx.doi.org/10.2307/4128346.

Insoll, T. 2004. *Archaeology, Ritual, Religion.* Themes in Archaeology. London: Routledge.

Isbell, W. H. 2000. "Repensando el Horizonte Medio." *Boletín de Arqueología. Huari y Tiwanaku: Modelos vs. Evidencias* 4: 9–68.

Kaulicke, P. 1993. "Evidencias paleoclimáticas en asentamientos del Alto Piura durante el Período Intermedio Temprano." *Boletín del Instituto Francés de Estudios Andinos* 22 (1): 283–311.

Kaulicke, P. 2000. "La Sombre de Pachacamac: Huari en la Costa Central." *Boletín de Arqueología PUCP* 4: 313–58.

Kroeber, A. 1937. *Archaeological Explorations in Peru/Cañete,* vol. 4. Chicago: Field Museum Press.

Mac Kay, M. 2007. *Contextos funerarios de la Huaca 20: Reconstrucción del ritual funerario y la vida cotidiana del Valle del Rímac en los Inicios del Horizonte Medio.* Lima: Letras y Ciencias Humanas, Pontificia Universidad Católica del Perú.

Mauricio, A. C. 2011. "The Huaca 20 Site in the Maranga Complex: Human-Environment Interactions, Household Activities, and Funerary Practices on the Central Coast of Peru." Master's thesis, Quaternary and Climate Studies, University of Maine, Orono, ME.

Menzel, D. 1964. "Style and Time in the Middle Horizon." *Ñawpa Pacha: Journal of Andean Archaeology* 2 (1): 1–105. http://dx.doi.org/10.1179/naw.1964.2.1.001.

Mogrovejo, J., and K. Makowski. 1999. "Cajamarquilla y los Mega Niños en el pasado Prehispánico." *Íconos* 1: 46–57.

Mogrovejo, J. D., and R. S. Llanos. 2000. "El Horizonte Medio en el Conjunto Arquitectónico Julio C. Tello de Cajamarquilla." *Boletín de Arqueología PUCP* 4: 565–82.

Narváez Luna, J. J. 2006. *Sociedades de la antigua ciudad de Cajamarquilla: investigaciones arqueológicas en el sector XI del Conjunto Tello y un estudio de la colección tardía del Conjunto Sestieri.* Lima: Ediciones Avqi.

Ochatoma Paravicino, J., and M. Cabrera. 2000. "Arquitectura y Areas de Actividad en Conchopata." *Boletín de Arqueología PUCP* 4: 449–88.

Rodriguez, C. 2015. "Caracterización de la Cerámica Cerro de Oro." BA thesis, Faculta de Letras y Ciencias Humanas, Pontificia Universidad Católica del Perú, Lima.

Rosenfeld, S. A. 2012. "Animal Wealth and Local Power in the Huari Empire." *Ñawpa Pacha: Journal of Andean Archaeology* 32 (1): 131–64. http://dx.doi.org/10.1179/naw.2012.32.1.131.

Rostworowski de Diez Canseco, M. 2004. *Costa peruana prehispánica*, 2nd ed. Lima: IEP.

Ruales, M. 2000. "Investigaciones en Cerro del Oro, Valle de Cañete." *Boletín de Arqueología PUCP* 4: 359–99.

Ruales, M. 2001. *Informe Final del Proyecto de Investigación Arqueológico Cerro de Oro*. Lima: Ministerio de Cultura.

Shimada, I., C. Shaaf, L. Thompson, and E. Mosley-Thompson. 1991. "Implicaciones culturales de una gran sequía del siglo d.C en los Andes peruanos." *Boletín de Lima* 13 (77): 33–56.

Silverman, H., and D. A. Proulx. 2002. *The Nasca*. Oxford: Wiley-Blackwell. http://dx.doi.org/10.1002/9780470693384.

Stumer, L. 1971. "Informe preliminar sobre el recorrido del Valle de Cañete." In *Arqueología y Sociedad*, 23–35. Lima: Museo de Arqueología y Etnología de la Universidad Nacional Mayor de San Marcos.

Tello, J. C. 1923. "Wira Kocha." *Inca* 1: 93–320, 583–606.

Thompson, L., E. Mosley-Thompson, and B. Morales Arnao. 1984. "El Niño–Southern Oscillation Events Recorded in the Stratigraphy of the Tropical Quelccaya Ice Cap, Peru." *Science* 226 (4670): 50–53. http://dx.doi.org/10.1126/science.226.4670.50.

Uceda, S., and J. Canziani. 1993. "Evidencias de grandes precipitaciones en diversas etapas constructivas de la Huaca de la Luna, Costa Norte del Perú." *Boletín del Instituto Francés de Estudios Andinos* 22 (1): 313–43.

Wallace, D. T. 1963. "Early Horizon Ceramics in the Cañete Valley of Perú." *Ñawpa Pacha: Journal of Andean Archaeology* 1 (1): 35–38. http://dx.doi.org/10.1179/naw.1963.1.1.003.

9

TERMINAL RITUALS AND SITE ABANDONMENT

The authors in this volume are consistent in highlighting the performative nature of rituals. If they can be understood as activities performed in a regular and systematic way, then, as Rick states in this volume, they should be interpreted primarily as a form of communication. We agree with Rick (this volume) that rituals are structured around "customary actions that are effective in obtaining outcomes over which the participants have little or no controlling power" and with Nielsen and his colleagues (this volume) that even though most of the specific actions that take place during rituals are designed to address non-human agents, they suppose the materialization of terrestrial outcomes. In this sense the mobilization of political expectations is a constitutive component of ritual activities in which certain social outcomes are expected as the result of a correctly performed ceremony.

Among the different social outcomes that can be expected as the result of particular ritual performances, the abandonment of public buildings is heavily related to political changes in the organization of past societies. This particular type of ritual is known in the literature as terminal rituals, deliberate and systematic performances that may or may not occur with the end of a site occupation where, per Stanton, artifacts or structures are destroyed, burned, or broken (Stanton, Brown, and Pagliaro 2008:234–36). Stross (1998:37) distinguishes

The Demise of the Ruling Elites

Terminal Rituals in the Pyramid Complexes of Panquilma, Peruvian Central Coast

Camila Capriata Estrada
and
Enrique López-Hurtado

DOI: 10.5876/9781607325963.c009

between two types of ritual: dedicatory (animation) and termination (de-animation). The aim of animation rituals is for objects to acquire a soul, while terminal rituals are those associated with the killing of the object, which in some way liberates its soul. The distinction between these rituals can be recognized in the archaeological record by the presence of specific patterns in the disposal of artifacts. In the case of terminal rituals, Mock (1998:5) expresses that "termination actions, although difficult to separate in all instances and often embedded in dedication events, generally include the defacement, mutilation, breaking, burning, or alteration of portable objects (such as pottery, jade or stone tools), sculptures, stellae, or buildings." Stanton and colleagues (2008:237) also mention the presence of deposits containing destroyed material culture, such as smashed ceramic pot caches, which may be associated with site or structure abandonment and may symbolize reverential ritual activity.

Some terminal rituals can be seen as a part of life cycles, like those cases associated with the end of a construction phase. The ritual destruction of artifacts or architectural features may indicate the end of a building episode and thus mark the beginning of a new phase. However, these events could also mark an end, without implicating any rebirth or regenerating process, as in the case of the abandonment of a particular building. Most of the examples of terminal rituals in Maya sites are presented as a *continuum*, usually associated with the construction of a new building, where "killing" the old structure was a means of containing its accumulated power (Mock 1998:10).

These rituals have been broadly studied for the Mayas, among whom dedicatory and terminal rituals were very common (Dahlin 2000; Freidel 1998; Harrison-Buck, McAnany, and Storey 2007; Mock 1998; Stanton, Brown, and Pagliaro 2008). Mock mentions several cases for the site Chalcatzingo in the Morelos Valley, where altars and other monuments were partially destroyed and the broken sections were sometimes moved to other areas of the same site. She suggests that these actions were performed to "neutralize [the] supernatural powers contained in the monuments and left uncontrolled by the ruler's death" (Mock 1998:5).

Intentional destruction constitutes a powerful and symbolic act. However, in what social contexts should we expect to encounter this type of behavior? Although these actions are often related to social, political, or economic factors, in all cases they seem to have a strong ritual component as well. It becomes crucial, then, to determine if these events are related to the partial or total abandonment of the site. Abandonment may occur on different scales; it can comprise entire regions, settlements, or just a few structures within a site. In addition, abandonment can be gradual when it is planned or abrupt when it is unexpected, temporal, or permanent (Joyce and Johannessen 1993; Schiffer 1996). Settlements that have been abandoned abruptly will not usually contain great amounts of trash but may contain particular items that, under other circumstances, would have been transported during evacuation. The opposite occurs during planned abandonments.

The ritual nature of this action is highlighted by the fact that it was deliberate, targeted, and systematic and that its main objective was to prevent the further use of buildings designated specifically for rituals. Settlements can be abandoned for various reasons, and their destruction usually constitutes a secular event (e.g., war, political conflict, drought, invasion). Exploring the relationship between terminal rituals and site abandonment would shed light on the context leading to this particular scenario.

CONTINUITY AND CHANGE IN MONUMENTAL ARCHITECTURE

The appearance of monumental architecture is strongly related to the increase of social stratification in complex societies (Clark and Martinsson-Wallin 2007; Moore 1996; Stanish 2001; Trigger 1990). The most distinctive attribute of these buildings is that their construction exceeds the pure practical needs of a specific human group, representing the most visible structures in a particular landscape. Furthermore, the visibility of monumental architecture may reflect sociopolitical interaction among different sites, where activities such as rituals may be oriented to large masses or to a select group of people (Chicoine et al., this volume). As Trigger (1990:126) explains, these buildings "constituted the most public material embodiment of the power of the upper classes," despite the fact that their meaning may not have been understood by everyone (Moore 1996).

Like many of the other authors in this volume, we suggest that monumental buildings symbolize the materialization of power of certain ruling groups (DeMarrais, Castillo, and Earle 1996). The monumentality of these buildings reflects the ability of local ruling elites to control labor (Abrams and Bolland 1999; Trubitt 2000) and is used to display their power and legitimacy over the population. The buildings' deterioration or destruction, however, implies a weakening of the religious or political institutions within a particular society. Terminal rituals involving the destruction or burning of structures generally occur within specific buildings that denote political and religious power in a particular community.

In this context terminal events would involve permanent changes to the architectural pattern, in many cases associated with the total or partial abandonment of the structure. Nevertheless, minor changes can take place while the building is still in use. However, some short-term architectural changes could be a consequence of moments of crisis within a society (Driessen 1995). Driessen distinguishes three types of changes: (1) a decrease in the energy used in the construction and maintenance of specific buildings, (2) a change in the original architectural layout of a site, and (3) a change in the use of certain spaces. In addition, in the case of religious buildings these changes seem to be more notorious because of their ideological significance. In both cases mentioned, the alterations of architectural features in monumental buildings reflect sociopolitical changes in a community. Monumental buildings have the ability to represent the power of local leaders; consequently, their destruction has a great impact at the social and political level. It remains to be determined, however, what situation would have triggered these events and who was responsible for these actions. As discussed later, it seems that in most cases some faction within the local population would have taken the lead in the execution of these rituals.

ABANDONMENT AND DESTRUCTION IN ANDEAN SETTLEMENTS

Terminal rituals, in which the destruction of monumental architecture is associated with the abandonment of at least part of a site, are very common in the Andean region. The level of destruction involved seems directly related to the magnitude of the events leading to the abandonment. Some scholars suggest that site destruction should be seen as part of a long-term process, as opposed to an isolated and unique event (Zuckerman 2007:3), and that it can shed light on some of the activities that were taking place at these sites prior to their final abandonment.

The Moche site of Pampa Grande, located in the Lambayeque Valley, presents evidence of the simultaneous abandonment of different buildings around AD 700, in an event most likely related to the demise of the Moche V polity (Shimada 1994). Archaeological excavations have revealed that a selected set of buildings was intentionally burned and abandoned. The fire caused the floors to harden, and some parts of the plaster from the roof vitrified because of the high temperatures. Moreover, the specific buildings that were burned had architectural styles reflecting some kind of political or religious power. The evidence presented by Shimada suggests that this burning and abandonment might have been part of a terminal ritual. Shimada presents two models that might explain this "systematic attack on and rejection of the material symbols of power and order" (ibid.:252). The first one concerns internal conflicts over political issues, while the second proposes an external factor that led to a shift in political control of the site. In Shimada's first model, an internal revolt as a result of competing factions within the bureaucratic system would have led to violent actions taken against buildings that symbolized power and the ruling elite. The second model involves a possible conquest of the site by the Wari polity during the Middle Horizon (ibid.).

In the case of the site of Túcume, a settlement in the Lambayeque Valley that dates from the Lambayeque period (AD 250–1000) to the second half of the sixteenth century, two buildings showed evidence of intentional destruction. One of the major buildings known as Huaca Larga exhibits three construction phases. In the central Inka building, dating to the last construction phase (fifteenth century AD), some rooms were intentionally filled while others were destroyed in an event probably dating to the first years of Spanish occupation of the area. The Stone Structure, also dating to the Inka period, suffered two major burning episodes (Narváez 1995).

Another building in the same sector, also destroyed intentionally, was the Temple of the Sacred Stone. The name of this temple derives from the upright stone (*huanca*) in the middle of the structure that was most likely the central shrine of the temple (ibid.). The building also contained three altars corresponding to different construction phases and associated with this huanca, as well as several offerings. During the abandonment of the temple at the end of the last construction phase, the tops of the walls were knocked over, the central chamber was filled, the huanca was covered, and the columns were burned. This event must have taken place contemporaneous to the destruction episode at Huaca Larga (ibid.). Despite the discussion of the possibility that these acts were caused by weather, local people, or the Spaniards, evidence confirms that they were intentional.

A more elaborate abandonment ceremony seems to have taken place at the site of Cerro Baúl, a Wari settlement in Moquegua. While this site appears to have been abandoned abruptly, evidence demonstrates that several terminal rituals were conducted prior to the final evacuation. This is reflected in the fact that most of the rooms were very clean when found. Nevertheless, researchers have noticed that some spaces were used for rituals during the abandonment. Among these terminal ceremonies, the most elaborate seems to be the one recorded in the brewery, a room containing artifacts associated with the preparation of *chicha,* an alcoholic beverage known to have been used in ceremonies across the Andean region. Consequently, this would have been a space of great importance related to the performance of rituals and feasting activities. As part of the site's abandonment, residents would have performed a ritual that would have included chicha. Evidence suggests that once they had consumed the beverage, the room was burned and the *keros*, used to drink it, were smashed and thrown into the fire (Moseley et al. 2005). A similar "highly ritualized abandonment ceremony" was performed at Pataraya, another Wari settlement in the Nasca region. The ritual included the placement of large rocks obstructing access to some rooms, the caching of entire ceramic vessels, and the intentional burying of some areas (Edwards, this volume).

In the examples given, several structures seem to have been intentionally destroyed. As long as these buildings were functioning, they continued to represent symbols of power, but as soon as they were destroyed or abandoned, they stopped serving this purpose. In the specific case of religious buildings, the connotation of their destruction was even greater since they constituted sacred spaces and were imbued with religious symbolism. In the case of Pampa Grande, the fire was used to attack formal constructions representing an existing religious and sociopolitical order (Shimada 1994:252). The same occurred at Túcume, where selected buildings with the same function were destroyed (Narváez 1995).

It can be debated whether local or foreign people were responsible for these destructions. The question that remains is, how elaborate and selective were these processes of destruction and the consequent abandonment, as it seems in fact that too much effort was put into these actions for them to be blamed on foreigners unaware of the ritual symbolism involved. In the case of Cerro Baúl, it is clear that the actions were part of an elaborate ceremony, probably presided over by the local ruling elite, prior to the final abandonment of the site. All the cases mentioned seem to have been local reactions to adjustments within the sociopolitical structure, especially during periods of regional change. The terminal destruction of a site, however, may also have been a secular action with no ritual components. This seems to be the case with the Omo 10 settlement in Moquegua on the Peruvian South Coast.

The site of Omo 10 is composed of a residential area, a temple, and a large cemetery; it was occupied during AD 725–950. The Tiwanaku polity colonized this settlement during its expansion period (AD 725–1000). Evidence suggests that the site was destroyed shortly after its final abandonment (Goldstein 1993). During the destruction of the site, structures were demolished indiscriminately, and many tombs in the cemetery were opened and looted. In fact, some rock slabs that were originally part of the structures destroyed were reused for sealing the tombs. The event occurred before colonial times, as it appears stratigraphically below a thick layer of ash left by the volcano Huayna

Putina, which erupted in February 1600. Goldstein (ibid.) suggests that this destructive event was related to the collapse of the Tiwanaku polity and that a local group rebelling against the Tiwanaku state probably destroyed the site. At Omo 10 the destruction included a series of structures serving different functions. Since this action was not targeted or systematically repeated, it is not considered a terminal ritual. The fact that several tombs were opened and looted further suggests that it was not a ritual action (ibid.).

BURNING PYRAMIDS AT PANQUILMA

At Panquilma, a multi-component settlement located in the left bank of the Lurín Valley on the Peruvian Central Coast (figure 9.1), the targeted destruction and consequential abandonment of specific areas within the monumental compounds appear to have been terminal rituals. The site occupies the surface of a dry ravine, extending approximately 150,000 m^2 at 400 m above sea level. It is 28 km up-valley from Pachacamac, one of the most important religious centers of the ancient Andes (Bueno Mendoza 1983; Eeckhout 1997; Jiménez Borja 1983; Jiménez Borja and Bueno Mendoza 1970; López-Hurtado 2011; Paredes Botoni 1991; Rostworowski de Diez Canseco 2002, 2004; Shimada 1991; Ühle 1991). The site is also part of a group of settlements associated with the Ychsma polity that occupied the Lurín Valley during the Late Intermediate Period (LIP), which extended from AD 1000 to AD 1476 (Menzel 1977; Rowe 1963). Most of these sites continued to be occupied during the Late Horizon (LH) (AD 1476–1535), when the Inkas conquered the area. At Panquilma, evidence recovered from excavations suggests that the site was occupied continuously during the LIP and the LH, but so far no evidence indicates an occupation during the early colonial period.

The settlement is composed of three sectors (López-Hurtado 2011; López-Hurtado and Capriata 2013; Marcone Flores and López-Hurtado 2002). Sector 1 was identified as the site's public sector and consists of three monumental compounds, each containing a type of building known in this region as a pyramid with ramps (Bueno Mendoza 1983; Eeckhout 1995, 1999a, 1999b, 2000a, 2000b; Franco Jordán 1993; Jiménez Borja and Bueno Mendoza 1970; Paredes Botoni and Franco Jordán 1987; Paredes Botoni et al. 1983) and a series of rooms and plazas associated with the main buildings. Tall perimeter walls surround these compounds whose access ways are restricted by a series of narrow corridors. Sector 2 consists of fifteen habitation complexes composed of a series of domestic structures, including dwellings, storage facilities, and patios that are also surrounded by perimeter walls. Finally, Sector 3 corresponds to

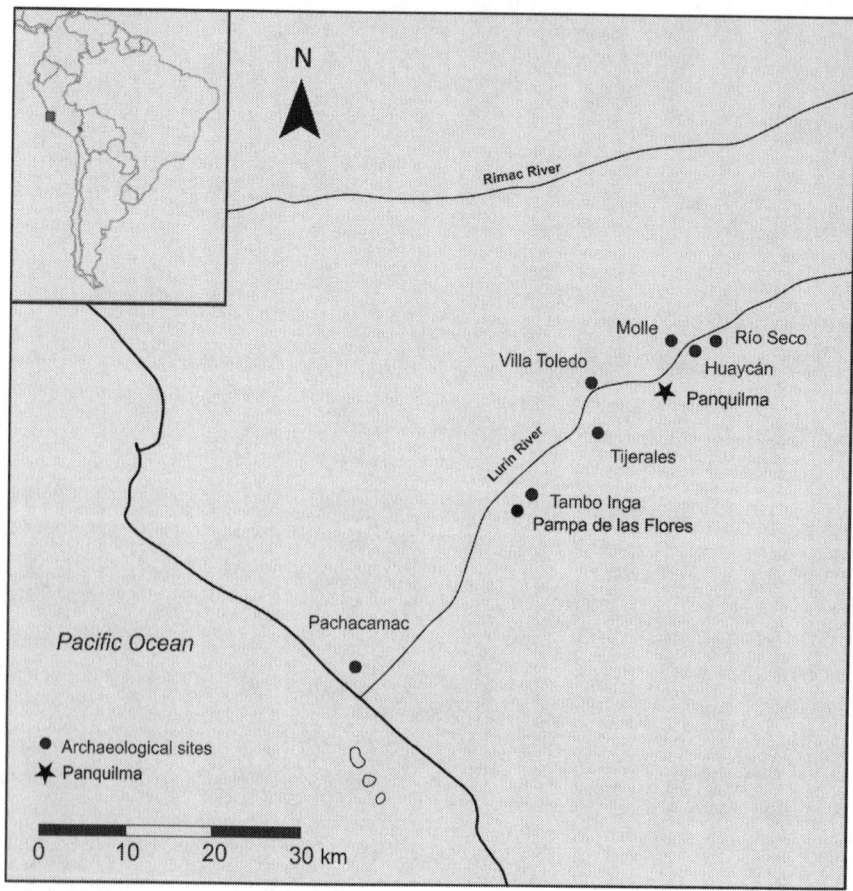

FIGURE 9.1. *Map indicating location of Panquilma*

the marginal areas of the site and is composed of a series of isolated structures, terraces, and tombs.

Between 2003 and 2013, excavations took place within the domestic and public sectors of the site (López-Hurtado 2010, 2011; López-Hurtado and Capriata 2013; Marcone Flores and López-Hurtado 2002). In the public area, units were placed within pyramid complexes 1 and 3—more specifically, within the plazas, platforms, and adjacent rooms (figure 9.2). During these excavations, we identified two different architectural components in these buildings: a public component that included large plazas and elevated platforms and a residential component formed by a series of adjacent rooms, patios, and storage facilities.

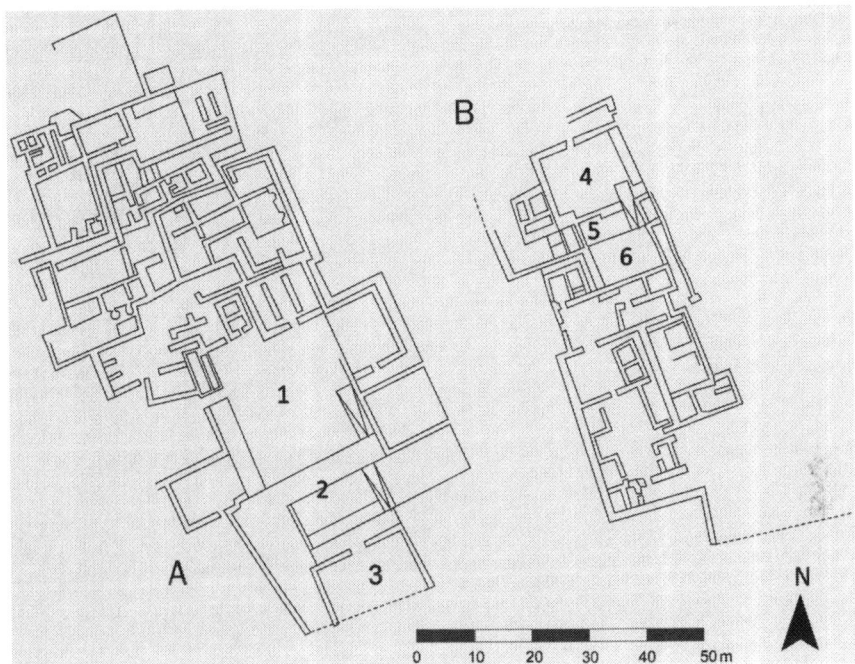

FIGURE 9.2. *(A) Pyramid 1: 1. plaza; 2. intermediate platform; 3. upper platform. (B) Pyramid 3: 4. plaza; 5. intermediate platform; 6. upper platform, Panquilma*

Data recovered at the main plaza of Pyramid 1 provided evidence of the ritual nature of these buildings' public component. Excavations here showed a sequence of occupational floors with a series of pits associated with the different levels. The floors were very clean, and their fine plastered surface differed greatly from ones identified in the site's domestic compounds. The pits were no bigger than 30 cm in diameter and were originally dug without any particular organization. In fact, some of them intrude into previous ones associated with earlier floors. We also found pits located in the center of the plaza, among all the occupational floors, that contained offerings such as ceramic figurines and *Spondylus princeps* valves, among others (figures 9.3, 9.4). The pits located in the peripheral areas of the plazas contained only ceramic fragments or were empty.

A similar pattern was identified at Pyramid 3. Here we were able to identify a similar succession of floors and pits. However, in this building the pits containing offerings were disturbed during a later occupation when the plaza was reused as a trash deposit. We have interpreted these findings as evidence of a process in which Panquilma's ritual areas were de-sacralized.

In addition, the excavation of the main platforms of Pyramids 1 and 3 indicated the abrupt end of the life of these buildings. In both cases these spaces had two access ways: one through the lateral ramps coming from the plazas and one through the adjacent rooms. Also, both had benches that ran parallel to the back walls that were originally covered by a roof. In both cases the roofs, made of canes (*Gynerium sagittatum*) tied together with ropes and supported by wooden posts, were burned and had consequently collapsed over the floor. The fire had been intense; therefore, some parts of the floors and the plaster over the benches and adjacent walls had turned orange. However, despite the intensity of the fire, it seems it was contained to the platforms without compromising the adjacent structures. No artifact remains associated with these events were found. The burning of these platforms corresponded with the end of the use of at least the public component of these buildings. In both cases the burned roofs were found directly under a layer of collapsed walls and over clean floors, indicating that the burning was probably the last event that took place at the pyramid before final abandonment (figures 9.5, 9.6).

FIGURE 9.3. *Ceramic figurine*

Finally, the discovery of walls in the last excavated layers indicates that the pyramid was probably constructed during the last phase of occupation. Although it is not possible to determine the spatial configuration of the first building, we established that there were at least two construction phases. Also, the presence of subsequent floors indicates a series of remodeling events associated with the last construction phase. The presence of large construction fills points to significant effort in its execution, probably to allow the pyramid to

FIGURE 9.4. *Spondylus valves*

gain altitude and the platforms to be built at different levels. Thus, the burning events we recorded marked the end of the life of a building that went through important transformations during its existence.

The excavation of the residential component of Pyramid 3 revealed that in addition to its public ritual function, these buildings were also the residences of Panquilma's ruling elites. A series of rooms and associated midden deposits excavated in the back part of the building revealed the special status of the people living there. One of the rooms excavated seemed to have served as a dwelling. The size of the room, its plastered walls and floor, and a bench that covered over 70 percent of the room's area support this hypothesis. The most important artifacts recovered here consisted of fragments of *Spondylus* beads and a decorated Ychsma head-jar, probably broken intentionally when the pyramid was abandoned. In addition, one storage facility that was excavated next to the upper platform of the pyramid and adjacent to this building's residential area still contained remains of *aji* peppers and maize cobs.

Finally, a unit placed behind the wall surrounding one of the inner patios of the residential area of Pyramid 3 showed evidence of large deposits of trash. A statistical analysis of the artifacts revealed a drastic change in the relationship between fine ceramics and serving vessels. Our analysis revealed that during the first occupational phase, in the public sector the number of fine ceramics and serving vessels was almost equal, while during the second phase, right before the pyramids' abandonment, there were almost four times

FIGURE 9.5. *Upper platform of Pyramid 1 at Panquilma showing evidence of intense burning over the floor.*

as many serving vessels as fine ceramics. This drastic change in the proportion of fine ceramics to serving vessels has been interpreted as an indicator of an increase in feasting activities in the elite's residential area before its abandonment (López-Hurtado 2011).

Some scholars suggest that feasting is a type of "commensal politics" or a specialized form of political competition in which a relationship of obligation, retribution, and loyalty is established between host and guest (Dietler 1996). Feasting can also be seen as a type of ritual practice conducted systematically or spontaneously by a society as a way to diffuse social tension. Based on the higher proportion of serving vessels and preferred food remains among the elites, such as *ají* peppers and maize, we suggest that competitive feasting took place on this patio (López-Hurtado 2011). The size of this space and its location within the private area of the pyramid, however, indicates that the feasts were performed for a small, select audience.

POLITICAL LANDSCAPE IN THE LURÍN VALLEY

Pyramids with ramps have been identified in several sites along the lower and middle Lurín Valley. Eeckhout (2003a) mentions the presence of at least

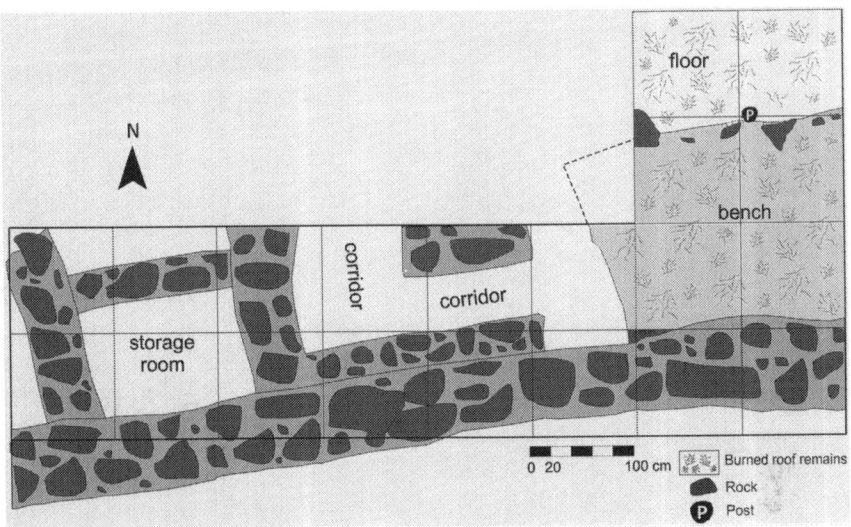

FIGURE 9.6. *Drawing of unit placed on Pyramid 3 showing burned room remains over the bench and the floor of the upper platform*

forty-three pyramids, with the vast majority located at the sites of Pachacamac and Pampa de Flores, both in the lower valley. While most of the pyramids share similar features, such as superimposed platforms connected by a ramp, a main plaza area, and several rooms associated with the platforms, they vary in size and complexity. In addition, there is variation in the position of the ramps that connect the platforms to the main plaza. At Panquilma, the three pyramids located in Sector 1 have what Eeckhout calls "offset ramps." As opposed to the majority of pyramids at Pachacamac and Pampa de Flores, which have a central ramp, pyramids at Panquilma have ramps located on one side of the main plaza (see figure 9.2).

Based on excavations at Pachacamac, Eeckhout suggests that central ramp pyramids were mainly used as palaces or elite residences, serving primarily administrative and residential functions (Eeckhout 2003a, 2003b). The occupants of the pyramids would have offered banquets to and performed ceremonies for a select audience. He indicates that most plazas contained storage vessels, hearths, and food remains, suggesting that these spaces were used primarily for processing food intended for the elite residents and sporadically for a greater number of people attending the feasts (Eeckhout 2003a). The buildings also had rooms dedicated to the production of crafts, such as textiles and ceramics, and several storage facilities, probably for the accumulation of residents' wealth (Eeckhout 2003b). Pyramids would have been continuously occupied while the main resident was alive and abandoned and sometimes ritually closed when he died. This approach implies a dynastic succession among rulers, in which the pyramids served as palaces used for a brief amount of time and did not function simultaneously (ibid.).

In addition, Eeckhout was able to identify events related to changes in the life use of ramp pyramids at Pachacamac. He discovered elite burials in three platforms excavated in the pyramids. These data are consistent with his theory of the use of pyramids by residential elites and a dynastic succession, which would explain the sudden abandonment of these palaces when the main resident died. Eeckhout also mentions that the abandonment of these pyramids could have been voluntary, as evidenced by the presence of ritual activity, which consists of the blockage of entrances, the covering of structures with fine sand, and the burial of offerings containing *Spondylus princeps* shells, among others (Eeckhout 2003a). Moreover, a new building was sometimes constructed on top of the old one (López-Hurtado 2011). As mentioned, this implies that most of the buildings in Pachacamac would have been abandoned before the Inka arrival, which, according to Eeckhout's model, also suggests that only one pyramid would probably have been functioning at that time: the one with the current ruler. It also implies that these events were not necessarily related to drastic disruptions of the sociopolitical order. On the contrary, the construction of new pyramids on top of the abandoned one can be interpreted as indicating continuity of the existing power structures.

However, the evidence found at Panquilma contrasts with Eeckhout's theories. First, excavations in Pyramids 1 and 3 suggest that even if the construction of Pyramid 3 might have been slightly older, the two were probably contemporaneous. In both buildings ceramic fragments associated with Late Ychsma A and B styles were found, which suggests they were used at the same time (ibid.). A small proportion of Inka-style ceramics was also associated with these occupations, indicating that the buildings were at some point also used during the Late Horizon, although this does not necessarily imply an Inka presence at the site.

Second, no evidence of public feasting was found in either of the excavated plazas in pyramid complexes 1 and 3. As opposed to what Eeckhout found at Pachacamac, these spaces in Panquilma seem to have served different functions. While both cases demonstrate that plazas represented the largest inner precincts in the pyramids and would have held a greater number of people, at Panquilma these areas were used for ritual practices that involved the placement of offerings during ceremonies probably presided over by ruling elites (ibid.; López-Hurtado and Capriata 2013). These inconsistencies may be a result of the different spatial configurations of the buildings, indicating that pyramids with an offset ramp served different purposes than those with a central ramp.

Finally, the abandonment of the buildings seems to have been more abrupt at Panquilma than at Pachacamac. In Pachacamac, the pyramids were used to bury the main occupant, which implies continuity as these spaces transformed from residential palaces to mausoleums (Eeckhout 2003a). The burning episodes at Panquilma, however, demonstrate that specific areas of the pyramids were targeted for destruction prior to final abandonment. Moreover, this destruction appears to have been systematic and deliberate, as we only found evidence of burning in the upper platforms of Pyramids 1 and 3. Given that this burning was targeted to specific areas of the pyramids, the destruction was most likely performed advisedly.

During the LIP, the Lurín Valley was populated by a series of groups forming the Ychsma polity, with the religious center of Pachacamac located in the lower section of this valley. Based on research carried out at Panquilma, it appears that Pachacamac did not have a strong influence on the political configuration of the valley (López-Hurtado 2011). Each settlement seems to have had its own political administration run by local ruling elites. Still, Pachacamac played a leading role in the ideological landscape of the valley, as it represented the largest religious center in the area (Astuhuamán Gonzáles 2000; Bueno Mendoza 1982; Cieza de León 1985; De La Calancha 1975; Guamán Poma de Ayala 2002; Rostworowski de Diez Canseco 2002).

The arrival of the Inkas to the Central Coast brought significant changes to the political landscape. Pachacamac was probably one of the first sites occupied. Inka authorities built a number of administrative and residential structures at the site, including the Temple of the Sun, the Acllahuasi, and the Tauri Chumpi Palace. Evidence indicates that most ramp pyramids were no longer used as residences for the elite but instead became temporary dwellings for pilgrims visiting the site (Eeckhout 2010; López-Hurtado and Nesbitt 2010). As Pachacamac gained importance during the Late Horizon as one of the empire's major religious and administrative centers, the political organization of some settlements in the valley was radically affected, perhaps as a consequence of these changes.

In this context, evidence indicates that Panquilma continued to be occupied during the LH, but its political importance may have diminished, as explained later. Evidence recovered in the domestic and private sectors of the site shows the presence of cultural material related stylistically to the Inka polity, appearing in contexts contemporaneous with the local Late Ychsma style. In addition, excavations at one of the isolated structures in Sector 3 displayed a vast amount of Inka-style ceramic fragments, more than found in the domestic sectors or the pyramid complexes. Further studies will determine whether this isolated structure was built during the LH or reoccupied at that time.

At Huaycán de Cieneguilla, another Ychsma settlement 2 km northeast of Panquilma, a series of architectural modifications with clear Inka influence took place during the LH, including the construction of a public building known as the "room of four windows" (López-Hurtado and Nesbitt 2010). Huaycán de Cieneguilla is the only site in the Lurín Valley that presents a monumental Inka-style architecture (Marcone Flores 2004). Marcone suggests that this evidence reflects indirect control by the Inkas, where they would have acquired control in the area through local rulers. In the case of Huaycán, this would have been the point at which the site gained hierarchical superiority over previously more important sites such as Panquilma (ibid.).

Given this evidence of Inka expansion in the Lurín Valley, it is possible to say that the arrival of the Inkas had an impact on Ychsma local populations. However, how did local ruling elites at Panquilma deal with the foreigner presence in the valley in terms of political control of the settlement? Prior to the arrival of the Inkas, Panquilma seems to have been ruled by different elite groups. These factions would have coexisted while competing against each other for prestige and, consequently, for control over the population. Evidence of feasting activities in the privately located patios of the pyramidal complexes demonstrates the competition between various elite groups. At the same time, ruling elites would have interacted with local populations by conducting rituals involving the placement of offerings in the main plazas of the pyramids. During these ceremonies the elite groups would have sat on the benches of the upper platforms in the pyramidal complexes, probably with their backs to the audience while this select entourage deposited offerings.

The evidence presented suggests that the political organization at Panquilma differed from the one at Pachacamac and that this may be reflected in the different configuration of the buildings as well as in their different use. At Panquilma, local ruling elites did not host banquets or feasts for commoners. As it has been established that the two pyramids may have functioned simultaneously, we propose that ruling groups had two ways of interacting with the rest of the population. In the first way, relationships with commoners occurred in the plazas where the rulers conducted ceremonies for a select audience, while the relationship among elite groups would have occurred through feasting activities carried out in private patio areas inside the pyramids. In this sense, although a ritual component of these banquets cannot be ruled out, given the evidence recorded in these spaces, the primarily mundane nature of these activities became very clear. Presuming the ritual nature of every communal activity homogenizes the varied ways in which mundane and ideological factors interacted in the history of Andean societies. In the second way of interacting, the relationship between Panquilma's elite and the rest of the population was the opposite of the first. Evidence recorded in the plazas and platforms on top of the three pyramids at the site highlighted the primarily ritual nature of these ceremonies.

CONCLUSION

The events leading to the abandonment of the pyramids at Panquilma occurred during the Late Horizon, when social and political changes were developing in the valley; consequently, they may be attributed to the arrival of the new Inka polity. But how did this affect the political power of local ruling groups at Panquilma? Did they refuse to align with the new political order? Those questions remain for further investigations.

As argued for the cases of Pampa Grande, Túcume, Cerro Baúl, and Panquilma, terminal rituals seem to have been a common practice in the Andean world. In all cases the events revealed different levels of complexity, but they always reflected important changes in the sociopolitical landscape at a regional level. Furthermore, the local ruling class seems to have played an important role in these processes. Nevertheless, not all intentional destructions and abandonments in the Andes would have had a ritual component, as has been demonstrated for the Omo 10 site in Moquegua.

While terminal rituals can result from endogenous conflict in Andean society, it seems probable that a violent and extensive ritual response reflects the collective trauma caused by large-scale exogenous factors (e.g., conquest, coercion). All of the events mentioned above were triggered by violent events such as invasions or threats of invasion. In this context terminal rituals were caused by external factors and the need to resist them. Consequently, they were probably performed by local elites, the original administrators of rituals in these precincts. It seems clear that in addition to the ritual implications of these actions, the common goal was to destroy things either to prevent their future illegitimate use by others or to "kill" them in a metaphoric way, thus undermining and denying legitimacy to imposed authority.

While it has been stated that Panquilma continued to be occupied during the Late Horizon, its political scenario suffered, directly or indirectly, from the impact of the Inka conquest. As other settlements such as Huaycán de

Cieneguilla gained importance with this new political situation, Panquilma lost its place in the valley hierarchy. The evidence of sudden destruction of the platforms in the pyramidal complexes points to an abrupt end of this polity. However, this intentional destruction does not appear to have been executed by foreigners. The fact that the burning events were confined to areas used by ruling elites to preside over ceremonies highlights the preeminent ritual nature and the probable existence of preconceived "culturally constructed concepts of how living and ritual spaces should be appropriately abandoned" (Edwards, this volume). Moreover, we found no evidence that suggests that outsiders were participants in these events. If this was a consequence of an invasion, the burning and destruction would have been more extensive. On the contrary, the burning events followed certain guidelines more in accordance with those proposed for terminal rituals. Within this context, the selection of spaces, the recurrence, and evidence indicating that these actions took place in spaces linked to ritual activities inside a monumental building support this argument. In addition, the effort and precision that went into these actions may suggest that local ruling groups were involved in this burning event, which suggests that they still had control over ritual practices at the site, even near the demise. Finally, the collapse of burned roofs over clean floors and the presence of these very clean spaces in the surrounding areas may also indicate a planned evacuation. In this scenario the ruling elites would have known that the end was coming and would have packed their belongings and ritually closed their sacred spaces.

ACKNOWLEDGMENTS

The 2008 field season was funded by a dissertation research grant from the National Science Foundation (award no. 0713828) and the University of Pittsburgh Center for Latina American Studies. Excavations took place during 2012 and 2013 as part of the Instituto de Estudios Peruanos Archaeological Research Program. Jorge Capriata kindly agreed to proofread this chapter before submission, and we also thank the editors for their comments and observations, which certainly made this chapter better. Finally, we give special thanks to our wonderful field and lab crew during the excavations in 2008, 2012, and 2013.

REFERENCES CITED

Abrams, E. M., and T. W. Bolland. 1999. "Architectural Energetics, Ancient Monuments, and Operations Management." *Journal of Archaeological Method and Theory* 6 (4): 263–91. http://dx.doi.org/10.1023/A:1021921513937.

Astuhuamán Gonzáles, C. 2000. *Ruta de los Dioses: de Jauja a Pachacamac*, vol. 2. Lima: Fondo Documentario de la Cultura Peruana Patrimonio Cultural del Perú.

Bueno Mendoza, A. 1982. *El antiguo valle de Pachacamac: espacio, tiempo y cultura*. Lima: Editorial Los Pinos.

Bueno Mendoza, A. 1983. "El antiguo valle de Pachacamac: espacio, tiempo y cultura (segunda parte)." *Boletín de Lima* 25 (5): 5–26.

Cieza de León, P. 1985 [1554]. *Crónica del Perú (segunda parte)*. Lima: Pontificia Universidad Católica del Perú / Academia Nacional de la Historia.

Clark, G., and H. Martinsson-Wallin. 2007. "Monumental Architecture in West Polynesia: Origins, Chiefs, and Archaeological Approaches." *Archaeology in Oceania* 42 (1): 1–30. http://dx.doi.org/10.1002/j.1834-4453.2007.tb00006.x.

Dahlin, B. H. 2000. "The Barricade and Abandonment of Chunchucmil: Implications for Northern Maya Warfare." *Latin American Antiquity* 11 (3): 283–98. http://dx.doi.org/10.2307/972179.

De La Calancha, A. 1975 [1638]. "Crónica Moralizada del Orden de San Agustín en el Perú, con successos ejemplares vistos en este Monarquía." In *Crónicas del Perú*, vols. 4–6. Lima: Edición Ignacio Prado Pastor.

DeMarrais, E., L. J. Castillo, and T. Earle. 1996. "Ideology, Materialization, and Power Strategies." *Current Anthropology* 37 (1): 15–31. http://dx.doi.org/10.1086/204472.

Dietler, M. 1996. "Feasts and Commensal Politics in the Political Economy: Food, Power, and Status in Prehistoric Europe." In *Food and the Status Quest: An Interdisciplinary Perspective*, ed. P. W. Wiessner and W. Schiefenhövel, 85–125. Providence, RI: Berghahn Books.

Driessen, Jan. 1995. "'Crisis Architecture'? Some Observations on Architectural Adaptations as Immediate Responses to Changing Socio-Cultural Conditions." *Topoi* 5 (1): 63–88.

Eeckhout, P. 1995. "Pirámide con rampa n°3, Pachacamac: Resultados preliminares de la primera temporada de excavaciones (zonas 1 y 2)." *Bulletin de l'Institut Français d'Études Andines* 24 (1): 65–106.

Eeckhout, P. 1997. "Pachacamac (Côte Centrale du Pérou): Aspects du fonctionnement, du développement et de l'influence du site durant l'Intermédiaire récent (ca 900–1470)." PhD dissertation, Faculté de Philosophie et Lettres, Orientation histoire de l'art et archéologie, Université Libre de Bruxelles, Brussels.

Eeckhout, P. 1999a. *Pachacamac durant l'Intermédiaire recent: Etude d'un site monumental préhispanique de la Côte centrale du Pérou*. BAR International Series 747. Oxford: British Archaeological Reports.

Eeckhout, P. 1999b. "Pirámide con rampa n°III, Pachacámac: Nuevos datos, nuevas perspectivas." *Bulletin de l'Institut Français d'Études Andines* 28 (2): 169–214.

Eeckhout, P. 2000a. "Los antecedentes formales y funcionales de las 'Pirámides con Rampa' de la Costa Central del Perú en los tiempos prehispánicos." *Boletín Americanista* 50: 39–60.

Eeckhout, P. 2000b. "The Palaces of the Lords of Ychsma: An Archaeological Reappraisal of the Function of Pyramids with Ramps at Pachacamac, Central Coast of Perú." *Revista de Arqueología Americana* 17–19: 217–54.

Eeckhout, P. 2003a. "Ancient Monuments and Patterns of Power at Pachacamac, Central Coast of Perú." *Beiträge zur Allgemeinen und Vergleichenden Archäologie* 23: 139–82.

Eeckhout, P. 2003b. "Diseño arquitectonico, patrones de ocupación y formas de poder en Pachacamac, Costa central del Perú." *Revista Espanola de Antropologia Americana* 33: 17–37.

Eeckhout, P. 2010. "Las pirámides con rampa de Pachacamac durante el horizonte tardío." In *Arqueología en el Perú: nuevos aportes para el estudio de las sociedades andinas prehispánicas*, ed. R. Romero Velarde and T. P. Svendsen, 415–34. Lima: Universidad Nacional Federico Villarreal.

Franco Jordán, R. 1993. "Excavaciones en la Pirámide con rampa n°2, Pachacamac." Tesis de Licenciatura, Universidad Nacional Mayor de San Marcos, Lima.

Freidel, D. A. 1998. "Sacred Work: Dedication and Termination in Mesoamerica." In *The Sowing and the Dawning: Termination, Dedication, and Transformation in the Archaeological and Ethnographic Record of Mesoamerica*, ed. S. B. Mock, 189–93. Albuquerque: University of New Mexico Press.

Goldstein, P. 1993. "Tiwanaku Temples and State Expansion: A Tiwanaku Sunken-Court Temple in Moquegua, Peru." *Latin American Antiquity* 4 (1): 22–47. http://dx.doi.org/10.2307/972135.

Guamán Poma de Ayala, F. 2002 [1615]. *El primer Nueva Corónica i Buen Gobierno*. Copenhagen: Real Biblioteca de Copenhague.

Harrison-Buck, E., P. A. McAnany, and R. Storey. 2007. "Empowered and Disempowered during the Late to Terminal Classic Transition: Maya Burial and Termination Rituals in the Sibun Valley, Belize." In *New Perspectives on Human Sacrifice and Ritual Body Treatments in Ancient Maya Society*, ed. V. Tiesler and A. Cucina, 74–101. New York: Springer. http://dx.doi.org/10.1007/978-0-387-48871-4_4.

Jiménez Borja, A. 1983. "Pachacamac." *Boletín de Lima* 38: 40–54.

Jiménez Borja, A., and A. Bueno Mendoza. 1970. "Breves notas acerca de Pachacamac." *Arqueología y Sociedad* 4: 13–25.

Joyce, A. A., and S. Johannessen. 1993. "Abandonment and the Production of Archaeological Variablility at Domestic Sites." In *Abandonment of Settlements and Regions: Ethnoarchaeological and Archaeological Approaches*, ed. C. M. Cameron and

S. A. Tomka, 138–54. Cambridge: Cambridge University Press. http://dx.doi.org/10.1017/CBO9780511735240.011.

López-Hurtado, E. 2010. "Pachacamac y Panquilma: Relaciones de Poder Durante el Período Intermedio Tardío." In *Arqueología en el Perú*, ed. R. Romero Velarde and T. P. Svendsen, 311–26. Lima: Universidad Nacional Federico Villareal.

López-Hurtado, E. 2011. "Ideology and the Development of Social Hierarchy at the Site of Panquilma, Peruvian Central Coast." PhD dissertation, Department of Anthropology, University of Pittsburgh, Pittsburgh, PA.

López-Hurtado, E., and C. Capriata. 2013. *Informe Final del Proyecto de Investigación Arqueológica Panquilma*. Lima: Programa de Investigaciones Arqueológicas del IEP.

López-Hurtado, E., and J. Nesbitt. 2010. "Provincial Religious Centers in the Inka Empire: Propagators of Official Ideology or Spaces for Local Resistance?" In *Comparative Perspectives on the Archaeology of Coastal South America*, ed. R. E. Cutright, E. López-Hurtado, and A. J. Martin, 214–29. Pittsburgh, Lima, and Quito: Center for Comparative Archaeology, Department of Anthropology, University of Pittsburgh / Fondo Editorial de la Pontificia, Universidad Católica del Perú / Ministerio de Cultura del Ecuador.

Marcone Flores, G. 2004. "Cieneguilla a la llegada de los Incas: Aproximaciones desde la historia ecológica y la arqueología." *Bulletin de l'Institut Francais d'Études Andines* 33 (3): 715–34. http://dx.doi.org/10.4000/bifea.5330.

Marcone Flores, G., and E. López-Hurtado. 2002. "Panquilma y Cieneguilla en la discusión arqueológica de la Costa Central." *Boletín de Arqueología PUCP* 6: 375–95.

Menzel, D. 1977. *The Archaeology of Ancient Peru and the Work of Max Uhle*. Berkeley: R. H. Lowie Museum of Anthropology, University of California.

Mock, S. B. 1998. *The Sowing and the Dawning: Termination, Dedication, and Transformation in the Archaeological and Ethnographic Record of Mesoamerica*. Albuquerque: University of New Mexico Press.

Moore, J. D. 1996. *Architecture and Power in the Ancient Andes: The Archaeology of Public Buildings*. New Studies in Archaeology. Cambridge: Cambridge University Press. http://dx.doi.org/10.1017/CBO9780511521201.

Moseley, M., D. J. Nash, P. R. Williams, S. D. deFrance, A. Miranda, and M. Ruales. 2005. "Burning Down the Brewery: Establishing and Evacuating an Ancient Imperial Colony at Cerro Baúl, Peru." *Proceedings of the National Academy of Sciences of the United States of America* 102 (48): 17264–71. http://dx.doi.org/10.1073/pnas.0508673102.

Narváez, V. A. 1995. "The Pyramids of Tucume: The Monumental Sector." In *Pyramids of Tucume: The Quest for Peru's Forgotten City*, ed. T. Heyerdahl, D. H. Sandweiss, and V. A. Narváez, 79–130. New York: Thames and Hudson.

Paredes Botoni, P. 1991. "Pachacamac." In *Los Incas y el Antiguo Perú, 3000 años de Historia*, ed. S. Purín. Madrid: Centro Cultural de la Villa de Madrid.

Paredes Botoni, P., and R. Franco Jordán. 1987. "Pachacámac: Las Pirámides con Rampa: Cronología y Funcción." *Gaceta Arqueológica Andina* 13: 5–7.

Paredes Botoni, P., R. Franco Jordán, and C. Rivera. 1983. *Pirámide con Rampa n°2: Pachacamac: Excavaciones, Conservación, y Restauro Parcial: Informe Final*. Lima: Instituto Nacional de Cultura.

Rostworowski de Diez Canseco, M. 2002. *Pachacamac y el Señor de los Milagros / Señoríos indígenas de Lima y Canta*. Lima: Instituto de Estudios Peruanos.

Rostworowski de Diez Canseco, M. 2004. *Costa peruana prehispánica*, 2nd ed. Lima: Instituto de Estudios Peruanos.

Rowe, J. H. 1963. "Inca Culture at the Time of the Spanish Conquest." In *Handbook of South American Indians*, vol. 2: *The Andean Civilizations*, ed. J. H. Steward, 183–330. New York: Cooper Square.

Schiffer, M. B. 1996. *Formation Processes of the Archaeological Record*. Salt Lake City: University of Utah Press.

Shimada, I. 1991. "Pachacamac Archaeology: Retrospect and Prospect." In *Pachacamac*, ed. M. Ühle, viii–xviii. University Museum Monograph 62. Philadelphia: University Museum of Archaeology and Anthropology, University of Pennsylvania.

Shimada, Izumi. 1994. *Pampa Grande and the Mochica Culture*. Austin: University of Texas Press.

Stanish, C. 2001. "The Origin of State Societies in South America." *Annual Review of Anthropology* 30 (1): 41–64. http://dx.doi.org/10.1146/annurev.anthro.30.1.41.

Stanton, T. W., M. K. Brown, and J. B. Pagliaro. 2008. "Garbage of the Gods? Squatters, Refuse Disposal, and Termination Rituals among the Ancient Maya." *Latin American Antiquity* 19 (3): 227–47.

Stross, B. 1998. "Seven Ingredients in Mesoamerican Ensoulment: Dedication and Termination in Tenejapa." In *The Sowing and the Dawning: Termination, Dedication, and Transformation in the Archaeological and Ethnographic Record of Mesoamerica*, ed. S. B. Mock, 31–39. Albuquerque: University of New Mexico Press.

Trigger, B. G. 1990. "Monumental Architecture: A Thermodynamic Explanation of Symbolic Behaviour." *World Archaeology* 22 (2, Monuments and the Monumental): 119–32. http://dx.doi.org/10.1080/00438243.1990.9980135.

Trubitt, M.B.D. 2000. "Mound Building and Prestige Goods Exchange: Changing Strategies in the Cahokia Chiefdom." *American Antiquity* 65 (4): 669–90. http://dx.doi.org/10.2307/2694421.

Ühle, M. 1991 [1903]. *Pachacamac*. Philadelphia: University Museum of Archaeology and Anthropology, University of Pennsylvania.

Zuckerman, S. 2007. "Anatomy of a Destruction: Crisis Architecture, Termination Rituals, and the Fall of Canaanite Hazor." *Journal of Mediterranean Archaeology* 20 (1): 3–32. http://dx.doi.org/10.1558/jmea.v20i1.3.

10

Reconstructing Early Colonial Andean Ritual Practice at Pukara, Peru

An Architectural Approach

Sarah Abraham

As the chapters in this volume demonstrate, the ancient Andes had a long and diverse history of religious traditions and ritual practices—one that did not end with the arrival of the Spanish in 1532. In the Andes, the introduction of Christianity during the early colonial period often resulted in a complex religious reality in which Christianity was added to, but did not necessarily replace, local beliefs. During this time aspects of Old and New World religious traditions became intertwined, and a new Andean Christian practice emerged. This entanglement can be seen at La Quinta, an early colonial chapel at Pucará, located in the northwestern Lake Titicaca Basin of Peru. Built on top of the Pukara ruins, La Quinta features a mix of European and Andean architectural traditions. By examining the use and reuse of the built environment, this chapter demonstrates how architecture can help identify past ritual behavior and discusses how hybrid architectural styles may be indicative of novel forms of worship. By studying the built environment and its place in the large cultural and sacred landscape, we can better understand the nature of ritual at Pukara during this crucial time in the development of Andean Christianity.

COLONIAL ANDEAN RELIGION

Although undoubtedly chaotic and destructive, the Spanish conquest of the Andes did not signal the abrupt dissolution of indigenous religions or their immediate

DOI: 10.5876/9781607325963.c010

replacement with European Christianity (Gose 2003; Mills 1997; Salomon and Urioste 1991; Van Buren 2010:176). In fact, missionization of the Andes was a long, protracted process. While the Inka state religion—which had only been around for a hundred years or so—had been effectively stamped out by the early 1700s, the older, regional religious rituals and traditions persisted and were far more difficult for the Spanish to extinguish (MacCormack 1991:4–5).

The introduction of Christianity elicited mixed responses from Andean peoples. Many saw an advantage in believing in a new, foreign, and seemingly all-powerful god, but most struggled with conversion and the demand to relinquish their traditional beliefs and ritual practices. While some openly embraced Christianity after conquest, others rejected it outright—in some cases, violently so. Far more added only the aspects of this new religion that they found appealing and dropped them when they no longer worked within their rapidly changing worldview. As Mills (1994:116) relates, "Aspects of the Europeans' faith became elements in the Andean religious framework by a fluctuating agenda, varying from place to place, individual to individual, and usually without clearly eclipsing the existing religious connections." It is this tangle of European and Andean beliefs and practices that was woven together, whether deliberately or inadvertently, to lay the foundation of Andean Christianity.

Andean Christianity in the early colonial period was inchoate and flexible. It was marked by religious compromise and co-option as well as uneven, fitful, and unpredictable change (Mills 1997:5). To varying degrees, aspects of indigenous belief and ritual practice were incorporated into Andean Christianity—at both an institutional and individual level—from its very inception: "The interaction of Christianity with native American religions in the colonial era (and indeed subsequently) was characterized by reciprocal, albeit asymmetrical, exchange rather than the unilateral imposition of an uncompromising, all-conquering and all-transforming monotheism" (Griffiths 1999:1). Andean Christianity was not purely indigenous or European—the reality was far more fluid than those binary categories suggest. Much like the hybrid colonial culture emerging at this time, the negotiation of religious identity in the Andes resulted in an "in-betweeness" of faith and ritual practice (Bhabha 1994).

The entanglement of Spanish Catholicism and traditional Andean belief systems produced new religious practices during the early colonial period (Gose 2003; Lara 2004; MacCormack 1991; Mills 1997; Wernke 2007, 2011). This hybridity was not practiced uniformly across the Andes and in some cases was not sanctioned by the church. New traditions in religious music, art, and festivals emerged, reflecting the complex cultural interactions that created them (Nair 2007:52). For instance, to the east of the Andes, the traditional songs and dances of the Guarani were adapted after contact to worship the Christian god (Bailey 2005:242). In addition, Catholic feast days became aligned with events on the Andean ritual calendar, producing new ritual traditions (MacCormack 1991; Mills 1997). For example, the timing of the Catholic festival of Corpus Christi corresponded with that of the Inka solstice celebration of Inti Raymi; the coinciding ritual procession through the streets of Cusco became an important event in the colonial period and featured aspects of both religious traditions (MacCormack 1991:180, 1998). Many hybrid religious practices started in these early years and contributed to the syncretic nature of Andean Christianity that is still practiced today.

Along with ecclesiastical music and art, new colonial forms of religious architecture also emerged. Many of the first colonial structures were churches built to facilitate conversion, and in rural areas, provisional chapels were constructed. Churches and chapels were the first permanent presence of Spanish culture and religion for many Andeans, as well as the materialization of Spanish conquest (Fraser 1990:82). While the Spanish may have been interested in creating architectural and stylistic forms that would have been somewhat familiar to indigenous populations, it is important to remember that Andeans were active participants in the creation of these new forms. As Abercrombie (1998:263) argues, "Much as we might like to attribute such facts to the conversion strategies of wily priests, we must also recognize that Andeans themselves were adept at the process of cultural translation." Analyzing colonial places of worship—in terms not only of how but also of where they were built on the landscape—can provide insight into the earliest practices of Andean Christianity.

Religious architecture can be used to examine ritual practice in a number of ways (Capriata Estrada and López-Hurtado, Chicoine et al., Vega-Centeno Sara-Lafosse, this volume). First, rituals routinely occur in specially prepared spaces, many of which were created specifically for that purpose. As the loci of ritual activity, religious buildings are designed and constructed to accommodate ceremonies, and this function is reflected in the architecture and the use of space. These special-purpose buildings are often distinguishable from their domestic counterparts in terms of layout, scale, architectural elements, and the labor invested in their construction (Moore 1996b:139; Renfrew 1985). Embedded with cues that communicate culturally coded information, religious architecture can also shape ritual experience (Moore 1996a:790, 1996b:221). As Moore (1996b:3)argues, "Architecture is more than a passive product of potential labor investment; it reflects other dimensions of public life, and in turn, helps shape the nature of social interaction." For example, Fogelin's (2007:62) examination of Buddhist architecture in India demonstrates how variations in spatial organization shape the ritual participation of priests and the audience. Thus, ritual structures not only reflect religious practice but also play a role in shaping it (ibid.; Moore 1996a:798; Wernke 2011:79).

Beyond architectural components, the placement of the religious structure within the local landscape is also indicative of its ritual role. As Low (1995:748) argues, "The symbolic importance of the built environment is found in its interpretation as an expression of culturally shared mental structures and embodied processes. By their configuration, content, and associations, the spatial or physical attributes establish a system of relationships that represent aspects of social life . . . The examination of the built environment, then, can provide insights into meanings, values, and processes that might not be uncovered through other observations."

Not coincidently, colonial religious structures were often placed in meaningful places in an attempt to map onto the indigenous sacred landscape. This appropriation also included the reuse of ancient religious architecture. In many parts of the Andes, indigenous shrines had to be "converted" as well as the people. Temples, plazas, and other pre-Columbian ritual sites were sometimes incorporated into colonial chapels and churches. This reshaping and reconfiguring of the built environment was perceived by the Spanish as an aid to conversion; "keeping existing shrines intact allowed the Spanish to bring people to God in a familiar place" (Lara 2008:20) as well as to provide a sense of continuity between Andean faith and Christianity (Bailey 2005:218). It is also possible, as Low (1995:758) argues, that "the spatial relationships maintained by building on ruins, using the same stones and foundations, allowed elements of indigenous politico-religious system to remain" and that "these latent meanings were not necessarily acted upon publicly, but they may have been useful in reinforcing aspects of indigenous identity, self-esteem, and spiritual power that helped to preserve indigenous folkways, beliefs, and practices."

However, not all religious architecture with elements of both Spanish and indigenous traditions is evidence of new syncretic practices. There is a difference between building a church on top of a temple and building a chapel that incorporates aspects of local religious architecture. Examples of the former are found throughout the Andes, including the Santo Domingo convent in Cusco, the cathedral of Vilcashuamán, and the San Juan Bautista church in Huaytará. In these cases, building on top of sacred sites was not only a symbol of the new Christian religious and social order but a physical demonstration of dominance. MacCormack (1991:252) argues that it was intended to be a "display of Spanish superiority over Andean weakness and error" and thus a way to establish physical hegemony (Lara 2008:21).

RELIGIOUS ARCHITECTURE IN THE COLONIAL ANDES

Spanish conquest of the Andes brought distinct religions and forms of worship into contact. The first Europeans in western South America found a seemingly infinite number of indigenous religions, from the Inka state religion to small hunter-gatherer belief systems, each with its own foreign worldviews, religious practices, rituals, and deities. However, the Spanish became quickly aware that in many regions, public rituals took the form of open-air worship and were conducted in spatially designated spaces and places. From Caral to the Inka, many Andean cultures built religious architecture in the form of large plazas and sunken courts where outdoor ceremonies took place, often in front of temples or *huacas*. Rituals involved speeches, music, and dance that Moore (1996a:791) believes "fused communities, validated social distinctions, and restated cosmologies." Many smaller-scale societies also had ritual spaces but often had no formally defined architectural space for ritual.

Andean religious traditions at the time of contact stood in stark contrast to how the Spanish practiced Christianity back in Europe. As Catholics, they were accustomed to rituals such as mass that took place indoors. As McAndrew (1965:205, original emphasis) stresses, "From its beginning the Christian religion had been one where worship took place *inside* a building," continuing that "the essential rite was the Mass, and its symbolism and traditions demanded that it take place indoors." In fact, "Christian architecture had from the first emphasized the interior of its churches rather than the exterior: where Mass was to be celebrated, a fine setting ought to be provided and the setting had to be indoors" (ibid.). European churches were architecturally distinct structures, with architectural canons that were followed across Europe. This included a cruciform floor plan that consisted of an apse and nave that symbolized the cross on which Christ died. The altar, located in the apse, was always oriented east—in the direction Jesus would rise again. Other architectural canons were added to the basic cruciform model, creating regional and temporal styles.

Old World religious practices and their corresponding architectural canons are visible in the religious architecture of the early colonial period. The arrival of the Spanish coincided with an explosion of church construction (Fraser 1986:325). This included the introduction of Christian religious architecture like the cruciform floor plan, as well as rites and rituals such as mass and baptism. As in other parts of Latin America, the earliest chapels in the Andes were temporary adobe buildings or repurposed existing structures that were used until a Spanish town could be founded and a formal church constructed (Lara 2004:36). However, the introduction of European religious architecture was also coupled with the appearance of new colonial forms adopted in the Andes after contact, including atria and open chapels. These new forms of religious architecture—originally developed in New Spain as part of a larger evangelization complex (see ibid.:29)—were constructed in response to the needs of a new colonial Andean society and included structures built to accommodate large crowds receiving religious instruction and witnessing mass.

Walled patios, or atria, were large, enclosed rectangular spaces built alongside churches and chapels. They ranged from a simple quadrangle to more elaborate spaces with an atrial cross or fountain in the center and multiple gateways (ibid.:18). Both churches and chapels opened up to atria, and this enclosed outdoor space is where Andeans gathered to learn Christian doctrine. Although they may have served more than one purpose, atria were conceived as transitional spaces between the church and the town as well as a continuation of the church (Gutiérrez et al. 1978:75), and they served as open-air naves. As many have noted, the use of atria for open-air worship relates not only to necessity (large-scale conversion) but also to prehispanic religious practice (Ballesteros 1975; Gisbert and de Mesa 1985; Gutiérrez et al. 1978; Lara 2004).

Open chapels, also referred to as Indian chapels or external chapels, were similarly common in the Andes in the sixteenth century. These chapels were sometimes referred to as *guayronas*, the Quechua word for wind, implying an open-air religious experience (Donahue-Wallace 2008:28). They tended to be small, roofed structures with one or more sides opening onto a plaza or atrium (Ballesteros 1975:118). This architectural plan created two distinct spaces of worship; while the priest gave mass under the protection of the roofed structure, large congregations gathered in the open plaza or atrium to participate in mass and religious instruction (Ballesteros 1975:117; Lara 2004:21). In larger towns open chapels were built alongside the main church, providing the Spanish and indigenous with their own spaces for worship because worship was segregated in many towns and cities during the early colonial period (Donahue-Wallace 2008:28). However, in smaller villages, especially those with no or very small Spanish populations, open chapels were standalone structures that served as rural houses of worship in the absence of a formal church.

Ballesteros (1975) identifies two common types of colonial Andean open chapels. The first consists of a chapel built next to or attached to a church and that opens onto a small enclosed atrium. This type of open chapel is found in the Collao region, where most were constructed during the 1570s through the 1590s (ibid.:119). Many remain unstudied and undocumented, in part because so many have been remodeled, destroyed, or deteriorated (ibid.:114). This is especially true of the open chapels of the Titicaca Basin because they were built with adobe bricks and thatch. However, it is possible to interpret the building materials as a reflection of the perceived intended use of these structures: temporary structures to be used only while indoctrination took place. Once formal churches were constructed and the indigenous population began worshipping indoors, these early structures were abandoned and quickly succumbed to the harsh Titicaca elements (Donahue-Wallace 2008:28).

The second type of open chapel is a second-story balcony on the church facade that is common in Cusco but can be found throughout the Andes (Ballesteros 1975:115, 119–20). Like their Titicaca cousins, these balconies were constructed to facilitate groups larger than the chapel itself could accommodate. The town's population could gather in the open air and witness the celebration of mass. Unlike their southern counterparts, the open chapels of Cusco tend to be made of more permanent materials (ibid.:114). The greater investment in labor and materials suggests that these structures were likely more than provisional constructions and possibly served a disparate role from the open chapels of the altiplano. One of the best-preserved examples of this type of open chapel can be found in Andahuaylillas. Another example is the balcony of Santo Domingo de Cusco, built on top of the Coricancha.

Both atria and open chapels reflected the practice of open-air worship, a clear departure from the Old World Christian tradition of indoor worship and the emphasis on the interior in Christian architecture (McAndrew 1965:205). Colonial Andean atria were unlike their European precursors because they were used to hold mass and were used regularly (ibid.). Priests preached in the open air in Europe but did so infrequently, and not in a specially constructed area. Nor was it customary to give mass outdoors. Outdoor Eucharistic liturgy was rare in Old World Christianity; thus, this architectural form appears to be a New World invention.[1] Without direct European antecedents, these new canons more closely paralleled plazas, sunken courts, and other places of open-air worship native to the Andes. The appropriation of Andean ritual practices such as open-air traditions may have been a compromise between Spanish missionary goals and local beliefs to facilitate the conversion process (Gisbert and de Mesa 1985:130; Gutiérrez et al. 1978:71). Thus, from the very beginning, religious architecture in the colonial Andes was similar to yet distinct from both European and pre-Columbian traditions. In combining indigenous and Christian spaces and practices, new types of ritual experiences were created.

However, documenting the full extent of these hybrid forms and their associated rituals is hampered by the preservation state of most early colonial sites; many of the first chapels have been destroyed or extensively remodeled, or they have deteriorated. This spotty record has diverted scholarly attention to the extant architecture of the later colonial period (Bailey 2010; Ballesteros 1975; Gisbert and de Mesa 1985; Gutiérrez et al. 1978). Recent studies, including excavations at Magdalena de Cao (Quilter 2010) and recently published work on Torata Alta in the Moquegua Valley (Rice 2012), have found that while these new forms fell out of favor, there is archaeological evidence that some aspects of pre-contact Andean ritual practice continued in European-style churches well after contact.

Although early colonial chapels are relatively rare, recent studies of extant structures have contributed to a more comprehensive understanding of the early ecclesiastical architecture and its associated rituals. Such research includes archaeological investigations of Colca Valley chapels built by the Franciscans prior to the 1570s (Wernke 2007, 2011). Some of the earliest standing chapels in Peru, these structures are open chapels built to accommodate outdoor worship. The chapels are strategically located near Inka structures and plazas—an attempt by the Spanish to create "a spatial analogy that linked and leveraged built-in spaces of Inka state-sponsored ceremonials with new forms of Christian ritual" (Wernke 2011:86). Wernke (2007:179) concludes that the interaction between the Spanish and the Collaguas people of the Colca Valley created new hybrid places and spaces that "were the creation of both but not controlled entirely by either." This is similar to findings at San Miguel de Piura, the first church built in South America (Astuhuamán Gonzáles 2012; Villanueva Domínquez et al. 2002). Constructed soon after Pizarro's arrival, this rectilinear structure consists of European architectural features such as a bell tower, baptismal fountain, altar, and sacristy. However, the church's location shows clear ties to the local sacred landscape—it was built partially on prehispanic architecture and is adjacent to a prehispanic stepped platform. Astuhuamán Gonzáles argues that San Miguel and its deliberate placement are reflections of a brief transitional period, between 1534 and 1548, during which European and indigenous ecclesiastical structures stood side by side in religious coexistence (Astuhuamán Gonzáles 2012:198).

PUKARA'S PREHISTORIC RELIGIOUS ARCHITECTURE

The archaeological site of Pukara, just south of the modern town of Pucará,[2] has a long history as a ritual center (figure 10.1). While its occupational history reaches back thousands of years, the site became the civil-ceremonial center of the Pukara culture during the Late Formative period (500 BC–AD 200). During this period the Pukara culture rose to prominence and was one of the

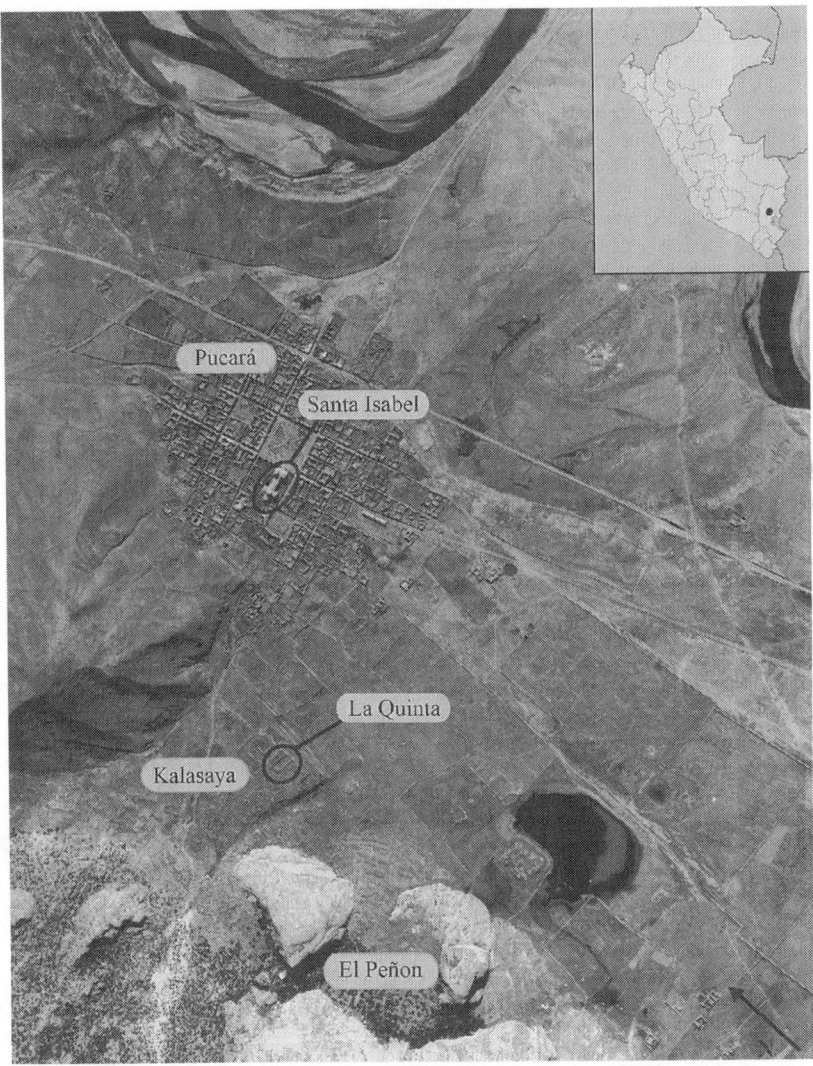

FIGURE 10.1. *Aerial photo of Pukara and its surroundings, showing the location of sites discussed in the text*

first complex societies to develop in the Titicaca Basin (see Klarich 2005). At the heart of this regional polity stood the Kalasaya, a large stepped platform that rises up from the pampa at the base of El Peñon, a massive red sandstone outcrop. On top of the Kalasaya are multiple subterranean stone-lined courts

FIGURE 10.2. *Site of Pukara with El Peñon in the background. Photo by Elizabeth Klarich.*

ringed by small rectilinear structures (figure 10.2). Sunken courts served as ritual spaces across the Southern Andes and were the dominant form of religious architecture during the Late Formative and Middle Horizon (Kolata 1993:104). Given their small size and restricted location, these sunken plazas would have been used for small, intimate ritual gatherings (see Moore 1996a).

By AD 400 the Pukara polity had collapsed; while the sunken courts may have fallen into disuse, ritual continued at the site in other areas. The post-Pukara occupation has been pieced together by Wheeler and Mujica (1981). During the Late Intermediate Period (AD 1100–1450), the Colla people lived near the Kalasaya and used the ruins as a cemetery. The dead were placed in communal burial towers, or *chulpa*, located on the terrace just below La Quinta. Like most Andean groups, the Colla venerated their ancestors, who were often visited and given offerings in rituals of remembrance that strengthened the lineage and its ties to the land (see Cobo 1997). Later, the Inka conquered the Colla and modified the Kalasaya as a demonstration of their newly established control. Imperial additions to the Kalasaya include rectilinear buildings, a double-jambed trapezoidal niched wall, and a new, rerouted stairway and entry (and sealing of the Late Formative entrance). Although much of the architecture from this period has since been destroyed, some of the structures the empire constructed were probably spaces for ritual. In the Inka provinces outside the capital of Cusco, large trapezoidal plazas were commonly constructed to hold public ceremonies, including state-sponsored feasting rituals. The fall of the Inka in the 1530s, however, did not mark the end of Pukara's ceremonial significance; the site continued to play an important role in local ritual after Spanish contact.

LA QUINTA AND PUKARA'S COLONIAL RELIGIOUS ARCHITECTURE

In the early decades of the colonial period, the La Quinta[3] chapel was constructed on top of the monumental terraces between two of the Late Formative sunken courts (figures 10.3, 10.4).[4] It was one of the first physical manifestations of the Spanish empire in this area, as well as the last stage in the occupational history of this important Andean site. La Quinta is composed of a chapel and an enclosed atrium. The chapel is a trapezoidal structure measuring roughly 27 m by 8 m and is oriented east-west, with the eastern end abutting the sealed Formative entryway and a niched Inka wall and the western end containing the apse (figure 10.5).

The architectural components of the chapel consist of an apse that opens onto a possible chancel (a rectilinear patio with a paved floor) with a set of stairs that connects this elevated section to a sunken nave. The single entrance is located on the north wall of the chancel. The nave's south wall features a row of arched niches, and a possible baptismal fountain can be found in the northwest corner of the nave. La Quinta's walls were constructed with a combination of adobe and undressed fieldstones (possibly borrowed from the nearby Inka structures) placed in irregular courses. However, more labor went into the construction of the apse: some of the rocks were shaped, and the interior walls were covered in red plaster. Overall, the construction materials and

FIGURE 10.3. *Late Formative sunken court. Photo by Elizabeth Klarich.*

techniques suggest that La Quinta was one of the early rudimentary chapels built in the early decades after conquest.

The atrium, accessed from the chapel's single entry, is a roughly 12 m by 18 m enclosed area. The perimeter wall is made of mud bricks and roughly shaped field stones and has been severely weathered by the elements. The access point to the Kalasaya is not clear, as the wall is missing in more than one place. A small square enclosure—with a single small window on its north wall—is located near the northeast corner of the atrium, but its function is unknown. The enclosure appears in photographs taken by Kidder in the 1920s and so is not a recent construction.[5] To the south of the atrium is a wall that runs along the edge of the Kalasaya. It is made of roughly shaped fieldstones and is composed of double-jambed niches. Between this wall and the edge of the terrace is a line of column foundations. The relationship of the niched wall to the chapel and atrium is not clear.

Architectural analysis shows that La Quinta was not a purely colonial construction but the result of multiple building events, starting in the prehistoric era. Based on wall alignments and masonry styles, a rectilinear Inka structure

FIGURE 10.4. *La Quinta chapel*

(once referred to as a *kallanka*) was reused and remodeled to serve as the apse of the chapel. The four original corners are evident, indicating that the apse was originally a standalone structure. The remains of two evenly spaced doorjambs along the east wall follow a standard Inka floor plan. Other Inka architectural features include the gables on the north and south walls, which indicate that the building had a gabled roof. Colonial modifications include the removal of the east wall, the addition of apertures in the north and south walls, the addition of two buttresses on the west wall, and construction of the nave, chancel, and atrium. The windows that were added to the apse may have been built to allow those outside La Quinta chapel to still witness the priest delivering mass. Moreover, the buttresses were probably added on to the structure to provide additional support for the roof, perhaps to compensate for the removal of the east wall. Although it is clear that the apse was roofed, there is no architectural evidence of roofing in the nave; no buttresses were constructed and no gables or niches for support beams are present. This absence of Andean and European roofing features strongly suggests that the nave was left open.

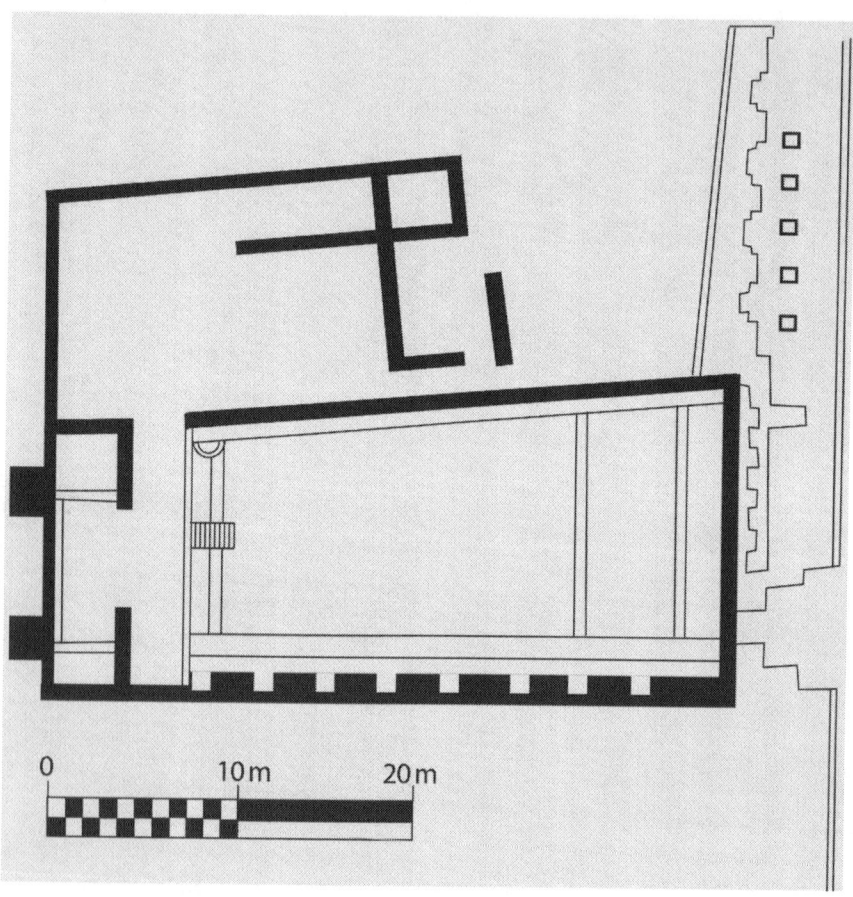

FIGURE 10.5. *Plan of La Quinta and surrounding architectural features, after Wheeler and Mujica 1981*

La Quinta also has architectural features that, while prehispanic in origin, were constructed during the colonial era. For instance, the floor plan of the chapel is trapezoidal, a hallmark shape of Inka plazas built across the empire to hold state rituals. The nave may have been open, which would more closely resemble Andean open-air worship traditions than the indoor Catholic ones. The chapel was constructed following the Kalasaya's alignment and does not follow the European canon of an east-facing altar. The double-jambed niched wall is also of Inka design. Double-jambed niched walls in the capital were signifiers of an important building (Niles 1987). However, the construction technique is more similar to the colonial aspects of La Quinta than the original Inka period structure. Thus, it is possible that this prehispanic architectural canon was built after contact. Lastly, the sunken nave is not a feature of European or Inka religious architecture but most closely resembles the surrounding Late Formative subterranean patios of the Kalasaya. In fact, it is possible that La Quinta was built on the remains of a sunken court.

Most of the colonial modifications to the chapel are of Spanish architectural features. The apse, chancel, nave, buttresses, and baptismal fountain have no Andean precedent and represent Old World canons. The line of columns in front of the niched wall is another colonial addition, as columns are uncommon in Inka architecture. Together with the double-niched wall, the columns may have been a patio or some version of a balcony open chapel seen in other parts of Peru during the colonial period. People could have gathered on the terraces and the principal staircase below to witness mass, receive religious instruction, or view other rituals. A balcony would have allowed the gathering of large numbers of people, well exceeding the capacity of the chapel and its atrium.

There is architectural evidence of other new forms of religious architecture at La Quinta. The atrium and arched niches cannot be traced back clearly to a European or prehispanic architectural tradition. As discussed in the previous section, atria were a new architectural feature first introduced in colonial Mexico that was subsequently adopted throughout the Americas. On the other hand, the arched niches are not well-known in the Andean architectural record. However, if we break down the form to its essential parts, we are left with the most dominant architectural symbol of each of these groups; the arch is a defining element of European architecture, whereas the trapezoidal niche is the hallmark of Inka architecture.

La Quinta may be an early example of an open chapel, in that it served to create a space for open-air worship that was familiar to the indigenous population. However, it is unlike any known open chapel and thus may have been built to meet the unique needs of the surrounding community. The nave's high walls would have prevented the congregation from seeing out or bystanders from seeing in. These changes drastically altered the nature of the ritual at the site and served to create a Christian religious experience in a once pagan place. The combination of Andean and European features created a new type of ritual space that allowed for a new kind of ritual experience, one that was both Andean and European. Like other architectural forms that emerged during the period, it may have served as a way to introduce Christianity in a traditional Andean manner and setting.

Thus, the trapezoidal floor plan, the open and sunken nave, and the arched niches found at La Quinta make it a unique amalgam of architectural elements. Together with its strategic location on top of the Kalasaya, La Quinta created a built environment that shaped but also reflected ritual experience at Pukara. La Quinta's architecture does not represent a drastic shift or complete replacement of indigenous traditions with Spanish ones. In fact, the architecture suggests that the religious practices that took place within its walls were also hybrid in nature. The open nave formed a ritual experience not entirely Catholic but a mix of European and Andean religious traditions. Moreover, because La Quinta incorporates aspects of local religious architecture, it is clear that its construction atop the Kalasaya was not solely an act of dominance. Instead, the architecture suggests a process of accommodation and compromise between Spanish and Andean interests. How this process was negotiated is not clear in the archaeological record; neither are the details about who was involved in the construction of La Quinta. However, given the demographics of the altiplano during this time, it can be safely assumed that the builders of the chapel were probably exclusively native Andeans. They were tasked by a priest or *encomendero* with constructing a type of building they had never seen to house rituals they had never experienced. This lack of familiarity with European religious architectural tradition may offer some explanation as to why the chapel deviates from that canon. But as the creators of La Quinta, Andean builders and their motivations cannot be discounted. As Bailey (2010:4) argues, the builders of La Quinta may have been able "to transform these imposed iconographies and religious practices so that they reflected their own beliefs and worldviews." To suggest that the architectural style of La Quinta was solely the work of "wily" Spanish priests or merely a poor translation of a Christian chapel would be to ignore the role Andeans played in the development of new forms of religious architecture at Pukara.

LA QUINTA AND SANTA ISABEL

La Quinta occupied a brief moment in time. The early colonial period in the Andes was over by 1610, marked by a distinct change in Andean Christianity and its material correlates. Initial attempts at evangelization were abandoned after the church realized that Andeans were not giving up their ancestral religions but merely adding Christianity to their belief system. In response, the church decided to shift its ecclesiastical energies toward eradicating idolatry in the Andes (see Andrien 1991; MacCormack 1991; Mills 1997).

This shift in strategy can be traced in the material record. Starting with the Toledan reforms of the 1570s, ecclesiastical architecture in the Andes became permanent and more homogeneous as populations were resettled in Spanish-style towns with churches constructed on the main plaza (Fraser 1986). In these new towns the church was the geographical and ideological focus of village life and represented not only a new spiritual order but a new social, political, and economic order as well (Cummins and Rappaport 1998; Fraser 1990:82; MacCormack 1991:141). At Pukara and its environs, churches built during this period are remarkably uniform in plan and are characterized by a simple nave, apse, bell tower, and arched portals with facades that featured elements of classical European architecture (Gutiérrez et al. 1978). In both architecture and landscape, the Spanish were trying to stamp out pre-contact (and thus pagan) influences in colonial Andean life.

The transition from the early colonial to the colonial is evident at Pukara. The colonial town of Pukara was founded during the Toledan era, and the surrounding reduced populations were moved into the new Spanish-style town. At the center of this new settlement were the main plaza and the Santa Isabel church (figure 10.6). The completion of Santa Isabel in 1607 marked the end of La Quinta and also the end of its new religious architectural features. Unlike La Quinta, considerable time and resources went into the construction of Santa Isabel—it was built to last. Also unlike the chapel, Santa Isabel was built in the classical European cruciform floor plan, featured traditional European architectural canons, and showed no Andean influence. While the original construction may have included an open chapel to take advantage of the colonial town's well-known market—one of the biggest in the region— to preach to a large group on market days (Sundays), Santa Isabel is a clear departure from La Quinta (Gutiérrez et al. 1978:72). Its architecture reflects a wholly Catholic place and space and suggests that the rites conducted within its walls were similarly Catholic in nature. In Santa Isabel, the architecture helps focus attention during Catholic ritual on the clergy at the apse and altar. In an overtly Spanish-style church during a time of a massive idolatry campaign, there is little chance that the rituals that took place in Santa Isabel had indigenous Andean religious overtones.

Moreover, Santa Isabel's architecture and relation to the surrounding landscape would have created a new ritual experience for the indigenous population at Pucará. The ritual experience at Santa Isabel would have been different from that at La Quinta because of the two structures' disparate relations to the surrounding landscape. By building the church away from the Kalasaya and in the heart of Spanish Pucará, the ties to Pukara—and its centuries of occupation and ritual importance—and El Peñon were broken (or at least weakened) and replaced with new ties to the Spanish state and the Catholic Church.

FIGURE 10.6. *Santa Isabel church, Pucará. Drawing (below) adapted from Gutiérrez et al. 1978. Photo by Elizabeth Klarich.*

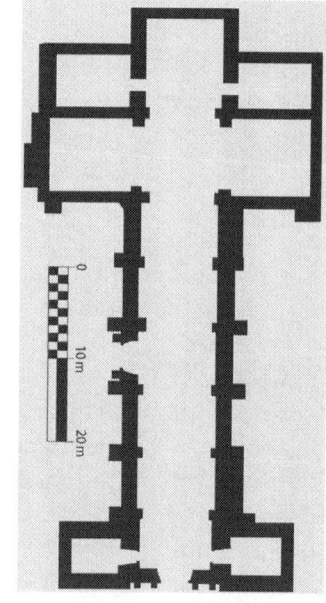

The architecture of Santa Isabel and its place on the landscape suggest a process very different than the one of accommodation and compromise seen at La Quinta. In the way La Quinta reflects the chaotic but more open times of the early colonial period, Santa Isabel mirrors the era in which it was built: a time of expiration campaigns and increasingly restrictive evangelization policies. While the nature of public ritual at Pukara may have changed, there is little doubt that traditional beliefs still persisted but were no longer played out in public; many traditional practices at this time were driven underground or relegated to the private sphere (see Gose 2003, 2008; MacCormack 1998; Mills 1997). In some areas of the Andes, indigenous beliefs actually grew stronger as a result of the idolatry campaigns, while some even campaigned to purge the newly adopted Christian beliefs, arguing that conversion had been a mistake and was responsible for the dire conditions in which most of the indigenous population lived at the time. In fact, the Toledan reforms coincide with the rise of Taki Onkoy, an indigenous messianic resistance movement that spread across most of the Southern Andes and sought to reject all aspects of Spanish life and reinstate pre-Columbian beliefs (Cummins 2002:144; Gose 2003, 2008; Mills 1997).

CONCLUSION: THE NATURE OF ANDEAN CHRISTIANITY

The religious architecture at Pukara demonstrates the dynamic nature of Andean Christianity. La Quinta's architectural amalgamation, as well as its placement on top of the Kalasaya and reuse of its place within the local sacred landscape, created a new and uniquely colonial ritual space. Ultimately, the new architectural forms and spaces, along with their corresponding rituals, were part of a short-lived experiment in religious hybridity. While architectural analysis at La Quinta suggests that some Andean religious practices continued into the early colonial period, the construction of Santa Isabel suggests that they were later relegated to the private sphere. They did not, however, disappear altogether. Across the Andes, traditional beliefs continued in household rituals and were practiced in clandestine locations outside the purview of the church. They, like their Christian counterparts, changed to fit the post-contact reality of their practitioners and have continued to evolve to the present day. In fact, many prehispanic rituals and beliefs continue today, and the Catholicism the vast majority of Andeans practice today is disparate from its Spanish parent. As Bailey (2010:4) states, "People who deny the vitality of indigenous religions during the colonial era—and there have been many—cannot have witnessed firsthand the degree to which much of the apparatus of Andean religion still coexists with Christianity."

ACKNOWLEDGMENTS

I owe a special debt of gratitude to Elizabeth Klarich, who invited me to study La Quinta chapel during her 2010 field season at Pukara. She was also very kind to allow the use of her site photos in this chapter. Aileen Balasalle provided invaluable help with analysis and mapping in the field, for which I am sincerely grateful. This chapter benefited from the volume's two anonymous reviewers, and I am thankful for their comments. Finally, I would like to thank Stefanie Bautista and Silvana Rosenfeld for inviting me to participate in this volume.

NOTES

1. Although see Lara (2004:24–25) for some possible Old Word antecedents.

2. The modern town is Pucará, but the archaeological site and culture are called Pukara.

3. Although it is called La Quinta today, the colonial name of the chapel is unknown.

4. According to Wheeler and Mujica (1981), Lumbreras excavated nine structures on the other side of the Kalasaya in the 1970s and concluded that they were domestic buildings constructed during the colonial period. Unfortunately, there are no further notes or data from those excavations, and the structures no longer exist. In addition, Wheeler and Mujica report that COPESCO (Comisión especial para coordinar y supervigilar el plan turístico y cultural Perú-UNESCO) excavated at least one test pit in La Quinta, but the results were never published.

5. Some Pucará residents have reported that the structure was built as a tool shed by COPESCO in the 1970s. Although it may have been used for that purpose, the photographic evidence suggests it predates the project.

REFERENCES CITED

Abercrombie, T. A. 1998. *Pathways of Memory and Power: Ethnography and History among an Andean People*. Madison: University of Wisconsin Press.

Andrien, K. J. 1991. "Spaniards, Andeans, and the Early Colonial State in Peru." In *Transatlantic Encounters: Europeans and Andeans in the Sixteenth Century*, ed. K. J. Andrien and R. Adorno, 121–48. Berkeley: University of California Press.

Astuhuamán Gonzáles, C. 2012. "Informal Final: Proyecto de investigación arqueológica de San Miguel de Piura, temporada 2011." Unpublished archaeological field report.

Bailey, G. A. 2005. *Art of Colonial Latin America*. London: Phaidon.

Bailey, G. A. 2010. *The Andean Hybrid Baroque*. South Bend, IN: University of Notre Dame Press.

Ballesteros, J. B. 1975. "Capillas abiertas en las parroquias andinas del Peru en los siglos XVI–XVII." *Arte y Arqueologia* 3: 113–30.

Bhabha, H. K. 1994. *The Location of Culture*. New York: Routledge.

Cobo, B. 1997 [1653]. *Inca Religion and Customs*, 3rd ed. Trans. R. Hamilton. Austin: University of Texas Press.

Cummins, T.B.F. 2002. *Toasts with the Inca: Andean Abstraction and Colonial Images on Kuero Vessels*. Ann Arbor: University of Michigan Press.

Cummins, T.B.F., and J. Rappaport. 1998. "The Reconfiguration of Civic and Sacred Space: Architecture, Image, and Writing in the Colonial Northern Andes." *Latin American Literary Review* 26 (52): 174–200.

Donahue-Wallace, K. 2008. *Art and Architecture of Viceregal Latin America, 1521–1821*. Albuquerque: University of New Mexico Press.

Fogelin, L. 2007. "The Archaeology of Religious Ritual." *Annual Review of Anthropology* 36 (1): 55–71. http://dx.doi.org/10.1146/annurev.anthro.36.081406.094425.

Fraser, V. 1986. "Architecture and Imperialism in Sixteenth-Century Spanish America." *Art History* 9 (3): 325–35. http://dx.doi.org/10.1111/j.1467-8365.1986.tb00204.x.

Fraser, V. 1990. *The Architecture of Conquest: Building in the Viceroyalty of Peru, 1535–1635*. Cambridge: Cambridge University Press.

Gisbert, T., and J. de Mesa. 1985. *Arquitectura andina: Historia y análisis*. La Paz, Bolivia: Talleres-Escuela de Artes Gráficas del Colegio Don Bosco.

Gose, P. 2003. "Converting the Ancestors: Indirect Rule, Settlement Consolidation, and the Struggle over Burial in Colonial Peru, 1532–1614." In *Conversion: Old Worlds and New*, ed. K. Mills and A. Grafton, 140–74. Rochester, NY: University of Rochester Press.

Gose, P. 2008. *Invaders as Ancestors: On the Intercultural Making and Unmaking of Spanish Colonialism in the Andes*. Toronto: University of Toronto Press.

Griffiths, N. 1999. "Introduction." In *Spiritual Encounters: Interactions between Christianity and Native Religions in Colonial America*, ed. N. Griffiths and F. Cervantes, 1–42. Lincoln: University of Nebraska Press.

Gutiérrez, R., R. C. Pernaut, G. Viñuales, H. Rodríguez Villegas, R. Vallin Magaña, B. E. Benavides, E. Kuon Arce, and J. Lambarri. 1978. *Arquitectura del altiplano peruano*. Buenos Aires: Libros de Hispanoamérica.

Klarich, E. A. 2005. "From the Monumental to the Mundane: Defining Early Leadership Strategies at Late Formative Pukara, Peru." PhD dissertation, Department of Anthropology, University of California, Santa Barbara.

Kolata, A. 1993. *The Tiwanaku: Portrait of an Andean Civilization*. Cambridge: Blackwell.

Lara, J. 2004. *City, Temple, Stage: Eschatological Architecture and Liturgical Theatrics in New Spain*. South Bend, IN: University of Notre Dame Press.

Lara, J. 2008. *Christian Texts for Aztecs: Art and Liturgy in Colonial Mexico*. South Bend, IN: University of Notre Dame Press.

Low, S. M. 1995. "Indigenous Architecture and the Spanish American Plaza in Mesoamerica and the Caribbean." *American Anthropologist* 97 (4): 748–62. http://dx.doi.org/10.1525/aa.1995.97.4.02a00160.

MacCormack, S. 1991. *Religion in the Andes: Vision and Imagination in Early Colonial Peru*. Princeton, NJ: Princeton University Press.

MacCormack, S. 1998. "Time, Space, and Ritual Action: The Inka and Christian Calendars in Early Colonial Peru." In *Native Traditions in the Postconquest World*, ed. E. Hill Boone and T.B.F. Cummins, 295–343. Washington, DC: Dumbarton Oaks.

McAndrew, J. 1965. *The Open-Air Churches of 16th Century Mexico: Atrios, Posas, Open Chapels, and Other Studies*. Cambridge, MA: Harvard University Press. http://dx.doi.org/10.4159/harvard.9780674186354.

Mills, K. 1994. "The Limits of Religious Conversion in Mid-Colonial Peru." *Past and Present* 145 (1): 84–121. http://dx.doi.org/10.1093/past/145.1.84.

Mills, K. 1997. *Idolatry and Its Enemies: Extirpation and Colonial Andean Religion, 1640–1750*. Princeton, NJ: University of Princeton Press.

Moore, J. D. 1996a. "The Archaeology of Plazas and the Proxemics of Ritual: Three Andean Traditions." *American Anthropologist* 98 (4): 789–802. http://dx.doi.org/10.1525/aa.1996.98.4.02a00090.

Moore, J. D. 1996b. *Architecture and Power in the Ancient Andes: The Archaeology of Public Buildings*. New Studies in Archaeology. Cambridge: Cambridge University Press. http://dx.doi.org/10.1017/CBO9780511521201.

Nair, S. 2007. "Witnessing the In-visibility of Inca Architecture in Colonial Peru." *Buildings and Landscapes: Journal of the Vernacular Architecture Forum* 14 (1): 50–65. http://dx.doi.org/10.1353/bdl.2007.0006.

Niles, S. A. 1987. *Callachaca: Style and Status in an Inca Community*. Iowa City: University of Iowa Press.

Quilter, J. 2010. "Cultural Encounters at Magdalena de Cao Viejo in the Early Colonial Period." In *Enduring Conquests: Rethinking the Archaeology of Resistance in Spanish Colonialism in the Americas*, ed. M. Liebmann and M. S. Murphy, 103–25. Santa Fe: SAR Press.

Renfrew, C. 1985. *The Archaeology of Cult: The Sanctuary at Phylakopi*. London: Thames and Hudson.

Rice, P. M. 2012. "Torata Alta: An Inka Administrative Center and Spanish Colonial Reducción in Moquegua Peru." *Latin American Antiquity* 23 (1): 3–28. http://dx.doi.org/10.7183/1045-6635.23.1.3.

Salomon, F., and G. L. Urioste. 1991. *The Huarochiri Manuscript: A Testament of Ancient and Colonial Andean Religion*. Austin: University of Texas Press.

Van Buren, M. 2010. "The Archaeological Study of Spanish Colonialism in the Americas." *Journal of Archaeological Research* 18 (2): 151–201. http://dx.doi.org/10.1007/s10814-009-9036-8.

Villanueva Domínquez, L., F. V. Cossío, A. Navarro Guzmán, and D. Rivera Gámez. 2002. "La ciudad de San Miguel del Piura, primera fundación española en el Perú." *Revista Espanola de Antropologia Americana* 32: 267–94.

Wernke, S. A. 2007. "Analogy or Erasure? Dialectics of Religious Transformation in the Early *Doctrinas* of the Colca Valley, Peru." *International Journal of Historical Archaeology* 11 (2): 152–82. http://dx.doi.org/10.1007/s10761-007-0027-5.

Wernke, S. A. 2011. "Convergences: Producing Early Colonial Hybridity at a *Doctrina* in Highland Peru." In *Enduring Conquests: Rethinking the Archaeology of Resistance in Spanish Colonialism in the Americas*, ed. M. Liebmann and M. S. Murphy, 77–102. Santa Fe: SAR Press.

Wheeler, J., and E. Mujica. 1981. "Prehistoric Pastoralism in the Lake Titicaca Basin, Peru (1979–1980 Field Season)." Report submitted to the National Science Foundation.

11

A key theoretical debate in archaeology and other social sciences today concerns the notion that in practice, agency is a faculty that can be displayed by non-human beings, which, depending on worldview and context, may include anything from ghosts to places or artifacts (Gell 1998; Knappett and Malafouris 2008; Latour 2005; Walker 2009). Since agency—or the various capacities encompassed by this concept—is a fundamental quality on which taxonomies of being are based, knowing how it is attributed to various entities in different cultures is central to understand the cosmologies involved and, more specifically, their underlying ontologies. The far-reaching implications of this debate have led some scholars to speak of an "ontological turn" in social theory (Alberti et al. 2011; Henare, Holbraad, and Wastell 2007; Olsen 2010).

The current interest in non-human agencies has a lot in common with what is usually encompassed under the category of *religion*, particularly if we embrace Horton's (1960:212) definition of this concept as "an extension of social relationships beyond the confines of purely human society," to include "personified" non-humans that have an influence on people's lives and destiny. Building on this idea and on the tradition that conceives of ritual as religious practice, we can tentatively define *ritual* as *social action that addresses non-human agents who have a significant influence on human fate*. This definition encompasses important aspects of ritual that have been stressed by the many authors who have written about the subject,

Ritual as Interaction with Non-Humans

Prehispanic Mountain Pass Shrines in the Southern Andes

Axel E. Nielsen,
Carlos I. Angiorama,
and Florencia Ávila

DOI: 10.5876/9781607325963.c011

including its communicative dimension, the formality and repetition it shares with any communication code, and its use to achieve outcomes that are beyond the control of practitioners because they depend on the actions of the powerful non-humans addressed (see Rick, this volume). Thus conceived, rites and the archaeological contexts created by them afford an important opportunity for learning about the non-humans that inhabited the worlds of past peoples. After all, both pragmatism and relationality indicate that spirits, like any other social entity (kin, enemies, pets, gods), become what they are through their interactions—in this case, with people. Furthermore, by construing the subject matter of religion and ritual as one among other forms of social interaction and relationship—instead of a metaphysical construct such as "the sacred" (Eliade 1996) or reified "society" (Durkheim 2001)—this view makes it possible to take advantage of valuable ideas originally developed to account for non-religious phenomena, such as communication or exchange.

An approach of this kind requires addressing a series of complex issues, such as, what is an "agent"? What kind of practices reveal that the people involved inferred the presence of such a being? What would be the archaeological evidence for such an interpretation? Since there is no possibility of discussing them here in any detail, we will summarize our position on these matters as an outline of the theoretical foundation for this chapter. We chose a relatively restrictive definition, which departs from Latour's (2005) notions of "actant" and similar ideas associated with symmetrical archaeology and artifact agency (Jones and Boivin 2010; Olsen 2010), because we want to narrow our discussion to practices that involve entities which humans understand as sentient beings. An agent is anything to which human practice accords *power* (capacity to alter a course of events), *awareness* (based on a particular understanding of the world), *intentionality* (goals, interest, values, affects, or desire), *choice* (possibility of acting otherwise [Giddens 1984]), and, therefore, *responsibility* of some sort. Some form of choice on the part of non-human agents is crucial in this context because this is what compels practitioners to interact with deities, who may decide to harm or ignore human needs if the proper social protocol is not observed.

To translate these ideas into pragmatic terms, we use the concept of *ritual gestures*, that is, simple actions that mark certain places, moments, and objects, indicating the presence of an interacting non-human alter. We base the concept of ritual gesture on Bell's (1992:74) notion of "ritualization," defined as culturally specific strategies for setting some activities off from others, "ascribing such distinctions to realities thought to transcend the power of human actors." Unlike Bell, however, we take the relationship with those "transcendental agencies" to be the central quality of ritual as a distinctive kind of human practice. A semiotic analysis of these gestures offers archaeology a way of exploring the nature of deities and the relationships they entertain with people, a point of entry into those "worlds otherwise," to borrow Alberti and colleagues' expression (Alberti et al. 2011). Exploring that nature is an interpretative task that, unlike reading texts, must rely on the indexical and iconic modes of representation (e.g., function, provenience, life history, association, performance characteristics, bundling, reuse, depositional mode [Joyce and Pollard 2010; Keane 2005; Richards and Thomas 1984; Schiffer 1999; Walker 1995]) that characterize the communicative properties of material culture. It is known that, since they do not respond to universal or necessary causal mechanisms, these semiotic connections need to be verified through the identification of homologous patterns that may reveal important symbolic conventions. As in other interpretative exercises, the resulting inferences are more sound if they can parsimoniously account for significant variability in terms of a few simple generative principles.

Focusing on the archaeology of mountain passes of the Southern Andes as an example, this chapter discusses the potential of these ideas for exploring the kinds of beings that inhabited the world of past peoples. The first part characterizes the rituals presently conducted on mountain passes of the Southern Andes, highlighting the religious importance of these places for travelers. The second part presents other archaeological evidence documented on mountain passes across the area, putting emphasis on offering pits, also known as "sepulchers" (Nielsen 1997) or "artificial hollows" (Pimentel 2009) in the literature. Interpreting these sites as *shrines*—places where non-humans are addressed—the third section discusses their possible meanings and the agencies they may have engaged.

PRESENT-DAY MOUNTAIN-PASS RITUALS IN THE SOUTH ANDEAN HIGHLANDS

Ethnographic and ethnohistorical studies support the notion that Andean peoples share an animistic ontology (cf. Descola 2013), that is, they believe the world is inhabited by countless non-human agents and interpret numerous phenomena that we (Moderns) attribute to natural mechanisms as effects of their intentional actions. These sentient beings can be a variety of things, including plants, celestial bodies, rocks, artifacts, places, or relatively abstract but omnipresent entities, such as *Pachamama*. Human life unfolds in a web of heterogeneous social relationships; every task, from building a house to healing, from farming to hosting a feast, requires interacting and negotiating with

FIGURE 11.1. *Invoking the assistance of mountains (*Mallkus*), San Rafael (the invisible drover), and* Pachamama *during departure ceremony of a llama caravan in Cerrillos, Sud Lípez, Bolivia, 1995*

different kinds of non-human agents through proper ritual protocols (Allen 1988; Martínez 1983; Ricard Lanata 2007; Van Kessel 1988, among others).

Long-distance travel is no exception. Depending on the region and period, travel rituals reported in the literature may engage different kinds of non-humans, including ancestors and accompanying spirits, *Pachamama*, mountains, outcrops, springs, archaeological sites (*chullpas*), special objects (e.g., figurines, amulets), pack animals (if they are used), and the road itself (Lecoq 1987; Mariscotti de Görlitz 1978; Nielsen 1997; Pimentel 2009; West 1981, among others). Since these agents have their own characters and can affect people in different ways, they are addressed through a variety of ritual actions that have to be performed in specific contexts.

During their caravan journeys to the eastern valleys, for example, the pastoralists (*llameros*) of Lípez in the southern Bolivian altiplano conduct different rituals at these places: (1) houses, upon departure and arrival; (2) *talvarita*, a cairn located on high terrain near the house from where the road is clearly visible (upon departure and arrival); (3) mountain passes; (4) dangerous places along the way, such as narrow passages (*punkus*) and the beginnings of steep slopes; (5) resting areas located every third or fourth day of the march; and (6) when entering the Tarija Valley—their final destination—from the Sama high plateau. The agents they interact with in each case vary from a single being (e.g., a scary-looking rock) to a host of non-human persons, as in the departure ceremony (figure 11.1), where llamas, caravan emblems (e.g., bells worn by leaders of the caravan, ropes), trade goods, San Rafael (the invisible herder), the road (*ñan*), *Pachamama*, the local *Mallku* (Tres Cerrillos), and the main mountains to be sighted along the way are all invoked and engage in different kinds of exchanges. This translates into considerable variation in the ritual actions carried out in each place, which range from a simple gesture—such as pouring alcohol (*ch'alla*) or naming while marching—to complex ceremonies that last for hours, as in the main *kowaco* held near the middle of the journey. In 1995, a caravan we traveled with from the southern altiplano to the Tarija Valley carried two bulky bundles containing ritual paraphernalia to perform the necessary rituals along the journey, including eight *kichiras* (dried llama hearts stuffed with clippings from different parts of the bodies of sacrificed animals), *kowa* (an aromatic shrub commonly burned in ritual contexts) incense, lard and cornmeal to shape llama figurines (*virauñas*), miniature bags filled with maize kernels and cornmeal, flamingo feathers, *unkuñas* (ceremonial textiles for altars), red yarn to "dress the altars," coca leaves, alcohol, and wine, among other elements (Nielsen 2011).

Mountain passes, or *abras*, are consistently reported as important ritual places in the Andes (Allen 1988:27; Ambrosetti and Debenedetti 1917:111; Galdames 1990:14, among others). There may be several material traits that justify this or, relationally speaking, "performance characteristics" (Schiffer 2011) that passes "afford" (Gibson 1979) travelers, accounting for this phenomenon. First, they open into a new view, frequently the first or last point from where significant landmarks—potentially perceived as animated, like mountains, caves, towns, outcrops, and lakes—can be sighted. They also divide watersheds; given the importance of water in the South Andean deserts, discontinuities in its behavior are powerful landscape signifiers. For those traveling on foot, mountain passes represent the culmination of particularly strenuous stretches of the road, thus marking a sharp inflection in bodily experience. Finally, the topographic constraints that define mountain passes create high redundancy in traffic, making the archaeological traces of previous transit and of ritual actions that may have been carried out at these points particularly noticeable, thus endowing them with particular mnemonic properties. Given these facts, it is hardly surprising that travelers in other parts of the world have also marked mountain passes as shrines (e.g., Muhonen 2012; Valli and Summers 1994).

The most common ritual presently conducted at abras in the Andes involves adding rocks to the *apachetas,* cairns developed on the highest point of the trail by the repetition of this gesture over time. Formed in this way, apachetas vary significantly in size and number; passes used intensively or for a long time may have several of these features, which may be up to 8 m high (Boman 1991 [1908]:483). Travelers may also leave wads of coca leaves they have been chewing on the way up (*acullico*), partake in a short libation (ch'alla), and even "smoke with the apacheta," often lighting two cigarettes and sticking one of them in the cairn. If time and weather permit, people may stop briefly at this point to catch their breath, enjoy the view, and consume a snack. According to most authors, the deposition of rocks, acullicos, and other objects (e.g., old sandals or clothes) is meant to release the traveler from fatigue, while alcohol and cigarettes are offered to invoke the favors or protection of *Pachamama* and nearby mountains, or *Mallkus* (Galdames 1990; Girault 1958). These entities are often addressed through songs and prayers that make explicit the ambiguous character of these agents, which can help or harm people (Mariscotti de Görlitz 1978:69–70), hence the need to negotiate with them socially.

Apachetas are restricted to the Andean highlands, but they are found in other locations in addition to mountain passes, including road intersections, points where two rivers meet (*palcas* in Quechua), and other places where travelers experience significant changes in the environment—for example, sharp slope changes or locations where a road leaves a plain to enter a narrow valley. This suggests that abras may be pragmatically understood as instances of a more general category of places in which contrasted things are brought together or divided, that is, thresholds or gates—punkus (Cruz 2006)—whose liminality demands similar ritual precaution.

Even when apachetas are invariably associated with roads, they are revered not only while people are traveling. People visit apachetas at other important moments of the annual cycle—toward the end of the rainy season, for carnival (*enflorada*), and in August, a month devoted to worshipping *Pachamama*. On these occasions they offer cornmeal, alcoholic beverages, coca leaves, and cigarettes; they "plant" bunchgrasses and branches of different plants (e.g., maize) in the interstices between rocks; and they "dress" the cairns, tying colored yarn around sticks or stones, particularly those that mimic the shape of camelids (figure 11.2).

The apacheta ritual was described in early colonial sources (De Albornoz 1988 [1584]:168; Polo de Ondegardo 1916 [1571]:189–90). Murúa (2004 [1590]:vol. 2,

FIGURE 11.2. *Apacheta in Abra de Sepulturas (Quebrada de Humahuaca) "dressed" during an enflorada ceremony. Note the camelid-shaped rock at the foreground, to the left, which has been ornamented with orange yarn, just like the animals in the corral, which have had their ear tassels (flores) renewed.*

f. 104v) and Hyslop (1984:311) report Inka ceramics and structures associated with these features. This demonstrates that these practices—or some of them—are of pre-Hispanic origin, at least in the Central Andes. Based on the frequent presence of chronologically diagnostic artifacts next to these features in the Southern Andes, it has been proposed that apachetas date to the time of the Inkas or earlier (Pimentel 2009:15). The lack of conclusive evidence of association between early artifacts and cairns, however, and the absence of these features along important pre-Hispanic roads leave open the possibility that these practices arrived at some regions of the Southern Andes only after the European invasion in the mid-sixteenth century (Berenguer et al. 2005; Nielsen, Berenguer, and Sanhueza 2006).

OFFERING PITS IN MOUNTAIN PASSES

Over the past twenty-five years we have been able to examine a fair number of mountain passes in a vast area of the Southern Andes, from the Western

Cordillera that divides the altiplano from the Atacama Desert to the Eastern Cordillera that dips into the forested valleys of the Yungas region. The archaeological traces found in these small sites show interesting patterns when compared interregionally. Table 11.1 summarizes surface evidence recorded systematically on twenty-two abras spread across the highlands of the "triple frontier" of Bolivia, Chile, and Argentina (figure 11.3). Except for Abra del Altar (3,650 meters above sea level [masl]), all of them are situated between 4,000 m and 5,100 masl. Only passes that present remains other than apachetas—and common refuse generated by their use, such as broken glass or cigarettes—are included to put into focus different ritual practices conducted at these places for which there is little published information. Those shrines located in the Argentine and Bolivian parts of the High Lakes region and along the border between Bolivia and Chile south of Salar de Uyuni were found during systematic survey designed to identify archaeological evidence of trans-Andean traffic (Nielsen 2011). We have also made less systematic observations in other passes, mentioned later in the argument since in some cases they offer important data with which to interpret these contexts.

One-third of these passes shown on the map have no apachetas; these are mainly on the Western Cordillera or in the López region, and some of them are associated with the Inka road (Qhapaqñan) that links the altiplano with the Atacama Desert. Berenguer and colleagues (2005) also noted the absence of apachetas along significant segments of the Inka road in the Loa River region. Almost two-thirds of the passes in our sample have offering pits (figure 11.4), invariably associated with crushed greenstone, among other items. Offering pits are found in all the cases without apachetas; when both types of features are present, they seem to represent independent contexts and activities. In the wide Abras of Cerro Blanco, Ascotán, and de la Laguna, for example, the offering pits are situated between 40 m and 100 m away from the apachetas and are associated with traces of different trails, possibly used in different periods. The idea of a chronological difference between these practices is supported by at least one observation made at Abra de la Cruz, a pass that connects the headwaters of Quebrada de Humahuaca with the eastern valley of Iruya (see figure 11.3), where road construction sectioned an old apacheta. The profile exposed a layer with greenstone (crushed and worked into beads) beneath the cairn, demonstrating that the apacheta covered an earlier deposit. This case raises the possibility that similar overlaps may have taken place in other passes, where no pits are visible but apachetas occur simultaneous with greenstone offerings.

Offering pits are present all across the Andes at this latitude, a fact that supports their association with long-distance traffic. Pimentel (2009) recently

TABLE 11.1. Archaeological remains recorded on mountain passes of the triple frontier area

Mountain Pass (abra)	Region	Features				Greenstone			Whitestone		Ceramics		Lithics		Other, Comments
		Apacheta	Hollow	Windbreak	Pavement	Fragments	Beads	Bead Frags.	Beads	Bead Frags.	Fragments	Groups	Type	Material	
1. Cerro Blanco	QH-EV	1	4	1	—	X	2	1	—	1	33	Hum	pp	obs	
2. Wayra Apacheta	QH-EV	1	—	3	—	X	1	10	1	1	30	Yavi	—	—	
3. Del Pueblo	QH-EV	1	—	—	—	X	3	—	2	4	—	—	—	—	
4. Chisca (Aparzo)	QH	2	—	—	—	X	1	—	—	1	27	Hum	pp	obs	disturbed
5. Cosmate	QH	2	1	—	—	X	6	4	1	4	39	Hum, Yavi	3 pp	cht	
6. Del Altar	QH	1	—	—	—	X	—	—	—	1	65	Hum, Yavi	1 fk	cdn	Qhpaqñan
7. Lipán sur	QH-PNW	2	—	—	—	X	—	—	—	—	22	Hum	—	—	
8. Sepulturas	QH-GC	6	—	—	—	X	1	—	—	—	—	—	—	—	disturbed
9. Rachaite	GC	1	—	—	—	X	1	—	—	—	5	Yavi	—	—	disturbed
10. Cabalonga	GC	1	1	—	1	X	2	1	—	—	—	—	1 pp, 1 inst	cht, and	
11. Granada	GC-AO	1	1	—	—	X	—	2	—	1	—	—	1 inst, 7 fk	cht, blt	
12. Tinte	GC-AO	1	3	—	—	X	5	32	1	9	—	—	—	—	disturbed
13. Río Amargo	OA-SEL	—	1	—	—	X	1	1	—	—	—	—	—	—	sulfur
14. Río Blanco	OA-SEL	—	2	—	—	X	1	—	—	—	—	—	—	—	

continued on next page

TABLE 11.1.—continued

Mountain Pass (abra)	Region	Features				Greenstone			Whitestone		Ceramics		Lithics		Other, Comments
		Apacheta	Hollow	Windbreak	Pavement	Fragments	Beads	Bead Frags.	Beads	Bead Frags.	Fragments	Groups	Type	Material	
15. Chaxa	OA	—	2	—	—	X	5	2	12	7	—	—	—	—	—
16. Toro Muerto 1	OA-GC	—	3	1	—	X	2	1	9	24	—	—	1 pp, 2 fk	obs	ceramic tube, marine shell frg, Qhpaqñan
17. Paso del Inka	LR-NL	—	1	4	3	X	1	1	—	—	20	Mku, Loa	—	—	Qhpaqñan
18. Ascotán	LR-NL	1	1	—	—	X	1	—	—	—	—	—	—	—	horseshoes
19. Lagunita	NL-LR	—	1	2	—	X	1	5	—	—	86	Mku, Loa, Inka	—	—	Qhpaqñan
20. Tomasamil	NL-LR	—	1	—	—	X	—	—	—	—	31	Inka	—	—	disturbed, Qhpaqñan
21. Sora	NL	1	—	—	—	X	2	1	—	1	48	Mku	1 pp, 11 fk	obs, cht, blt	—
22. De la Laguna	NL	—	1	—	—	X	1	—	—	—	2	Mku	2 inst, 2 fk	cht, cdn and	hoe, knife

Notes. Ceramic groups: Hum = Humahuaca, Yavi = Yavi/Chicha, Mku = Mallku/Hedionda, Loa = Loa/San Pedro, Inka = Imperial or Provincial Inka. Lithic types: pp = projectile point, inst = instrument other, fk = debitage. Lithic materials: obs = obsidian, cht = gray chert, cdn = calcedony, blt = basalt, and = andesite (hoes only).

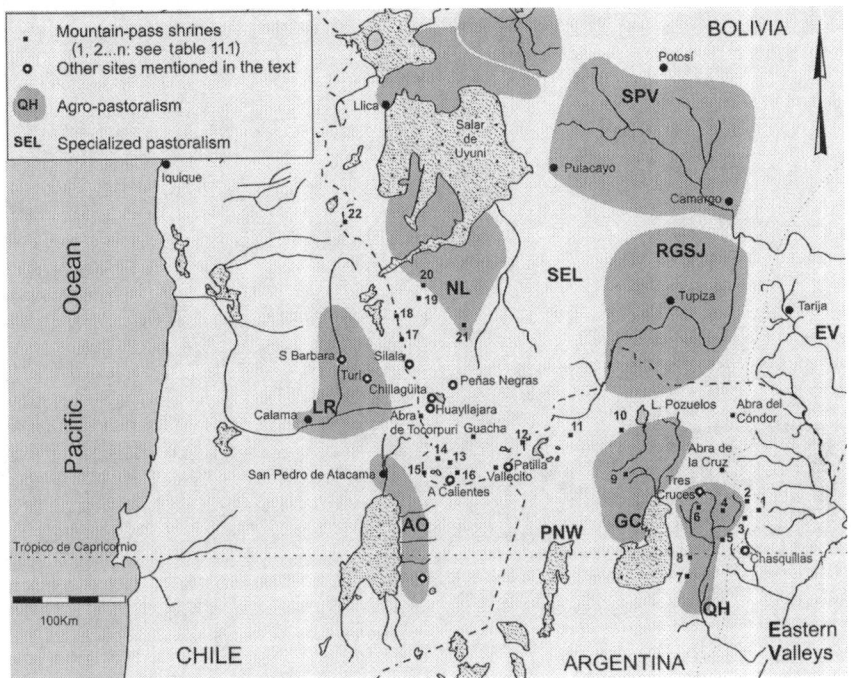

FIGURE 11.3. *Location of sites mentioned in the text*

Note to figure 11.3. Regions: QH = Quebrada de Humahuaca, GC = Doncellas-Guayatayoc, RGSJ = Río Grande de San Juan, SPV = southern Potosí valleys, PNW = northwest Puna, SEL = southeast Lípez, NL = northern Lípez, LR = Loa River, AO = Atacama oases.

recorded five more cases in the Atacama Desert, including one below 1,000 masl on a route that connects the Middle Loa River with the Pacific Coast. Given the lack of a specifically oriented survey, it is not known at present how far these sites extend to the north and south of our study area. All of the chronologically diagnostic artifacts (decorated pottery, projectile points) recorded in association with these features belong to the Late Intermediate Period (LIP, AD 1000–1450) or the Inka period (AD 1450–1550). This observation is consistent with a radiocarbon date of 800 ± 40 AP (Beta 275739) obtained by Pimentel (ibid.:19) from a wood sample recovered through the excavation of one of these features in the Atacama Desert.

The pits range from 0.5 m to 3 m in diameter and can be up to 1 m deep. We have observed up to thirteen of them aligned on the same pass (Abra del Toro Muerto, Bolivia). They are commonly surrounded by the rocks and dirt extracted from the excavation—often mixed with greenstone and whitestone,

FIGURE 11.4. *Artificial hollow at Abra del Toro Muerto 1*

attesting to the periodic reactivation of the pits—and they sometimes show a circle made of stones demarcating the depressed interior of the feature. At Abra Lagunita, where the substrate is formed by exposed bedrock, a low (0.3 m) wall was erected to circumscribe an elliptic area, inside of which the offerings were deposited.

Many offering pits show traces of recent excavations, motivated by the widespread belief that these features hide fabulous treasures. According to a legend told frequently by the herders of Lípez, there was an Inka king (Incarrey) who lived on the summit of Licancabur, near San Pedro de Atacama. Since he had no legs, he was carried throughout the region on a litter. This task was so difficult and straining that sometimes, when they reached a mountain pass, his porters would die of exhaustion. The Inka would bury them there with metal treasures as a sign of gratitude for their service. This is why they call these features *tapados*, or "sepulchers," although excavations have yet to reveal evidence of the presence of human burials at these sites.

Local people suspect the existence of hidden treasures in offering pits because of the invariable presence of greenstone on their surface. It appears as raw material (from fist-size rocks to tiny pieces) or worked into beads of various shapes and sizes, discarded whole or as fragments. Most of these stones are copper minerals (e.g., malachite, azuryte, atacamite), but petrographic analysis has shown that in some cases they are chert or other rocks with no copper,

Figure 11.5. *Common offerings at artificial hollows: greenstone, green and white beads and yellowstone (sulfur). Surface assemblage from Sepulcros de Chillagüita.*

suggesting that color rather than metal was the signifying quality of these items. Usually, there is also "whitestone," mostly volcanic ash, which also appears as beads and what seems to be debris generated during manufacture (e.g., cylindrical pre-forms, pieces broken while drilling the central orifice). Indeed, as table 11.1 shows, 65 percent of the beads in the systematically collected sample (N = 178, both colors) are broken (figure 11.5). These materials appear inside and around the hollows but also as light scatters that fan to the east, as if they had been "sprinkled" from above and dispersed by the dominant west winds before reaching the ground. In passes without pits, greenstone and whitestone offerings are usually found around apachetas, but it is unclear if they are associated with these features or were deposited before the cairns were formed. On a few occasions we have also recorded "yellowstone" in the form of unshaped pieces of sulfur (also found by Pimentel 2009 in some of the hollows he studied) and once—in Abra de Tocorpuri—small gold foil trimmings.

Other features found on occasion are circular stone pavements (1.5–3 m in diameter) and semicircular windbreaks (0.8 m high, 2 m in diameter, maximum) expediently made of dry stones. This suggests that travelers occasionally spent some time at passes, building these precarious refuges to protect themselves from the gelid wind. In Paso del Inka, two of the windbreaks are directly attached to the pavement, as if they were meant to protect people carrying out activities on these prepared surfaces.

Other artifacts commonly associated with pits and windbreaks are ceramic fragments, lithic instruments (e.g., projectile points, retouched flakes, and hoes or hoe fragments), and debitage. In some cases these materials may have been obtained in the region where the site is located, particularly in the Western Cordillera where lithic materials are relatively abundant, but the obsidian and gray chert discarded in the sites around Quebrada de Humahuaca came from a considerable distance, hundreds of kilometers away. By contrast, the diagnostic ceramics are usually from adjacent regions, as is the case with the Mallku (northern López) and Loa (Atacama Desert) groups in the western sites and the Yavi (Río Grande de San Juan) and Humahuaca (Quebrada de Humahuaca) sherds recorded on the eastern passes. As expected, Inka ceramics are found in some shrines associated with the Qhapaqñan. We have observed other perishable materials in recently disturbed sites not listed in table 11.1 (Abra del Toro Muerto 2, Vallecito, and Guacha; see figure 11.3), including tropical bird feathers, llama and vicuña wool, pieces of yarn, rope, and textiles.

DISCUSSION: GESTURE, METAPHOR, AND AGENCY

We believe archaeological research on ritual should start with a "behavioral" focus, emphasizing patterns of bodily interaction between humans and the material world rather than the hermeneutic or discursive renderings of these activities, pragmatics rather than semiology. This should be seen not as a limitation but as an opportunity for archaeology to bring to the fore a distinctive aspect of religious life that is often missed in the textual evidence privileged by the anthropology of religion and ritual under the influence of the linguistic turn. The patterns that can be recognized in ritual deposition, the gestures involved, and the nature of the non-humans abduced (sensu Gell 1998) become apparent at spatial and temporal scales, which are very different from those revealed by ethnography. Ethnographers and historians working with texts or participant observation may find variations in a ritual (e.g., in the interpretations given by different subjects, in the ways things are done each time), which archaeologists get to know through a single material signature.

The presence of pre-Hispanic remains other than apachetas on mountain passes of the Southern Andes has been identified recently, and their variability is just beginning to be explored, so any interpretation of them can only be preliminary at this point. The data presented in the previous section demonstrate that many passes across the Andes between 20° and 24° S Latitude (at least), from the Atacama Desert to the last mountain ranges above the eastern valleys, show traces of ritual deposition—mainly of green and white beads, together with what seems to be the debris produced by their manufacture. This material was frequently sprinkled over, placed in, or buried in pits, often demarcated by stone circles. Other materials that frequently accompanied these offerings were maize, *Geophrea* and *Prosopis* fruits, wool (spun or not) and textiles, feathers, marine shell, ceramics, and chipped stone. On occasion, people spent some time at these places carrying out activities that involved flintknapping and the manipulation of ceramic containers, for example, preparing and consuming food and beverages. Stone-paved circles protected by windbreaks in some passes suggest that other activities took place on these features, but there are no elements to define them at this point. These activities took place during the LIP and the Inka period, but they may have started during the first millennium AD and could have persisted into colonial times.

In this part of the Andes, apachetas seem to have been later than offering pits, perhaps introduced from the Central Andes in early colonial times, but the possibility of both ritual practices being contemporaneous should not be ruled out. Moreover, although in some passes apachetas may have covered offering pits—as observed in Abra de la Cruz—the frequent presence of greenstone and beads next to cairns raises the possibility that these were among the offerings made to apachetas as well, at least in some cases or periods. The persistence of similar practices among travelers until colonial times is revealed by blue/green glass beads found in at least two caravan campsites in the area (Patilla and Vega de Tres Cruces; see figure 11.3).

The connection between offering pits and long-distance caravans indicated by the association of these features with important interregional routes is also supported by the invariable presence of greenstone and beads at almost every caravan campsite with pre-Hispanic occupation that has been investigated in this part of the Andes (Berenguer 2004; Nielsen 1997, 2013; Pimentel et al. 2011). Independent proof of the high value travelers assigned to these colored stone offerings comes from a burial excavated at Los Amarillos, one of the largest

LIP residential sites known in Quebrada de Humahuaca. The body of an adult male had been tied with ropes and a wooden toggle (distinctive drovers' artifacts) and interred with a half-gourd containing minuscule fragments of greenstone (atacamite in this case) and white volcanic ash (Angiorama 2007).

Moving away from mountain passes, pits with greenstone and whitestone offerings (i.e., raw mineral and beads) have been found in three other kinds of contexts: caravan overnight stops, water springs, and mid-altitude mountaintops. Offering pits have been recorded at four way-sites associated with interregional routes of the triple frontier. Two of them (Huayllajara and Peñas Negras) are consecutive campsites along a llama caravan trail that connects San Pedro de Atacama with the southeastern corner of the Uyuni salt flat. The other two are next to Inka way stations associated with the Qhapaqñan. One of them is Tambo Chasquillas (east of Quebrada de Humahuaca), located next to a mountain pass; the other is Aguas Calientes (west of San Pedro de Atacama), where the hollow is 100 m away from the buildings, near a water spring.

This brings us to the second kind of location where ritualized pits occur: water springs. This association is also found in Silala 3, a campsite with traces of use since the late Formative period (500 BC–AD 500) located next to a spring on a natural route that connects the southern altiplano with the ancient caravan hub of Santa Barbara (Berenguer 2004). Even the rocks at the place where the water surges have been painted with a green substance or thick paint probably made with copper mineral. Volcanic ash beads have also been found at Baños de Turi, in the Upper Loa region (Gallardo, personal communication, 2009). A variation on this pattern is found at Chillagüita, near the west shore of Laguna Colorada (southwest Lípez), where four large pits with abundant greenstone, whitestone, and yellowstone (sulfur) offerings crown a small hill overlooking the lake.

Relatively low mountains (3,300–4,500 masl) in areas densely settled during the LIP and the Inka period served as stages for similar rituals on their summits. A pit with the usual colored offerings is located on Cerro Agua Colorada, across the river from the town of Rodero (Quebrada de Humahuaca). Systematic survey recently conducted in the southern part of Laguna Pozuelos (Jujuy, Argentina) identified shrines with greenstone offerings on the tops of six highly visible mountains in the area (table 11.2, figure 11.6). These sites are not directly associated with interregional routes but are close to settled areas, so it is likely that the offerings were made by the local population. No chronologically diagnostic artifacts were found in the shrines, but the survey revealed that the main occupation of the region took place in the period AD 1200–1600 (Angiorama 2012). Nearby sites include rock art representations

TABLE 11.2. Archaeological remains recorded on mountain tops of the Southern Pozuelos Basin (Jujuy, Argentina)

Site	Features		Greenstone			Whitestone		Lithics	
	Apacheta	*Hollow*	*Fragments*	*Beads*	*Bead Frags.*	*Beads*	*Bead Frags.*	*Type*	*Material*
San José 155	1	—	X	—	—	—	—	1 flake	obsidian
Peñas Blancas 9	2	—	X	—	1	1	3	—	
Cerro León Chico 2	—	3	X	—	6	—	2	—	
Cerro Chiquito 10	1	1	X	1	4	1	—	—	—
Cerro León Grande 12	2	—	X	1	7	3	2	—	—
Pan de Azúcar	2	3	X	22	8	7	10	1 instrument	andesite

of llama caravans, so it is reasonable to think the local pastoral communities were actively involved in long-distance traffic and may have been among those making offerings in different mountain passes.

Another region where homologous contexts have been found in association with residential settlements is the Middle and Upper Loa River. The features known as "walls and boxes" (*muros y cajas*) are shrines formed by rows of slab-lined square pits ("boxes") protected by windbreaks ("walls") and facing the main surrounding mountain peaks (Berenguer 2004). Some of the offerings found in the boxes resemble those recorded in offering pits—for example, greenstone fragments and beads, whitestone beads, marine shell, feathers, wool, ceramics, lithic debris, and fragments of sandals, among others. Interestingly, these shrines are sometimes found on the outskirts of LIP villages (e.g., Lasana, Santa Bárbara) in direct association with caravan trails that connect the main settlements (Calama, Chiu-Chiu, Lasana) or lead to the altiplano—one of the reasons they have been associated with interregional caravan traffic (Berenguer 1994; Pimentel 2013; Sinclaire 1994). This location is analogous to present-day *talvaritas*, rock cairns placed on high places near the herders' houses where family members see the caravan off on the day of departure and come to meet the travelers two or three months later, when they return from the valleys (Nielsen 2001). If the analogy is valid, both *talvaritas* and walls-and-boxes shrines would operate as thresholds between the domestic space and the road.

What can we learn from these contexts about the entities travelers were addressing in mountain passes and related places and about their relationships

FIGURE 11.6. *Artificial hollow with greenstone offerings on the top of Cerro Pan de Azúcar, Pozuelos Basin, Jujuy, Argentina*

with humans? We propose three, non-exclusive interpretations at this point. First, they could mean or anticipate through ritual the union of resources from multiple productive and cultural areas that long-distance traffic intends to achieve (Nielsen 1997:355). This would account for the fact that in the walls and boxes and offering pits with the best preservation of organic remains, the offerings include items that reference every eco-zone of the Southern Andes: marine shell, copper minerals, camelids (dung, fiber, bones, textiles), maize, *Prosopis*, *Geoffrea*, feathers of flamingoes and tropical birds, among others.

Second, the repetition of the gesture of sprinkling and introducing into the earth greenstone and whitestone beads and the debris produced during their manufacture suggests more broadly that passes, water springs, mountain summits, and walls and boxes had something in common, since they shared the same form of "structured deposition" (Joyce and Pollard 2010; Richards and Thomas 1984). Perhaps they were all conceived as animated entities in themselves, sentient gates or thresholds, punkus between reality domains—that is, different views or "watchers" (Allen 1988:25), divergent water flows, underworld and surface, earth and sky, house and trail. The "ceremonial trash" (Walker 1995) found there would be the material traces of transactions travelers made with these "place spirits," securing their permission to continue through the gift of goods that were highly valued by humans and non-humans alike.

Another possibility is that these "openings" put people in contact with other beings who were the actual recipients of the gifts or the partners in these exchanges. Focusing on the walls and boxes of the Loa River, for example, Berenguer (2004) interprets copper minerals (greenstone) and other colored offerings as South Andean versions of *mullu* that people fed to the local mountains (*Mallkus*) and to *Pachamama* during ritual meals, committing their reciprocity in the form of health and fertility in general and particularly good fortune for their journeys. But perhaps these liminal places exposed travelers to other, less "Christianized," whimsical spirits of the underworld, or *ukhupacha* (see Van Gijseghem and Whalen, this volume), which demanded special ritual protection. Pimentel (2013:328) notes that the Quechua word for bead (*huallca*) is related to the term *shield* (*huallccacancca* [González Holguín 1952 [1608], libro 4, 172]), both sharing a semantic field articulated around the concept of protection. The only pre-Hispanic shield known from northwest Argentina, found at the late pre-Hispanic site Angualasto (San Juan), is made of *Prosopis sp.* wood, and its front surface is covered with 3,811 malachite and turquoise beads that contrast sharply with a series of red feldspar plaques that sketch a curvilinear design against the light-green background of the beads, a "ceremonial shield" according to González (1967). The piece was presumably associated with—among other things—wooden snuff trays and related paraphernalia. These trays—perhaps as portals or punkus into other states of consciousness—frequently have green (copper minerals), white (shell), and red (*Spondylus*) beads as inlays surrounding the cavity in which the hallucinogenic substances were placed.

Could we account historically for aspects of these rituals in terms of a "genealogy of practices" (Pauketat 2001)? Recall that the use of the green-white color contrast goes back—at least—to the early Formative period (1500–500 BC), when communities of pastoralists-hunters like those at Tulán 54 (Núñez et al. 2006) manufactured large quantities of greenstone (copper minerals) and whitestone (marine shell) beads for interregional trade, probably already using llamas as pack animals. Although there is no evidence to sustain the idea that mountain passes were ritualized at this time, it is clear that many of the routes where the late pre-Hispanic shrines described in this chapter are located had been regularly traveled since the late Archaic period—or earlier—by hunter-gatherers who articulated the valleys/oases on both sides of the Andes with the altiplano through seasonal movements ("transhumance" sensu Núñez 1989).

By the end of the first millennium AD, this chromatic structure was transposed to new practices: offerings of green and white huallcas (beads/shields) "to" or "through" artificial hollows placed on mountain passes, summits, springs, and other punkus, perhaps with an ambiguous propitiatory and protective intent. This would be more in accordance with the whimsical nature of pre-Hispanic non-human agents, who were probably less predictable than those who inhabited heaven/*hananpacha*, earth/*kaypacha*, and hell/*ukhupacha*, a cosmological structure that seems strongly influenced by Christianity (Bouysee-Cassagne and Harris 1987). Following this line of reasoning, it seems hardly accidental that this change in the form of deposition of green and white beads took place at approximately the same time agro-pastoral communities were moving from vulnerable to fortified villages and pukaras across the south Andean highlands. The defensive attitude implied by the repetition of this "protective" ritual gesture in every punku along the way or wherever unpredictable evil forces could be stalking people seems attuned to the climate of social unrest that characterized the LIP in the area.

This understanding of things apparently persisted in some parts of the Southern Andes during the Inka period—as attested by the association between offering pits and segments of the Qhapaqñan—and into the colonial era, as revealed by the presence of blue/green glass beads in caravan campsites. It may have even more recent echoes in the aesthetics of two curious offerings we observed during our fieldwork. One of them was found in Pozuelos (San José 155, table 11.2), where among the greenstone spread around an apacheta on the top of a hill, someone had deposited fragments of an unidentified plastic object of the same color. The second was a set of nine plastic beads—two orange, seven green—attached to a pin left on a large apacheta in Abra del Cóndor in the Eastern Cordillera (figure 11.7). What did these gestures mean to those who performed them? What do they tell us about the way such "diachronic homologies" or ritual traditions are reproduced in practice?

The myths that associate offering pits with the Inka—the leg-less Incarrey who honored the service of his porters or the one who hid his treasures from the Spaniards (Pimentel 2009:20)—are good examples of the unique ways these features entangle the practices of current Andean highland travelers. Like other *saqra* places, these "sepulchers" mobilize the imagination of local peasants, who can spend hours remembering—telling "urban stories" about— old acquaintances who left the community because they contracted a mysterious disease while excavating tapados or found fabulous treasures that allowed them to buy a taxi or set up some other business in the city, where they now lived enjoying their riches.

FIGURE 11.7. *Offering of plastic beads at the apacheta of Abra del Cóndor, Jujuy, Argentina*

The archaeological study of shrines and ceremonial refuse can help us explore the heterogeneous sociality that involves a past and present "other" life. We believe that in this way, from the archaeology of ritual, we can contribute significant insights about the nature of non-human agencies in the ancient Andean world. This knowledge would be as important as that provided by ethnography and anthropological history, but it is unique because of its focus on the practical entanglements of cosmology with matter.

ACKNOWLEDGMENTS

The field research on which this chapter is based was funded in part by Consejo Nacional de Investigaciones Científicas y Técnicas, Argentina (PIP 6243), the National Geographic Society (Grant 7552-03), and Fondecyt, Chile (grant 1010327 for international cooperation, directed by José Berenguer).

REFERENCES CITED

Alberti, B., S. Fowles, M. Holbraad, Y. Marshall, and C. Witmore. 2011. "'Worlds Otherwise': Archaeology, Anthropology, and Ontological Difference." *Current Anthropology* 52 (6): 896-912. http://dx.doi.org/10.1086/662027.

Allen, C. J. 1988. *The Hold Life Has: Coca and Cultural Identity in an Andean Community*. Smithsonian Series in Ethnographic Inquiry. Washington, DC: Smithsonian Institution Press.

Ambrosetti, J. B., and S. Debenedetti. 1917. *Supersticiones y Leyendas*. Buenos Aires: La Cultura Argentina.

Angiorama, C. 2007. "¿Una ofrenda 'caravanera' en Los Amarillos? Minerales y tráfico de bienes en tiempos prehispánicos." In *Producción y Circulación Prehispánicas de Bienes en el Sur Andino*, ed. A. E. Nielsen, M. C. Rivolta, V. Seldes, M. Vázquez, and P. Mercolli, 383–92. Córdoba, Argentina: Editorial Brujas.

Angiorama, C. 2012. "La ocupación del espacio en el sur de Pozuelos (Jujuy, Argentina) durante tiempos prehispánicos y coloniales." *Estudios Sociales del NOA* 11: 125–42.

Bell, C. M. 1992. *Ritual Theory, Ritual Practice*. New York: Oxford University Press.

Berenguer, J. 1994. "Asentamientos, caravaneros y tráfico de larga distancia en el Norte de Chile: el caso de Santa Bárbara." In *De Costa a Selva*, ed. M. E. Albeck, 17–50. Tilcara, Argentina: Instituto Interdisciplinario Tilcara.

Berenguer, J. 2004. *Caravanas, Interacción y Cambio en el Desierto de Atacama*. Santiago de Chile: Ediciones Sirawi.

Berenguer, J., I. Cáceres, C. Sanhueza, and P. Hernández. 2005. "El Qhapaqñan en el Alto Loa, Norte de Chile: Un estudio micro y macromorfológico." *Estudios Atacameños* 29: 7–39.

Boman, E. 1991 [1908]. *Antigüedades de la Región Andina de la República Argentina y del Desierto de Atacama*. San Salvador de Jujuy: Universidad Nacional de Jujuy.

Bouysee-Cassagne, T., and O. Harris. 1987. "Pacha: En torno al pensamiento aymara." In *Tres Reflexiones Sobre el Pensamiento Aymara*, ed. T. Bouysee-Cassagne, 11–59. La Paz: Hisbol.

Cruz, P. 2006. "Espacios permeables y espacios peligrosos: Consideraciones acerca de *punkus* y *qaqas* en el paisaje altoandino de Potosí, Bolivia." *Boletín del Museo Chileno de Arte Precolombino* 11 (2): 35–50.

De Albornoz, C. 1988 [1584]. "Instrucción para descubrir todas las guacas del Pirú y sus camayos y haziendas." In *Fábulas y mitos de los incas by C. de Molina and C. de Albornoz*, ed. H. Urbano and P. Duviols, 161–98. Madrid: Historia 16.

Descola, P. 2013. *Beyond Nature and Culture*. Chicago: University of Chicago Press.

Durkheim, É. 2001 [1912]. *The Elementary Forms of Religious Life*. New York: Oxford University Press.

Eliade, M. 1996 [1953]. *Patterns in Comparative Religion*. Lincoln: University of Nebraska Press.

Galdames, L. 1990. "Apacheta: La ofrenda de piedra." *Diálogo Andino* 9: 11–25.

Gell, A. 1998. *Art and Agency*. Oxford: Clarendon.

Gibson, J. J. 1979. *The Ecological Approach to Visual Perception*. Boston: Houghton Mifflin.

Giddens, A. 1984. *The Constitution of Society: Outline of the Theory of Structuration*. Cambridge: Polity.

Girault, L. 1958. "Le culte des apacheta chez les Aymara de Bolivie." *Journal de la Société des Americanistes* 47 (1): 33–46. http://dx.doi.org/10.3406/jsa.1958.1149.

González, A. R. 1967. "Una excepcional pieza de mosaico del Noroeste Argentino." *Etnia* 6: 1–28.

González Holguín, D. 1952 [1608]. *Vocabulario de la lengua general de todo el Perú, llamada Quechua*. Lima: Edición del Instituto de Historia, Universidad Nacional de San Marcos.

Henare, A., M. Holbraad, and S. Wastell. 2007. "Introduction: Thinking through Things." In *Thinking through Things: Theorizing Artefacts Ethnographically*, ed. A. Henare, M. Holbraad, and S. Wastell, 1–31. London: Routledge.

Horton, R. 1960. "A Definition of Religion, and Its Uses." *Journal of the Royal Anthropological Institute* 90 (2): 201–26.

Hyslop, J. 1984. *The Inka Road System*. Orlando: Academic.

Jones, A., and N. Boivin. 2010. "The Malice of Inanimate Objects: Material Agency." In *The Oxford Handbook of Material Culture Studies*, ed. D. Hicks and M. C. Beaudry, 333–50. Oxford: Oxford University Press.

Joyce, R., and J. Pollard. 2010. "Archaeological Assemblages and Practices of Deposition." In *The Oxford Handbook of Material Culture Studies*, ed. D. Hicks and M. C. Beaudry, 291–309. Oxford: Oxford University Press.

Keane, W. 2005. "Signs Are Not the Garb of Meaning: On the Social Analysis of Material Things." In *Materiality*, ed. D. Miller, 182–205. Durham, NC: Duke University Press. http://dx.doi.org/10.1215/9780822386711-008.

Knappett, C., and L. Malafouris. 2008. *Material Agency: Towards a Non-Anthropocentric Approach*. Cambridge: Springer. http://dx.doi.org/10.1007/978-0-387-74711-8.

Latour, B. 2005. *Reassembling the Social: An Introduction to Actor-Network Theory.* Oxford: Oxford University Press.

Lecoq, P. 1987. "Caravanes de lamas, sel et échanges dans une communauté de Potosi, Bolivie." *Bulletin de l'Institut Français d'Études Andines* 16 (3–4): 1–38.

Mariscotti de Görlitz, A. M. 1978. *Pachamama Santa Tierra: Contribución al Estudio de la Religión Autóctona en los Andes Centro-Meridionales.* Indiana Supplement 8. Berlin: Gebr. Mann Verlag.

Martínez, G. 1983. "Los dioses de los cerros en los Andes." *Journal de la Société des Americanistes* 69 (1): 85–115. http://dx.doi.org/10.3406/jsa.1983.2226.

Muhonen, T. 2012. "Faith in Stones: Accumulating Stone Heaps as Cross-Cultural Phenomenon." *Material Religion: The Journal of Objects, Art, and Belief* 8 (4): 539–40. http://dx.doi.org/10.2752/175183412X13522006995132.

Murúa, M. d. 2004 [1590]. *Códice Murúa: Historia y genealogía de los reyes Incas del Perú (Códice Galvin).* 2 vols, ed. J. M. Ossio. Madrid: Testimonio Compañía Editorial.

Nielsen, A. E. 1997. "El tráfico caravanero visto desde la *jara*." *Estudios Atacameños* 14: 339–71.

Nielsen, A. E. 2001. "Ethnoarchaeological Perspectives on Caravan Trade in the South-Central Andes." In *Ethnoarchaeology of Andean South America: Contributions to Archaeological Method and Theory*, ed. L. Kuznar, 163–201. Ann Arbor: University of Michigan Press.

Nielsen, A. E. 2011. "El tráfico de caravanas entre Lípez y Atacama visto desde la Cordillera Occidental." In *En Ruta: Arqueología, Historia y Etnografía del Tráfico Sur Andino*, ed. L. Núñez and A. E. Nielsen, 83–109. Córdoba, Argentina: Encuentro.

Nielsen, A. E. 2013. "Circulating Objects and the Constitution of South Andean Society (500 BC–AD 1550)." In *Merchants, Trade, and Exchange in the Pre-Columbian World*, ed. K. Hirth and J. Pillsbury, 389–418. Washington, DC: Dumbarton Oaks.

Nielsen, A. E., J. Berenguer, and C. Sanhueza. 2006. "El *Qhapaqñan* entre Atacama y Lípez." *Intersecciones en Antropología* 7: 217–34.

Núñez, L. 1989. "Hacia la Producción de Alimentos y la Vida Sedentaria (5.000 a.C. a 900 d.C.)." In *Culturas de Chile: Prehistoria, desde sus Orígenes hasta los Albores de la Conquista*, ed. J. Hidalgo, V. Schiappacasse, H. Niemeye, C. Aldunate, and I. Solimano, 81–105. Santiago: Andrés Bello.

Núñez, L., I. Cartajena, C. Carrasco, and P. de Souza. 2006. "El templete Tulán de la Puna de Atacama: emergencia de complejidad ritual durante el Formativo Temprano (norte de Chile)." *Latin American Antiquity* 17 (4): 445–73. http://dx.doi.org/10.2307/25063067.

Olsen, B. 2010. *In Defense of Things: Archaeology and the Ontology of Objects.* Lanham, MD: Altamira.

Pauketat, T. 2001. "Practice and History in Archaeology: An Emerging Paradigm." *Anthropological Theory* 1 (1): 73–98. http://dx.doi.org/10.1177/14634990122228638.

Pimentel, G. 2009. "Las huacas del tráfico: Arquitectura ceremonial en rutas prehispánicas del desierto de Atacama." *Boletín del Museo Chileno de Arte Precolombino* 14 (2): 9–38.

Pimentel, G. 2013. "Redes viales prehispánicas en el Desierto de Atacama: viajeros, movilidad e intercambio." PhD dissertation, Postgrado de Antropología, Universidad Católica Del Norte–Universidad de Tarapacá, San Pedro de Atacama, Chile.

Pimentel, G., C. Rees, P. de Souza, and L. Arancibia. 2011. "Viajeros costeros y caravaneros: Dos estrategias de movilidad en el Período Formativo del desierto de Atacama, Chile." In *En Ruta: Arqueología, Historia y Etnografía del Tráfico Sur Andino*, ed. L. Núñez and A. E. Nielsen, 43–81. Córdoba, Argentina: Encuentro.

Polo de Ondegardo, J. 1916 [1571]. *Instrucción contra las ceremonias y ritos que usan los indios, conforme al tiempo de su infidelidad.* Colección de libros y documentos referentes a la historia del Perú, vol. 3., ed. H. Urteaga. Lima: Imprenta y Librería Sanmartí.

Ricard Lanata, X. 2007. *Ladrones de Sombra: El Universo Religioso de los Pastores del Ausangate.* Lima: IFEA, Centro Bartolomé de Las Casas. http://dx.doi.org/10.4000/books.ifea.611.

Richards, C., and J. Thomas. 1984. "Ritual Activity and Structured Deposition in Later Neolithic Wessex." In *Neolithic Studies: A Review of Some Current Research*, ed. R. Bradley and J. Gardiner, 189–218. BAR International Series 133. Oxford: British Archaeological Reports.

Schiffer, M. B. 1999. *The Material Life of Human Beings: Artifacts, Behavior, and Communication.* London: Routledge.

Schiffer, M. B. 2011. *Studying Technological Change: A Behavioral Approach.* Salt Lake City: University of Utah Press.

Sinclaire, C. 1994. "Los sitios de 'muros y cajas' del Río Loa y su relación con el tráfico de caravanas." In *De Costa a Selva: Producción e Intercambio entre los Pueblos Agroalfareros de los Andes Centro-Sur*, ed. M. E. Albeck, 51–76. Tilcara, Argentina: Instituto Interdisciplinario Tilcara.

Valli, E., and D. Summers. 1994. *Caravans of the Himalaya.* Washington, DC: National Geographic Society.

Van Kessel, J. 1988. "Tecnología Aymara: Un enfoque cultural." *Hombre y Desierto* 2: 58–88.

Walker, W. H. 1995. "Ceremonial Trash?" In *Expanding Archaeology*, ed. J. M. Skibo, W. H. Walker, and A. E. Nielsen, 67–79. Salt Lake City: University of Utah Press.

Walker, W. H. 2009. "Warfare and the Practice of Supernatural Agencies." In *Warfare in Cultural Context: Practice, Agency, and the Archaeology of Violence*, ed. A. E. Nielsen and W. H. Walker, 109–37. Tucson: University of Arizona Press.

West, T. 1981. "Llama Caravans of the Andes." *Natural History* 90 (12): 62–73.

12

Mining, Ritual, and Social Memory

An Exploration of Toponymy in the Ica Valley, Peru

HENDRIK VAN GIJSEGHEM
AND VERITY H. WHALEN

[Humans] know that although speech alone cannot materially transform nature, it can direct attention, organize insignificant entities into significant composite wholes, and in so doing, make things formerly overlooked—and hence invisible and nonexistent—visible and real. (Tuan 1991:685)

In this chapter we examine the relationship among ancient mining, landscape perceptions, and ritual through the intersection of archaeological and linguistic data. More specifically, we consider contemporary place names in the Upper Ica Valley of southern Peru to be a link between ancient landscapes and past beliefs about mining. We propose that places where ancient mining was performed may have been regarded as special and perhaps dangerous, as recent archaeological evidence of ritual activity in mines indicates. Furthermore, we suggest that these perceptions carried over into the historical period and became embedded in (1) the maintenance of ancient place names or their translation during times of important societal change (such as Inka and Spanish conquest) and (2) the persistence of these beliefs into the historical period, whereby landscape locations were given equivalent names in contemporary languages.

First, we review the kinds of evidence that lead us to make this argument. We provide a general discussion of the practice of place naming and the meanings of

DOI: 10.5876/9781607325963.c012

toponyms. We also explore how mining, as the extraction of the earth's substance for human use, is embedded in Andean attitudes and beliefs toward the landscape. While much information about these practices comes from the ethnographic present, we argue that they are anchored in the pre-colonial past. We do this by drawing from studies that highlight the continuity and transmission of Andean dispositions about landscape, mountains, caves, and the subterranean realm. We argue that changes in political regimes and population relocation caused by Inka or Spanish colonialism are unlikely to have erased general patterns of autochthonous landscape cognition. By examining the language policies under Inka and Spanish domination of the Ica Valley, we provide a context for the persistence of ancient place names and place-name categories. Finally, we evaluate the likelihood that a prehispanic set of beliefs about mining existed that was analogous to the beliefs and practices documented ethnographically. While the study of toponyms yields reliable but imprecise results, we argue that these results tend to support the hypothesis that ancient mining practices had an effect on landscape cognition. Moreover, by examining toponyms in combination with the archaeological data we collected from survey in the Upper Ica Valley during 2010, we suggest that prehispanic landscape cognition had a lasting effect on place names as they exist today.

TOPONYMY AND THE TRANSMISSION OF SOCIAL MEMORY

Here, we underline the major dimensions and attributes of place names and their role in the transmission of social memory. There are several reasons we should at least explore the possibility that toponyms are embedded within ancient attitudes toward landscape and exhibit some components of social memory. At the outset, the attribution of a name is a central part in the process of place making (Tuan 1991) because it reflects people's partitioning of space and the definition of its major characteristics. For this reason toponyms are a ubiquitous and enduring component of human society, communicate information to people who use them, and are a product of both cultural creativity and social consensus. As the "shared remembrance" from which people construct identities (Alcock 2002:1), social memory is inscribed in place names and landscape cognition among many modes of persistence and transmission. Toponyms, for instance, are "constructors of ... social memory" (Nash 2012:16) and as such constitute a unique point of intersection among language, landscape, cultural aesthetics, and ontological concerns. A review of literature on place names and how they are shared further reveals these themes.

1. *Toponyms are universal in human society.* While claims about the existence of "universals" are regarded with some skepticism, we can still perhaps assert that all humans give names to places. Ever since humans acquired complex cognitive abilities and language, they have anchored their lived experiences in landscape meanings and classifications that required them to name places (Hunn and Meilleur 2010:17). This process generates associative information about those places, if for no other reason than to communicate. People select what is deemed nameable out of the continuous spectrum that is their known world. They assign names to subjectively defined entities and, most important, what the name should refer to or what information it highlights. The semiotic content of these names varies tremendously. The mundane "Round Hill," the commemorative "The Place Where a Historical Event Took Place," the quaint "Greendale," the blissful "Heaven," the threatening "Death Valley," and the evocative "Pulltrouser Swamp" were all named according to some explicit or implicit intent and design. In a comprehensive analysis of place names in the United States, Stewart (1970) distinguishes among ten classes of place-name origins, including those that are based on description, association, and commemoration.[1]

2. *Toponyms are a polysemic source of information to the people who use them.* This is the most fundamental and instrumental quality of place names (Basso 1996). From this perspective place names are a component of landscape knowledge that reveals characteristics of the land, primarily in distinguishing different ecotopes by evoking categories of plants, animals, and other resources found in certain places. They anchor ethnogeography in the description of some sensorial characteristic of certain features—often, but not necessarily, a visual characteristic. This information is transmittable among people and from generation to generation. It also structures spatial cognition by ordering the landscape into a manageable number of shorthand categories (Hunn and Meilleur 2010:18). These toponyms may equally serve as direction, indication, or warning and sometimes evoke myths and histories. Particularly in non-literate societies, the lived landscape gives structure to these stories, and cues contained in the cognitive map assist narration. The landscape, therefore, constitutes a type of mnemonic device akin to a text (Johnson 2007; Thomas 2001:175). Place names, as textual cues, play a central role in communication and social memory.

3. *Toponyms are the product of cultural creativity.* Like other cultural creations (such as art, iconography, and architectural styles), the semiotic content of place names is culturally contingent and their associative nature vastly subjective (Vuolteenaho and Berg 2009). For this reason place names may exhibit patterns of associations among name types or categories that are appropriate for analysis and interpretation (Hunn and Meilleur 2010:15; Johnson and Hunn 2010). Landscape cognition is socially constructed, and place names carry subjective perceptions of landscape. As such, we argue that place names "map out" to some degree past ontologies and resonate in myth, history, worldview, and heritage. Although we may not entirely decipher the exact content of the toponymic discourse, general patterns emerge and may be confronted with other sources of data. In this study we draw upon archaeological and geologic data.

4. *Toponyms are the product of a social consensus.* More often than not, place names grow somewhat organically. They are established in common practice through everyday conversations rather than through the agency of a small number of people. Moreover, politically imposed place names tend to disappear if they are not wholly embraced in daily parlance. In many cases the original place name reappears, suggesting that place names exist and persist mostly by virtue of their vernacular nature (Tuan 1991:688).

5. *Toponyms are resilient.* While political powers may attempt to impose new place names in an act of dominance, people often ignore such place names. Tucker (2011:172) evokes the example of Cuba, which was renamed "Juana" by Columbus and subsequently "Fernandina" by King Fernando. Both names were received with some indifference, and neither came close to impacting the vernacular language. Natives and Spaniards alike quickly reverted to the native name, Cuba, in both unofficial and official documents, and it is still used today. Place names are resilient in part because of their orthodox and collective nature (see Henshaw 2006) and deeply emotional associations (Kearney and Bradley 2009). They are easily inherited from generation to generation and largely go unquestioned, except in exceptional circumstances (Tuan 1991; Tucker 2011). How many average North Americans, for example, know the origin of their town name, the nearby river, or a hill? Yet throughout history, these names have very rarely changed, and the extremely large number of Native American place names Euro-Americans routinely use attests to this.

6. *Toponymy as a component of social memory.* In light of the previously developed points, it emerges that toponymy is a powerful structuring agent of the landscape. It is shared and inherited through narratives that have landscape referents. Toponymy's associative content constitutes a central part of social memory beyond its instrumental quality of orientation and information (Alderman and Inwood 2013:213). Tringham (2000) and others (e.g., Horsfall 2002; Joyce 2000) emphasize that social memory is anchored in physical space and places from houses to landscapes, which serve as mnemonics (Schmidt 2006). As central components of landscape cognition, the role of toponyms exceeds mere description: they anchor oral narratives on visible or imagined landscape features. Toponyms structure landscape maps that ensure the transmission of oral narratives across generations (Henshaw 2006). Toponyms thus reveal the existence of a "past within the past" (see Alcock 2002; Bradley 1991, 2002; Van Dyke and Alcock 2003). In fact, toponymy's demonstrated resilience through social, political, and even linguistic changes situates it as a unique group of data existing in its own distinctive temporal frame. Following Braudel (1969), we can conceptualize time on several levels: the longue durée or "geographical" time that operates at the level of environmental change, the "social" time that registers particular histories of groups of people, and the "individual" time that is more properly conceptualized as a history of actual events (Bradley 1991:210). Toponyms exist in an intermediary temporal space between "individual time" and "geographical time." While the time frame of toponyms generally operates beyond direct social memory (Braudel 1969) because the knowledge associated with place names is often lost, this knowledge can nonetheless be preserved, reproduced in mnemonics: monuments, commemorations, and culturally constructed landscapes preserved in place names. Moreover, we can recover some areas of this knowledge, we argue, from the analysis of those ancient mnemonics.

Toponymy is a mnemonic form of communication, and because of the permanence of landscape, it is precisely one of the main cultural mechanisms of recognition and transmission of knowledge. Schmidt (2006:92) echoes this sentiment when he argues that "social memory linked to place and maintained through storytelling—myth—has an interactive, recursive capacity to reactivate ancient places as renewed centers of ritual power and authority." Basso (1996:55) termed the recursive relationship in which people animate the landscape and create places through experience, memory, and emotion "interanimation." By examining Ica's place names, we are attempting to better understand some of the meanings held by these place names, which were possibly inherited from ancient times.

MINING, RITUAL, AND LANDSCAPE: AN ANDEAN PERSPECTIVE

The initial interest for this research came from an extended reflection on the relationship among Andean mining, landscape, and ritual. A complete discussion can be found in another article (see Van Gijseghem et al. 2013) but is briefly summarized here. Ample ethnohistorical and ethnographic evidence in the Andes indicates that mining is regulated by common principles of Andean reciprocity and that the extraction of minerals from the earth necessitates payment to chthonic forces (Cobo 1890–95 [1653]:bk. 13, ch. 11, cited in Rowe 1946:246; Ramirez 1994:95). These beliefs and practices take many forms, all of which involve a rich set of ritual practices surrounding mining and invoke the inherent spiritual implications involved with the extraction of subterranean resources. In Oruro, Bolivia, the miners of Potosí invoke a supernatural force known as Tío, or alternatively Supay, who lives in the mines (Bouysse-Cassagne 2005:447; Gil García and Fernández Juárez 2008; Gose 1986; Harris 2000:24; Nash 1972; Taylor 1980). Miners maintain that propitiatory gestures and offerings to Tío are necessary in exchange for high-quality minerals and the safety of the workers. In some narratives Tío is equated with the Roman Catholic Devil and is the consort of the local saint known as the "Virgin of the Mineshaft," who tempers his sedition. Local Aymara historiography suggests that Tío is the incarnation of a prehispanic demon named Tiw, who dwelled in mines and was responsible for natural resources. According to local folklore, only later was Tiw inserted into the Roman Catholic narratives and his name modified as Tío, the Spanish cognate for "uncle" (UNESCO 2001).

There is little doubt that these beliefs are syncretic versions of prehispanic attitudes toward mining, especially considering Andean populations' complex relationship with the earth and mountains (Gose 1986; Nielsen, Angiorama, and Ávila, this volume; Reinhard 1985). Archaeological evidence, while scarce, exists for prehispanic rituals associated with mining (Shimada 1994; Van Gijseghem et al. 2011, 2013; Vaughn et al. 2013 (both sources)). While the details of regional beliefs may have varied, the extraction of the earth's substance requiring compensation in the form of rituals and offerings is absolutely consistent with our understanding of prehispanic cultures. Gose (1986:303) describes mining as the "culminating violation of the most central manifestation of the apu:[2] the mountain itself. It represents a quantum leap beyond any other productive activity in the intensity of relations between people and *apus*, and constitutes a definite strain on both." It should come as no surprise, then, that mines were endowed with powerful supernatural characteristics and housed spirits that had the potential to be malevolent. Regardless of whether we wish to employ the somewhat tired term *Gates to the Underworld*, historical and ethnographic evidence suggests that prehispanic mines were perceived as liminal spaces embodying the chthonic outside/inside, or light/darkness duality, and that potentially dangerous beings lived within them (Bouysse-Cassagne 2005; Cobo 1890–95 [1653]:bk. 13, ch. 11; MacCormack 1984). We review this evidence below.

ENDURING BELIEFS IN COLONIAL CONTEXTS, LANGUAGE, AND MINING

How likely is it that these attitudes and beliefs remain imprinted on the landscape in toponymy after centuries of imperial and colonial regimes, population replacement, and linguistic change? After all, the impacts of Spanish colonialism on the native peoples of South America were severe. Yet the endurance of indigenous Andean belief and practice in the face of conquest and conversion is well documented (e.g., Andrien 2001; Hill Boone and Cummins 1998). In the Qollahuaya region, Bastien (1978) observed ancestral graves carved into the local mountainside. During the Spanish conquest, Catholic missionaries burned the mummies that had been placed in these graves, leaving behind the empty niches carved in the rock. The symbolic importance of these empty graves remains centuries later, and diviners sprinkle the niches with animal blood and fat during contemporary ritual practices to honor the mountain and their ancestors (ibid.:21). Christian missionaries taught the indigenous residents that baptism was necessary to get into heaven, but as Bastien (ibid.:87) states, they "had little interest in going to heaven; rather, they wished to remain forever on their mountain." The writings and drawings in Felipe Guaman Poma de Ayala's conquest-era manuscript demonstrate a similar pattern: European subjects, even religious officials, are often depicted with subversive elements of indigenous Andean symbolism (Pratt 1991:36; see also Scott 2012). Such examples illustrate the continuity in belief and practice that transcended the prehispanic and post-conquest eras. Given the central role of landscape in the Andean worldview, the continuation of such beliefs likely included attitudes toward landscape and mining.

At the same time, multiple eras of colonialism and political reorganization have dramatically shaped the Andean social landscape. As Lockhart

(1998:41) notes, the traditionally highland-oriented nature of pre-conquest Andean society, combined with the rapid and extensive depopulation of the coast, created a post-conquest Peru that consisted of a Spanish-African coast and an indigenously populated interior. Many Quechua speakers on the coast were displaced highlanders who had migrated to work for the Spanish (Lockhart 1968:217–18). Southern Peru, previously linguistically heterogeneous, was fused into a socially cohesive "oppressed nation" under Spanish colonial rule (Mannheim 1998:384). This has obvious implications for our discussion of the endurance of cultural traditions and attitudes toward mining in the coastal Ica Valley. If there were considerable relocations of indigenous groups, continuity in belief and practice may have been interrupted between the prehispanic and modern eras. Evidence suggests, however, that the more deep and basic elements of worldview were widely shared and persistent in the Andean universe (see Bastien 1978). The presence of pre-Quechua place names on twenty-first-century maps, despite the successive Inka and Spanish conquests, at the very least supports the endurance of some areas of cultural construction.

TOPONYMY AND LANGUAGE POLICIES

While the Inka never made a clear attempt to establish Southern Peruvian Quechua as the administrative language of the empire, Spanish colonial policy sought the establishment of one dominant indigenous language in addition to Spanish (Mannheim 1998:384). Evidence such as the combination of Quechua verb structure with Spanish stems (see the Huarochirí manuscript; Lockhart 1998:43) early in the post-conquest era, however, suggests that indigenous people began linguistically syncretizing Quechua, and potentially other indigenous languages, with Spanish starting shortly after conquest. Syncretization continues in contemporary society, as evidenced by hybrid literacies in rural communities composed of bilingual speakers of Quechua and Spanish (e.g., De La Piedra 2009). The existence of entirely Spanish or Quechua place names, in addition to place names that are syncretizations of Quechua and Spanish, thus does not conflict with the hypothesis that these names have prehispanic roots. They may have been converted to Spanish, Quechua, or both beginning early in the post-conquest era but still retained a meaning that reflects indigenous South Coast worldview and landscape perceptions. Therefore, we suggest that some salient elements of worldview transcend languages and linguistic change.

ENDURING ATTITUDES ON MINES AND MINING: THE CASE FOR CONTINUITY

We should be careful not to blindly assign to prehispanic populations beliefs that may have been post-conquest phenomena (e.g., Shimada 2013; Taussig 1980). Scott (2008:1859–60) underlines how the colonial experience, particularly forced labor in mines, "transformed the subterranean realms in Andean imaginations into spaces associated with evil." It is clear that Roman Catholic symbols, particularly the Manichean good/evil duality, were incorporated in native discourse on the relationship between people and minerals. However, in the foregoing discussion we make a case for the existence of a set of beliefs that is largely indigenous. We suggest that those beliefs have parallels in the prehispanic period, as indicated by the archaeological contexts previously mentioned. While the colonial encounter rendered a view of subterranean spaces as evil, prehispanic mines were seen as no less powerful, embodying the potential for both good and evil in customary Andean cognitive fluidity and flexibility (Gil García and Fernández Juárez 2008:106). Cobo (1890–95 [1653]:bk. 13, ch. 11) offers compelling insights by invoking a native category of sacred places to describe mines, stating that they were *huacas* to which the Andeans prayed and held festivals. Similarly, the Spanish jurist Solórzano y Pereira (1972 [1648]:vol. 1, 277) wrote in the seventeenth century that the mines of Huancavelica were thought to have been inhabited by frightening and demonic apparitions that guarded the mineral wealth preserved underground.

Bastien (1978) outlines several areas of overt continuity and reproduction in an Andean community's ritual observances regarding mountains, conceived metaphorically as biological beings whose mouths are caves. In consequence, caves are the object of various rituals and offerings as the mountain is ritually fed (ibid.:48). The reciprocal relationship is manifest: "if we don't feed the mountain, it won't feed us" (ibid.:xix); a quote that stands in conceptual contrast with the somewhat more foreboding statement recorded in the Potosí ethnography by Nash (1979): "we eat the mines and the mines eat us."

MINING IN THE UPPER ICA VALLEY

We turn to the Upper Ica Valley in southern Peru and argue that collectively, toponyms incorporate ancient attitudes, perceptions, and beliefs about certain landscape characteristics and the communally understood forces they incarnate. Even if they are relatively recent Spanish toponyms, we contend that some of them were affixed to places in accordance with beliefs and attitudes that have their roots in the prehispanic period, as the "lived" landscape is continually produced and reproduced by human involvement. Based on our conceptual framework, the endurance of these Spanish place names attests to the fact that they were often in agreement with the previous prehispanic meanings. If they were not in agreement, history suggests they likely would have been cast off in favor of the old place names, as was the case with Cuba. In particular, we explore the relationship that exists among ancient mining, ritual, and landscape perceptions as illustrated by place names. While recognizing that the exact meaning of the patterns we are finding is probably forever lost, we maintain that landscape locations where mining would have been possible in the past have often received names that are qualitatively different than the names of non-mining locations. In some cases we have demonstrated that prehispanic mining was not just possible in these locations but actually occurred (see Van Gijseghem et al. 2011, 2013; figure 12.1). The associated place names either have negative, ambiguous, or powerful connotations, or they refer to things or events other than ecological or visual characteristics of the place. Sometimes these place names incorporate verbs. We propose that this phenomenon indicates that the referent is part of a more complex and dynamic narrative than are the names of non-mining places, which more often than not are somewhat mundane (e.g., landform, visual characteristic, indigenous plant/animal resource). In short, we argue that the data support the idea that mining place names are more likely to be metaphorical or allegorical rather than descriptive, and vice-versa. This, we suggest, opens a rare window onto ancient landscape ethnocategories.

While gold is mined today in the Upper Ica Valley, copper remains the principal mineral mined in this region. The natural forces of tectonic uplift, land erosion, and weathering have affected the local cretaceous diorite formations, exposing seams of oxidized material notable for their green and blue colorations. The minerals that accompany copper ore (e.g., carbonates and silicates such as azurite, malachite, and chrysocolla) were probably the first to have been harvested by past populations (Van Gijseghem et al. 2013). We have found evidence of ancient mining dating to the Early Horizon (ca. 300 BC–AD 1), which appears to have intensified during the Late Intermediate Period (ca. AD 1000–1476; Van Gijseghem et al. 2011, 2013). Mining operations today, with a few exceptions, have remained relatively modest and are unlikely to have erased all traces of past activity (see figure 12.2). By contrast, in more economically significant mining regions such as Cerro Verde in Huancavelica, most archaeological evidence for ancient mining is more likely to have been obliterated by recent developments in infrastructure.

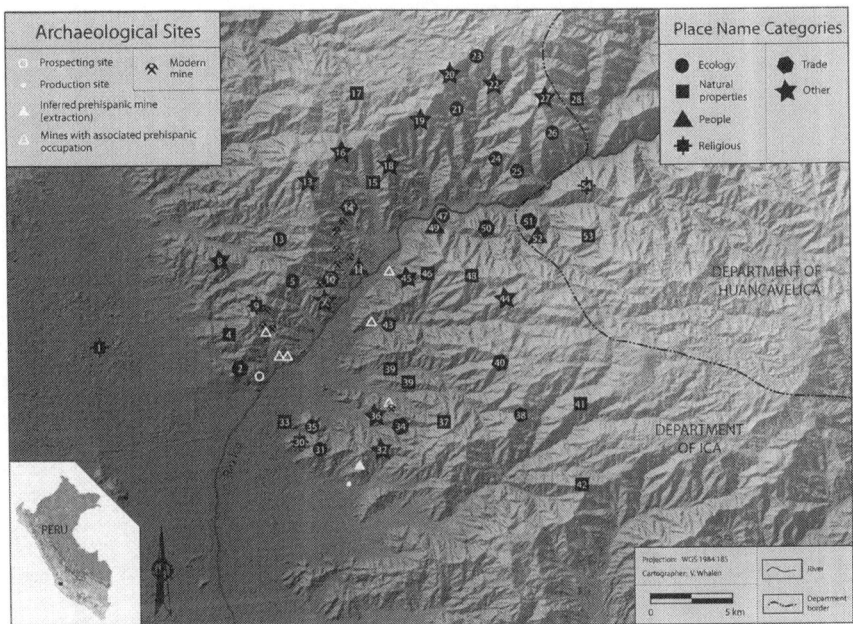

FIGURE 12.1. *Upper Ica Valley. The numbers associated with places refer to table 12.1.*

UPPER ICA PLACE NAMES

Here we describe the place names of the Upper Ica Valley and their relationship with the region's numerous but generally small-scale copper and gold mines. The majority of toponyms in Ica are Spanish or Quechua. Some place names are syncretizations composed of entire words from both languages (e.g., Jatun Diablo). In addition, two place names are believed to be from the pre-Quechua language spoken in parts of the South Coast, a language referred to as Jaqui/Aru, part of the Aymaran language family (Hardman 1966; Silverman 2002). We considered without distinction the names of localities (e.g., mines, towns, agricultural concessions, quebradas, and mountains and hills) found on various maps of the area,[3] in particular the official maps produced by Peru's National Geographic Institute (Reference: Guadalupe; 1:100,000 scale, Edition 3-IGN, Series J631, Sheet 28L), the online geologic map of Ica produced by INGEMMET, Peru's Geology, Mining, and Metallurgy Institute, and some place names as they appear on Google Earth. The Quechua names were translated and cross-referenced in several dictionaries (see table 12.1 for references).

In general, the existence of Quechua and Jaqui/Aru place names testifies to the relative resilience of place names across time, especially in the case of the

FIGURE 12.2. *Mina Azurita, a mining complex with prehispanic and post-colonial occupations and architecture, looking northwest, with the Quebrada Llancay Grande at the bottom*

latter since it is no longer spoken and the meanings of those place names are lost. In addition, we argue that some post-conquest Spanish or syncretized names may have been either translations of pre-conquest names or new toponyms given to places in accordance with pre-conquest landscape perceptions. For example, there is a mine in Nasca located in a mountain called Cerro Quitacalzón, meaning "remove underwear" in Spanish. The nearby agricultural concession is called Huarasaca. The only translation we were able to conjure was a syncretic usage of the Quechua term *Huara*, meaning "pants," to which the Spanish word *saca*, meaning "to remove," was affixed. It appears that in this case, by the time the map was created, the Spanish name for the mountain had been adapted from an older native form of the word and syncretized as Huarasaca and that for some reason, native landscape cognition associated this place with the removal of pants. This example, incidentally, also illustrates the relationship we found in Ica between mines and toponyms that evoke ideas not strictly related to the local ecosystem but that seem to incorporate metaphors pointing to associative narratives.

In Ica we collected fifty-four place names. Of these, four are religious and typically a saint's name, seven refer to some trade or tool, twelve refer to the visual or morphological properties of the place, twelve bear the name of a species of plant or animal, three were named after people or the relationship between people (e.g., Mina Dos Hermanos, which means "two brothers mine" in Spanish), and three could not be translated, including the two Jaqui/Aru names (i.e., Quiojate and Tiojate). Finally, thirteen place names fit in no particular category. They translate as "volcanic fume/small oven," "serpent," "fortune/mercy," "misstep," "great devil," "to work/toil" or "to devastate," "acne/pimple," "parent of an illegitimate child," "shivering/trembling," "rascal," "stitches," "cowardly," and "strangle." The word for "serpent" was included here because of the serpent's privileged status in both Roman Catholic and Andean thought. All place names and translations, language, and spatial association with mines can be consulted in table 12.1.

Although there is no exact correspondence between any name category and an association with mines, the "other" category is overrepresented on the west side of the valley, where most mining occurs (nine out of thirteen and nine out of twelve if we were to exclude Carhuas, whose translation is equivocal). We performed exploratory chi-square tests on several variations of the associations among geographic location, place-name category, and local mining, and none showed this relationship to be statistically significant. We are neither disappointed nor surprised by this. A few reasons led us to doubt the possibility of reaching statistical significance. For one thing, not all ancient place names are expected to have survived, and not all ancient mines are expected to have borne names that are negative or ambiguous. In addition, several modern mining locations do not bear ambiguous or negative names, and it is impossible at this time to know if they were exploited in ancient times. For these reasons and undoubtedly many others, the relationship between name type and mines is muddled and clouded; there is too much interference in the place-name data for us to expect a strong statistical correlation. However, the data highlight the intersection among mining, ritual practice, and landscape cognition if we look at individual cases while examining the region under coarser resolution.

The first six of the place names that belong in the "other" category cited above ("volcanic fume," "serpent," "fortune/mercy," "misstep," "devil," and "to work/toil") are directly associated with mines, some of which are decidedly prehispanic (Van Gijseghem et al. 2011, 2013). Of these, all but one ("to work/toil") are located on the northwest side of the valley. The one exception is the name of a wide, barren quebrada called Llancay Grande, which leads to Mina Azurita (see figure 12.2), a large copper mining complex on which prehispanic material and architecture has been found. Post-conquest architecture

TABLE 12.1. Toponyms of the Ica Valley. Toponyms assigned to the "other" category are in bold.

#	Place Name	Side	Language	Associated Mines	Topographic Feature	Meaning[a]	Category
1	Pampa de Guadalupe	W	Spanish		Pampa	Religious	Religious
2	Cerro Soldado	W	Spanish		Mountain	Soldier	Trade
3	Tiojate	W	Jaqui/aru		Mountain	N/A	N/A
4	Cerro Blanco	W	Spanish	X	Mountain	White	Natural properties
5	Coquimbana	W	Spanish	X[b]	Mines	Cactus	Ecology
6	Quiojate	W	Jaqui/aru	X[b]	Mountain	N/A	N/A
7	**Mina Hornitos**	W	**Spanish**	X	Mines	**Small volcanic fume, small oven?**	**Other**
8	**Cerro Serpiente**	W	**Spanish**	X	Mountain	**Serpent**	**Other**
9	**San Miguel Rescate**	W	**Spanish**	X	Mine / quebrada	**Rescue / recovery**	**Religious**
10	Mina Cuartillos	W	Spanish	X	Mines	Quarts (like pints)	Trade
11	Mina Dos Hermanos	W	Spanish	X	Mines	Two brothers	People
12	Cerro Guanaco	W	Quechua	X	Mountain	Guanaco	Ecology
13	**Mina Fortuna / cerro fortuna**	W	**Spanish**	X	Mine / mountain	**luck, fortune, mercy**	**Other**
14	Casa Blanca	W	Spanish	X	Mine / quebrada	White house	Trade
15	Quebrada Cuesta Vieja	W	Spanish	X	Quebrada	Old slope / incline	Natural properties
16	**Cerro Mal Paso**	W	**Spanish**	X	Mountain	**Misstep**	**Other**

continued on next page

TABLE 12.1.—continued

#	Place Name	Side	Language	Associated Mines	Topographic Feature	Meaning[a]	Category
17	Cerro Pedregal	W	Spanish	X	Mountain	Scree	Natural properties
18	**Cerro Suche**	W	**Quechua**		Mountain	Suchi = acne/pimple; Suchiy = donation, present; suchu = paralytic, limping; such'u = disabled at the feet; Suchuy = to trip, to drag, failure	Other
19	Huahuancan-cha	W	Quechua		Place?/mountain	Wawa = child; Wawani = parent of an illegitimate child	Other
20	Cerro Chaupican-cha	W	Quechua		Mountain	Chawpi = middle, among, center; Chanka Chawpi = gore, gusset (triangular piece of cloth)	Other
21	Sauche	W	Quechua		Mountain	Sawsi = willow	Ecology
22	**Cerro Chiriticancha (?)**	W	**Quechua**		**Mountain**	Chirichi = shivering, trembling	Other
23	Cerro Huamandioja	W	Quechua		Mountain	Waman = falcon; dioja = ? tioja(te?)	Ecology
24	Cerro Guinda	W	Spanish		Mountain	Cherry	Ecology
25	Cerro Huancasa	W	Quechua		Mountain	Wanka = stone	Ecology
26	Cerro Ramadillas	W	Spanish		Mountain	Small branch	Ecology
27	**Cerro Tuno**	W	**Spanish**		**Mountain**	Rascal	Other
28	Pongo	W	Quechua		Place/quebrada	Punku = gate	Natural properties
29	Fribay	E	N/A	X[b]	Locality	N/A	N/A

continued on next page

TABLE 12.1.—continued

#	Place Name	Side	Language	Associated Mines	Topographic Feature	Meaning[a]	Category
30	Cerro Santa Rosa	E	Spanish		Mountain	Religious	Religious
31	Cerro Cordero	E	Spanish		Mountain	Lamb	Ecology
32	**Cerro Los Puntados**	**E**	**Spanish**		**Mountain**	**Stitches**	**Other**
33	Cerro Cerrillo	E	Spanish		Mountain	Hill	Natural properties
34	Quebrada La Mina	E	Spanish	X	Quebrada	Mine	Trade
35	Cerro Yunque	E	Quechua		Mountain	Yunka = forest / valley	Ecology
36	Quebrada Llancay	E	Quechua	X[b]	Quebrada	To work, to toil, to devastate	Other
37	Cerros Altos Mina Zurita	E	Spanish	X[b]	Mountain	Zurita = Azurita	Natural properties
38	Cerro Rompe Trapo	E	Spanish	X	Mountain	Plant	Ecology
39	Cerro / Quebrada La Yesera	E	Spanish	X[b]	Mountain / quebrada	Gypsum factory (yeso)	Natural properties
40	Cerro Trapiche	E	Spanish		Mountain	Mill	Trade
41	Cerro Jatun Loma	E	Quechua		Mountain	Long / tall hill	Natural properties
42	Cerro Jatun Ccasa	E	Quechua	X	Mountain	Ice	Natural properties
43	Quebrada Tortolita	E	Spanish	X[b]	Quebrada	Turtledove	Ecology
44	**Loma Carhuas**	**E**	**Quechua**		**Quebrada**	Karwa = yellow / steinbock / goat / cowardly / recreant	**Other**
45	**Huarcaya**	**E**	**Quechua**		**Locality**	Warkuy = strangle / hang up	**Other**

continued on next page

TABLE 12.1.—continued

#	Place Name	Side	Language	Associated Mines	Topographic Feature	Meaning[a]	Category
46	Cerro La Bandera	E	Spanish		Mountain	Flag	Natural properties
47	Huamani	E	Quechua		Locality	Waman = hawk / falcon	Ecology
48	Cerro Loma Redonda	E	Spanish		Mountain	Round knoll, round hill	Natural properties
49	Chiliano Cabrera	E	Spanish		Locality	Name	People
50	La Canteria / Cerro Canteria	E	Spanish		Locality / mountain	Stonework	Trade
51	Zapatero	E	Spanish		Locality	Shoemaker	Trade
52	Cerro Cervantes	E	Spanish		Mountain	Name	People
53	Cerro Buena Vista	E	Spanish		Mountain	Good view	Natural properties
54	Cerro San Cristobal Macho	E	Spanish		Mountain	Religious	Religious

a. All translations were made using a variety of dictionaries, including Cordero Crespo (2010 [1892]), *Webster's Online Dictionary*, and the *Babylon Quechua Dictionary Index*.

b. Prehispanic mine.

that appears to follow a prehispanic architectural convention was also encountered at Mina Azurita, testifying to the maintenance of prehispanic practices and attitudes into the historical period (Van Gijseghem et al. 2011, 2013). Given the absence of agriculture or habitations in this quebrada, we suggest that the "work" in question refers to the only obvious work that would have been possible in the area, which is mining. Excluding Llancay Grande, the other five place names have a decidedly negative or at least ambiguous connotation, especially "devil," "misstep," and "serpent," although even "fortune/fate" is loaded with something ominous.[4] We suggest that all of these meanings, combined with the location of the associated places on the northwest side of the valley where mining now and in prehistory is and was most intense, arise from their spatial association with mines.

Another example includes a small-scale mine near which we have identified prehispanic exploitation called San Miguel Rescate, meaning "Saint Michael" and "rescue," "ransom," or "redemption" in Spanish. This specific aspect of Saint Michael is not a commonly recognized icon in Latin America or elsewhere, as we have found no reference to it. However, in various parts of the Andes, from Bolivia to the North Coast, the figure of Saint Michael leads dancing devils in processions as they are ceremonially cast out of the mines and publicly ridiculed (Harris 2000:63; Millones 1998). Roman Catholic hagiography describes Saint Michael alternatively as the archangel that leads God's armies in the eternal battle against Satan or as the angel of death who wrestles the souls of the deceased from the Devil to carry some of them to heaven (Holweck 1911). It is a decidedly ambiguous figure whose realm is the liminal space between good and evil, light and dark, damnation and salvation. Its associations with devils in Andean festivals, as well as with Bolivian mines and this one in Ica, testify to the equally ambiguous, liminal, and powerful character of mines (see Scott 2012). This is a Spanish, Roman Catholic toponym, but it evokes timeless beliefs about mining and landscape. It appears that Saint Michael was specifically selected from Roman Catholic hagiography because it is one of those infrequent figures that evolve in the ambiguous realm between good and evil.

All of the place names in the "other" category that are associated with mines are Spanish, except the Quechua Llancay discussed above and the syncretized Jatun Diablo (where Jatun = "great, large, notable" in Quechua and Diablo = "devil" in Spanish). This Spanish bias may stem from the fact that mining locations still play a significant role in the local economy of the Ica Valley. As such, mines are perhaps more present in people's routine experiences and are consequently more likely to have been given names in most people's vernacular language.

FIGURE 12.3. *Panoramic ground-level view of the west side of the Ica Valley, with mining locations and prominent landscape features and toponyms*

Perhaps examining these associations from the admittedly Western and modern perspective of the Cartesian mapping of spatial associations also does disservice to the data (see Thomas 2001:173). From a phenomenological perspective, it is from the thin fertile ribbon that is the Ica River that landscape may have to be appreciated (see Johnson and Hunn 2010:2). The valley bottom and narrow cultivation plain are the focus of settlement and daily social experience in all periods of Ica prehistory and history. It is from this perspective that landscape was routinely perceived and experienced. In this light, wherever one stands at the base of the Ica Valley looking toward ancient mining sites, one is most likely to be looking at a landform that bears an ambiguous or negatively charged place name (figure 12.3). Social memory through the bias of place names would associate mining in the mental map with an ambiguous place name: Cerro Serpiente ("serpent mountain"), Jatun Diablo ("great devil"), Cerro Mal Paso ("misstep mountain"). The opposite is not true. A person looking toward a non-mining area is more likely to be looking at something whose name refers to landforms or some ecological character associated with that place: Cerro la Bandera ("flag mountain"), Loma Redonda ("round hill"), Cerro Buena Vista ("good view mountain"), La Canteria ("stonework"). In addition, the phenomenological perspective reveals that on the northwest side of the valley, visible landmarks bear negative or ambiguous names, which is not the case on the southeast side of the valley. We suggest that this is neither a coincidence nor the Andean expression of a type of left/right duality. We are unaware of any examples of good/bad duality expressed on the landscape as different sides of the valley. Instead, we propose that because of the intersection of mineral availability on the northwest side of the valley and mining's symbolic associations, the negatively charged place names reveal ancient perceptions of landscape. These are powerful places, ambiguously perceived and potentially dangerous, the abode of mysterious forces, and the focus of extraction of precious materials but also of circumspect rituals. Although there are mines on the southeast side of the valley, our survey shows that they are few and far between. Mineral availability is much more pronounced on the northwest side, where virtually every quebrada is marked with modern and ancient mine shafts. These perceptions were carried over into the historical period, and the places were in some cases given Spanish names.

The importance of landscape features in Andean ritual, myth, and memory is well-known (Farrington 1992; Nielsen, Angiorama, and Ávila, this volume; van de Guchte 1999). Either through the existence of huacas, the spatio-temporality associated with Cusco's *ceque* systems (Bauer 1998), and arguably other landscape modifications such as the Nasca lines (Lambers 2006) or sacred mountains united by complex narratives and genealogies, the place and landscape play a central part in the formation of group identity. In non-literate societies, landscape acts as a text on which narratives are inscribed. Narratives are not strictly linear tales. They are inscribed in space, and storytelling requires gestures and references to direction, distance, and sightlines (see Tuan 1991). The physicality of narration is part of its performance as it is reproduced, modified, and reinterpreted through generations. Take, for example, this well-known myth recorded by Rossel Castro (1977) in Nasca, in which landscape elements are central:

> Cerro Blanco is the wife of the highland lord, Illa-kata . . . During a visit to Illa-kata, Tunga, who was the lord of the coast, fell in love with Cerro Blanco and convinced her to leave Illa-kata and go to the coast with him. Illa-kata discovered that he had been betrayed and searched for the fleeing couple. When Tunga realized that he and his loved one were not able to flee fast enough, he covered Cerro Blanco with a layer of corn flour, successfully hiding her from Illa-kata. Illa-kata, in a vengeful rage, created cataclysmic events to destroy all mountains, subsequently turning Cerro Blanco and her corn flour covering into a giant sand dune. Tunga was also transformed. In his case, he became a black iron mountain currently located in Marcona. (Nieves 2007:179)

We thus contend that through the narratives toponyms reflect, such dimensions of landscape cognition act as central components of social memory and shape the ways groups of people produce and reproduce shared histories (French 1995:9).

CONCLUSION

We have explored a potential source of information that could contribute to reconstructions of the past because it is composed of elements that are resilient, evocative, comparable, and idiosyncratic. Toponyms constitute a distinctive window into the past. This research should be seen as an experiment in landscape ethnogeography and an interpretive exercise of a data set that has been given relatively little attention by archaeologists, in contrast to other disciplines. While we believe there is some promise in the systematic analysis of toponyms in archaeological interpretation, our research also highlights its difficulties. We argue that in some instances the meanings behind place names might transcend historical processes such as colonialism, religious conversion, and linguistic change. However, the meaning associated with a certain place in the landscape often does not endure, making the link between modern toponyms and prehispanic attitudes toward the landscape tenuous. Like archaeological remains on a regional scale, a map is a palimpsest, the legacy of different periods fixed in time by the priorities of modernity. In this chapter we have attempted to read this palimpsest and extract from it the legacy of prehispanic landscape cognition and attitudes toward the supernatural character of mines. We have also been as diligent as possible in documenting the likelihood that these sorts of pre-colonial beliefs survived in one form or another through time and were transferred onto the palimpsest.

While the results may not be as robust as we would have wished, they do reveal a qualitative association between mineral-rich areas of the Upper Ica Valley and modern place names, which makes these places stand out from the valley-wide inventory of toponyms. We have found that most modern place names in Upper Ica are generic descriptors out of which it is difficult to extract deeper meaning, although surely these meanings may exist. The referents in these cases at least appear to be fairly straightforward: the place's biotic or physical character. If, as Vuolteenaho and Berg (2009:11) observe, "place names frequently become 'shorthands' for broader cultural meanings," then the "non-descriptive" place names of the northwest side of the valley reflect a perception of these landscape portions or general directions that involves concepts that are not strictly geographical in the Western sense. These referents may be narrative and metaphorical rather than ecological in a strict modern sense, and most of Ica's small-scale mines are found in these places or are visually associated with them. We propose that this association is not a coincidence and that it is related to the supernatural dangers involved with mines and mining. The perceptions and discourses associated with these dangers and the special status of mining places are revealed to us by the perseverance of place names.

What emerges from this exploration of toponymy as a palimpsest for ancient attitudes toward landscape is its unique potential as a data set. Because landscape cognition cradles all human experiences, it should not be divorced from the ritual practice it structures. But achieving an understanding of landscape cognition remains a delicate intellectual exercise that requires the intersection of several lines of evidence. In this chapter we have explored the suitability of toponymy as one form of evidence. It reveals a scale of analysis that links the individual, local, immediate scale of ritual practice that is visible archaeologically with the collective, supra-individual, regional, timeless scale of landscape perception. Regional toponymic analysis holds the potential to reveal some dimensions of the text, character, and narratives in which ritual imperatives may be anchored. In this regard, any attempt at reconstructing landscape cognition reveals less about ritual practice's content than about its context. It attempts to uncover its ontological underpinnings rather than the substance of ritual gestures.

On a more speculative note, the pattern we have observed may reveal ancient landscape classificatory schemes that articulate mundane/extraordinary, lived space/dangerous space, civilized/wild ontological oppositions. Where many sedentary cultures perceive the forest/town duality (Johnson 2000), perhaps the ancient dweller of the Ica Valley had similar ontological categories that hinged upon mining/non-mining, safe/dangerous landforms, and the powerful/quotidian and that these categories are still perceptible today through the heritage of place names.

ACKNOWLEDGMENTS

We thank the editors, Stefanie Bautista and Silvana Rosenfeld, for organizing the Society for American Archaeology conference that led to this volume. Canada's Social Sciences and Humanities Research Council grant to Van Gijseghem funded attendance to the conference. This research and the survey that generated it were made possible by a National Geographic Society grant to Kevin J. Vaughn, to whom we are grateful for opening up this opportunity. Gratitude goes to Ruben Garcia Soto and Susana Arce Torres of Ica's Ministry of Culture who, as always, have been highly generous with their support and to Moises Linares Grados, a perpetually valuable colleague. Conversations with Jorge Olano Canales, who participated in the Ica Valley survey, established the foundation for this exploration of toponymy. We thank the scholars who took time to carefully review this work and provide valuable criticisms. We remain responsible for the proverbial shortcomings this work may contain.

NOTES

1. Stewart's (1970) complete classification distinguishes among (1) descriptive: name given as a result of some distinguishing characteristic; (2) association: name related to a descriptive name by association; (3) possessive: based on ownership by a person or group; (4) incident: based on a specific event; (5) commemorative: name honoring a person or an abstract moral value; (6) commendatory: name having a positive association to attract settlers; (7) manufactured: name composed of parts of other names; (8) transfer: name imported from another location; (9) folk-etymology: name modified through language change; and (10) mistake: name resulting from human error.

2. *Apus* are sacred mountains in Andean thought.

3. We are aware of the many caveats in our methodology, not the least of which is that modern maps represent a desperately biased and momentary snapshot of landscape knowledge. We do not know where these compendiums ultimately came from, who the informants responsible for communicating place names to mapmakers were, and whether their own knowledge represented the collectivity's (e.g., we are aware that a hunter, a miner, and a priest may know certain places under different names; feuding families may have derogatory terms for each other's lands, and so on). The identity and agency of the mapmaker's informants is therefore critical because of their role in the "final" crystallization of a potentially fluid and contextual spatial cognition. Another possible source of error lies in the translation of Quechua names. Neither of us is a native Quechua speaker, and the different forms of spelling and pronunciation that exist in Quechua's written forms (e.g., the existence of regional variants and the potential presence of spelling errors within the map itself) contribute to make it impossible to be completely confident in our translations. For the purposes of the present exploration into toponymy, however, we accept that we will deal with these weaknesses, and we have made efforts not to let our hypotheses bias the results of the translations.

4. It is highly tempting to suggest that the (Aymara) Jaqui/Aru toponym Tiojate, also located on the west side of the valley and associated with ancient mining, has its root in the Aymara devil Tiw, discussed above, hispanicized as Tío, the spirit/demon lurking within (Aymara) Bolivian mines. Admittedly, we lack evidence to support the idea that the phonemic similarity is anything other than a coincidence.

REFERENCES CITED

Alcock, S. E. 2002. *Archaeologies of the Greek Past: Landscape, Monuments, and Memories.* Cambridge: Cambridge University Press.

Alderman, D. H., and J. Inwood. 2013. "Street Naming and the Politics of Belonging: Spatial Injustices in the Toponymic Commemoration of Martin Luther King Jr." *Social and Cultural Geography* 14 (2): 211–33. http://dx.doi.org/10.1080/14649365.201 2.754488.

Andrien, K. J. 2001. *Andean Worlds: Indigenous History, Culture, and Consciousness under Spanish Rule, 1532–1825*. Albuquerque: University of New Mexico Press.

Basso, K. H. 1996. *Wisdom Sits in Places: Landscape and Language among the Western Apache*. Albuquerque: University of New Mexico Press.

Bastien, J. W. 1978. *Mountain of the Condor: Metaphor and Ritual in an Andean Ayllu*. Prospect Heights, IL: Waveland.

Bauer, B. S. 1998. *The Sacred Landscape of the Inca: The Cusco Ceque System*. Austin: University of Texas Press.

Bouysse-Cassagne, T. 2005. "Las Minas del centro-sur andino, los cultos prehispanicos y los cultos cristianos." *Bulletin de l'Institut Francais d'Études Andines* 34 (3): 443–62. http://dx.doi.org/10.4000/bifea.4988.

Bradley, R. 1991. "Ritual, Time, and History." *World Archaeology* 23 (2): 209–19. http://dx.doi.org/10.1080/00438243.1991.9980173.

Bradley, R. 2002. *The Past in Prehistoric Societies*. London: Routledge.

Braudel, F. 1969. *Écrits sur l'Histoire*. Paris: Flammarion.

Cobo, B. 1890–95 [1653]. *Historia del Nuevo Mundo*. Seville: E. Rasco.

Cordero Crespo, L. 2010 [1892]. *Diccionario Quichua–Castellano Castellano–Quichua*, sexta edición revisada. Quito: Corporación Editora Nacional.

De La Piedra, M. T. 2009. "Hybrid Literacies: The Case of a Quechua Community in the Andes." *Anthropology and Education Quarterly* 40 (2): 110–28. http://dx.doi.org/10.1111/j.1548-1492.2009.01031.x.

Farrington, I. S. 1992. "Ritual Geography, Settlement Patterns, and the Characterization of the Provinces of the Inka Heartland." *World Archaeology* 23 (3): 368–85. http://dx.doi.org/10.1080/00438243.1992.9980186.

French, S. A. 1995. "What Is Social Memory?" *Southern Cultures* 2 (1): 9–18. http://dx.doi.org/10.1353/scu.1995.0049.

Gil García, F. M., and G. Fernández Juárez. 2008. "El culto a los cerros en el mundo andino: Estudios de caso." *Revista Espanola de Antropologia Americana* 38: 105–13.

Gose, P. 1986. "Sacrifice and the Commodity Form in the Andes." *Man* 21 (2): 296–310. http://dx.doi.org/10.2307/2803161.

Hardman, M. J. 1966. *Jaqaru: Outline of Phonological and Morphological Structure*. The Hague: Mouton.

Harris, O. 2000. *To Make the Earth Bear Fruit: Essays on Fertility, Work, and Gender in Highland Bolivia*. London: Institute of Latin American Studies.

Henshaw, A. 2006. "Pausing along the Journey: Learning Landscapes, Environmental Change, and Toponymy amongst the Sikusilarmiut." *Arctic Anthropology* 43 (1): 52–66. http://dx.doi.org/10.1353/arc.2011.0047.

Hill Boone, E., and T. Cummins, eds. 1998. *Native Traditions in the Postconquest World*. Washington, DC: Dumbarton Oaks Research Library and Collection.

Holweck, F. 1911. "St. Michael the Archangel." In *The Catholic Encyclopedia*. New York: Robert Appleton. Accessed 1 June 2011. http://www.newadvent.org/cathen/10275b.htm.

Horsfall, N. 2002. "The Poetics of Toponymy." *Literary Imagination* 4 (3): 305–17. http://dx.doi.org/10.1093/litimag/4.3.305.

Hunn, E. S., and B. A. Meilleur. 2010. "Toward a Theory of Landscape Ethnoecological Classification." In *Landscape Ethnoecology: Concepts of Biotic and Physical Space*, ed. L. M. Johnson and E. S. Hunn, 15–26. Oxford: Berghahn Books.

Johnson, L. M. 2000. "'A Place That's Good,' Gitksan Landscape Perception and Ethnoecology." *Human Ecology* 28 (2): 301–25. http://dx.doi.org/10.1023/A:1007076221799.

Johnson, L. M., and E. S. Hunn. 2010. "Introduction." In *Landscape Ethnoecology: Concepts of Biotic and Physical Space*, ed. L. M. Johnson and E. S. Hunn, 1–14. Oxford: Berghahn Books.

Johnson, M. 2007. *Ideas of Landscape*. New York: John Wiley and Sons. http://dx.doi.org/10.1002/9780470773680.

Joyce, R. A. 2000. "Heirlooms and Houses: Materiality and Social Memory." In *Beyond Kinship: Social and Material Reproduction in House Societies*, ed. R. A. Joyce and S. D. Gillespie, 189–212. Philadelphia: University of Pennsylvania Press.

Kearney, A., and J. J. Bradley. 2009. "'Too Strong to Ever Not Be There': Place Names and Emotional Geographies." *Social and Cultural Geography* 10 (1): 77–94. http://dx.doi.org/10.1080/14649360802553210.

Lambers, K. 2006. *The Geoglyphs of Palpa, Peru: Documentation, Analysis, and Interpretation*. Aichwald, Germany: Lindensoft Verlag.

Lockhart, J. 1968. *Spanish Peru: 1532–1560*. Madison: University of Wisconsin Press.

Lockhart, J. 1998. "Three Experiences of Culture Contact: Nahua, Maya, and Quechua." In *Native Traditions in the Postconquest World*, ed. E. H. Boone and T. Cummins, 31–54. Washington, DC: Dumbarton Oaks Research Library and Collection.

MacCormack, S. 1984. "From the Sun of the Incas to the Virgin of Copacabana." *Representations* 8 (Fall): 30–60. http://dx.doi.org/10.2307/2928557.

Mannheim, B. 1998. "A Nation Surrounded." In *Native Traditions in the Postconquest World*, ed. E. H. Boone and T. Cummins, 383–420. Washington, DC: Dumbarton Oaks Research Library and Collection.

Millones, L. 1998. *Los Demonios Danzantes de la Virgen de Tucume*. Lima: Fundacion El Monte.

Nash, J. 1972. "Devil in Bolivia's Nationalized Tin Mines." *Science and Society* 36: 221–33.

Nash, J. 1979. *We Eat the Mines and the Mines Eat Us: Dependency and Exploitation in Bolivian Tin Mines.* New York: Columbia University Press.

Nash, J. 2012. "Naming the Aquapelago: Reconsidering Norfolk Island Fishing Ground Names." *Shima: International Journal of Research into Island Cultures* 6 (2): 15–20.

Nieves, A. C. 2007. "Between the River and the Pampa: A Contextual Approach to the Rock Art of the Nasca Valley (Grande River System, Department of Ica, Peru)." PhD dissertation, Department of Art and Art History, University of Texas, Austin.

Pratt, M. L. 1991. "Arts of the Contact Zone." *Profession*: 33–40. www.jstor.org/stable/25595469.

Ramirez, S. E. 1994. "Ethnohistorical Dimensions of Mining and Metallurgy in Sixteenth-Century Northern Peru." In *In Quest of Mineral Wealth: Aboriginal and Colonial Mining and Metallurgy in Spanish America*, ed. A. C. Craig and R. C. West, 93–108. Geoscience and Man 33. Baton Rouge: Louisiana State University Press.

Reinhard, J. 1985. "Sacred Mountains: An Ethno-Archaeological Study of High Andean Ruins." *Mountain Research and Development* 5 (4): 299–317. http://dx.doi.org/10.2307/3673292.

Rossel Castro, A. 1977. *Arqueologia del Sur del Peru.* Lima: Editorial Universo.

Rowe, J. H. 1946. "Inca Culture at the Time of the Spanish Conquest." In *Handbook of South American Indians,* vol. 2: *The Andean Civilizations,* ed. J. H. Steward, 183–330. New York: Cooper Square.

Schmidt, P. R. 2006. *Historical Archaeology in Africa: Representation, Social Memory, and Oral Traditions.* Oxford: Altamira.

Scott, H. V. 2008. "Colonialism, Landscape, and the Subterranean." *Geography Compass* 2 (6): 1853–69. http://dx.doi.org/10.1111/j.1749-8198.2008.00164.x.

Scott, H. V. 2012. "The Contested Spaces of the Subterranean: Colonial Governmentality, Mining, and the Mita in Early Spanish Peru." *Journal of Latin American Geography* 11 (2S special): 7–33. http://dx.doi.org/10.1353/lag.2012.0029.

Shimada, I. 1994. "Pre-Hispanic Metallurgy and Mining in the Andes: Recent Advances and Future Tasks." In *In Quest of Mineral Wealth: Aboriginal and Colonial Mining and Metallurgy in Spanish America*, ed. A. C. Craig and R. C. West, 37–74. Geoscience and Man 33. Baton Rouge: Louisiana State University Press.

Shimada, I. 2013. "Discussion: Mineral Resources and Pre-Hispanic Mining." In *Mining and Quarrying in the Ancient Andes: Sociopolitical, Economic, and Symbolic Dimensions,* ed. N. Tripcevich and K. J. Vaughn, 335–53. New York: Springer. http://dx.doi.org/10.1007/978-1-4614-5200-3_16.

Silverman, H. 2002. "Nasca Settlement and Society on the Hundredth Anniversary of Uhle's Discovery of the Nasca Style." In *Andean Archaeology I: Variations in Sociopolitical Organization*, ed. W. H. Isbell and H. Silverman, 121–58. New York: Kluwer. http://dx.doi.org/10.1007/978-1-4615-0639-3_5.

Solórzano y Pereira, J. d. 1972 [1648]. *Política indiana 1*. Madrid: Atlas.

Stewart, G. R. 1970. *American Place-Names: A Concise and Selective Dictionary for the Continental United States of America*. New York: Oxford University Press.

Taussig, M. T. 1980. *The Devil and Commodity Fetishism in South America*. Chapel Hill: University of North Carolina Press.

Taylor, G. 1980. "Supay." *Amerindia* 5 (3–6): 47–63.

Thomas, J. 2001. "Archaeologies of Place and Landscape." In *Archaeological Theory Today*, ed. I. Hodder, 165–86. Cambridge, MA: Blackwell.

Tringham, R. 2000. "The Continuous House: A View from the Deep Past." In *Beyond Kinship: Social and Material Reproduction in House Societies*, ed. R. A. Joyce and S. D. Gillespie, 115–34. Philadelphia: University of Pennsylvania Press.

Tuan, Y.-F. 1991. "Language and the Making of Place: A Narrative-Descriptive Approach." *Annals of the Association of American Geographers* 81 (4): 684–96. http://dx.doi.org/10.1111/j.1467-8306.1991.tb01715.x.

Tucker, G. R. 2011. "Place-Names, Conquest, and Empire: Spanish and Amerindian Conceptions of Place in the New World." PhD dissertation, Transatlantic History, University of Texas, Arlington.

UNESCO [United Nations Educational, Scientific, and Cultural Organization]. 2001. *The Carnival of Oruro*. Proclamation, List of the Intangible Cultural Heritage of Humanity. Paris: UNESCO.

van de Guchte, M. 1999. "The Inca Cognition of Landscape: Archaeology, Ethnohistory, and the Aesthetic of Alterity." In *Archaeologies of Landscape*, ed. W. Ashmore and A. B. Knapp, 149–68. Malden, MA: Blackwell.

Van Dyke, R. M., and S. E. Alcock, eds. 2003. *Archaeologies of Memory*. Oxford: Routledge. http://dx.doi.org/10.1002/9780470774304.

Van Gijseghem, H., K. J. Vaughn, V. H. Whalen, M. L. Grados, and J. O. Canales. 2011. "Prehispanic Mining in South America: New Data from the Upper Ica Valley, Peru." *Antiquity* 85 (328): http://www.antiquity.ac.uk/projgall/gijseghem328/.

Van Gijseghem, H., K. J. Vaughn, V. H. Whalen, M. L. Grados, and J. O. Canales. 2013. "Economic, Social, and Ritual Aspects of Copper Mining in Ancient Peru: An Upper Ica Valley Case Study." In *Mining and Quarrying in the Ancient Andes: Sociopolitical, Economic, and Symbolic Dimensions*, ed. N. Tripcevich and K. J. Vaughn, 275–98. New York: Springer. http://dx.doi.org/10.1007/978-1-4614-5200-3_13.

Vaughn, K. J., H. Van Gijseghem, M. L. Grados, and J. W. Eerkens. 2013. "Hematita en la Costa Sur del Perú: Investigaciones Arqueológicas en Mina Primavera." *Chungará: Chilean Journal of Anthropology* 45 (1): 131–42.

Vaughn, K. J., H. Van Gijseghem, V. H. Whalen, J. W. Eerkens, and M. L. Grados. 2013. "The Organization of Mining in Nasca during the Early Intermediate Period: Recent Evidence from Mina Primavera." In *Mining and Quarrying in the Ancient Andes: Sociopolitical, Economic, and Symbolic Dimensions*, ed. N. Tripcevich and K. J. Vaughn, 157–82. New York: Springer. http://dx.doi.org/10.1007/978-1-4614-5200-3_8.

Vuolteenaho, J., and L. D. Berg. 2009. "Towards Critical Toponymies." In *Critical Toponymies: The Contested Politics of Place Naming*, ed. J. Vuolteenaho and L. D. Berg, 1–18. Burlington, VT: Ashgate.

13

Rituals of the Past

Final Comments

Jerry D. Moore

A rich ethnohistorical record documents the importance of ritual in traditional Andean societies, documentation largely created during efforts to extirpate idolatry. Among the more sympathetic accounts is the famous work *Nueva Cronica y Buen Gobierno* by Felipe Guaman Poma de Ayala (1993 [1615]), who summarized the calendar of Inka religious practices:

> The first month January [is] Capac Raymi Caymi Quilla. This month they made sacrifices and fasts and penance, and they covered themselves in ashes and put ash on their doorways, just as the Indians do today; and they had processions [to the] places of the temples of the Sun and of the Moon and to the huaca vilca and to other huaca idols in each temple; and they went from hilltop to hilltop, conducting ceremonies and weeping, and they were led by high priests, wizards, and confessional priests, paying homage to the said huacas of Huanacauri and Pacaritambo and the other idols they had. And it was commanded that the same sacrifices were to be done in all this kingdom during the said month of January, according to the law and command of the king, and those who did not [do them] were condemned to death and eaten. And it was commanded that the fasts and penances and weeping in their temples and idols, conducting ceremonies and sacrifices, and not laying with their women throughout this kingdom. (ibid.:177; my translation)

DOI: 10.5876/9781607325963.c013

And so it went throughout the Inkan year. In February the Inka king and all his realm sacrificed great quantities of gold and silver and camelids to the *huacas* for the Sun, the Moon, the stars, and the highest mountain peaks during a season of scarcity and hunger. March was a time of plenty and the month to sacrifice black llamas in ceremonies led by priests and by the *layaconas* "wizards who speak with demons," who avoided salt, sex, and fruit during this month (ibid.:180). Multicolored llamas (*carneros pintados*) were sacrificed in April, a month of fiestas and celebrations marked by songs sung to the llamas and to rivers (ibid.). May was a month of smaller fiestas, as this was the time of harvest; camelids of every color were offered and agrarian oddities—such as a two-eared maize cob or a double-lobed potato—were venerated (ibid.:183).

June was the winter solstice and the fiesta of Inti Raymi, when the Sun received offerings of gold, silver, and *Spondylus* shells (*mullu*), and children were sacrificed at shrines throughout Tawantinsuyu (ibid.). July was devoted to preparing fields for planting, accompanied by sacrifices to the Sun and river systems so they would not damage future crops, offerings that included 100 blood-red llamas and 1,000 white guinea pigs who were burned in the public plaza in Cusco (ibid.:186). Farm fields were tilled and planted in August, and throughout the kingdom local huacas were offered guinea pigs, mullu, maize gruel, *chicha*, and children (ibid.). September was devoted to the fiesta of the Moon, the Wife of the Sun and the Queen of all the planets and stars; this was also when the Inka king deployed his armies to drive out pestilence from the land, which they did by shouting for the disease to leave and hurling burning embers from their slings (ibid.:186–88). October was devoted to rites focused on rainfall in ceremonies involving weeping: the elderly and infirm cried for rain, dogs were beaten until they howled, and a herd of black llamas was tethered in the plaza and intentionally starved until the animals bleated in hunger, adding their cries to the pleadings for rain (ibid.:189). Feasts for dead ancestors were held in November; mummies of ancestors were visited in their tombs, given food and chicha, sung to, and danced with. This was also the month when the Inka king visited the provinces—reviewing troops, giving out women to be married, and reviewing the stockpiles in state storehouses. In December was the Capac Inti Raymi, "the great and solemn festival of the Sun ... Lord of the Heavens and all the Planets," who was honored with sacrifices of great quantities of gold, silver, fine vessels, mullu, camelids, and 500 boys and girls (ibid.:192).

In light of this abundant evidence for the importance of ritual practice in Andean societies, it is surprising that archaeologists working in the Andes have been rather late in making ritual a central focus of archaeological inquiry. As Rosenfeld and Bautista note in their introduction to this volume, "Though ritual has long been important to [sociocultural] anthropologists . . . archaeologists have only more recently recognized the importance of studying ritual and its role in past societies." Tamara Bray (2015:3) has made a similar point, writing:

> In contrast to the plethora of archaeological studies focused on presumably secular aspects of society like subsistence practices, the economy, and political organization, investigations into the realm of the sacred have been much less common. This is not to suggest that all peoples past and present compartmentalize the sacred and secular in the way we tend to do in the west. Rather, it is acknowledgement of the fact that archaeologists have tended to steer clear of anything beyond the quotidian concerns of human societies. Yet today, a decade and a half into the twenty-first century, it remains abundantly clear that much of the world's population lead [sic] lives in which basic questions about diet, housing, education, social interaction, and so on are structured by the dictates of religion and spiritual devotion.

Further, archaeology provides the possibility—incompletely realized at this juncture—of understanding how such dictates and actions emerged and changed over time. And these are the issues explored throughout the chapters of this book.

As is made abundantly clear by the studies in this volume, ritual in the prehispanic Andes occurred at multiple scales of social life and was directed to varied purposes and intents. (It is worth realizing that Guaman Poma's ritual calendar only listed the major, formal, and public rites.) Throughout the Andes, ritual engaged with sacred things and places called *wak'as*, including origin places affiliated with ethnic and kin groups known as *pacarisca wak'as*. In his circa 1568 *Instrución para descubrir todas las guacas del Pirû y sus camayos y haziendas* (in Duviols 1967:20), the ecclesiastic Cristobal de Albornoz wrote that "the principal class of wak'as they had before [been] subjugated by the Inkas are called *pacariscas*, which is to say 'Creator of their Natures.' Depending on the province, these have different forms and names: some are stones, others springs and rivers, others caves, others animals and birds and trees and plants, and despite these differences they insist that they are the offspring and descendents from such things." Instructing his fellow extirpators, Albornoz orders: "You must understand that not a single kin group (*parcialidad*)—whether small or large—of these natives lacks a *wak'a pacarisca*" (ibid.). Albornoz proceeds with a list of known wak'a pacarisca from north of Quito to south of Cusco; 169 mountains, springs, lakes, stones, islands, and other features on the landscape are listed. Even this was not an exhaustive list; Albornoz cautions, "One must understand that these said huacas are the major ones in this kingdom, which the Inkas rebuilt, adored, and provided [with] riches and service. And that in each province there are many more" (ibid.:35).

In 1621 the Jesuit Pablo Jose de Arriaga (1968) published a chapter in *The Extirpation of Idolatry in Peru* titled "What the Indians Worship Today and of What Their Idolatry Consists." From the Spanish cleric's point of view, it was a daunting list. "In many places, especially in the sierra," he begins, "they worship the sun"; then he notes other astral and atmospheric phenomena: the moon, the Pleiades, and lightning (ibid.:22–23). The sea, *mamacocha*, and the earth, *mamapacha*, were worshipped, as were streams and springs "especially when water is scarce, begging them not to dry up" (ibid.:23). When crossing a river, the Indians would cup riverwater in their hands and "talk to the river, asking it to let them cross over without being swept away" (ibid.). The hills and mountains—and even large stones—were named and revered and were the subjects of "numerous fables about their changes and metamorphoses" (ibid.:24). The ruins of ancient people were revered as the houses of ancient giants, the *huaris*. The places of ancestral origins, the *pacarinas*—which could be caves, hills, streams, or rivers—were worshipped. Arriaga describes the movable objects of veneration: the huacas affiliated with *ayllus*, the mummies of their ancestors, the incredible variety of icons and amulets known as *conopas*, the respect for unique ears of corn or double potatoes. Arriaga then details the various offerings made to these subjects of worship and veneration: chicha, llamas, guinea pigs, silver, coca, llama fat, espingo seeds, colorful feathers, *Spondylus* shells, powders of colorful minerals, wads of cornmeal, and eyelashes, "which they pull out and blow toward the huacas as an offering" (ibid.:46). Later in his treatise, Arriaga (ibid.:115) admits that "some of these huacas are hills and high places that time cannot consume," and his frustration is still palpable centuries later. Arriaga's frustration reflected the deep resiliency of Andean ritual, the broad corners of life in which ritual occurred, the embeddedness of religious belief, and the constant enactment of ritual through practice.

This broad engagement of ritual with the Andean world is clearly evident in the study by Axel E. Nielsen, Carlos I. Angiorama, and Florencia Ávila (this volume), who define ritual as "social action that addresses non-human agents that have a significant influence on human fate." Influenced in part by the "ontological turn" in anthropological theory and related fields (e.g., Descola 2013; Gell 1998; Latour 2005), Nielsen and colleagues explore the rituals Andean peoples deployed to engage with entities they consider sentient beings capable of power, awareness, intentionality, choice, and some form of responsibility. In their fascinating and careful study, Nielsen and colleagues discuss archaeological evidence from the Southern Andes for a specific but incompletely understood ritual gesture in which pits were excavated at key locations: mountain passes but also at camps along llama caravan routes, water springs, and mid-altitude (3,300–4,500 m) mountains peak that were not on caravan routes but near populated areas. Intriguingly, these pits also contained offerings of green and white minerals, stones, and beads, with the green offerings particularly distinctive and widespread. Based on diagnostic ceramics and absolute dates, this ritual practice may be earlier than another well-recorded ritual gesture: piles of stone offerings placed at mountain passes known as *apachetas*. The authors suggest that the pit and greenstone offerings date from the Late Intermediate Period (ca. AD 1000–1450) and continued to be created in the Late Horizon/Inka period (AD 1450–1550) as well as into the colonial period, while the discovery of apachetas covering Late Intermediate Period pit offerings at Abra de la Cruz, Argentina, may indicate that creating apachetas was a relatively late ritual gesture and in some regions may have only occurred in Colonial and modern times.

In addition to ritual objects and offerings, Andean peoples engaged the cosmos with words, whether creating sophisticated astronomies or imbuing landscape with myths and legends (e.g., Urton 1988, 2011). This semiotic class of ritual engagement is explored by Hendrik Van Gijseghem and Verity H. Whalen (this volume), who argue that "because landscape cognition cradles all human experiences, it should not be divorced from the ritual practice it structures. But achieving an understanding of landscape cognition remains a delicate intellectual exercise that requires the intersection of several lines of evidence." Their own version of this "delicate exercise" examines the distribution of toponyms in the Ica Valley on the South Coast of Peru, a research project influenced by previous work documenting ritual and other aspects of copper mining in the Upper Ica Valley (Van Gijseghem et al. 2013). Van Gijseghem and Whalen suggest a possible—if not absolutely conclusive—relationship between mining zones and negative or ambiguous place names in the Upper Ica Valley, toponyms of "powerful places, ambiguously perceived and potentially dangerous, the abode of mysterious forces, and the focus of extraction of precious materials but also of circumspect rituals."

The chapters by Nielsen and colleagues and Van Gijseghem and Whalen are the only case studies in this volume to examine archaeological evidence for ritual outside of the prehispanic built environment. Having written extensively about built environments and ritual in the prehispanic Andes (e.g., Moore 1996a, 1996b, 1999, 2004, 2005, 2006, 2010a, 2010b), I do not doubt the value of archaeological studies of rituals within or relating to architecture. And yet, our emphasis on ritual within and directed toward architecture is a scholarly bias worth mentioning, especially given the wide range of "natural" places and features that were the objects of and places for Andean ritual practices, as listed by Guaman Poma, Albornoz, Arriaga, and others. I return to this issue at the close of this chapter.

The Andean engagement with the built environment—whether in its creation, use, maintenance and renewal, or destruction—was deeply embedded in ritual practice. Sacred architecture anchored and enhanced ritual practice (Humphrey and Vitebsky 1997). John W. Rick's long-term study of the Chavín de Huántar, Ancash, Peru, has supported earlier interpretations of the site as a temple complex while deepening our understanding of ritual activities at the site (Rick, this volume). Rick argues that "Chavín's [architectural] configuration is a strategic attempt to create a physical context that would generate desired psychological states in inductees and participants in the evident cult of Chavín." The monumental constructions at Chavín de Huántar were undoubtedly places where rituals occurred, practices that involved offerings of fine artifacts and camelids and the intentional manipulation of water. Processions took place in outdoor rectangular and sunken circular plazas. Within the temple mound the dark, mysterious interior *galerías* were threaded by extensive canals of flowing water, which not only created an audial effect but the canals were also given offerings of "highly decorated pottery, large fragments of camelid bone representing relatively few animals, drug-related paraphernalia, or other categories of ritual material." Some canals moved water in distinctive ways, including creating junctions of broader, low-energy flows with narrower, high-energy flows—perhaps constructed metaphor for the nearby confluence of the Mosna and Wacheqsa Rivers, a hydraulic convergence locally referred to as *tinku* or *tinkuy*. These terms, Rick writes, have "complex meaning in the Andes." Citing the work of Catherine Allen and H. D. Webb, Rick observes that tinku and tinkuy reference not only "encounters, often violent, between watercourses or between people" but also "issues of complementary and opposing, even opposite forces or dualistic entities, their intermingling and sometimes turbulent coexistence. Structurally, the Chavín canal conjunctions could conceivably represent, on a small, controlled scale, the large *tinku* at which Chavín was built, in the similarly positioned pattern of unequal size and water energy." Thus, the canals of Chavín might be seen as constructed, flowing metaphors of confluence and conflict at multiple levels of ritual practice.

In addition to the temple mound, other constructed spaces were settings for the focus of ritual practice at Chavín de Huántar, such as the Mito-style chamber discovered 300 m west discussed by Daniel A. Contreras (this volume). Previously, the Mito Tradition was known from the Central Andean highlands and was thought by the archaeologist Elisabeth Bonnier to date to ca. 2500–2000/1800 BCE, although Richard Burger and Lucy Salazar-Burger argued that this architectural form continued to be influential in the Early Horizon (Bonnier 1997; Bonnier and Rozenberg 1988; Burger and Salazar-Burger 1980, 1985). It is now known that Mito-style chambers were still in use in 1000–500 BCE and were more widely distributed, including in coastal sites in the Santa, Casma, and Supe Valleys (e.g., Montoya Vera 2007). Based on Contreras's excavations and absolute dates, the Mito-style structure was coeval with the monumental core (900–500 BCE) at Chavín de Huántar. This discovery leads Contreras to suggest a pattern of "ritual eclecticism and diversity" and to raise the possibility that there were multiple loci of ritual practice at Chavín. He writes, "The persistence of the Mito Tradition alongside these later developments [was] not, apparently, as a marginalized survivor among a population resisting the changes but rather was incorporated into institutionalized ceremonial practices." As Contreras notes, only a small portion of the residential area at Chavín has been excavated, and the actual evidence for ritual within the Mito-style chamber is limited to deposits of obsidian flakes and fragments of an anthracite mirror. Contreras's research broadens and deepens understanding of the diversity of ritual practice during the Formative period in the Andes. However, Contreras slightly misrepresents a hypothesis I suggested in 1996: I did *not* suggest that small ritual spaces were *replaced* by the creation of monumental ceremonial architecture at circa 1800–1400 BCE but rather argued that smaller ritual chambers were incorporated into ceremonial centers. I wrote: "After 1800–1400 BC, this changes. Although intimate ritual spaces were maintained, they become auxiliary to larger monumental constructions" (Moore 1996b:226). Rather than refute this then "untested hypothesis" (ibid.), Contreras's important discovery of a Mito-style chamber coeval with the temple complex at Chavín actually lends it support.

David Chicoine, Hugo Ikehara, Koichiro Shibata, and Matthew Helmer (this volume) apply methods of visual analysis to explore how elites in the Nepeña Valley may have manipulated ritual architecture during the Formative period. Their sophisticated study spans a fascinating and pivotal period in Central Andean prehistory from ca. 1500–1100 cal BC to 450–150 cal BC. The earlier centuries were characterized by centers such as Cerro Blanco (1100–800 cal BC). Chicoine and colleagues write that these centers incorporated "a style of monumental architecture and public visual art that shows symbolic and stylistic similarities with Chavín and Cupisnique-related religious ideologies."

They add, "The Late and Final Formative periods were times of great ritual diversity. Chavín was only part of a very complex series of related developments that included regional and interregional changes that intertwined different styles of architectural design, religious ideology, and public art." At circa 800–450 cal BC, monuments and friezes at Cerro Blanco and Huaca Partida were extensively remodeled, while monumental buildings at both sites were abandoned circa 450–150 cal BC. Chicoine and colleagues use methods of visual analysis to explore these complex and varied changes, arguing that "leaders, architects, and builders in Nepeña were using ceremonial monuments as tools for multiple purposes, including social control, political integration, and inter-communal competition."

Along analytically similar lines, Rafael Vega-Centeno Sara-Lafosse (this volume) applies access analysis to understand the potential movements of people through the multi-room construction known as Huaca A at Pampa de las Llamas-Moxeke, drawing on excavations and analyses by Thomas and Shelia Pozorski. Vega-Centeno Sara-Lafosse's analysis is somewhat puzzling; although he questions the Pozorskis' interpretation of Huaca A as an "administrative structure," he provides no evidence for its use as a place or object of ritual practice; nor is it clear how his analysis of access patterns substantively clarifies the functions of Huaca A at Pampa de las Llamas-Moxeke.

Sarah Abraham (this volume) provides an elegant analysis of changing religious architecture at Pukara during the colonial era at the sites of La Quinta and Santa Isabel. La Quinta is the earlier construction, an open chapel that literally incorporated indigenous architectural features (walls and sunken courts), a trapezoidal plan, and a nave that may have been unroofed, an accommodation to native practices of open-air worship—literally, religious architecture that embodied hybridity. By the late sixteenth century, such efforts to incorporate indigenous religious customs had ended: the broad realization that decades of proselytizing efforts had produced a veneer of Christianity over fundamentally unchanged native practice led to the extirpation campaigns mentioned at the beginning of this chapter. Paralleling the Toledan reforms and the campaigns against Taki Onkoy (a native revitalization movement that rejected Spanish customs and reinstated native culture and rituals), the architectural hybridity of La Quinta was replaced by the church of Santa Isabel, erected on the main plaza in Colonial Pukara and "built in the classical European cruciform floor plan, [which] featured traditional European architectural canons and showed no Andean influence." While Abraham has the scholarly advantage of having a rich historical record regarding changes in religious practice in Colonial Peru, her archaeological study exemplifies what we can learn from nuanced studies of architecture associated with religious practice.

Ritual architecture is not only the *space* in which rites occurred, but it may also be the *object* and *subject* of ritual practice. Interestingly, several of the chapters in this volume discuss archaeological evidence for ritual burial or termination of buildings. As mentioned by Yoshio Onuki (this volume), this practice was observed at the site of Kotosh in the Upper Huallaga Valley, Peru, in which successive stages of dismantling, filling, and rebuilding temples led Izumi and Matsuzawa (1967) to dub this process "temple entombment." This practice has an intriguingly widespread and enduring legacy, apparently from the Archaic period to the Late Horizon, involving rites "relating to the creation, renewal, and termination of ancient built environments" (Gamboa Velásquez 2015:100). Reviewing the evidence for such rites at Moche sites, Gamboa Valásquez argues that "the available evidence points toward the association of events of dedication, renewal, and termination with political changes and responses to natural phenomena" (ibid.).

In this volume, Onuki reiterates "a hypothesis that involves the ideology of temple renovation as a prime mover of the social development of the Formative period." To summarize his earlier argument, Onuki (1993:92–93) proposed that episodic renovation of ceremonial centers would have stimulated new sociopolitical arrangements, as larger constructions demanded larger labor pools supported by increasing quantities of food and drink, more elaborate craft and artistic production, and greater interregional exchange. In this volume, Onuki expands on his hypothesis:

> The requirement of renovation after a certain time lapse generated accelerating change in various aspects of culture, such as technology, social organization, and religion or cosmology. The competition among the settlements or villages, or certain social groups responsible for taking charge of the ritual, may have played a role in accelerating the process of enlargement and sophistication, and eventually a kind of massive public building worth calling a temple was constructed. The renovation of the temple together with competition for prestige ignited a process of ever-increasing activities, such as population growth, technological improvement of food production, planning of architecture and labor investment, and sophistication of religious concepts and ritual itself together with ritual paraphernalia. In this process ideology was formed on the basis of cosmology, and elites began to manipulate it to lead society.

This is a plausible hypothesis, but I want to pose two related cautions regarding ritual entombment and its sociopolitical impacts. First, we have ethnographic counter-examples in which recurrent ritual entombments and mound reconstructions do *not* result in the juggernaut of sociocultural intensification Onuki envisions. For example, Tom Dillehay and colleagues have written extensively about Araucanian mound-building practices as practiced by the Mapuche of Chile, ritual practices beginning between AD 1200 and 1500 and continuing into the twentieth century (Dillehay 1986, 1990, 1995, 2007, 2014). The Mapuche hold a "mound-capping" ceremony (*cueltun*) in which a local leader's grave is annually covered with earth, an act of commemoration by kinfolk and allies in which the connections between the living and the dead are maintained and instantiated with layers of earth. Through time, the mound, or *kuel*, is transformed into a part of the cultural landscape, increasing in height and size as the nearest kinfolk and supporters diminish in number. In some instances, two or more kuel will be constructed on leveled ridges or hilltops, mound complexes known as *rehuekuel* that become the settings for Mapuche ceremonies—preeminently the *nguillatun* ceremony, which ensures agricultural fertility, is attended by hundreds of Mapuche, and unifies distinct patrilineages from different communities. Dillehay (2007:42) writes, "The Araucanian's religious ideology is associated with a cognitive map or imagery of sacred routes and places . . . that connects historically meaningful landscapes and spiritual locations of the real physical world and the spiritual or esoteric worlds, that is, other regions of levels of the cosmos . . . Taken together, *kuel* and *rehuekuel* form a social and aesthetic physical arrangement of spaces, pathways, meanings, and objects that keep alive the memories of the individuals and lineages that make Araucanian history." And yet, these extensive coordinated constructions did not create inter-community competition, changes in food production, or the other innovations Onuki's hypothesis suggests. Second, it is possible that archaeologists are conflating under the term *ritual entombment* superficially similar activities motivated by distinct cultural conceptions and ritual intentions. I suggest that we should consider some empirical distinctions as we look at the archaeological evidence.

For example, Camila Capriata Estrada and Enrique López-Hurtado (this volume) discuss evidence for ritual at the Late Intermediate Period/Late Horizon site Panquilma, in the Lurín Valley, Peru. The archaeological evidence points to two classes of rite. First, a series of superimposed, well-made, and clean floors in plazas associated with Pyramids 1 and 3 also contained pits interpreted as offerings; the pits in the center of the plazas contained valuable items such as *Spondylus* shells and ceramic figurines, whereas pits on the periphery simply contained potsherds. In addition, the elite residential areas associated with the pyramids were subject to intentional burning restricted to the upper platforms of the pyramids; the structures' roofs were torched, the reed and wood roofing fell and intensely burned the floor, but the fire did not spread to adjacent areas. This seems to have occurred in an unsettled political landscape as the Inkas expanded into the Lurín Valley, incorporated Pachacamac, and conquered other regional centers. Essentially seeing the end of their political autonomy looming, the elites of Panquilma terminated their ancestral seat. Capriata Estrada and López-Hurtado argue that in common with other Andean cases such as Pampa Grande, Túcume, and Cerro Baúl, Panquilma experienced acts that "were probably performed by the local elites who were the original administrators of rituals within these precincts. It seems clear that in addition to the ritual implications of these actions, the common goal was to destroy things either to prevent their future illegitimate use by others or to 'kill' them in a metaphoric way, thus undermining and denying legitimacy to imposed authority."

At Cerro de Oro in the Cañete Valley, Francesca Fernandini and Mario Ruales (this volume) present evidence for termination rituals, burials, and other ritual acts, a "broad spectrum of ritual that spans from small-scale domestic practices to large-scale ceremonies." Their fundamental argument is sound: "we intend to move beyond the dualistic distinctions that segregate ritual and domestic as two apparently incommensurable realms of social life . . . by exploring ritual as a relational practice. We propose that ritual practices are better understood from a multi-scalar approach that emphasizes the way meanings, social rules, and relations are embedded within the recurrent practices that produce and reproduce their material habitus . . . In this way the nature of ritual can be seen as a process in which repetitive actions socialize people into particular dispositions; in turn, these dispositions establish a recursive relationship with rituals in which social meaning is produced and reformulated through repetition."

And yet, not everything in an archaeological site is the product of ritual. Fernandini and Ruales describe pits with offerings that include "specially selected material such as partial/complete animals, decorated sherds, musical instruments, and frieze fragments, among other things" in areas that also have evidence for food preparation. They suggest that such structured depositions were "intrinsically associated with the presence of cooking and storage areas, establishing a particular link among unconsumed, consumed, and disposed food." The authors also discuss evidence for termination rituals incorporating burning events. A specific example comes from Fernandini's excavations in the SE Area, where a 35–40 cm thick stratum of ash and organic material covered a floor associated with the Cerro de Oro/Middle Horizon occupation (for a detailed discussion, see Fernandini 2015:135–39). Fernandini reports that the floor surface showed evidence of burning and that the ash contained a high density of both ceramics—sherds from serving vessels and cooking pots—and organic materials, which include maize cobs, gourd fragments, reed cordage, cotton fibers, and a textile described as "a large plain cloth made of thick beige cotton S-twist threads, in warp face 1 × 1, with evidence of recurrent repairs" (ibid.:137). The apparently good condition of the organic materials leads one to wonder whether the ash deposit was associated with an in situ burning event or rather was re-deposited midden used as architectural fill before Cerro de Oro was rebuilt.

A different class of ritual practice is described by Matthew J. Edwards (this volume) in his discussion of termination rituals at the Wari installation of Pataraya, in the Nasca Valley circa AD 950, a relatively small enclosure built according to canons of Wari architecture. Activities within Pataraya were spatially segregated, and movement through the compound was channeled via narrow corridors. Edwards proposes a detailed sequence of abandonment rituals. The first offering consists of a cache of nine Wari vessels placed upside down on the floor of a small room—which (in terms of access patterns) was also the most remote space in Pataraya; this was then covered with a deposit of clean river sand and *Spondylus* shells. Next was a sequence of burned offerings—indicated by small ash features—and single Wari vessels (cups and a jar) smashed next to the burned features; all of these were also covered with clean river sand. At this point a large boulder was rolled into place, blocking access to this residential sector of Pataraya. Another deposit of burned offerings and smashed vessels was followed by another boulder rolled into place, which blocked access to the enclosure. Ritually sealed, the Wari inhabitants broke numerous vessels in front of the now-closed enclosure at Pataraya. The obstructing boulders and layer of river sand may parallel termination rites known from other Wari sites. Although the Wari inhabitants abandoned Pataraya as the Wari Empire waned, that community was not under eminent threat. Rather, the Wari inhabitants engaged in a deliberate sequence of ritual gestures before Pataraya "was carefully abandoned and then quietly forgotten." The access patterns at Pataraya and the blockage of nodal passages allow for a clear sequence of termination rituals.

As Silvana A. Rosenfeld and Stefanie L. Bautista discuss in the introduction to this volume, identifying ritual practice in the archaeological record poses real challenges (vis. Fogelin 2007; Swenson 2015), but these challenges do not only afflict Andeanists. For example, the identification of specific sets of features and artifacts at British archaeological sites as "structured deposits"—some interpreted as the product of ritual actions—has been discussed by Duncan Garrow (2012). Garrow provides a very useful overview of the development of this idea, pointing to an early (1984) use by Colin Richards and Julian Thomas, followed by the broad use of the concept—especially but not exclusively—by post-processual archaeologists. For example, Richard Bradley (2000:122) wrote of

> the sheer complexity of the phenomenon that has become known as structured deposition. The placing of objects in the ground involved a whole series of references—to the origins of objects, to their history and to the significance of particular places in the landscape—and it involved a series of conventions about which kinds of material might be associated together and which needed to be kept apart. It also merged artefacts with human and animal remains in a way that cut across [the] stereotyped division between culture and nature. Thus, human remains could be passed about the landscape in the same way as portable objects. Each of these deposits might have encapsulated basic ideas about the world.

And yet, as Garrow (2012:114–15) suggests, perhaps we should question alternative hypotheses rather than assume that *all* such deposits were, in fact, the structured results of ritual practice—which is not to say that *none* were (see also, Jones 2015). As Garrow (2012:109–10; italics in the original) states, "I do not want to argue here against the suggestion that *material culture patterning* was not in the past, and cannot be today, *explicitly* meaningful. It can. However, I do think that in attributing enhanced meaningfulness to all patterning, we have foreclosed other interpretive possibilities."

Rather than assume that specific archaeological features are the products of ritual (e.g., see Moore 2010b:410 for my interpretation of cairns), perhaps we Andeanists should formulate explicit ways to apply the characteristics of ritual as discussed by Bell (1997:138–69): formality, traditionalism, disciplined invariance, rule-governance, sacral symbolism, and performance. While not all rituals will intersect with all of these domains, we might expect several to be present. Recalling Edwards's study of ritual closing at Pataraya, we seem to see evidence of *formality* (e.g., the sequence of burned offerings, the partial blocking of passageways with boulders), *traditionalism* (analogous deposits known from other Wari sites), *disciplined invariance* (the regular deposits of burned vessels and a single Wari vessel), and obviously *performance*—while the evidence for sacral symbolism is less clear. Similarly, such measures could be applied to other archaeological features interpreted as structured ritual deposits in the various studies in this book.

Finally, it is clear that we Andeanists need to consider ritual settings that occurred *outside* constructed spaces. The range of ritual practices conducted in constructed spaces is extraordinarily important, as the chapters in this volume demonstrate. To repeat, I am not suggesting that ceremonial architecture is unimportant or that rites associated with constructing or using buildings are irrelevant (for a fascinating study of modern construction rituals in Europe, see van den Ende and van Marrewijk 2014). Yet given the broad engagement of Andean rituals, it seems obvious that we need to broaden our inquiries. As we look for models about how such research might proceed, it may be profitable to examine studies by colleagues working on ritual and landscape in the Mayan region, such as Lucero's work on water and cenotes (Lucero and Kinkella 2015), Brown's studies of hunting shrines (Brown 2005; Brown and Emery 2008), and studies of caves by Moyes (2014) and others.

The case studies in this collection demonstrate the breadth and detail of Andean peoples' engagement with their cosmos through ritual practice. The challenge we archaeologists now face is to develop research agendas and analytical methods of similar scope and nuance. A great deal of exciting and demanding research awaits us as we Andeanists broaden and deepen our analytical gaze.

REFERENCES CITED

Arriaga, P.J.d. 1968. *The Extirpation of Idolatry in Peru.* Trans. L. C. Keating. Lexington: University of Kentucky Press.

Bell, C. M. 1997. *Ritual: Perspectives and Dimensions.* Oxford: Oxford University Press.

Bonnier, E. 1997. "Preceramic Architecture in the Andes: The Mito Tradition." *Archaeologica Peruana* 2: 120–44.

Bonnier, E., and C. Rozenberg. 1988. "Del Santuario al Caserío: Acerca de la Neolitización en la Cordillera de los Andes Centrales." *Bulletin de l'Institut Français d'Études Andines* 17: 1–12.

Bradley, R. 2000. *An Archaeology of Natural Places.* New York: Routledge.

Bray, T. L. 2015. "Andean Wak'as and Alternative Configurations of Persons, Power, and Things." In *The Archaeology of Wak'as: Explorations of the Sacred in the Pre-Columbian Andes*, ed. T. L. Bray, 3–19. Boulder: University Press of Colorado. http://dx.doi.org/10.5876/9781607323181.c001.

Brown, L. A. 2005. "Planting the Bones: Hunting Ceremonialism at Contemporary and Nineteenth-Century Shrines in the Guatemalan Highlands." *Latin American Antiquity* 16 (2): 131–46. http://dx.doi.org/10.2307/30042808.

Brown, L. A., and K. F. Emery. 2008. "Negotiations with the Animate Forest: Hunting Shrines in the Guatemalan Highlands." *Journal of Archaeological Method and Theory* 15 (4): 300–337. http://dx.doi.org/10.1007/s10816-008-9055-7.

Burger, R. L., and L. Salazar-Burger. 1980. "Ritual and Religion at Huaricoto." *Archaeology* 33 (6): 26–32.

Burger, R. L., and L. Salazar-Burger. 1985. "The Early Ceremonial Center of Huaricoto." In *Early Ceremonial Architecture in the Andes: A Conference at Dumbarton Oaks, 8th to 10th October 1982*, ed. C. Donnan, 111–35. Washington, DC: Dumbarton Oaks.

Descola, P. 2013. *Beyond Nature and Culture*. Chicago: University of Chicago Press.

Dillehay, T. D. 1986. "Cuel: Observaciones y comentarios sobre los túmulos en la cultura Mapuche." *Chungara (Arica)* 16–17: 181–93.

Dillehay, T. D. 1990. "Mapuche Ceremonial Landscape: Social Recruitment and Resource Rights." *World Archaeology* 22 (2): 223–41. http://dx.doi.org/10.1080/00438243.1990.9980142.

Dillehay, T. D. 1995. "Mounds of Social Death: Araucanian Funerary Rites and Political Succession." In *Tombs for the Living: Andean Mortuary Practices*, ed. T. D. Dillehay, 281–313. Washington, DC: Dumbarton Oaks.

Dillehay, T. D. 2007. *Monuments, Empires, and Resistance: The Araucanian Polity and Ritual Narratives*. Cambridge: Cambridge University Press. http://dx.doi.org/10.1017/CBO9780511499715.

Dillehay, T. D. 2014. *The Teleoscopic Polity: Andean Patriarchy and Materiality*. New York: Springer Science and Business Media. http://dx.doi.org/10.1007/978-3-319-03128-6.

Duviols, P. 1967. "Un inédit de Cristobal de Albornoz: La instrucción para descubrir todas las guacas del Pirú y sus camayos y haziendas." *Journal de la Société des Americanistes* 56 (1): 7–39. http://dx.doi.org/10.3406/jsa.1967.2269.

Fernandini, F. 2015. "Beyond the Empire: Living in Cerro de Oro." PhD dissertation, Department of Anthropology, Stanford University, Stanford, CA.

Fogelin, L. 2007. "The Archaeology of Religious Ritual." *Annual Review of Anthropology* 36 (1): 55–71. http://dx.doi.org/10.1146/annurev.anthro.36.081406.094425.

Gamboa Velásquez, J. 2015. "Dedication and Termination Rituals in Southern Moche Public Architecture." *Latin American Antiquity* 26 (1): 87–105. http://dx.doi.org/10.7183/1045-6635.26.1.87.

Garrow, D. 2012. "Odd Deposits and Average Practice: A Critical History of the Concept of Structured Deposition." *Archaeological Dialogues* 19 (2): 85–115. http://dx.doi.org/10.1017/S1380203812000141.

Gell, A. 1998. *Art and Agency*. Oxford: Clarendon.

Guaman Poma de Ayala, F. 1993 [1615]. *Nueva Cronica y Buen Gobierno*. Trans. J. Szeminski. Mexico City: Fondo de Cultura Economica.

Humphrey, C., and P. Vitebsky. 1997. *Sacred Architecture, Models of the Cosmos, Symbolic Form, and Ornament: Traditions of East and West*. Boston: Duncan Baird.

Izumi, S., and T. Matsuzawa. 1967. "Early Preceramic Cultist Culture of the Central Andes: The Kotosh Mito Phase." *Latin American Studies* 8: 39–69.

Jones, A. M. 2015. "Ritual, Rubbish, or Everyday Life? Evidence from a Middle Bronze Age Settlement in Mid-Cornwall." *Archaeological Journal* 172 (1): 30–51. http://dx.doi.org/10.1080/00665983.2014.985016.

Latour, B. 2005. *Reassembling the Social: An Introduction to Actor-Network Theory*. Oxford: Oxford University Press.

Lucero, L. J., and A. Kinkella. 2015. "Pilgrimage to the Edge of the Watery Underworld: An Ancient Maya Water Temple at Cara Blanca, Belize." *Cambridge Archaeological Journal* 25 (1): 163–85. http://dx.doi.org/10.1017/S0959774314000730.

Montoya Vera, M. 2007. "Arquitectura de la 'Tradición Mito' en el valle medio del Santa: sitio 'El Silencio.'" *Bulletin de l'Institut Français d'Études Andines* 36 (2): 199–220. http://dx.doi.org/10.4000/bifea.3795.

Moore, J. D. 1996a. "The Archaeology of Plazas and the Proxemics of Ritual: Three Andean Traditions." *American Anthropologist* 98 (4): 789–802. http://dx.doi.org/10.1525/aa.1996.98.4.02a00090.

Moore, J. D. 1996b. *Architecture and Power in the Ancient Andes: The Archaeology of Public Buildings*. New Studies in Archaeology. Cambridge: Cambridge University Press. http://dx.doi.org/10.1017/CBO9780511521201.

Moore, J. D. 1999. "Le Place Dans les Andes Anciennes: Le Contrôle des Espaces Ouverts dans les Villes Précolombiennes." In *La Ville et le Pouvoir en Amérique: Les formes de l'autorité*, ed. J. Monnet, 35–50. Paris: Edition L'Harmattan.

Moore, J. D. 2004. "The Social Basis of Sacred Spaces in the Prehispanic Andes: Ritual Landscapes of the Dead in Chimú and Inka Societies." *Journal of Archaeological Method and Theory* 11 (1): 83–124. http://dx.doi.org/10.1023/B:JARM.0000014348.86882.50.

Moore, J. D. 2005. *Cultural Landscapes in the Ancient Andes: Archaeologies of Place*. Gainesville: University Press of Florida.

Moore, J. D. 2006. "The Indians Were Much Given to Their Taquis: Drumming and Generative Categories in Ancient Andean Funerary Processions." In *Archaeology of Performance: Theaters of Power, Community, and Politics*, ed. T. Inomata and L. A. Coben, 47–69. Lanham, MD: Altamira/Rowman and Littlefield.

Moore, J. D. 2010a. "Architecture, Settlement, and Formative Developments in the Equatorial Andes: New Discoveries in the Department of Tumbes, Peru." *Latin American Antiquity* 21 (2): 147–72. http://dx.doi.org/10.7183/1045-6635.21.2.147.

Moore, J. D. 2010b. "Making a Huaca: Memory and Praxis in Prehispanic Far Northern Peru." *Journal of Social Archaeology* 10 (3): 398–422. http://dx.doi.org/10.1177/1469605310381550.

Moyes, H., ed. 2014. *Sacred Darkness: A Global Perspective on the Ritual Use of Caves*. Boulder: University Press of Colorado.

Onuki, Y. 1993. "Las actividades ceremoniales tempranas en la cuenca del Alto Huallaga y algunos problemas generales." In *El mundo ceremonial andino*, ed. L. Millones and Y. Onuki, 69–96. Senri Ethnological Studies 37. Osaka: National Museum of Ethnology.

Richards, C., and J. Thomas. 1984. "Ritual Activity and Structured Deposition in Later Neolithic Wessex." In *Neolithic Studies: A Review of Some Current Research*, ed. R. Bradley and J. Gardiner, 189–218. BAR International Series 133. Oxford: British Archaeological Reports.

Swenson, E. R. 2015. "The Archaeology of Ritual." *Annual Review of Anthropology* 44 (1): 329–45. http://dx.doi.org/10.1146/annurev-anthro-102214-013838.

Urton, G. 1988. *At the Crossroads of the Earth and the Sky: An Andean Cosmology*. Austin: University of Texas Press.

Urton, G. 2011. *The History of a Myth: Pacariqtambo and the Origin of the Inkas*. Austin: University of Texas Press.

van den Ende, L., and A. van Marrewijk. 2014. "The Ritualization of Transitions in the Project Life Cycle: A Study of Transition Rituals in Construction Projects." *International Journal of Project Management* 32 (7): 1134–45. http://dx.doi.org/10.1016/j.ijproman.2014.02.007.

Van Gijseghem, H., K. J. Vaughn, V. H. Whalen, M. L. Grados, and J. O. Canales. 2013. "Economic, Social, and Ritual Aspects of Copper Mining in Ancient Peru: An Upper Ica Valley Case Study." In *Mining and Quarrying in the Ancient Andes: Sociopolitical, Economic, and Symbolic Dimensions*, ed. N. Tripcevich and K. J. Vaughn, 275–98. New York: Springer. http://dx.doi.org/10.1007/978-1-4614-5200-3_13.

Contributors

SARAH ABRAHAM
Affiliated anthropologist
Department of Anthropology
University of California, Santa Barbara

CARLOS I. ANGIORAMA
Consejo Nacional de Investigaciones
　Cientificas y Tecnicas (CONICET)
Instituto Superior de Estudios Sociales,
　San Miguel de Tucumán, Argentina

FLORENCIA ÁVILA
Consejo Nacional de Investigaciones
　Cientificas y Tecnicas (CONICET)
Instituto Nacional de Antropología y
　Pensamiento Latinoamericano, Buenos Aires, Argentina

STEFANIE L. BAUTISTA
Doctoral candidate
Department of Anthropology
Stanford University, Stanford, CA

CAMILA CAPRIATA ESTRADA
Proyecto Qhapaq Ñan
Ministerio de Cultura, Peru

DAVID CHICOINE
Associate professor
Department of Geography and
　Anthropology
Louisiana State University, Baton Rouge

DANIEL A. CONTRERAS
Postdoctoral research fellow
Institut Méditerranéen de Biodiversité et d'Ecologie marine et continentale (IMBE) / Groupement de recherche en économie quantitative d'Aix-Marseille (GREQAM), Aix-Marseille Université, Marseille

MATTHEW J. EDWARDS
Cultural Resources program director
SWCA Environmental Consultants, Salt Lake City

FRANCESCA FERNANDINI
Pontificia Universidad Católica del Perú, Lima

MATTHEW HELMER
Doctoral student
Sainsbury Research Unit for the Arts of Africa, Oceania, and the Americas
University of East Anglia, UK

HUGO IKEHARA
Departamento de Humanidades
Pontificia Universidad Católica del Perú, Lima

ENRIQUE LÓPEZ-HURTADO
Associate researcher
Instituto de Estudios Peruanos (IEP), Peru, Lima

JERRY D. MOORE
Professor and chair
Department of Anthropology
California State University, Dominguez Hills

AXEL E. NIELSEN
Consejo Nacional de Investigaciones Cientificas y Tecnicas (CONICET), Instituto Nacional de Antropología y Pensamiento Latinoamericano, Argentina, Buenos Aires

YOSHIO ONUKI
Emeritus professor
University of Tokyo, Japan

JOHN W. RICK
Associate professor
Department of Anthropology
Stanford University, Stanford, CA

SILVANA A. ROSENFELD
Assistant professor
Department of Anthropology
University of South Dakota, Vermillion

MARIO RUALES
Conservación, Cultura y Desarrollo–Proyectos SAC
Lima, Peru

KOICHIRO SHIBATA
Associate professor
Hosei University, Japan

HENDRIK VAN GIJSEGHEM
Visiting assistant professor
Dickinson College, Carlisle, PA

RAFAEL VEGA-CENTENO SARA-LAFOSSE
Associate professor
Pontificia Universidad Católica del Perú, Lima

VERITY H. WHALEN
Visiting assistant professor
Wake Forest University, Wake Forest, NC

Index

abandonment, 13, 113, 123–25, 151, 153–57, 159–64, 178, 180–83, 188–89, 193–99, 202–6, 209, 306
abra, 245–52, 254–55, 260–61, 299
access, 12, 22, 26–27, 38–39, 45, 67–71, 107–9, 111–12, 116–20, 130–31, 135, 137–38, 144, 151, 153, 157–59, 163, 179, 184, 198–99, 202, 228, 302, 306
actant, 242
Acullico, 246
agency, 7, 14, 241–43, 254, 261, 270, 289
Aja, 155–56
Albornoz, Cristobal de, 246, 297–98, 300
altar, 56, 61–62, 194, 197, 221, 224, 230, 233, 245, 248–49
Altiplano, 223, 232, 244–45, 248, 256–57, 259
Alto Piura, 180
Aluvión, 35, 52
Amazonia, 85
Anaconda, 85–86
Ancash, 3, 12, 123–24, 300
Andahuaylillas, 223
Andean Christianity, 217–19, 232, 235
Andes mountains, 154
animism, 243
Apacheta, 10, 246–50, 257, 260–61. *See also* cairn worship
apse, 221, 227, 229, 231, 233
Apu, 7, 10, 272–73, 289
Araucanian. *See* Mapuche
architecture, 5, 10–13, 21, 23, 25, 27, 39, 46–47, 51–56, 59, 65, 67, 69, 71, 73, 80, 84–85, 87–88, 95, 97–99, 103, 105, 107, 109, 111, 113–15, 117, 119–20, 125–32, 134–35, 139, 144–45, 156, 179–81, 183, 195–96, 208, 217, 219–24, 226–27, 231–35, 278–79, 300–3, 306, 308; ceremonial, 10, 12, 27, 51, 56, 59, 67, 71, 73, 74, 76, 77, 80, 84, 87, 95, 107, 144, 301, 308, 309
ArcMAP, 135
Argentina, 6, 10, 14–15, 190, 248, 256–59, 261, 299
Arriaga, Pablo Jose de, 298, 300, 308
Asia, 174–75, 190
Atacama Desert, 248, 251, 254–55
Agustino, 92, 99
authority, 5, 12, 14, 44, 65–66, 71–72, 124, 127, 141, 207, 209, 271, 305

Bahía de Samanco, 131
baptism, 7, 221, 273
Basso, Keith, 269, 271
Bastien, Joseph, 4–5, 273–75
Bautista, Stefanie, 164, 235, 288, 297, 306
beads, 32, 113, 182, 203, 248–50, 252–53, 255–61, 299
Bell, Catherine, 6–8, 93, 224, 233, 242, 245, 307–8
Black and White phase, 37, 47
blackware, 46
Bolivia, 6, 10, 14, 244, 248, 251, 272, 284

bones, 24, 28, 30, 35, 43, 112, 177–78, 182–83, 258, 308
Bonnier, Elisabeth, 51, 55–56, 58, 62, 66, 73, 83–85, 95, 301, 308
Bourdieu, Pierre, 6, 104, 169, 177, 190
Bradley, Richard, 7, 152, 164, 270–71, 307–8
Braudel, Fernand, 271
Bray, Tamara, 5, 11, 160, 164, 297, 308
Brown, Linda A., 84, 193–94, 308
built environment, 217, 220, 232, 299–300, 303
Burger, Richard L., 21, 46–47, 52, 55–56, 59, 61, 65–68, 73, 93, 95, 109, 113, 125–26, 135, 145, 301

Cabrera, Martha, 178, 283
cairn worship, 10
Cajamarca, 85–87, 93, 97–99, 172
Cajamarquilla, 179
canals, 10–11, 25, 27–28, 30–31, 35–45, 53, 69–70, 89–90, 174, 300. *See also* canal systems
canal systems, 35–37, 39, 43–44, 174
Cañete Valley, 13, 170, 173–74, 305
Capilla Gallery, 35
Caracoles Gallery, 58
Caral, 56, 59, 61–62, 85–86, 97–98, 221
caravan, 244–45, 255–57, 260, 299
Central Coast, 13, 59, 135, 155, 186, 188–89, 193, 199, 207
central hearth, 55, 58–59
ceremony, 21, 23, 56, 66, 69, 124, 132, 139, 151, 153–55, 157, 159–64, 169–70, 176, 178, 190, 193, 197–98, 205–6, 208–10, 219, 221, 227, 244–45, 247, 295–96, 304–5
Cerro Blanco, 87–88, 94, 97–98, 125–29, 134, 136–42, 144–45, 248–49, 280, 286, 301–2; legend, 286; phase, 94, 126, 128, 129, 137, 138, 139, 141, 144, 145; site, 97, 98, 100, 121, 125, 127, 128, 129, 134, 136, 137, 139, 140, 141, 145, 147, 148, 301, 302
Cerro de Oro, 13, 169–79, 181–85, 187–90, 305–6; occupation, 170, 172, 175–76, 181, 183–84
Chakipampa, 172, 179
ch'alla, 245–46
chapel, 13–14, 35, 217, 219–24, 227–33, 235–36, 302
Chavín de Huántar (site), 3–4, 11, 21–24, 26–27, 42, 46, 51, 94, 98, 300–301
chicha, 3, 197–98, 250, 296, 298

Chile, 6, 10, 14, 248, 304
Christianity, 13–14, 217–21, 223, 231–32, 235, 260, 302
church, 3, 14, 218–24, 232–35, 302
Colca Valley, 224
Colla (culture), 227
Collao, 222
collapse, 29, 151, 161, 163–64, 199, 210
collective action, 3, 145
Colonial period, 80, 199, 218–19, 221–22, 224, 227, 231–32, 234–36, 299. *See also* Early Colonial period
colonnaded patios, 126, 130–31
Complejo Maranga, 180
compounds, 130–32, 134, 138, 171–72, 180–81, 183–84, 188, 199, 201
concentric cline, 67–68
Conchopata, 47, 178
Connerton, Paul, 104, 106
conopas, 298
Contreras, Daniel, 6, 11, 26, 29, 36, 42, 44, 46–47, 51–52, 54–56, 58–59, 63–66, 68, 70, 72, 125, 144–45, 301
controlled landscape, 175
Copa, 87–89, 91
Copper, 252, 256, 258–59, 276–77, 279, 299
Coricancha, 223
Corpus Christi (festival), 219
cosmology, 7, 11, 14, 79, 85–86, 89, 96–97, 99, 221, 241, 261, 303
Crumley, Carol L., 72
Cuba, 270, 276
cueltun, 304
Cupisnique, 87–88, 90, 93–94, 123, 125–27, 141, 301
Cusco, 219–20, 223, 227, 286, 296–97

Daggett, Richard, 127, 132–34
daily (quotidian) life, 6–7, 151, 169, 176–78, 288, 297
diachronic, 12, 14, 260
Diessl, Wilhelm, 52, 54
Digital Elevation Model (DEM), 135
Dillehay, Tom, 5, 180, 190, 304
dismounted architecture, 180
disposal space, 176
diversity, 11, 36, 42, 44, 51, 59, 65, 68, 70–71, 73, 125, 127, 145, 301–2

Early Colonial period, 13–14, 199, 217–18, 221–24, 232–35, 246
Early Horizon, 66–67, 73, 124, 276, 301
Early Intermediate Period, 127, 155, 170
Eastern Cordillera, 248, 260
Eastern valleys, 244, 255
Ecuador, 10, 92, 161
Eeckhout, Peter, 199, 204–7
elites, 13, 45, 99, 193, 195, 203–10, 301, 303, 305
El Niño, 44
entanglement, 8, 217–18, 261
environmental, 9, 44, 179–80, 190, 271
epicausto, 83–84
Estrella, 172
ethnicity, 65, 156, 163, 297
evangelization, 222, 232, 234

farming, 3, 144, 155, 243
feasting, 5, 32, 127, 164, 177, 197, 204, 206, 208, 227
fills, 11, 27–30, 33, 37, 55, 57–58, 61, 83, 91, 134, 159, 177, 180–83, 202, 306
Formative, 12, 21, 43, 45–46, 51, 66, 71, 79–80, 85–87, 93–94, 103–4, 109–10, 119–20, 123–29, 131–37, 139–41, 145, 181, 224, 226–28, 231, 256, 259, 301–3
Franco, Régulo, 164, 180, 199
friezes (murals), 97–98, 112, 125–26, 130–31, 133–34, 138–39, 144, 171, 180, 302

galleries, 11, 21, 25, 30, 33–36, 52, 67–71, 157–59
Gamma Analysis, 103, 107, 108, 116, 117
Garrow, Duncan, 307
Geographic Information Systems (GIS), 6, 12, 124
Gold, 12, 88–93, 99, 254, 276–77, 296
González Moreno, Marino, 24
Gose, Peter, 10, 153, 218, 234–35, 272
Guaman Poma de Ayala, Felipe, 273, 295
Guarani, 219

Hanson, Julianne, 103, 107–8, 116, 158
hearth, 5, 23, 55, 58–59, 61, 64–65, 81, 83–85, 176, 205
heterarchy, 65, 68, 71–72
hierarchy, 42, 65–66, 67, 68, 71–72, 103, 107–8, 115, 116, 119–20, 139, 158, 175, 208, 210
Higuchi, Tadahiko, 134
Hillier, Bill, 103, 107–8, 116, 158

Horton, Robin, 241
Huaca 20, 180
Huaca de los Reyes, 94
Huacaloma, 62, 85–88, 93–94, 97–99
Huaca Malena, 175, 186, 188, 190
Huaca Partida, 125–26, 128–29, 134, 136–42, 144–45, 302
Huacas de Moche, 180
huaico, 44. *See also* landslides
Huallaga, 59, 65, 79–80, 97, 303
Huambocayán (phase), 125–26, 144
Huanca, 197
Huancarpón, 126, 132–34, 136–39, 141, 143, 145
Huancavelica, 275–76
Huánuco, 5, 79–80, 87, 94
Huaycán, 208–9
Huaycoloro (or Jicamarca), 179
Huaytara, 220
hybridity, 218, 235, 302
hybridization, 172

Ica Valley, 14, 267–69, 271, 273–77, 279–80, 284–85, 287–89, 299
ideology, 8, 11–12, 14, 65, 79, 94, 97–99, 109, 125, 127, 152–53, 155, 164, 301–4
Idolatry, 232–33, 235, 295, 298, 308
Idolo phase, 87, 89, 94–95, 98
Incarrey, 252, 260
Inka, 5, 8, 10, 13, 45, 197, 199, 205–9, 218–19, 221, 224, 227–31, 247–48, 250–52, 254–56, 260, 267–68, 274, 295–99, 305
Inti Raymi, 219, 296
intrusive funerary contexts, 181, 183, 186
isovistas, 12, 135–39, 141, 144. *See also* viewsheds

Janabarroid/Janabarroide, 29–30, 46, 56
Jaqui/Aru, 277, 280, 289
Jicamarca. *See* Huaycoloro

Kalasaya, 225, 227–8, 230–33, 235–6
Kembel, Silvia, 24, 47, 56, 59, 66–67, 70–72
Kertzer, David, 104–6
kichira, 245
kipu, 175
Kolar, Miriam, 34
Kolata, Alan, 67, 180, 190, 226
Kotosh religious tradition, 55, 59, 64–67, 95
kowaco, 245
Kroeber, Alfred, 170

kuel, 304
Kuntur Wasi, 12, 79, 86–89, 91–92, 94, 97–99
Kushipampa, 126, 132–34, 136, 138–39, 141, 143–45

La Galgada, 51, 56, 60, 65, 86
Laguna Pozuelos, 256
Lake Titicaca, 5, 217
landscape, 7, 10–12, 25, 37, 47, 123–24, 134–35, 141, 174–75, 188, 195, 204, 207, 209, 217, 219–20, 224, 233–35, 245, 267–76, 278–79, 284–89, 297, 299, 304–5, 307–8
landslides, 26, 35, 44
Lanzón Gallery, 34, 69
La Quinta chapel, 13, 229–30, 235
Late Formative period, 51, 66, 123, 224, 256
Late Horizon, 13, 170, 181, 199, 206–7, 209, 299, 303–4
Late Intermediate Period, 13, 139, 159, 170, 176, 181, 199, 227, 251, 276, 299, 304
Layzón, 87, 97–99
Lima, 47, 90, 99, 163, 172, 180, 190
Lípez, 244, 248, 251, 252, 254, 256
lithic (art/sculpture), 52, 68, 159, 249–50, 254, 257
llameros, 244
Loa River, 248, 251, 257, 259
Lockhart, James, 273–74
Loco Gallery, 35
Los Amarillos, 255
Lucero, Lisa J., 308
Lumbreras, Luis, 21, 24–25, 30, 33, 36–37, 44, 46, 52, 58, 65–66, 68, 109, 125, 156, 236
Lurin Valley, 305

Magdalena de Cao, 224
maize, 125, 182, 203–4, 245–46, 255, 258, 296, 306
Mala, 174–75
Mallku, 244–46, 250, 254, 259
mamacocha, 298
mamapacha, 298
Manchay, 135
manioc, 86, 98
Mapuche, 304
Marcone, Giancarlo, 199–200, 208
Mass, 3, 175, 195, 221–23, 229, 231
material habitus, 169, 305
Mauricio, Ana Cecilia, 164, 180
Megalithic architecture, 52, 132, 134

Mesia, Christian, 46, 72
Mexico, 231
Middle Horizon period, 13, 155–58, 160–61, 170, 173, 179, 181–82, 186, 190, 197, 226, 305
mining, 6, 11, 13–14, 46, 267–68, 272–74, 275–84, 286–89, 299
Mito structure/tradition, 11, 51, 55–60, 65–69, 70–72, 300–301
Moche, 10, 58, 85, 127, 180, 196, 303
monumental, 6, 11, 21, 23–24, 26–29, 39, 42, 46–47, 51–56, 58, 67–68, 70, 107, 109, 125–34, 137–38, 145, 170–71, 174, 181, 195–96, 199, 208, 210, 227, 300–302
Moore, Jerry D., 4–6, 10, 14–15, 21–22, 66, 68, 73, 106, 127, 134–35, 139, 141, 164, 195, 219–21, 226, 295–96, 298–302, 304, 306–8
Moro, 127, 132, 141, 145
Mosna River, 39, 49, 54, 300
mountain pass shrines/ritual, 14, 243, 246, 256–57, 259, 261
mountain worship, 10
Moyes, Holly, 308
mullu, 259, 296
multi-scalar, 169, 305

ñan, 245
Narvaéz, Joaquín, 179
Nasca, 10, 13, 151, 154–56, 161, 163–64, 172, 181, 198, 278, 286, 306
Nash, June, 10, 158, 162–63, 268, 272, 275
Nave, 221–22, 227, 229–33, 302
Nepeña phase, 126, 128–29, 136–40, 145
Nepeña Valley, 12, 123, 127–29, 135, 141, 144, 301
nguillatun, 304
niche (architecture), 5, 55, 79–84, 97, 112–13, 117, 159, 184, 227–29, 231, 273
non-human agency, 14, 241, 261

obsidian, 28–29, 42, 44, 58, 160, 178, 250, 254, 257, 301
Ochatoma, José, 178
offering, 5, 7, 13–14, 24, 26, 30, 33, 38, 42, 45, 47, 58–59, 65, 71, 93, 106, 124, 151, 154, 159, 161–62, 178, 181, 183–85, 197, 201, 205–6, 208, 227, 243, 247–48, 252–53, 255–61, 272, 275, 296, 298–300, 304–7
Ofrendas Gallery, 24, 33, 58, 70
Ontological turn, 241, 298
ontology, 15, 190, 241, 243, 270

Open-air worship, 221–23, 230–31, 302
Open chapel, 222–24, 231, 233, 302

pacarinas, 298
Pachacamac, 180, 199, 205–8, 305
Pachamama, 7, 92, 243–46, 259
PACO, 170, 172, 175–76, 184
Pacopampa, 93–94, 97
palca, 246
Pampa de Flores, 205
Pampa de las Llamas–Moxeke, 12, 63, 103, 110–11, 113, 115, 117, 119–20, 302
Pampa Grande, 180, 196, 198, 209, 305
Panquilma, 13, 193, 195, 197, 199–210, 304–5
Paredes, Ponciano, 180, 199
Paredones, 126, 132, 134, 136, 138–39, 141, 143–45
pastoralists, 244, 259
Pataraya, 13, 151, 153–64, 198, 306–7
Pauketat, Timothy, 4, 15, 46, 259
performance, 9, 12, 86, 96, 103–4, 106, 113, 117–18, 130, 139, 144, 152, 162–63, 193, 197, 243, 245, 286, 307
pericausto, 83–84
Peru, 3–4, 6, 10–14, 21, 46–47, 64, 73, 79, 92, 123, 135, 145, 151, 155–56, 163, 217, 219, 221, 223–25, 227, 229, 231, 233, 235–36, 267, 269, 271, 273–75, 277, 279, 285, 287, 289, 298–300, 302–4, 308
PIACO, 170, 172, 176, 182, 184
platforms, 9, 85, 88–89, 97–98, 113, 115, 132–33, 158, 171–72, 175–76, 188, 200, 202–3, 205–6, 208–10, 305
Plaza Mayor, 30, 32–33, 37, 69, 131–32, 144
plazas, 23, 27, 37, 42, 59, 67–69, 71, 110, 113, 126, 130–33, 136, 139, 199–202, 205–6, 208–9, 220–21, 223–24, 226–27, 230, 300, 304
plurality, 68
polity, 13, 71, 111, 120, 123, 127, 145, 196–99, 206–7, 209–10, 225–26
Potosí, 251, 272, 275
pottery, 13, 24, 28–30, 32, 35–37, 44, 46, 80, 87–88, 91, 93–94, 97–99, 151, 161–62, 194, 251, 300. *See also* blackware
Practice theory, 6
pragmatism, 242
priest, 23, 219–20, 222–23, 229, 232, 289, 295–96
private, 66–67, 69, 104–5, 132, 159, 163, 204, 207–8, 234–35
processions, 24, 42, 58, 68–71, 106, 137–38, 151, 284, 295, 300

Proulx, Donald, 127, 132–33, 155, 181
public, 3, 10, 59, 66, 69, 85, 95, 97, 99, 104–5, 107, 109–10, 115, 123–25, 127–28, 130, 135–37, 140–41, 144, 193, 195, 199–203, 206, 208, 219, 221, 227, 234, 296–97, 301–3
Pukara, 13, 217, 224, 226–27, 232–36, 260, 302; culture, 226, 227, 236; site, 13, 217, 224, 232, 233, 234, 235, 236, 237, 302
Pucará (town), 224
Pulgar Vidal, Javier, 80
punku, 245–46, 258–60, 281
Punkurí, 144
Puno Region, 14

Qhapaqñan, 248, 254, 256, 260
Qhaya, 7
Quebrada de Humahuaca, 15, 190, 247–48, 251, 254, 256
Quechua, 222, 246, 259, 274, 277–78, 280–84, 289
Quelccaya ice cap, 180

Ramp Pyramid, 205, 207
Rappaport, Roy, 4–5, 9, 104–6, 233
Recuay, 127
rehuekuel, 304
relational practice, 169, 305
Religion, 4, 8, 15, 58, 66, 73, 79, 99, 105, 123–25, 127, 129, 131, 133, 135, 137, 139, 141, 145, 152–53, 155, 217–19, 221, 232, 235–36, 241–42, 254, 297, 303
Religious center, 23–24, 123, 199, 206–7
Religious tradition, 55, 59, 64–67, 95, 217, 219, 221, 232
reproduced, 175, 177, 183, 188–89, 260, 271, 276, 286
Richards, Colin, 243, 258, 307
Rick, John W., 5–9, 11, 21–22, 24, 26, 28, 30, 32, 34, 36, 38, 40, 42, 44, 46, 51, 55–56, 58–59, 64, 66–72, 123, 125, 144, 157, 193, 242, 300
ritual, 3–15, 21–39, 41–47, 51–53, 55–56, 58–59, 65–73, 79, 81, 83, 85–87, 89, 91, 93–99, 103–9, 111, 113, 115, 117, 119–20, 124–25, 127–30, 135–41, 144–45, 151–53, 157, 160, 162–64, 169–70, 175–76, 178, 183, 188–90, 193–99, 201–10, 217–21, 223–27, 229–35, 241–46, 248, 254–56, 258–61, 267, 269, 271–73, 275–77, 279, 285–89, 295–308; appropriation, 189; architecture, 11, 21, 51–53, 55, 59, 65, 67, 69, 71, 73, 107, 109,

INDEX 319

301, 303; gesture, 242, 260, 288, 299, 306; landscape, 308
ritualization, 7, 242
Rosenfeld, Silvana, 3–6, 8, 10, 12, 14, 65, 158, 164, 178, 235, 288, 297, 306
Rossel Castro, Alberto, 286
Rostworowski, María, 3–4, 170, 199, 207
Rowe, John, 67, 70, 199, 272

sacred, 5, 7, 51–52, 65, 67–69, 71, 144, 170, 178, 197–98, 210, 217, 220, 224, 235, 242, 275, 286, 289, 297, 300, 304, 308
sacred landscape, 217, 220, 224, 235
Sacrifice, 5, 11, 31, 38, 42, 44, 93, 295–96
Saint Michael, 284
Salitre, 133, 145
Samanco, 125–28, 131–32, 134, 136–42, 144–45; phase, 126, 128, 132, 141, 145; site, 127, 131, 132, 134, 136, 137, 138, 139, 140, 141, 142, 144, 145
San Miguel de Piura church, 224
San Pedro de Atacama, 252, 256
Santa Barbara, 256
Santa Isabel, 14, 232–35, 302
Santa Isabel Church, 233–34
Schmidt, Peter, 271
Scott, Heidi, 273, 275, 284
Sechín, 115, 135
Segura, Rafael, 179
semiotic analysis, 243
sepulchers, 243, 252, 260
settlement pattern, 123, 127, 145, 174–75
shrine, 6, 9, 13–14, 124, 197, 220, 241, 243, 245–48, 251, 253–57, 259, 261, 296, 308
slash-and-burn agriculture, 12, 79, 85, 96, 99
social action, 6, 9, 188, 241, 298
social landscape, 188, 273
social memory, 11, 14, 267–69, 271, 273, 275, 277, 279, 285–87, 289
social rules, 169, 305
Solórzano, Juan de, 275
South America, 4–6, 92, 221, 224, 273
Southern Andes, 226, 235, 241, 243, 247, 255, 258, 260, 299
Southern Nasca Region, 13
Space syntax analysis, 158
Spanish conquest, 214, 217, 219, 221, 267, 273–74, 292
Stanford Project, 24–26, 34, 52, 70, 72

Stewart, George, 269, 289
stone sculpture, 12, 88–91, 98
storage, 23, 34, 112–13, 158, 160, 172, 176, 178, 199–200, 203, 205, 305
stratigraphy, 87, 177
Strombus galeatus, 34
structured deposition, 11, 13, 258, 305, 307
Stumer, Louis, 170
sunken court, 13, 88–89, 221, 223, 226–28, 231, 302
Supay, 272
supernatural, 4, 7, 127, 144, 194, 272–73, 287
syncretic practice, 220
syncretism, 66, 72, 219–20, 272, 274, 277–78, 284

Taki Onkoy, 235, 302
talvarita, 244
tapados, 252, 260
Tello, Julio C., 25, 52, 58–59, 98, 112, 115, 125, 127–29, 170, 179–80
Tello's Obelisk, 98
Tembladera, 94
Temple of the Crossed Hands, 80–84
Temple of the Small Niches, 80, 83–84
tenoned head, 52
terminal ritual, 13, 162, 193–97, 199, 201, 203, 205, 207, 209–10
terrace, 28, 30, 37, 53–57, 69, 80–81, 83, 88, 97–98, 131–34, 200, 227–28, 231
Thomas, Julian, 243, 258, 269, 285, 302, 307
Tierras Blancas, 154–55, 157, 161
Tinku, 11, 41, 300
Tío, 272, 289
Titicaca Basin, 14, 217, 225
Tiwanaku, 15, 67, 198–99
Torata Alta, 224
Tres Cerrillos, 245
Tringham, Ruth, 271
Triple frontier, 248–49, 256
tropical forest/rain forest, 12, 85–86, 92, 94, 98–99, 190
Tucker, Gene, 270
Tulán 54, 259
Turner, Victor, 4–5, 26, 105–6, 153

ukhupacha, 259–60
unku, 186
U-shaped architecture, 42, 59, 70, 88, 112, 115, 119, 128

Venezuela, 10, 92
viewsheds, 12, 135, 141, 144–45. *See also* isovistas
Vilcashuaman, 220
Virahuanca Bajo, 126, 133–34, 136, 138–39, 141, 143–45
Virgen del Carmen, 3–4
Virgin of the Mineshaft, 272
Wacheqsa River, 39–40, 47, 300

Wak'as, 5, 297
Wallace, Dwight, 170, 222
Wari Empire, 13, 151, 161–63, 306
Western Cordillera, 248, 254
White Temple, 80–81

Ychsma, 199, 203, 206, 208
yunga, 80
Yungas, 248